This is an outstanding book ... the first high-quality academic work on religion and the psy disciplines in modern Japan. It covers the topics of modern religion and psychotherapy in Japan and connects them with the recent major crises of Aum Shinrikyo and the earthquake and tsunami of March 2011.

Akihito Suzuki, *Professor of History at Keio University, Japan*

Chris Harding and his fellow editors have brought together a significant set of essays examining the relationship between the 'psy disciplines' of psychiatry, psychology, and psychotherapy, and religion in Japan. Harding's overview takes us beyond the problematic definitional issues relating to religion to show how the 'psy disciplines' have helped shape the ways in which religion is manifested in modern Japan. The essays that follow introduce a wealth of Japanese scholarship in the field that will be of value to all who are interested in religion, psychotherapy, and Japanese culture in general.

Ian Reader, *Professor of Religious Studies at Lancaster University, UK*

A novel take on the role of religion in Japan, and another significant contribution to understanding religion in modern Japanese society. Instead of the usual image of Buddhist meditation as *zazen*, we find fascinating studies of various kinds of mental and psychological care, from naikan meditation to Morita therapy. These chapters show how modern psychotherapy and traditional religion are both utilized (though not always harmoniously) for dealing with 'spiritual' issues. This collection presents work by many of the best religious studies scholars in Japan today.

Paul L. Swanson, *Editor,* Japanese Journal of Religious Studies

# Religion and Psychotherapy in Modern Japan

Since the late nineteenth century, religious ideas and practices in Japan have become increasingly intertwined with those associated with mental health and healing. This relationship developed against the backdrop of a far broader, and deeply consequential meeting: between Japan's long-standing, Chinese-influenced intellectual and institutional forms, and the politics, science, philosophy, and religion of the post-Enlightenment West. In striving to craft a modern society and culture that could exist on terms with – rather than be subsumed by – western power and influence, Japan became home to a religion–psy dialogue informed by pressing political priorities and rapidly shifting cultural concerns.

This book provides a historically contextualized introduction to the dialogue between religion and psychotherapy in modern Japan. In doing so, it draws out connections between developments in medicine, government policy, Japanese religion and spirituality, social and cultural criticism, regional dynamics, and gender relations. The chapters all focus on the meeting and intermingling of religious with psychotherapeutic ideas and draw on a wide range of case studies including: how temple and shrine 'cures' of early modern Japan fared in the light of German neuropsychiatry; how Japanese Buddhist theories of mind, body, and self-cultivation negotiated with the findings of western medicine; how Buddhists, Christians, and other organizations and groups drew and redrew the lines between religious praxis and psychological healing; how major European therapies such as Freud's fed into self-consciously Japanese analyses of and treatments for the ills of the age; and how distress, suffering, and individuality came to be reinterpreted across the twentieth and early twenty-first centuries, from the southern islands of Okinawa to the devastated northern neighbourhoods of the Tohoku region after the earthquake, tsunami, and nuclear disasters of March 2011.

*Religion and Psychotherapy in Modern Japan* will be welcomed by students and scholars working across a broad range of subjects, including Japanese culture and society, religious studies, psychology and psychotherapy, mental health, and international history.

**Christopher Harding** is Lecturer in Asian History in the School of History, Classics and Archaeology, University of Edinburgh, UK.

**Iwata Fumiaki** is Professor in the Department of Social Science Education, Osaka Kyoiku University, Japan.

**Yoshinaga Shin'ichi** is Associate Professor at the Maizuru National College of Technology, Japan.

# Routledge Contemporary Japan Series

1  **A Japanese Company in Crisis**
   Ideology, strategy, and narrative
   *Fiona Graham*

2  **Japan's Foreign Aid**
   Old continuities and new directions
   *Edited by David Arase*

3  **Japanese Apologies for World War II**
   A rhetorical study
   *Jane W. Yamazaki*

4  **Linguistic Stereotyping and Minority Groups in Japan**
   *Nanette Gottlieb*

5  **Shinkansen**
   From bullet train to symbol of modern Japan
   *Christopher P. Hood*

6  **Small Firms and Innovation Policy in Japan**
   *Edited by Cornelia Storz*

7  **Cities, Autonomy and Decentralization in Japan**
   *Edited by Carola Hein and Philippe Pelletier*

8  **The Changing Japanese Family**
   *Edited by Marcus Rebick and Ayumi Takenaka*

9  **Adoption in Japan**
   Comparing policies for children in need
   *Peter Hayes and Toshie Habu*

10 **The Ethics of Aesthetics in Japanese Cinema and Literature**
   Polygraphic desire
   *Nina Cornyetz*

11 **Institutional and Technological Change in Japan's Economy**
   Past and present
   *Edited by Janet Hunter and Cornelia Storz*

12 **Political Reform in Japan**
   Leadership looming large
   *Alisa Gaunder*

13 **Civil Society and the Internet in Japan**
   *Isa Ducke*

14 **Japan's Contested War Memories**
   The 'memory rifts' in historical consciousness of World War II
   *Philip A. Seaton*

15 **Japanese Love Hotels**
A cultural history
*Sarah Chaplin*

16 **Population Decline and Ageing in Japan**
The social consequences
*Florian Coulmas*

17 ***Zainichi* Korean Identity and Ethnicity**
*David Chapman*

18 **A Japanese Joint Venture in the Pacific**
Foreign bodies in tinned tuna
*Kate Barclay*

19 **Japanese–Russian Relations, 1907–2007**
*Joseph P. Ferguson*

20 **War Memory, Nationalism and Education in Post-War Japan, 1945–2007**
The Japanese history textbook controversy and Ienaga Saburo's court challenges
*Yoshiko Nozaki*

21 **A New Japan for the Twenty-First Century**
An inside overview of current fundamental changes and problems
*Edited by Rien T. Segers*

22 **A Life Adrift**
Soeda Azembo, popular song and modern mass culture in Japan
*Translated by Michael Lewis*

23 **The Novels of Oe Kenzaburo**
*Yasuko Claremont*

24 **Perversion in Modern Japan**
Psychoanalysis, literature, culture
*Edited by Nina Cornyetz and J. Keith Vincent*

25 **Homosexuality and Manliness in Postwar Japan**
*Jonathan D. Mackintosh*

26 **Marriage in Contemporary Japan**
*Yoko Tokuhiro*

27 **Japanese Aid and the Construction of Global Development**
Inescapable solutions
*Edited by David Leheny and Carol Warren*

28 **The Rise of Japanese NGOs**
Activism from above
*Kim D. Reimann*

29 **Postwar History Education in Japan and the Germanys**
Guilty lessons
*Julian Dierkes*

30 **Japan-Bashing**
Anti-Japanism since the 1980s
*Narrelle Morris*

31 **Legacies of the Asia-Pacific War**
The Yakeato generation
*Edited by Roman Rosenbaum and Yasuko Claremont*

32 **Challenges of Human Resource Management in Japan**
*Edited by Ralf Bebenroth and Toshihiro Kanai*

33 **Translation in Modern Japan**
*Edited by Indra Levy*

34 **Language Life in Japan**
Transformations and prospects
*Edited by Patrick Heinrich and Christian Galan*

35 **The Quest for Japan's New Constitution**
An analysis of visions and constitutional reform proposals 1980–2009
*Christian G. Winkler*

36 **Japan in the Age of Globalization**
*Edited by Carin Holroyd and Ken Coates*

37 **Social Networks and Japanese Democracy**
The beneficial impact of interpersonal communication in East Asia
*Ken'ichi Ikeda and Sean Richey*

38 **Dealing with Disaster in Japan**
Responses to the Flight JL123 crash
*Christopher P. Hood*

39 **The Ethics of Japan's Global Environmental Policy**
The conflict between principles and practice
*Midori Kagawa-Fox*

40 **Superhuman Japan**
Knowledge, nation and culture in US–Japan relations
*Marie Thorsten*

41 **Nationalism, Political Realism and Democracy in Japan**
The thought of Masao Maruyama
*Fumiko Sasaki*

42 **Japan's Local Newspapers**
Chihōshi and revitalization journalism
*Anthony S. Rausch*

43 **Mental Health Care in Japan**
*Edited by Ruth Taplin and Sandra J. Lawman*

44 **Manga and the Representation of Japanese History**
*Edited by Roman Rosenbaum*

45 **Negotiating Censorship in Modern Japan**
*Edited by Rachael Hutchinson*

46 **EU–Japan Relations, 1970–2012**
From confrontation to global partnership
*Edited by Jörn Keck, Dimitri Vanoverbeke and Franz Waldenberger*

47 **Japan and the High Treason Incident**
*Edited by Masako Gavin and Ben Middleton*

48 **Diplomacy in Japan–EU Relations**
From the Cold War to the post-bipolar era
*Oliviero Frattolillo*

49 **Sound, Space and Sociality in Modern Japan**
*Edited by Joseph D. Hankins and Carolyn S. Stevens*

50 **Japanese Femininities**
   *Justin Charlebois*

51 **Japan's Foreign Aid to Africa**
   Angola and Mozambique within
   the TICAD process
   *Pedro Amakasu Raposo*

52 **Internationalising Japan**
   Discourse and practice
   *Edited by Jeremy Breaden,*
   *Stacey Steele and Carolyn S. Stevens*

53 **Heritage Conservation and Japan's Cultural Diplomacy**
   Heritage, national identity and national interest
   *Natsuko Akagawa*

54 **Religion and Psychotherapy in Modern Japan**
   *Edited by Christopher Harding,*
   *Iwata Fumiaki and*
   *Yoshinaga Shin'ichi*

# Religion and Psychotherapy in Modern Japan

Edited by Christopher Harding,
Iwata Fumiaki, and Yoshinaga Shin'ichi

LONDON AND NEW YORK

First published 2015
by Routledge
2 Park Square, Milton Park, Abingdon, Oxon OX14 4RN

and by Routledge
711 Third Avenue, New York, NY 10017

*Routledge is an imprint of the Taylor & Francis Group, an informa business*

© 2015 Christopher Harding, Iwata Fumiaki, and Yoshinaga Shin'ichi

The right of the editors to be identified as the authors of the editorial material, and of the authors for their individual chapters, has been asserted in accordance with sections 77 and 78 of the Copyright, Designs and Patents Act 1988.

All rights reserved. No part of this book may be reprinted or reproduced or utilized in any form or by any electronic, mechanical, or other means, now known or hereafter invented, including photocopying and recording, or in any information storage or retrieval system, without permission in writing from the publishers.

*Trademark notice*: Product or corporate names may be trademarks or registered trademarks, and are used only for identification and explanation without intent to infringe.

*British Library Cataloguing in Publication Data*
A catalogue record for this book is available from the British Library

*Library of Congress Cataloging in Publication Data*
Religion and psychotherapy in modern Japan / edited by
Christopher Harding, Iwata Fumiaki, and Yoshinaga Shin'ichi.
    pages cm. – (Routledge contemporary Japan series; 54)
    Includes bibliographical references and index.
    1. Psychotherapy–Japan. 2. Psychotherapy–Religious aspects.
    3. Psychology and religion–Japan. I. Harding, Christopher, editor.
    RC451.J3R45 2014
    616.89'1400952–dc23                                           2014011543

ISBN: 978-1-138-77516-9 (hbk)
ISBN: 978-1-315-77396-4 (ebk)

Typeset in Baskerville
by Wearset Ltd, Boldon, Tyne and Wear

**For all the lives lost and overturned on 11th March 2011**

# Contents

| | |
|---|---|
| *List of illustrations* | xv |
| *List of contributors* | xvi |
| *Acknowledgements* | xvii |
| *Note on Japanese names* | xviii |

| | | |
|---|---|---|
| | **Introduction**<br>CHRISTOPHER HARDING | 1 |
| 1 | **Religion and psychotherapy in modern Japan: a four-phase view**<br>CHRISTOPHER HARDING | 25 |
| 2 | **Psychiatry and religion in modern Japan: traditional temple and shrine therapies**<br>HASHIMOTO AKIRA | 51 |
| 3 | **The birth of Japanese mind cure methods**<br>YOSHINAGA SHIN'ICHI | 76 |
| 4 | **The mind and healing in Morita therapy**<br>KONDO KYOICHI AND KITANISHI KENJI | 103 |
| 5 | **The dawning of Japanese psychoanalysis: Kosawa Heisaku's therapy and faith**<br>IWATA FUMIAKI | 120 |
| 6 | **Doi Takeo and the development of the 'Amae' theory**<br>ANDO YASUNORI | 137 |
| 7 | **From salvation to healing: Yoshimoto Naikan therapy and its religious origins**<br>SHIMAZONO SUSUMU | 150 |

| | | |
|---|---|---:|
| 8 | Naikan and mourning: a Catholic attempt at Naikan meditation<br>TERAO KAZUYOSHI | 165 |
| 9 | Kawai Hayao's transnational identity and Japanese spirit<br>TARUTANI SHIGEHIRO | 181 |
| 10 | The contemporary view of reincarnation in Japan: narratives of the reincarnating self<br>HORIE NORICHIKA | 204 |
| 11 | A society accepting of spirit possession: mental health and shamanism in Okinawa<br>SHIOTSUKI RYOKO | 234 |
| 12 | Chaplaincy work in disaster areas<br>TANIYAMA YŌZŌ | 250 |
| | **Conclusion**<br>CHRISTOPHER HARDING | 267 |
| | *Index* | 291 |

# Illustrations

**Figures**

| | | |
|---|---|---|
| 2.1 | A waterfall therapeutic practice at Nissekiji Temple. Two *gōriki* hold a schizophrenic farmer (centre) for the duration of the bath | 56 |
| 2.2 | The building used for Yamamoto Kyūgosho, sometime before 1963 | 61 |
| 3.1 | Hara Tanzan's system of psychology: *kaku* appears shaded, *fukaku* in black | 81 |
| 12.1 | A Tohoku memorial service | 254 |
| 12.2 | Distributing Buddhist devotional materials | 257 |
| C.1 | Zen Buddhist monks pray with a Christian pastor amidst the debris in Miyagi Prefecture, 28th April 2011 | 268 |

**Table**

| | | |
|---|---|---|
| 10.1 | Analysis of experiences of past life therapy | 215 |

# Contributors

**Ando Yasunori** School of Health Sciences, Faculty of Medicine, Tottori University, Japan.

**Christopher Harding** Lecturer in Asian History, University of Edinburgh, UK.

**Hashimoto Akira** Department of Welfare Science, School of Education and Welfare, Aichi Prefectural University, Japan.

**Horie Norichika** University of Tokyo, Japan.

**Iwata Fumiaki** Department of Social Science Education, Osaka Kyoiku University, Japan.

**Kitanishi Kenji** Director of the Institute of Morita Therapy and Chair of the International Committee for Morita Therapy, Japan.

**Kondo Kyoichi** Medical Advisor to Chofu Hashimoto Clinic, Japan.

**Shimazono Susumu** Sophia University, Japan.

**Shiotsuki Ryoko** Atomi Gakuen Women's University, Japan.

**Taniyama Yōzō** Department of Practical Religious Studies, Tohoku University, Japan.

**Tarutani Shigehiro** Maizuru National College of Technology, Japan.

**Terao Kazuyoshi** St Catherine University, Japan.

**Yoshinaga Shin'ichi** Maizuru National College of Technology, Japan.

# Acknowledgements

The Editors would particularly like to thank the following for their help and support in the preparation of this volume: Carl Freire, Ioannis Gaitinidis, Hayashi Chine, Inoue Yoshinobu, Yumi Kim, Junko Kitanaka, Orion Klautau, Kosawa Yorio, Kosawa Makoto, Dylan Toda Luers, Justin B. Stein, Suzuki Akihito, and Mark Unno; the anonymous reviewers of our manuscript, and all at Routledge; the Kyūdōkaikan; and, of course, all our contributors to this volume.

Content from the following published works features in the chapters contained in this volume (see individual chapters for details):

Horie Norichika, 'Gendai no Rinne-tenshō-kan: Rinne suru Watashi no Monogatari' [The Contemporary View of Reincarnation: Narratives of the Reincarnating Self], in Tsuruoka Yoshio and Fukasawa Hidetaka (eds), *Supirichuariti no Shūkyōshi (Jōkan) [The Religious History of Spirituality (first volume)]* (Tokyo: Liton, 2010), pp. 421–463.

Kondo Kyoichi and Kitanishi Kenji, 'Kokoro: Morita ryōhō no Kokoro to Iyashi' [The heart and healing of Morita therapy], in Shintaro Tanabe *et al.* (eds), *Iyashi wo Ikita Hitobito: Kindaichi no Orutanatibu [Those who Lived as Healers: Alternatives in the Modern Age]* (Tokyo: Senshu University Press, 1990), pp. 129–164.

Shiotsuki Ryoko, 'Hyōi wo Kōteisuru Shakai – Okinawa no Seishin Iryōshi to Shamanism' [A society that accepts spirit possession: psychiatric history in Okinawa, and Shamanism], in *Hyoi no Kindai to Politics [Modern Age of Spirit Possession and Politics]* (Tokyo: Seikyusha, 2007), pp. 197–224.

Shimazono Susumu, 'Sukui kara Iyashi e: Yoshimoto Naikan to sono Shūkyōteki Kigen' [From salvation to healing: Yoshimoto Naikan therapy and its religious origins], in Shigehiko Araya *et al.* (eds), *Iyashi to Wakai: Gendai ni okeru Kea no Shosō [Healing and reconciliation: Varieties of care today]* (Tanasai-city: Harvest-sha, 1995) [page numbers not available].

Taniyama Yōzō, 'Saigai-toki no chapuren no ugoki: sono kanōsei to kadai' [Disaster chaplaincy and its task in the wake of the Great East Japan earthquake and tsunami], *Shūkyō Kenkyū [Journal of Religious Studies]*, 86/2 (2012).

Terao Kazuyoshi, 'Naikan to Hiai' [Naikan and grief], in Takada Nobuhiro (ed.), *Shūkyō ni okeru shiseikan to chōetsu [Transcendence and views of life and death in religion]* (Kyoto: Hojodo, 2013), pp.128–145.

# Note on Japanese names

In most cases Japanese names, including names of contributors to this volume and authors of cited works published in Japanese, appear in this book in the Japanese order: surname followed by personal name. The names of authors of cited works published in English appear in the English-language order: personal name followed by surname.

Macrons are used to indicate extended vowels, except in the case of place names (for example Tokyo, or Tohoku) and in the case of Japanese authors who do not themselves indicate extended vowels in their names with a macron.

# Introduction

*Christopher Harding*

When Yabe Yaekichi, one of Japan's earliest enthusiasts for psychoanalysis, met Sigmund Freud in Berlin in 1931, the latter was delighted to hear that Yabe and his colleagues had chosen *Beyond the Pleasure Principle* (1920) as one of the first of Freud's books to be translated into Japanese. The decision was made on the basis that the idea of life containing within it an impulse towards death – initially controversial in Freud's European circle – was supposedly common currency in Japan, due in part to the influence of Buddhist thought. Freud saw similar cause for optimism where acceptance of his earlier libido theory was concerned, remarking to Marui Kiyoyasu, Professor of Psychiatry at Tohoku Imperial University, that the Japanese seemed relatively free of the 'prejudices that have caused difficulties for psychoanalysis in Europe and America' – a likely reference to western prudishness about sex.[1] And yet Freud was also in for disappointment from his 'far-flung' Asian followers:[2] he found himself forced to defend the virtues of 'practical', clinical approaches over and above what he saw as the overly 'philosophical' approach of Girindrasekhar Bose, India's father of psychoanalysis based in Calcutta; and he remained stonily silent when the Japanese psychoanalyst and devout Buddhist Kosawa Heisaku handed him a thesis on the 'Ajase Complex' that was both a modification of the Oedipus idea (the better to suit the Japanese familial context) and a rejection, as hopelessly parochial, of the theory of religion found in Freud's *Totem and Taboo* (1913).[3]

Freud's highs and lows with his Japanese and Indian colleagues, as with associates closer to home such as Oskar Pfister and Romain Rolland, reflected the broader vicissitudes of a major modern cultural theme: complex interchange and overlap between professionalizing and expanding 'psy disciplines' – principally psychiatry, psychology, and psychotherapy – and the thinkers, leaders, and laypeople of the world's religions. Psy theories have been put forward to explain or to help 'cure' religious thinking and behaviour, or to sort doctrinal or ideological wheat from accumulated chaff; and psychotherapy has been widely touted as a distillation of the positive 'functions' of religion, into a form culturally acceptable to the disenchanted and helpfully systematized to meet the demands of busy people. Yet the coming together of psychotherapy and religion – perhaps, taking a longer historical view, we should talk of their *rapprochement* – has been rather more ambiguous a process than straightforward secularization and the co-option of religious ideas and practices by science and medicine, as Freud found to his cost in his dealings with Kosawa, Bose, and others. For one, psy approaches to religion have been far from uniformly deconstructionist in intent and effect, nor have they developed in a vacuum of socio-economic and cultural concerns, not to mention governmental and personal interests.

Religion, both in Japan and elsewhere, has tended to be re-shaped rather than always displaced by, or absorbed into, cognate areas of human life and knowledge, from the psy disciplines through to aesthetics, ethics, and the latest contender for hermeneutic supremacy, the neurosciences.[4] In many forms of Christianity and Buddhism, Freudian ideas have found themselves appropriated as part of a system of checks and balances that seeks to keep communal worship and private prayer or meditation as free as realistically possible of narcissism, interpersonal strife, counter-phobic strategies, and various forms of self-deception.[5] The Jungian contribution has been to highlight the continuing psycho-social necessity and potential of religious belief and praxis, while leaving open the question of their ultimate referent(s).

Modern rationalizing approaches towards our global religious inheritance, then, in which the psy disciplines continue to play a significant role, do not look like they will result in the whole lot ending up on the bonfire any time soon – for all that this outcome was once expected, and in some quarters fervently hoped for.[6] One might even argue that increasingly in the twenty-first century, the idioms of the psy disciplines and the neurosciences are showing themselves to be little match for the raw symbolic and emotional power of religious stories, hopes, and intuitions when it comes to grasping and tackling existential concerns, while at the same time religious individuals and institutions find they have more and more use for the insights of such things as developmental and dynamic psychology.[7] Recent initiatives in the UK and Japan are bringing religion and spirituality into psychiatry and into end of life care, and most recently, in the post-3/11 Japanese context, into disaster relief.[8]

Yet religion and the psy disciplines clearly do not always make happy or profitable bedfellows. Behind a phrase like 'religion–psy dialogue', which this book employs as shorthand, lurk complications, antagonisms (albeit sometimes creative ones), points of confusion, and instances of everything from governmental and cultic manipulation to the sort of cultural essentialism that remains a stubborn feature of commentary on countries such as India and Japan, both from without and within.[9] Besides this, religious traditions and the psy disciplines are both notable for their combination of all-encompassing claims about the nature and destiny of the human person with the use of powerful language, imagery, and practices whose sometimes enigmatic nature many are willing to tolerate, as necessary or harmlessly characteristic, rather than probe for clarification.

So it was that sociologists of religion in Japan found themselves caught out in 1995, alongside most of the rest of the Japanese population, when members of the religious group Aum Shinrikyō – which Tarutani Shigehiro has described as the 'child of … pop psychology and Buddhism'[10] – launched a sarin gas attack on the Tokyo subway and was revealed to have been planning further attacks.[11] Aum was just one of hundreds of new religious movements to appear in Japan since the 1920s, many of which drew on traditional or folk religious ideas and healing practices combined with psychology and psychotherapy – frequently, as Shimazono has pointed out, in an attempt to fill the modern vacuum of agreed ethical standards by offering, as the next best thing, technical methods of self-mastery designed to provide a modicum of peace of mind.[12]

There have been concerns, too, about the impact of the religion–psy encounter upon how people grow up learning to conceive of themselves, 'as ideally and potentially certain sorts of person'.[13] Junko Kitanaka's recent work on depression in Japan illustrates how acutely susceptible to shifts in politics, the law, and commercial imperatives are our most intimate and automatic interpretations of inner experience.[14] Similar concerns emerge in Nikolas Rose's work on the psy disciplines and governmentality, specifically a recent trend away from traditional, external modes of surveillance and coercion towards more internalized forms, which feel as though they have been freely chosen by us for our own good:

> Through self-inspection, self-problematization, self-monitoring and confession, we evaluate ourselves according to the criteria provided for us by others. Through self-reformation, therapy, and the calculated reshaping of speech and emotion, we adjust ourselves by means of the techniques propounded by experts of the soul.[15]

Broadly encompassing in its conceptual scope, deeply personal in its everyday reality, and phenomenologically complex – ideas and propositions blending with symbol, myth, feeling, memory, faith, presumed unconscious content, and meditative states – the religion–psy dialogue resists adequate description, critique, and evaluation via any single metalanguage. Instead, the task of reflecting upon this dialogue, and where it might be leading us, is in part one of understanding the transnational, institutional, intellectual, and personal circumstances in which it has come about: tracing its impact and ambiguities as they have played out in practice – amongst practitioners, clients, and others – and thereby offering as a counterpoint to its sometimes rather totalizing claims a vivid sense of its sheer historical contingency and diverse possible futures.

The present volume offers a contribution to this analytic project by exploring a particularly rich and complex case study in the encounter of religion with the psy disciplines: modern Japan, from the late nineteenth century through to the present day. Here the religion–psy encounter occurred against the backdrop of a far broader, and deeply consequential meeting: between Japan's long-standing, Chinese-influenced intellectual and institutional forms, and the politics, science, philosophy and religion of the post-Enlightenment West. Striving to craft a modern society and culture that could exist on terms with – rather than be subsumed by – western power and influence, Japan became home to a religion–psy dialogue inflected by pressing political priorities and rapidly shifting cultural concerns. What was the true intellectual and ethical worth to Japan of western science and biomedicine? Where, if anywhere, did the continued relevance lie of Japan's religious and philosophical traditions? If these required reform, what should it look like and what should be the aim? Where should Japanese people look for their core values? Was there such a thing as a 'Japanese' identity that could be located and asserted, as western influences appeared to creep into every area of life and thought? What sorts of aspirations, attitudes, and relationships were proper to Japanese men and women living in a new era – what did it now mean to be a *jinkakusha*, a person of true character[16] – and how could these things be nurtured and encouraged at social and individual levels?

It is with these political, socio-cultural, and personal contexts firmly in view that we present in this volume an introductory selection of newly commissioned and seminal pieces of Japanese scholarship in this emerging area of study. The bulk of current scholarship on psychiatry in general, and on religion and psychotherapy in particular, is Japanese, and for the most part only available in the Japanese language. Given the promise and pitfalls of the religion–psy dialogue discussed above the time seems right to introduce this scholarship to an English-language audience: for its own intrinsic interest, for the broader themes in Japanese history upon which it touches, and so that it may be set alongside scholarship on religion and the psy disciplines elsewhere in the world. Our focus in particular is upon the meeting and intermingling of religious with psychotherapeutic ideas: how temple and shrine 'cures' of early modern Japan fared in the light of German neuropsychiatry; how Japanese Buddhist theories of mind, body, and self-cultivation negotiated with the findings of western medicine; how Buddhists, Christians, and other organizations and groups drew and redrew the lines between religious praxis and psychological healing; how major European therapies such as Freud's fed into self-consciously Japanese analyses of and treatments for the ills of the age; and how distress, suffering, and individuality came to be reinterpreted across the twentieth and early twenty-first centuries, from the southern islands of Okinawa to the devastated northern neighbourhoods of the Tohoku region after the earthquake, tsunami, and nuclear disasters of March 2011.

This chapter prepares the ground for the specialized contributions that follow by looking at how the religion–psy dialogue intersects with related questions and areas of current study in Japanese history and anthropology. A four-phase introductory overview of religion and the psy disciplines in modern Japan follows in Chapter 1, intended for the benefit of readers relatively unfamiliar with the Japanese context.

## Major themes in the psy disciplines and religion in modern Japan

Up until fairly recently the history of mental health in Japan has been the preserve primarily of Japanese psychiatrists seeking to contextualize their professional concerns. However, in the last few years historians, sociologists, and anthropologists, writing mostly in Japanese, have begun to take up the challenge of examining the modern development of mental healthcare in Japan and attitudes towards mental health and illness more broadly. As English-language scholarship too gathers pace, including work by Akihito Suzuki, Junko Kitanaka, and Janice Matsumura, a number of themes and areas of focus are emerging in the combined Japanese and English literatures.

Institutional histories provide something of a historiographical backbone, with many universities and hospitals home to detailed sets of administrative records and correspondence, research notes, and client notes (known as *karute*, after the German *Karte*).[17] Allied to these are biographical accounts of major figures such as Kure Shūzō, hailed by many as the 'father' of Japanese psychiatry, and Kosawa Heisaku, similarly regarded as the father of psychoanalysis in Japan. 'Mothers' are all too scarce in the early years of modern mental healthcare, featuring more often as male psychological subject matter or as under-acknowledged assistants to husbands than as practitioners in their own right – although some work has been done on women psychiatric nurses, such as Ishibashi Haya.[18] The history of particular illness categories and patterns of behaviour is also being traced, from depression and schizophrenia through to so-called 'culture-bound syndromes' such as *hikikomori* (acute social withdrawal) and *taijinkyōfushō* (fear of interpersonal relations).[19]

Mental health and hygiene, with the attendant possibilities for creating new institutions and 'moulding Japanese minds',[20] was of great interest to policy makers and state builders during the period of the Meiji Emperor's reign (1868–1912) and their successors in later eras. Work by Janice Matsumura, Yu-chuan Wu and others looks at how politics and mental health came together both on the domestic front, and later in Japan's colonies and on her battlefields.[21] The experience of patients and clients is perhaps the most difficult for historians reliably to access, although anthropologists such as Kitanaka and Ozawa-de Silva have successfully explored the perspectives of particular social groups.[22]

While broad scholarly interest in the history of psychiatry in Japan is relatively recent, the intersection of mental health with shifting social and cultural norms has been the object of anthropological and sociological enquiry at least since the wartime work of Geoffrey Gorer and Ruth Benedict,[23] frequently attended by questions about the nature and purported 'uniqueness' of the Japanese psycho-social world. There has been considerable overlap here with a body of writing, both in Japanese and English, described in terms of *nihonjinron*, or 'theories about (the) Japanese people'. The origins of this kind of speculative theorizing, which Harumi Befu describes as one of Japan's favourite and enduring 'national pastimes',[24] are usually traced back to the *kokugaku* (national learning) school of thought in late eighteenth-century Japan, which sought to distinguish truly 'Japanese' from Chinese- and Buddhist-influenced scholarship and culture. After Japan's opening up to broad western influence in the 1850s and 1860s, a similar discriminating dynamic encouraged the use of religious and psy ideas to try to make sense of the new historical–cultural position in which Japan as a national community found itself, and to provide relief for the social and psychological distress to which it was seen to be giving rise. A partnership between the psy disciplines and general cultural reflection on 'Japan' and 'Japaneseness' thus emerged, epitomized early on by the linking of neurasthenia to the relentless pressures and ambiguous rewards of modern, westernized life in Japan[25] and forming part of the subtext for much of the pioneering work in religion and psychotherapy that followed over the next century or more. A key theme here was a sense that aspects of Japan's modernizing project grated upon – even placed under threat – something essential and valuable about Japan and the Japanese people, leading to a rise in psychological incapacitation alongside deviancy and delinquency of all sorts, in which government officials, writers, and the media took a powerful interest.[26]

These concerns re-emerged in new forms as the Japanese reflected upon their defeat in war after 1945, with a publishing peak for *nihonjinron* in the 1970s and 1980s. Since that time, *nihonjinron* have receded slightly and have been treated somewhat as sociological and anthropological curiosities in their own right – by Yoshino Kosaku and Harumi Befu respectively – as well as being subjected to outright critical attack by Peter Dale, amongst others.[27] Many of the recurring themes within *nihonjinron* live on, however, as watered-down assumptions or vague intuitions in Japanese popular culture: the importance of climate and ancestry in shaping Japanese society and psyche; Japan's supposed groupism and especially high evaluation of good relationships and non-verbal communication, juxtaposed with westerners' heavy, almost pedantic reliance upon Aristotelian logic and verbosity in apprehending the world and communicating within it;[28] and a Japanese 'spirit' much beloved of mid-twentieth century militarists. Books regarded as classics of the genre, such as Watsuji Tetsurō's *Fūdo* [*Climate*] (1935), continue to be strong sellers, to such an extent that an element of self-fulfilling prophecy seems to be at play where *nihonjinron* are concerned – a theme taken up at various points in the present volume.

It is impossible to look back on the intersection of religion and the psy disciplines since 1868 without considering the way in which writers and practitioners in both realms have contributed material, methodologies, and sometimes professional credibility to this theorizing about 'the Japanese' – in particular Doi Takeo, in the Freudian tradition, and Kawai Hayao, Japan's first Jungian, both of whom feature in this collection.[29] The large audiences that both Doi and Kawai found for their ideas reminds us of how mistaken we would be to assess the impact upon Japanese society and culture of psychodynamic theories and practices purely on the basis of practitioner and client numbers, which have been consistently small when set alongside the boom in Rogerian counselling in recent decades. We would be equally mistaken in imagining that the political and ethical concerns arising from the religion–psy dialogue's ties with *nihonjinron* can be addressed by drawing a clear line between fictitious parochialism on the one hand and legitimate, constructive social-psychological commentary on the other. As Befu has pointed out, examples of *nihonjinron* must instead be considered in the broader context of the particular episodes and moods in Japan's modern history from which they emerge.[30]

A third area of Japan's modern history upon which the religion–psy dialogue touches is the emergence of new and re-shaped concepts and disciplines in her intellectual and institutional life; their initially uncertain meanings and spheres of competence inspiring the experimentation with ideas and practices in the prewar period upon which the first part of the present volume focuses. As recent work by Gerard Godart, Isomae Junichi, and Jason Josephson has shown, the matching of Japanese to western words – *shūkyō* (宗教) for 'religion', and the neologisms *tetsugaku* (哲学) for 'philosophy', *seishin ryōhō* (精神療法) for 'mental therapy' (in psychiatric contexts), and *shinri ryōhō* (心理療法) for 'psychological therapy' – involved difficult debates about precisely what these concepts denoted and how they functioned in the western societies upon which Japanese thinkers sought to draw carefully and selectively.[31] As Isomae and Josephson have shown, *shūkyō* was closely modelled on Protestant Christianity, with deliberate attempts at identifying and eradicating 'superstitions' and emphasizing faith and conduct in their place. A number of practices aimed at the manipulation of the mind were squeezed out of the definition of *shūkyō*, finding their way instead into 'therapy' – just one example of the way in which, in western and Japanese modernities alike, 'religion' and 'psychotherapy' are relational entities.[32]

The formation of new concepts and associated fields of expertise – in the media, medicine, literature, and rapidly proliferating academic institutions – was heavily bound up with political ambitions, with the particular concerns and aspirations of a range of intellectuals, religious and medical practitioners, laities and clientele, and with influences carried over from earlier decades, including a broadly encompassing virtue of 'self-cultivation' recently explored by Janine Anderson Sawada.[33] Though in the West during the same period the legacy of European Pietism and Romanticism, alongside early liberal Christian theology (particularly Friedrich Schleiermacher[34]) and American New Thought, was helping to blur the boundaries of religion, philosophy, the experiential, and the therapeutic, the sheer range of fresh thought-forms entering Japanese culture over a short span of time meant that the religion–psy dialogue in the prewar Japanese context was as much about the formation of new conceptual and disciplinary boundaries as their blurring or crossing.[35]

An important outcome of this state of affairs is that, as Chikako Ozawa-de Silva and Emiko Ohnuki-Tierney have pointed out, to label a particular Japanese practice using the English word 'psychotherapy' is to risk inaccurately circumscribing it through inappropriate connotations – in terms of what is implied about its origins, its purposes, and its likely meanings to participants.[36] This is most clearly the case with Morita and Naikan therapies, both of which feature in this volume and for neither of which either 'psychotherapy' or 'religious practice' would be an entirely satisfactory tag. The same concern applies to Kosawa Heisaku's distinctly Buddhistic brand of psychoanalysis, about whose philosophical underpinnings and implications his secular-minded and American-influenced students had their distinct doubts after the Second World War – Doi Takeo most vocal amongst them. Moreover, while Morita Masatake, Yoshimoto Ishin (developers of Morita and Naikan therapies, respectively), and Kosawa were all influenced by Japanese Buddhism, they seemed to have been only partially resolved in their own minds about how – or whether – the therapies they were developing and practising fitted with the Buddhist cosmologies to which they were heirs. There is evidence to suggest that they did not regard theoretical resolution as a priority in the religion–psy dialogue, in addition to which Yoshimoto in particular was mindful of how he presented his therapy in a postwar context where State Shintō and the wartime collaboration of many (though not all) Japanese religious organizations continued to cast a shadow.[37]

Away from the Japanese context too, the coming together of religion and the psy disciplines has given rise to all manner of difficulties over nomenclature and connotation, most obviously with an uneasy consensus developing around the separation out of 'religion' from 'spirituality', often for the purpose of allowing people to declare themselves 'spiritual, not religious': attuned to the transcendent or sensitive to the existential yet relatively unencumbered by tradition, institution, or dogma (and perhaps aspiring to be less encumbered by wealth and possessions, if we accept that the meaning of 'spiritual' is partly constructed by a spiritual–material dichotomy).[38] As Horie Norichika has shown, in the Japanese case 'spiritual' became particularly important after the considerable damage done to the reputation of all things 'religious' by the Aum Affair (see below).[39] And as Taniyama Yōzō suggests in this volume, there is a useful and strategic distinction to be made between 'religious care' and 'spiritual care' in the context of disaster relief work.

It is tempting to conclude, on the basis of this brief discussion about words and concepts, that function and efficacy are what matter in exploring and evaluating the religion–psy dialogue; that our focus should be upon experience, change, and healing, and that tying ourselves up in semantic knots does no more than hamper progress and waste time. To an extent this is true. Morita Masatake lambasted psychoanalysis for having pretty theories and an abominable cure rate. Kosawa sailed all the way to Europe to escape his university mentor's lack of practical therapeutic awareness. And the majority of ideas and practices to emerge from the religion–psy dialogue in Japan and elsewhere often point the finger at thinking and rumination – too much, or the wrong sort – as the very essence of the modern malaise.

And yet words and categories clearly play a dynamic role in how any practice – even a completely silent one[40] – fits into and shapes the rest of everyday life. As the psychiatrist Gerald May pointed out in his study of psychiatry, psychotherapy, and spiritual direction in the American context, without clarity over terms it is all too easy for people to be misled: imagining, for example, that psychologists deal in some way with the same things as a spiritual director, failing to distinguish (or assuming that, on some ultimate level, the distinction doesn't matter) between anthropocentric and theocentric approaches to the healing or transformation of the self, or confusing techniques that purport to offer control with techniques designed to open the individual up to inspiration or external agency. May argues for a clearer separation of religion and psychotherapy at the level of words and concepts; if they are to be brought together at all, better that this take place in the hearts of practitioners, informing their expertise and manner of engagement with clients, rather than in grand theories[41] or airy and obfuscatory metaphor. A complicating factor, however, for which perhaps May did not sufficiently allow, is that increasing numbers of people in the contemporary world approach the religion–psy dialogue in a cautiously exploratory spirit, so that it is not always possible or valid to be categorical at the outset about what is at stake – personally, spiritually, metaphysically, theologically – where a particular practice or encounter is concerned. Perhaps we see here a modern manifestation of the vagaries of prayer, in the context of which, as Ignatius of Loyola insisted, accurate 'discernment' of what is happening inside one's mind or heart is vital: something between a skill and an art, requiring experienced assistance for its development.[42]

Of two final historiographical themes to consider here, the first concerns what the religion–psy encounter may or may not be able to tell us about the lines between the religious and the secular and civil in Japan, about whether Japan can meaningfully be said to be a decreasingly religious society, and about which scholarly methodologies are best suited to the tackling of such vexing questions.[43] Timothy Fitzgerald takes the idea that the designation of something as 'religious' is often a matter of ideology or of vested interest, and pushes this to radical lengths: 'it has long been one of the fundamental assumptions of the religion industry that Buddhist temples are religious places', he writes, 'though we don't know clearly why'.[44] Ian Reader counters that evidence at least as far back as the eighth century shows Japanese temples, shrines, and their functionaries enjoying special tax and legal statuses precisely on account of their associations with other 'beings' and 'realms'.[45]

Staking out the 'religious' in any given context is clearly no simple exercise: even apparently useful sub-concepts like 'worshipfulness' and 'trust' present challenges, since they feature across a range of areas of life – Fitzgerald gives the example of the attitude of *shin'yō*, 'trust', which in the Japanese context is deeply bound up with a sense of confidence that social relationships will function as expected.[46] Discerning and labelling the content of an action – the attitudes and motivations involved – is, in other words, a complex exercise in interpretation, whether that action be participation in ritual or use of an apparently religious object, such as an *ema* (wooden plaque, inscribed with wishes or prayers) in a Shintō context or images of the Bodhisattva *Jizō* whose use in disaster relief care Taniyama describes in this volume. Many scholarly methodologies struggle at this point, with statistical surveys criticized for asking rather general questions ('Do you use charms?'[47]) without any mechanism for following up and unpicking the answers, while in-depth interviews with small groups of people can be dismissed as anecdotal and unrepresentative. The value of interviews and of self-ascription as a marker for religious-vs-secular is, in any case, likely to be compromised by various forms of self-editing in which we all habitually engage – people in this case perhaps talking about *shūkan* (custom or habit) rather than *shūkyō* when explaining their behaviour, out of a desire not to be thought superstitious or otherwise socially/psychologically suspect, especially after the Aum Affair.[48] Even where self-editing is at a minimum, people are of course still constrained and shaped by concepts and their shifting valences when they think about and identify themselves.

The potential contribution to be made to these debates by studying the religion–psy dialogue lies in freeing us from having to rely either on some dubious notion of an 'essence of religion' (which the academic field of religious studies did away with some years ago) or on a rather blunt and unlikely assertion that 'religion' is simply a blank canvas upon which successive generations paint, with complete autonomy, whatever they like. By looking at the formation and fate of new conceptual and therapeutic constructs to emerge from the religion–psy dialogue, such as those upon which the chapters in this volume focus, we can instead observe in detail the boundary work that has gone on between religion and the psy disciplines over the course of the late nineteenth and twentieth centuries. We can look at the serious ways in which the precise meaning, object, and function of 'religion' has been explored by practitioners and clienteles, and the various social and cultural dynamics that have been at play in delineating the 'religious' from the therapeutic, medical, or everyday. Taniyama's contribution to this volume, on 'religious' versus 'spiritual' forms of disaster relief care, brings these observations fully up to date: by watching 'clinical clergy' experimenting in their work with different choices of spatial and institutional contexts, clothing, words, and deeds when they deal with disaster victims, and learning about the ways in which these choices are interpreted by the people they work amongst, we move towards a usefully concrete sense of what 'religion' means to particular Japanese communities in the present day.

In addition, it is reasonable to expect that a focus, across much of the religion–psy dialogue, upon awareness and the interpretation of one's internal states, may give rise to more acute (though not necessarily more accurate) reflection on the part of future fieldwork interviewees when they discuss their own impression of the interrelation of the religious, secular, and civil. We may also end up being able to say more about where 'culture' fits into the religious–secular debate in Japan: is it understood as the broad context in which boundary work between the religious and the secular plays out, or does it more often become a euphemism or stand-in for religion (as with the postwar *nihonjinron* boom) – a valued alternative to what are seen as historically 'western' forms of secularism, pressing upon contemporary Japan from all sides? Ozawa-de Silva has highlighted the potential for confusion, between religion and culture. She warns against making too close an identification between Japanese cultural values at any one time and the rather broader Buddhist philosophical and psychological ideas upon which Naikan and parts of Kosawa's work drew.[49] Some of the problems with Peter Dale's critique of Japanese psychoanalysis seem to bear this out: Dale relied heavily on postwar writing by students of Kosawa, including Okonogi Keigo and Doi Takeo, both of whom had sought to exchange Kosawa's religious preoccupations for secular scientific professionalism in fuller communion with the international psychoanalytic movement, combined with psychological explorations of Japanese society and culture.[50] Dale ended up reading Okonogi's and Doi's concerns back into Kosawa, missing the intergenerational conflict between master and students and largely missing, too, what Iwata Fumiaki shows in this volume to be the specifically religious element in Kosawa's modification of the Oedipus Complex – at once more universal and more deeply personal than 'culture' seems to allows for.

Finally, what kind of people, what kind of 'subjects', has the religion–psy dialogue helped to create in Japan? One must beware of attributing too much about modern Japanese selfhood to the religion–psy dialogue since, as suggested above, the dialogue itself was often profoundly shaped by the social mores and politics of a given period – so much so that Dale and others have accused Morita Therapy and the like of being little more than an instrument of social-psychological coercion, persuading people to live up to the expectations of their times and to cope with their situation as it was presented to them.[51] There is a tension, of course, in any religious tradition or form of psychotherapy between discovery and creativity – between finding out something about oneself or the world that was previously hidden, and constructing a new vision of, or attitude towards the world.[52] But the argument where Japan is concerned is that new, hybrid religion–psy constructs tended to be therapies of 'commitment', in Philip Rieff's terms:[53] answering psychological needs by enabling people to commit, or re-commit to their communities, rather than be liberated from them.

The sorts of subjects that were created by Morita or Naikan were certainly acutely aware of their debts to mothers, fathers, other family members, wider society, and Reality in a more abstract sense. The Jōdo Shinshū Buddhist roots of both Naikan therapy and Kosawa's psychoanalysis may be seen to have contributed to these forms of therapy an ideal of *shinjin*, true entrusting to Other-power (sometimes understood devotionally in terms of Amida Buddha; elsewhere more in terms of an Absolute), which clients might feasibly apply in any sphere of life from private conscience and interpersonal relations to broader social interactions and political commitments.[54] Similarly, one might turn around Shimazono Susumu's comment, referred to above, about what he calls a 'psycho-religious composite movement' filling a modern vacuum of agreed ethical standards with technical methods of self-mastery, and ask whether such movements encourage the persistence of the vacuum they purport to fill: by encouraging and perpetuating a vision of human life where the only realistic goal is to accommodate oneself to the existing order.

Liberation and commitment are not so easily discerned and distinguished from one another, of course: the wordlessness of Zen practice and Zen-like therapies offer a degree of liberation from concepts, constructs, and the average person's tedious internal verbalizing in general, while at the same time requiring a commitment to a practice, to the ideals that support that practice, and in some cases to traditions, texts, and authority figures. The major difficulty here, where the creation of what we might call 'psycho-religious subjectivities' is concerned, is a lack of strong empirical evidence about client experiences in therapy. One is far more likely to stumble across satisfied customers, because in many cases such people formed enduring relationships with their therapists, becoming friends or *deshi* ('disciples') of one sort or another – or, in the case of Morita, forming groups to publicize and further facilitate his therapy. The less impressed are all but invisible except – we might speculate – as one-time visitors recorded in client notes (in contrast to those who returned for regular treatment), or turning up in the client notes of one therapist complaining of an unhappy experience with another. Perhaps the principal shortcoming of the present volume, reflecting the scholarly field as it stands, is that our focus is overwhelmingly upon pioneering individuals, institutions, and ideas. Interesting and significant though these are, the relative lack of information about clients is notable and ought to be a major priority for future research.

The likelihood that clients contributed significantly to the shaping of new therapies is suggested in Kondo Kyoichi and Kitanishi Kenji's chapter on Morita in this volume, and in recent work by Sawada in a related area: she reveals the powerful influence exerted upon twentieth-century Zen Buddhism in Japan by lay practitioners who funded the upkeep of temples and their communities in return for regular training and education by Zen masters.[55] Lay activism was not, of course, a new feature of the modern period: as James C. Dobbins has shown, the theology and institutional organization of Jōdo Shinshū (around rural *dōjō*, or meeting places) from the thirteenth century onwards was remarkable for the respect and power enjoyed by ordinary believers.[56] But in Inoue Enryō's advocacy of the non-institutional lay practice of Buddhism (*zaike bukkyō*) and in Inagita Kōsen's revival of koji Zen (lay engagement in Zen koan and meditation) we see a clearly modern empowerment of religious laities: newly cash-strapped religious institutions, particularly Buddhist ones in the wake of government confiscation of property, and contemplative or reflective religious practices playing a role in respectable middle-class culture – often bound up with professional or commercial statuses and ties. That the religion–psy dialogue too has had its modern laities must be recognized and the details pursued by research in years to come.

## Organization of the present volume

The individual contributions to this volume are drawn from scholars working in the fields of the history of psychiatry, Buddhist and religious studies, sociology, and cultural anthropology, as well as the worlds of religious and psychotherapeutic practice in present-day Japan. Approaches and thematic concerns vary considerably, but a chronological arrangement allows readers to connect these specialized perspectives with the general trends laid out in Chapter 1. It also allows us to counter the lingering sense in much western scholarship that innovations such as Morita Therapy, Kosawa's Ajase Complex and Doi's *Amae* theory are mere 'cultural variants' of seminal happenings in the West: instead, we are able here to see their deep originality and their rootedness in Japanese traditions and changing socio-historical circumstances – with borrowings from western intellectual traditions often rather more superficial, ad hoc, or narrowly pragmatic than it might first appear.

Beginning at the turn of the twentieth century, Hashimoto Akira looks at the role of religious institutions, particularly temples and shrines, in caring for the mentally ill just as western medical and psychological ideas were starting to make their way into Japan. He finds that a combination of poor initial psychiatric provision in the new western paradigm, suspicion (often fuelled by newspaper reports) of what went on in mental hospitals, and growing public concern with mental health meant that traditional therapies survived far longer than is generally supposed – especially where they were found to be in some way consistent with newly imported modern methods such as hydrotherapy and psychotherapy. Hashimoto rejects the thesis of the modern and medical simply replacing the old and 'superstitious', as inadequate in accounting either for the serious interest taken by psychiatric researchers in whether and why some of these religious therapies were successful or the efforts of some religious institutions to update their work in line with new insights about mental illness, as opposed simply to closing their doors.

Continuing the theme of new western theories being evaluated alongside pre-existing Japanese approaches to the body and mental health, Yoshinaga Shin'ichi looks in Chapter 3 at the emergence of new 'mind cure' methods in the Meiji era, from the University of Tokyo's first lecturer in Buddhism, the Zen priest Hara Tanzan, through a Japanese hypnotism boom and on to the birth of *seishin ryōhō* in the 1910s – a concept heavy with the cultural and political baggage of the preceding years. Although many ultimately dismissed Hara's theories of mind as eccentric – the product of a fleeting moment of fusion between Japanized Dutch anatomy, Daoism, and reformist Buddhism – his was a first attempt at thinking through the possibilities and implications of a religion–psy dialogue, and through his students Hara helped to shape the next century or more of religion and psychotherapy in Japan. One of these students was Inoue Enryō, who helped to introduce hypnosis and psychotherapy into Japan at the turn of the twentieth century. In contrast to Hara, who intended a reformed Buddhism to pay closer attention to transformation of the heart, Inoue sought to formulate a rationalized religion that would help Japan stand up to the West in political and cultural terms. Yoshinaga contrasts the work of Inoue here with Kuwabara Toshio, showing how uncertain and even contradictory was the nature of the religion–psy dialogue at this time: desacralization and resacralization seemed to run in parallel, since unlike Inoue, who used hypnotism to interpret, psychologically, the 'superstitious' and the 'magical', Kuwabara used it to affirm and to explore the reality of the supernatural. Yoshinaga sets all this against the backdrop of general Meiji-era dilemmas over mind, materialism, and the concept of *seishin* – 'spirit'.

The next two chapters consider two major, contrasting contributions from within Japanese psychiatry to the religion–psy dialogue in prewar Japan: the new therapy created by Morita Masatake and the Buddhist-influenced psychoanalysis of Kosawa Heisaku. Both chapters highlight the critical importance of personal life stories in the emergence of these new therapeutic forms. In their insider analysis of Morita Therapy, the Morita practitioners Kondo Kyoichi and Kitanishi Kenji see Morita Masatake as a psychiatrist discerning in Japanese life a new phenomenon – *shinkeishitsu*, a nervous character or temperament – on the basis of his own troubles, and setting out to tackle it by systematizing the cure he developed for his own situation and for a number of his colleagues. This involved a rejection of psychoanalysis and a relative sidelining of the prevailing German neuropsychiatry paradigm, with strong intellectual links discernible instead to Mahayana Buddhist philosophy. Kondo and Kitanishi argue that Morita rooted 'cure' in an attentive appreciation of one's natural and social environment, and sought to set up a contrast between western, elite forms of psychotherapy, on the one hand, and Japanese, non-elite forms on the other. Placing himself firmly in the latter camp, Morita emphasized the importance of social and cultural congruence in a successful psychotherapeutic modality – a concern that readers may want to consider in the light of the discussions of *nihonjinron* offered above.

In contrast to Morita's dismissal of psychoanalysis, his psychiatrist colleague Kosawa Heisaku saw in the life and work of Freud an echo of the pioneering exploration of the inner world for which the founder of the Shin sect of Buddhism, Shinran, was widely celebrated in Japan. Iwata Fumiaki shows in his chapter how this religious dimension to Kosawa's work has been largely obscured both in the postwar psychoanalytic profession in Japan and in scholarly writing about psychoanalysis. He links Kosawa's reworking of Freudian theory – epitomized by the answering of Freud's Oedipus Complex with an 'Ajase Complex' based in Buddhist legend – to the influence upon Kosawa of a Buddhist priest and junior of Inoue Enryō: Chikazumi Jōkan. In this sense, Kosawa's psychoanalysis and his Ajase Complex cannot be understood solely as an adaptation of Freud for the Japanese social context; rather, Kosawa was deeply committed to securing cultural space for Buddhism within the Japanese psy disciplines and society at large.

Kosawa's difficult relationship with his student, Doi Takeo, symbolizes the break between prewar Japan and the American influences and the relative secularism of the postwar period. 'Relative' secularism because, as Ando Yasunori shows in his chapter, Doi's Catholicism was crucial to the development of his hugely influential *Amae* theory. Ando argues that Doi sought here not to create an artificially 'Japanized' psychoanalysis, but rather to highlight existing elements in Japanese culture that resonated with the insights of Freud. Much of this Doi achieved by exploring his own powerful feelings of culture shock during brief periods of study and work in the United States, at a time when – in Doi's view – American psychoanalysis had a strong tendency to treat patients as objects, making few allowances for the sorts of human needs that Doi's *Amae* theory sought to understand.

Doi's influence in the postwar Japanese psy disciplines ran alongside that of Yoshimoto Ishin and his 'Naikan therapy', which had its origins in the same Japanese Buddhist sect – Jōdo Shinshū – as the form of psychoanalysis that Doi so vehemently opposed in Kosawa. In this chapter perhaps the single most influential contributor to the study of the religion–psy dialogue in the Japanese context, Shimazono Susumu, offers a sociological analysis of Naikan, placing it in the context of a broader movement that he discerns in modern Japan: from 'salvation' to 'healing'. Shimazono picks up on the way that as a 'psycho-religious composite method', Naikan exhibits a certain fluidity, an uncertainty, about its own religious or metaphysical connotations, arising as it did out of Yoshimoto's personal Buddhist faith, on which he never turned his back. Shimazono also offers a parallel to cautions in Hashimoto's chapter, about assuming simple shifts from traditional to modern, and from religious to secular. He shows that the emergence of Naikan was very much the product of pre-modern ambiguities and divisions within Jōdo Shinshū, concerning practice and devotion; and although many took to Naikan as a secular–rational approach to healing, Yoshimoto himself retained a belief in reincarnation and late in life became a monk, turning his house, which had been a Naikan centre, into a temple.

Terao Kazuyoshi offers further insights into Naikan's liminal status with his account of how a Catholic priest, Fujiwara Naosato, experienced Naikan with Yoshimoto Ishin himself and has since sought to transform it into a Catholic meditation practice that helps people struggling with grief and sorrow. The importance of this experiment is underscored in Terao's brief survey of Japanese Christianity's postwar engagement with psychology and psychotherapy, which reveals its substantial debt to western pastoral psychology and its relative lack, thus far, of original contributions to the dialogue between religion and the psy disciplines in modern Japan. 'Catholic Naikan meditation', as it is called, is just one of a number of signs that this state of affairs is starting to change: Christian groups are increasingly and more systematically becoming involved in counselling and various forms of psychological care – including disaster relief care, as Taniyama Yōzō shows in the penultimate chapter of this volume. In his analysis of Catholic Naikan meditation, Terao links a number of major themes within religion and psychotherapy in modern and contemporary Japan: the dilemmas of Christian 'inculturation', the rich and sometimes confusing multivalence of 'salvation' across religious and psycho-therapeutic worlds, orthodoxy and its margins, and finally the immensely important work of mourning.

Alongside the notion of a 'psycho-religious composite method', which he applied to Naikan, another of Shimazono Susumu's contributions to scholarship on the religion–psy dialogue has been to highlight the importance of what he calls 'spiritual intellectuals'. This theme is taken up by Tarutani Shigehiro in his essay on the pioneering figure of Kawai Hayao, Japan's first Jungian and the 'spiritual intellectual' par excellence. In including the dynamic of transnationalism in his analysis, Tarutani is able to focus on an aspect of Kawai's life and work that is central to the experience of many of the other figures in this volume (Morita, Kosawa, Doi):

the sense of needing to find an accommodation between their own western and Japanese selves. This raises the difficult question of whether, in their writing, Kawai and others were partly creating the problem – of split cultural personalities amongst cosmopolitan Japanese – that they claimed needed to be resolved, or whether theirs was a genuinely worthwhile exercise, one whose lessons remain relevant in contemporary Japan. We return to this question in our Conclusion. Tarutani also looks at how Kawai's Buddhism was influenced by Jung's functional understanding of religion and of myth: how these latter two operate, and what they achieve in the lives of individuals and in digging beneath the surface of national cultures to find out what makes them tick.

In the two chapters that follow, Horie Norichika and Shiotsuki Ryoko take up the theme of how the modern religion–psy dialogue has given new life – an apt metaphor, in this context – to two of Japan's oldest religious themes: ancestors, spirits, and reincarnation (Horie), and the healing power of shamans (Shiotsuki). Presenting the results of extensive recent fieldwork, Horie links shifts in popular understandings of reincarnation to patterns of continuity and change in Japanese subjectivities, not least where major themes of responsibility, interpersonal relations, and self-development are concerned. Japanese theorization of and engagement with Past Life Therapy (PLT) – which involves regression to past lives in a psychotherapeutic setting – turns out to be richly revealing, from ideas about a reincarnating Self to the suspension or bracketing out of questions of 'truth', when it comes to the reality or otherwise of past lives, in the interests of the peace and healing that imagining them can bring to this present one.

Shiotsuki brings a cultural anthropologist's eye to her subject matter: the survival of the Okinawan shamanic ('*yuta*') tradition from the premodern into the contemporary world, and its accommodation within the new idiom of *iyashi* – healing – discussed in Chapter 1. Exploring the reasons why *yuta*, the majority of whom are women, continue to practise and to be respected by the public when shamanism has largely disappeared in most other parts of Japan, Shiotsuki homes in on Okinawa's legal and medical systems, looking at the relative historical scarcity in this part of Japan of competing modes of treatment for the mentally ill – such as confinement, isolation, and western-style hospital treatment (there were no psychiatric hospitals in Okinawa prior to the Second World War). Shiotsuki offers a complement to Hashimoto's analysis in Chapter 2 of how western psychiatric paradigms have interacted – at the level of institutions, the law, and public awareness – with older ideas about possession, purity, and mental health and illness, by showing how Okinawa's particular combination of circumstances has helped to prevent possession from coming to be regarded as pathological there.

Our final essay explores the religion–psy dialogue in the aftermath of Japan's triple disasters of March 2011. Taniyama Yōzō, a Buddhist monk with experience working as a 'disaster chaplain' in the Tohoku region – and now an associate professor at Tohoku University's Department of Practical Religious Studies, which was set up in the wake of 3/11 – presents fieldwork case studies from affected regions of northern Japan, illustrating some of the work being done by 'chaplains' from a range of faiths: contributing grief care, prayer, and counselling to populations in need. Taniyama sets these in the context of changing legal and public attitudes towards religion, and considers the practicalities and possible benefits of distinguishing 'religious' from 'spiritual' disaster relief care. He argues that having learned from the failings of the relief effort in the wake of the Kobe earthquake (1995), Japan's religious organizations must now learn too from the shortcomings after 3/11. Before the next disaster happens, Japan needs four things: (1) interfaith organizations and common standards for chaplains; (2) relationships of mutual trust with healthcare teams and government; (3) a systematic examination of the quality and effect of religious care; and (4) a system that takes into account the diversity of each community.

Our concluding chapter picks up a number of threads from these individual contributions, focusing first upon the potential for 'care' to be a means by which Japanese religions re-enter and secure for themselves a place in postwar and contemporary civil society and culture. It then homes in on three particular tensions that seem to be at the heart of the religion–psychotherapy encounter in Japan and to extend beyond it into Japan's experience of modernity and modernization more generally: the personal versus the (con)textual, creation versus discovery, and instrumentalism versus engrossment.

## Notes

1 Sigmund Freud, Letter to Marui Kiyoyasu, 10 November 1927. Sigmund Freud Archive, Library of Congress, Washington, DC.
2 On Freud's relationships with his Indian and Japanese colleagues, and his quasi-colonialist outlook when it came to the spread of psychoanalysis around the globe, see Harding, 'Sigmund's Asian fanclub?', p. 357.
3 See Iwata, this volume.
4 On conceptual invention and reinvention in modern Japanese religion, see Josephson, *The Invention of Religion in Japan*.
5 See Engler, 'Being somebody and being nobody'.
6 The tensions that exist within and surrounding the psychology of religion, as an academic discipline – revealed in how the aims of 'reduction' as a methodology are variously understood – are rather instructive on this point. See the Introduction in Wulff, *Psychology of Religion*.
7 On the potency and irreducibility of symbol and myth, see Ricoeur, *The Symbolism of Evil*. For a personal, heavily psychological account of the power of the Christian message, see Spufford, *Unapologetic*.
8 See Taniyama, this volume.
9 This is most highly developed, in the Japanese context, in *nihonjinron*: 'theories about the Japanese'.
10 Tarutani, 'Transcendence and Immanence', p. 107.

11 On the aftermath of the Aum Affair see the special issue of the *Japanese Journal for Religious Studies* (Vol 39, 2012). Erica Baffelli and Ian Reader note that in addition to heavy media criticism of religious studies academics, commentators wondered why an education at elite universities had not prevented a number of Aum devotees from being taken in by the cult's leader, Asahara. Baffelli and Reader, 'Impact and ramifications', pp. 5–6, 16–17. See also Reader, 'Scholarship, Aum Shinrikyō, and academic integrity'.
12 See Shimazono, *From Salvation to Spirituality*, especially Chapter 11: 'From religion to psychotherapy'; also Shimazono, *Iyasu Chi no Keifu*.
13 Rose, *Governing the Soul*, p. 11.
14 Kitanaka, *Depression in Japan*.
15 Rose, *Governing the Soul*, p. 11.
16 One young man sought out Kosawa Heisaku in 1946 with precisely this question on his lips. Christopher Harding, 'The therapeutic method of Kosawa Heisaku'.
17 See for example Okada's work on perhaps the most famous psychiatric institution in Japan, the Matsuzawa Hospital, attached to the University of Tokyo: Okada, *Shisetsu Matsuzawa Byōin-shi*. For a more general historical account: Matsushita and Hiruta (eds), *Seishin-iryō no Rekishi*.
18 On Kure, see Okada, *Kure Shūzo: Sono Shōgai to Gyōseki*, and, on Kure's links with Germany: Hashimoto, 'A "German world" shared among doctors'. On Kosawa: Blowers and Yang Hsueh Chi, 'Freud's deshi'; Takeda, *Seishin Bunseki to Bukkyō*; Harding, 'The therapeutic method of Kosawa Heisaku'; Iwata, this volume. On women in mental healthcare, see Urano's biography of the pioneering psychiatric nurse, Ishibashi Haya: *Ishibashi Haya Joshi no Kiseki*.
19 On *taijinkyōfushō* see Russell, 'Anxiety disorders in Japan'. On *hikikomori* see Horiguchi, 'Hikikomori'. On depression see Kitanaka, *Depression in Japan*.
20 The phrase comes from Garon, *Molding Japanese Minds*.
21 Matsumura, 'Mental health as public peace'. Wu, *A Disorder of Ki*.
22 See for example Ozawa-de Silva, 'Shared death'.
23 *Time Magazine* ran a piece on Gorer in August 1944, entitled 'Science: Why are Japs Japs?' See also Gorer, *Japanese Character Structure*. Benedict's controversial *The Chrysanthemum and the Sword*, a perennial bestseller in Japan, was first published in 1946.
24 Befu, *Hegemony of Homogeneity*. See also Ryang, *Japan and National Anthropology*; Dale, *The Myth of Japanese Uniqueness*.
25 See Hill, 'Exhausted by their battles with the world'. As Yu-chuan Wu has shown, a neurasthenia diagnosis was sometimes worn as a badge of honour – a sure sign of civic engagement and commitment to Japan's modernizing project – but people such as the journalist Ishikawa Hanzan, author of *Neurasthenia and Recovery* (1909), were also genuinely doubtful about Japan's cultural trajectory. Wu, *A disorder of Ki*, especially pp. 39–40.
26 See Ambaras, *Bad Youth*. Japanese journalism and literature of the early twentieth century offers a vivid resource for grasping the broad contours here, from mythologizing and romanticism about Japanese particularism, blood, the imperial institution, language, ecology, and spirit, to the rather more nuanced social and cultural commentary of writers such as Natsume Sōseki. See in particular the *shishōsetsu* ('I-novel') genre. Fowler, *The Rhetoric of Confession*.
27 Kosaku, *Cultural Nationalism in Contemporary Japan*; Dale, *The Myth of Japanese Uniqueness*. Not only is the understanding of Japan as a whole impoverished by *nihonjinron*: Befu notes that nuances of region, class, gender, rural, and urban tend to be lost, while Dale suggests that a stereotype of the West is perpetuated – as patriarchal, meat-eating, rationalist, alienating, and violent. See Befu, *Hegemony of Homogeneity*, p. 4; Dale, *The Myth of Japanese Uniqueness*, pp. 12–23.

28 Befu gives the example of Itasaka Gen, who found the western 'I love you' positively cumbersome in its requirement for constant reiteration – indicative of a culture that was deficient in 'intuitive understanding'. Itasaka, quoted in Befu, *Hegemony of Homogeneity*, p. 39. For Dale, this juxtaposition of prosaic western languages with poetic Japanese is nothing more than 'historical [Japanese] resentment' at the achievements of first China and then the West: 'sentimental revolt against the language of critical thinking' (pp. 100–101). The implication that exophoric, or content-dependent speech is all but unknown in the West is simply unfounded, he insists. Dale, *The Myth of Japanese Uniqueness*, Chapter 7: 'Silence and elusion'.

29 See Sharf, 'The Zen of Japanese nationalism'. Nagapriya, 'Poisoned Pen Letters?'

30 Befu, *Hegemony of Homogeneity*, pp. 123–141.

31 Godart, ' "Philosophy" or "religion"?'; Isomae, 'Kindai nihon ni okeru 'shūkyō' gainen no keiseikatei'; Josephson, *The Invention of Religion in Japan*, and 'When Buddhism Became a "Religion"'. See also Howland, 'Translating liberty in nineteenth-century Japan'. Related debates took place over how to translate as crucial a term as 'education'. Japan's Education Minister Mori Arinori promoted a distinction between *kyōiku* on the one hand, referring to the imparting of knowledge from a senior, and/or more learned party to a junior, as-yet-immature one, and *gakumon*, on the other: a more mature task of choosing and pursuing a particular interest of one's own. Sawada, *Practical Pursuits*, p. 94. See also Yoshinaga, this volume.

32 See Yoshinaga, this volume. On 'relational entities', see Harding (Conclusion), this volume.

33 Sawada, *Practical Pursuits*.

34 See Schleiermacher, *The Christian Faith* (1821).

35 On 'boundaries' see Ornatowski, 'On the boundary between "religious" and "secular" '. On 'boundary work' see Gieryn, 'Boundary-work'.

36 Ozawa-de Silva, *Psychotherapy and Religion in Japan*, p. 43. See also Ohnuki-Tierney, *Illness and Culture in Contemporary Japan*.

37 On Kosawa, see Harding, 'The therapeutic method of Kosawa Heisaku'; Harding, 'Japanese Psychoanalysis and Buddhism'; Iwata, this volume. On Yoshimoto, Ozawa-de Silva, *Psychotherapy and Religion in Japan*, and Shimazono, this volume; on Morita, Kondo and Kitanishi, this volume.

38 On the question of definitions, see Sutcliffe and Bowman (eds), *Beyond the New Age*.

39 Horie, 'Spirituality and the spiritual in Japan'. See also Horie, this volume.

40 See Sharf, 'The rhetoric of experience and the study of religion'.

41 May, *Care of Mind/Care of Spirit*, especially Chapter One: 'Heritage: history, definitions, and distinctions'.

42 The Jesuit writer Gerard Hughes has explored discernment in the context of contemporary life and psychology: *God of Surprises* (1986).

43 Hardacre, 'Religion and civil society in contemporary Japan'; Reader, 'Secularisation, RIP?' and 'What constitutes religious activity? (II)'.

44 Fitzgerald, 'Religion and the secular in Japan'.

45 Reader, 'Ideology, academic inventions, and mystical anthropology'.

46 Fitzgerald, 'Religion and the secular in Japan'. See also Fitzgerald, *Japanese Religion: A Critical Anthropology* (forthcoming, 2014).

47 Anderson, 'What constitutes religious activity? (I)'.

48 Reader, 'What constitutes religious activity? (II)'. Anderson, 'What constitutes religious activity? (I)'.

49 Ozawa-de Silva, 'Demystifying Japanese therapy', p. 429.

50 Doi, who was analyzed by Kosawa, particularly disliked the role played by

Buddhistic speculation and a motherly approach in Kosawa's therapeutic method. Doi, 'Kosawa Heisaku to Nihonteki Seishinbunseki'. See, in this context, Amy Borovoy's recent analysis of Doi's desire to 'reconcile prewar ideals of national community ... with postwar ideals of liberal democracy'. Borovoy, 'Doi Takeo and the Rehabilitation of Particularism in Postwar Japan', p. 265 and pp. 274–282.
51 See Dale, *The Myth of Japanese Uniqueness*. Practices like Morita Therapy, he claims, normalize certain patterns of development, emotion, and behaviour while pathologizing and 'treating' others. See pp. 22–23.
52 See Harding (Conclusion), this volume.
53 Rieff, *The Triumph of the Therapeutic*.
54 On Naikan here, see Ozawa-de Silva, *Psychotherapy and Religion in Japan*, especially Chapter 3 (Naikan confessions), and Shimazono, this volume; on Kosawa and *shinjin*, see Harding, 'The therapeutic method of Kosawa Heisaku', and Iwata, this volume.
55 Sawada, *Practical Pursuits*.
56 See Dobbins, *Jōdo Shinshū*.

## References

Ambaras, David R. *Bad Youth: Juvenile Delinquency and the Politics of Everyday Life in Modern Japan* (Berkeley: University of California Press, 2005).

Anderson, Richard W. 'What constitutes religious activity? (I)', *Japanese Journal of Religious Studies* 18, no. 4 (1991).

Baffelli, Erica and Reader, Ian. 'Impact and ramifications: the aftermath of the Aum Affair in the Japanese religious context', *Japanese Journal of Religious Studies* (Vol. 39, 2012).

Befu, Harumi. *Hegemony of Homogeneity* (Melbourne, Trans Pacific Press, 2001).

Blowers, Geoffrey H and Yang Hsueh Chi, Serena. 'Freud's deshi: the coming of psychoanalysis to Japan,' *Journal of the History of the Behavioral Sciences* 33, no. 2 (1997).

Borovoy, Amy. 'Doi Takeo and the rehabilitation of particularism in postwar Japan', *The Journal of Japanese Studies* 38, no. 2 (2012).

Dale, Peter. *The Myth of Japanese Uniqueness* (New York: St Martin's Press, 1986).

Dobbins, James C. *Jōdo Shinshū: Shin Buddhism in Medieval Japan* (Bloomington: Indiana University Press, 2002).

Doi Takeo. 'Kosawa Heisaku to Nihonteki Seishinbunseki (Kosawa Heisaku and Japanese Psychoanalysis)', short unpublished essay based on Doi's speech to the twenty-fifth conference of the Japan Psychoanalytic Society (1979). Tokyo: Kosawa Family Private Collection.

Engler, Jack. 'Being somebody and being nobody: a reexamination of the understanding of self in psychoanalysis and Buddhism', in Jeremy D. Safran (ed.), *Psychoanalysis and Buddhism: An Unfolding Dialogue* (Boston: Wisdom Publications, 2003).

Fitzgerald, Timothy. 'Religion and the secular in Japan: problems in history, social anthropology and the study of religion,' *Electronic Journal of Contemporary Japanese Studies* (July, 2003).

Fitzgerald, Timothy. *Japanese Religion: A Critical Anthropology* (London: Continuum, 2014).

Fowler, E. *The Rhetoric of Confession: Shishōsetsu in Early Twentieth-century Japanese Fiction* (Berkeley: University of California Press, 1988).

Garon, Sheldon. *Molding Japanese Minds: the State in Everyday Life* (Princeton: Princeton University Press, 1998).

Gieryn, Thomas F. 'Boundary-work and the demarcation of science from non-science: strains and interests in professional ideologies of scientists'. *American Sociological Review* (American Sociological Association) 48, 6 (1983).

Godart, Gerard Clinton. '"Philosophy" or "religion"? the confrontation with foreign categories in late nineteenth century Japan', *Journal of the History of Ideas* 69, no. 1 (2008).

Gorer, Geoffrey. *Japanese Character Structure* (New York: Institute for Intercultural Studies, 1942).

Hardacre, Helen. 'Religion and civil society in contemporary Japan', *Japanese Journal of Religious Studies* 31, no. 2 (2004).

Harding, Christopher. 'Sigmund's Asian Fanclub? The Freud franchise and independence of mind in India and Japan', in Robert Clarke (ed.), *Celebrity Colonialism: Fame, Power and Representation in Colonial and Postcolonial Cultures* (Newcastle upon Tyne: Cambridge Scholars Press, 2009).

Harding, Christopher. 'The Therapeutic Method of Kosawa Heisaku: "Religion" and "the Psy Disciplines"', *Japanese Contributions to Psychoanalysis Volume 4* (Tokyo: Japan Psychoanalytic Society, 2013).

Harding, Christopher. 'Japanese psychoanalysis and Buddhism: the making of a relationship', *History of Psychiatry*, 25, 2 (June 2014).

Hashimoto, Akira. 'A "German world" shared among doctors: a history of the relationship between Japanese and German psychiatry before World War II', *History of Psychiatry* 24, 2 (2013).

Hill, Christopher. 'Exhausted by their battles with the world: neurasthenia and civilization critique in early twentieth century Japan', in Nina Cornyetz and J. Keith Vincent (eds), *Perversion and Modern Japan: Psychoanalysis, Literature, Culture* (London: Routledge, 2010).

Horie, Norichika. 'Spirituality and the spiritual in Japan', *Journal of Alternative Spiritualities and New Age Studies* 5 (2009).

Sachiko Horiguchi. 'Hikikomori', in Roger Goodman, Yuki Imoto, and Tuukka Toivonen, *A Sociology of Japanese Youth* (London: Routledge, 2012).

Howland, D. 'Translating liberty in nineteenth-century Japan', *Journal of the History of Ideas* 62, no. 1 (2001).

Hughes, Gerard. *God of Surprises* (Luton: Andrews UK, 1986).

Isomae Junichi. 'Kindai nihon ni okeru "shūkyō" gainen no keiseikatei [The formative process of the category "shūkyō" in modern Japan]', *Nihon Joshi Daigaku Sōgō Kenkyūjō Nyūsu*, 8 (2000).

Josephson, Jason Ananda. 'When Buddhism became a "religion": religion and superstition in the writings of Inoue Enryō', *Japanese Journal of Religious Studies* 33, no. 1 (2006).

Josephson, Jason Ananda. *The Invention of Religion in Japan* (Chicago: University of Chicago Press, 2012).

Kitanaka, Junko. *Depression in Japan: Psychiatric Cures for a Society in Distress* (Princeton: Princeton University Press, 2011).

Yoshino Kosaku, *Cultural Nationalism in Contemporary Japan* (London: Routledge, 1992).

Matsumura, Janice. 'Mental health as public peace: Kaneko Junji and the promotion of psychiatry in modern Japan', *Modern Asian Studies* 38, no. 4 (2004).

Matsushita Masaaki and Hiruta Genshiro (eds). *Seishin-iryō no Rekishi [A History of Psychiatric Practice]*, Supplement No. 1 of the Encyclopaedia of Psychiatry (1999).

May, Gerald G. *Care of Mind/Care of Spirit: A Psychiatrist Explores Spiritual Direction* (San Francisco: Harper San Francisco, 1992).

Nagapriya, Dharmachari. 'Poisoned pen letters? D.T. Suzuki's communication of Zen to the West', *Western Buddhist Review* 5 (2008).

Ohnuki-Tierney, Emiko. *Illness and Culture in Contemporary Japan* (Cambridge: Cambridge University Press, 1984).

Okada Yasuo, *Shisetsu Matsuzawa Byōin-shi: 1879–1980 [Matsuzawa Hospital: A Private History, 1879–1980]* (Tokyo: Iwasaki Gakujutsu Shuppansha, 1981).

Okada Yasuo, *Kure Shūzo: Sono Shōgai to Gyōseki [The Life and Works of Kure Shuzo]* (Kyoto: Shibunkaku Shuppan, 1982).

Ornatowski, Gregory K. 'On the boundary between "religious" and "secular": the ideal and practice of neo-Confucian self-cultivation in modern Japanese economic life', *Japanese Journal of Religious Studies* 25, no. 3 (1998).

Ozawa-de Silva, Chikako. *Psychotherapy and Religion in Japan: the Japanese Introspection Practice of Naikan* (New York: Routledge, 2006).

Ozawa-de Silva, Chikako. 'Demystifying Japanese therapy: an analysis of Naikan and the Ajase Complex through Buddhist thought', *Ethos* 35, no. 4 (2007).

Ozawa-de Silva, Chikako. 'Shared death: self, sociality and internet group suicide in Japan', *Transcultural Psychiatry* 47, no. 3 (July 2010).

Reader, Ian. 'What constitutes religious activity? (II)', *Japanese Journal of Religious Studies* 18, no. 4 (1991).

Reader, Ian. 'Scholarship, Aum Shinrikyō, and academic integrity', *Nova Religio*, 3 (2000), pp. 368–382.

Reader, Ian. 'Ideology, academic inventions, and mystical anthropology: responding to Fitzgerald's errors and misguided polemics', *Electronic Journal of Contemporary Japanese Studies* (March, 2004).

Reader, Ian. 'Secularisation, RIP? Nonsense! The rush hour away from the gods and the decline of religion in contemporary Japan', *Journal of Religion in Japan* 1, no. 1 (2012).

Ricoeur, Paul. *The Symbolism of Evil* (New York: Harper & Row, 1967).

Rieff, Philip. *The Triumph of the Therapeutic: Uses of Faith After Freud* (New York: Harper & Row, 1966).

Rose, Nikolas. *Governing the Soul: Shaping of the Private Self* (London: Routledge, 1999).

Russell, John G. 'Anxiety disorders in Japan: a review of the Japanese literature on Shinkeishitsu and Taijinkyōfushō', *Culture, Medicine and Psychiatry* 13, no. 4 (1989).

Ryang, Sonia. *Japan and National Anthropology* (New York: Routledge, 2004).

Sawada, Janine Anderson. *Practical Pursuits: Religion, Politics, and Personal Cultivation in Nineteenth-Century Japan* (Honolulu: University of Hawai'i Press, 2004).

Schleiermacher, Friedrich. *The Christian Faith* (1821).

Sharf, R.H. 'The Zen of Japanese nationalism', *History of Religions* 33, no. 1 (1993): 1–43.

Sharf, R.H. 'The rhetoric of experience and the study of religion', *Journal of Consciousness Studies*, 7, no. 11–12 (2000).

Shimazono Susumu. *Iyasu Chi no Keifu* (Tokyo: Yoshikawa Kōbunkan, 2003).

Shimazono Susumu. *From Salvation to Spirituality* (Melbourne: Trans Pacific Press, 2004).

Spufford, Francis. *Unapologetic: Why, Despite Everything, Christianity Can Still Make Surprising Emotional Sense* (New York: HarperOne, 2012).

Sutcliffe, Steven and Bowman, Marion (eds). *Beyond the New Age: Exploring Alternative Spirituality* (Edinburgh: Edinburgh University Press, 2000).

Takeda Makoto. *Seishin Bunseki to Bukkyō [Psychoanalysis and Religion]* (Tokyo: Shinchōsha, 1990).

Shigehiro Tarutani. 'Transcendence and immanence: Buddhism and psychotherapy in Japan', in Mark Unno (ed.), *Buddhism and Psychotherapy Across Cultures: Essays on Theories and Practices* (Boston: Wisdom Publications, 2006).

Urano Shima. *Ishibashi Haya Joshi no Kiseki: Meiji, Taishō, Shōwa wo Kakenuketa Naichingeeru [Traces of Ms Ishibashi Haya: the [Florence] Nightingale of the Meiji, Taishō, and Shōwa era]* (Tokyo: Makino Shuppan, 1996).

Wu, Yu-chuan. *A disorder of Ki, Alternative Treatments for Neurasthenia in Japan, 1890–1945*, University College London dissertation (2012).

Wulff, David. *Psychology of Religion: Classic and Contemporary* (New York: John Wiley & Sons, 1997).

# 1 Religion and psychotherapy in modern Japan

A four-phase view

*Christopher Harding*

We may usefully divide the period covered by the present volume into four phases: the initial impact of Japan's modernizing reforms and its interaction with western politics and culture, from the late nineteenth century through to the early 1910s; the rise, from the 1910s to the late 1940s, of psychotherapies inspired by new scientific and medical ideas but rooted in – or making strategic use of – traditional Japanese religious or cultural forms; Japan's rebirth as a nation in the early 1950s and the renewed impact of western, particularly American, dynamic and developmental psychology; and finally a boom for new religious, spiritual, cultural, and psychotherapeutic discourses from the 1970s onwards – some cosmopolitan and outward looking, others echoing pre-war concerns about the cohesion of Japanese society and culture, and almost all of them seeking to offer alternative or corrective discourses and rationalities to the modernism of the previous period. All four periods have fed into present-day mental health priorities in Japan, including the provision of counselling in schools and universities, together with grief, terminal, and disaster care.

## Meiji-era religion and the psy disciplines: 1868–1912

Japan's dramatically expanding involvement with western modernity from the 1860s onwards, and the resulting intellectual and social tensions over whether and how modernization could practically be distinguished from westernization, was a major force shaping the emerging religion–psy dialogue in this first period. The position of Japanese religious ideas and institutions in such a climate was rather ambiguous. Japanese Buddhism in particular was vulnerable, linked to the power of the old regime and to what many modern intellectuals saw as Japan's historically weak polity and her humiliating scientific and technological backwardness. A period of anti-clerical violence at the end of the 1860s, as the early Meiji government's policy of *shimbutsu bunri* (separation of Shintō and Buddhism) degenerated into *haibutsu kishaku* (the eradication of Buddhism), confirmed high levels of popular anger against the Buddhist establishment and heightened the sense that Buddhism was inconsistent with the aspirations of the new society that was taking shape.[1]

And yet, in common with other non-western nations in the modern era, Japanese intellectuals and political leaders regarded their cultural inheritance as an important resource in establishing Japan as a powerful and sophisticated country in the eyes of western peers. As H. Gene Blocker and Christopher L. Starling have pointed out, Japanese leaders faced a dilemma here – alongside their counterparts in China and India – over whether their aims would be best achieved by reinterpreting and promoting indigenous culture in the terms of imported foreign disciplines and institutions, such as western philosophy and forms of political organization, or by eschewing foreign forms in favour of revivified local idioms.[2] As a number of the chapters in this volume show, the coming together of religion and psychotherapy in Japan was frequently a combination of these two approaches. The work both of the reforming Buddhist philosopher Inoue Enryō and the psychoanalyst Kosawa Heisaku was characterized by the conviction that the core of traditional religion and the cutting edge of western science were fully compatible and even complementary – helping to expose false religion and fraudulent science. Of the two individuals, Inoue was the more systematic in seeking to carve out areas of appropriate operation for religion and for science. He was assiduous in cultivating government and popular support for his schema: seeking to demonstrate, for example, that psychology could help in ridding Japan of harmful superstitions, for which real Buddhism had no time and bore no responsibility.[3]

A surge in Christian missionary activity in Japan, particularly in the generation beginning in the 1870s (when government restrictions on Christian activity were relaxed), further contributed to the reforms of Buddhism, encouraged by the likes of Inoue. Buddhist sects sending delegations to Europe and America around this time, to investigate Christianity's institutional, intellectual, and social dimensions, quickly found that various of the modern sciences offered powerful means of critiquing the tenets and practices of this religion that they so feared as a potential competitor (relatively large numbers of former samurai became Christians during the early part of the Meiji era). One of the advantages for Inoue and others in showing how easily Buddhism and science could be reconciled was that this further underlined what they regarded – and hoped to advertise to fellow Japanese – as Christianity's preposterousness and irreconcilability with science and with modernity more generally.[4]

This, however, was only one side of the story where Buddhist–Christian relations were concerned. Modernizing Buddhists began to emulate and even co-operate with some of the forms of education, outreach, and social work in which Christian groups engaged – something made all the more acceptable in social and political terms as Japanese Christians from the 1890s onwards sought to make the case for the compatibility of what the prominent Christian Uchimura Kanzō described as the two 'J's: Jesus and

Japan. This was to be important for future religion–psy dialogue in two ways. First, investment by some Japanese Buddhist organizations in the creation of school and dormitory facilities proved a highly successful means of engaging with new generations, helping to ensure that the modern rationalist dimensions of their education were complemented by an immersion in Buddhist culture. It was at one such Buddhist dormitory that a Jōdo Shinshū priest, Chikazumi Jōkan, met and influenced profoundly the life of the young Kosawa Heisaku.[5]

Second, Buddhist intellectual outreach made possible the beginnings of a positive three-way dialogue between Buddhism, Christianity, and science.[6] As Notto R. Thelle has pointed out, there were many in Japan at this time who experienced an attraction to both Buddhism and Christianity. Such people became pioneers of inter-religious study and Buddhist–Christian dialogue, with a Chair of Comparative Religion established at the University of Tokyo in 1889 and a Buddhist–Christian Conference taking place in 1896. Although Thelle cautions that these early encounters were rather rudimentary in philosophical terms, an intellectual and spiritual context was clearly taking shape in which religious ideas and practices were to be weighed and considered side by side.[7] Science became a part of this context initially in the form of evolutionary theory, with Buddhists taking an interest in Christian debates about Darwin – possibly with slight smiles on their faces: evolution was rather more of a problem for Christianity than for Buddhism since the former's anthropology and Old Testament narratives were still taught and understood in many quarters as (historically) literal. As Helen Ballhatchet has pointed out, the matter was most pressing of all for Japanese Christian converts, many of whom had initially been won over to Christianity as the apparent spiritual bedrock of western science and civilization.[8] Here already, then, we find key elements of inter-religious and religion–psy dialogue in the decades to come: the status of doctrine, metaphysics, rationality, faith, belief, and the weighing of conflicting claims, academic disciplines, and professional expertise.

Developments in Japanese medicine and science – rooted in far-reaching explorations of western knowledge and techniques after 1868, including the employment of foreign experts and periods of study abroad for significant numbers of promising young Japanese professionals[9] – shaped religion–psy dialogue both directly, in terms of new ideas, and indirectly, by creating legal frameworks, institutions, and professional hierarchies, within and often in opposition to which relatively informal psychotherapies and psycho-religious therapies then emerged. The two key pieces of mental healthcare legislation in the pre-war period were the 1900 Mental Patients' Custody Act and the 1919 Mental Hospitals Act. Up until the turn of the twentieth century, regulation in Japan was largely an extension of an early modern emphasis upon confining those regarded as dangerous lunatics to their homes or to secure municipal institutions. Responsibility rested with the person's family and with the local police, and it was only when news got out in the Japanese media in the 1880s that a powerful former feudal lord had been unjustly held on a pretext of lunacy that the call was raised for proper national legislation. The issue quickly got caught up with the Japanese political establishment's one abiding preoccupation: to demonstrate that Japan had risen to become the equal of western nations in any and all things. The resulting Act in 1900 was not, however, a watershed in psychiatric care in Japan: it provided for the regulation by law of the old system of confinement, with a requirement that a 'custodian' be appointed for anyone deemed dangerously ill and the criminalization of wrongful confinement. The custodian was usually a family member, since coping with this kind of mental illness was regarded most fundamentally as a family rather than a state responsibility. This custodian would apply for the imposition of custody at an approved location, often the family home, in which a cage-like secure room was installed, to be inspected now and again by local police and doctors.[10]

As this construal of mental illness in terms of the confinement of the dangerously insane gathered cultural and legal force in late nineteenth and early twentieth century Japan, a Japanese psychiatric establishment began to emerge that was heavily indebted to German systems and concepts[11] and centred around prestigious university departments, particularly at Japan's imperial universities: Tokyo, and later Kyoto, Tohoku, and Kyushu. Largely thanks to developments at the University of Tokyo, under the German doctor Erwin Baelz from 1879 and the German-trained Kure Shūzō after 1901, a professional psychiatric paradigm was established across Japan rooted in the categories and research focus of Kraepelinian neuropsychiatry. Japan's second major piece of mental health legislation of the pre-war era was directly influenced by this new medical and psychiatric expertise: the Mental Hospitals Act of 1919 was in part the result of successful lobbying by Kure and others for 'lunacy' to be seen not merely as a problem of law and order or public safety, but of illness; not merely the responsibility of families and the police, but of qualified doctors and hospitals. Under the new law, the emphasis shifted from confinement at home to hospitalization, partly using the private mental hospitals that had emerged in Japan to cater for those whose families could not look after them (local authorities footed the bill, making for a reasonably steady and lucrative line of business) and requiring the building in each of Japan's prefectures of a public asylum. Psychiatrists were accorded considerable respect under the new Act and in this period more generally: they were employed by government and the police as consultants, conducted the epidemiological surveys for which Kure became well known, and cooperated with various bodies in promoting mental hygiene in the general population.[12]

Hashimoto Akira has cautioned against overstating the extent to which these institutional and professional changes resulted in a neat shift in the popular understanding of mental health and illness, from traditional religious and folk to biomedical models. And Suzuki points out that these two major pre-war pieces of legislation on mental illness and care mostly codified existing practices (custody then hospitalization) rather than staking out new territory and imposing new ideals from above.[13] But undoubtedly the dissemination of neuropsychiatric models of mental health via hospitals and clinics, government policy, the law courts, and the popular media had powerful and mixed effects: alongside the humanitarian advantages of new forms of care ran fear over stigma and the potentially serious legal implications of some diagnoses,[14] together with a sense, albeit difficult to gauge, that when it came to emotional problems and psychological distress there was relatively little that Japanese psychiatry was inclined to say or do.

Alongside these themes of modernization, state-building, and new institutional and intellectual activity we find four major cultural dynamics in operation across this period: the power, especially since the early nineteenth century, of an encompassing paradigm of 'personal cultivation';[15] a concern of popular new religious movements around that same time with physical and spiritual healing; a post-1868 emphasis upon the importance of practical learning; and an interest in the making of psychological problems experienced by Japanese urbanites a kind of social or cultural barometer – a sign of the times.

The 'personal cultivation' paradigm, which Janine Anderson Sawada has noted was 'pervasive to the point of banality' in nineteenth-century Japan, covered much of what in the West at the time tended to be separated into 'religion', 'morality', 'divination', 'health', and 'education',[16] and was heavily concerned with *shugyō*: self-strengthening through various quasi-ascetic practices.[17] This cultivation ethic, reinforced in various areas of Meiji Japanese culture – from government initiatives and proclamations through to newspaper and magazine pieces – provided a means of connecting that which western-influenced conceptualization and institution-building tended to divide into distinct spheres of study or professional competence after 1868. Many pioneers and clients of new psychotherapies worked with these westernized concepts and institutions while at the same time drawing on this popularly familiar self-cultivation ethic and the intimate modes of interpersonal relationship and guidance that came with it. Japan's nineteenth-century 'new religions', including Kurozumikyō (founded in 1814) and Tenrikyō (1838), further helped ensure that the idea of self-cultivation, linked with physical and spiritual healing, loomed large in popular consciousness – to the point where, as Helen Hardacre has pointed out, designations of 'Shintō' or 'Buddhist' were of comparatively little concern.[18] These trends merged with an emphasis from the 1860s onwards upon the practical utility of ideas. This was most clearly associated with Fukuzawa Yukichi's concept of *jitsugaku*, or 'practical learning' (Fukuzawa memorably excoriated old-style Japanese Confucian scholars as mere 'rice-consuming dictionaries').[19] This dynamic made its way into Japanese religion thanks to reformers such as Hara Tanzan and Inoue Enryō, who combined stripped-down versions of old cosmologies with an emphasis on bodily and psychological exercises and the solving of immediate individual problems.[20]

Such was the level of stigma attached to mental illness within families, cynicism and fear in regard to what went on inside mental hospitals, and levels of doubt as to whether modern medicine could as yet do anything decisive for the afflicted, large numbers of people in Japan suffering from a range of emotional and psychological problems saw themselves – or sought to place themselves – outside the purview of psychiatry. In the search for alternative sources of relief they turned to the language of 'nerves', to emerging psychotherapies, and to religion. Talk of *shinkei-byō* (nerve illness) began to appear in Japanese newspapers from the 1870s onwards, accompanied by a variety of treatments, from warm mustard footbaths and special diets to *zazen* (sitting meditation). The role played by regulated breathing in a number of these treatments reflected their links to *shugyō* and to the Chinese-influenced *yōjō* concept of health: an emphasis upon the nurturing of life, viewing disease as an abnormal state resulting from an imbalance of one sort or another rather than as a 'thing' in itself, an intruder into or upon the body.[21] In some quarters, regulated breathing exercises were thought to help one's vital energy remain in proper relation to the surrounding atmosphere, without becoming blocked, stagnant, or otherwise 'constrained'; Chinese ideas of *ki* were being drawn upon here, but *ki* itself was rarely invoked in its pure form in these years, found instead in combinations including *seiki*, meaning life or vitality.[22] Elsewhere, and especially in Buddhist-influenced practices (which rarely used notions of *ki*), a more popular explanatory framework was that of the small individual self developing in relation to a larger 'self' such as Amida Buddha.[23]

Conditions such as 'nerves' were more than a state of affairs requiring a therapeutic solution, however: already in the early Meiji era their prevalence was being used as ad hoc sociological data for exercises in sociocultural self-reflection – of both negative and positive sorts. Japanese adoption of the diagnosis of neurasthenia offers a vivid example of this process. In keeping with the theories of the American neurologist G.M. Beard, who popularized the use of the term, neurasthenia became linked in Japan by the 1870s to urbanization and newly competitive living and working environments, attracting thereby a certain social cachet for the sufferer since it was thought to be a sure sign of busy and successful modern living. The neurasthenia memoir of the journalist Ishikawa Hanzan (*Neurasthenia and Recovery*, 1909) was the occasion for considerable boasting about the author's membership of more than 100 governmental and social organizations, together with his 1,000 public speeches across Japan. These efforts at education and enlightenment of ordinary people had left him, he confessed, utterly exhausted. However, as

Yu-chuan Wu has pointed out, the Ishikawa memoir was more than just a thinly disguised exercise in self-promotion: later in the book he expressed doubts about the real value of the work he had done and the ideals for which he had sacrificed his health.[24] In any case, as work by Akihito Suzuki has shown, it is difficult to interpret the available statistics on mental illness in the pre-war Japanese population in terms of modernization and urbanization. Tokyo shows an increasing rate of mental illness in this period, but Japan's second-largest city, Osaka, shows a very low level, while rural areas such as Iwate and Okinawa show relatively high levels. Suzuki suggests that a general rise in rates of recorded mental illness from the early 1900s up to the 1940s (an approximate doubling, across the general population) is likely to have been connected instead with increased awareness and detection.[25]

Finally, of critical importance in the evolution of religion–psy interaction in Japan, in this period and beyond, was the way that relational subjectivity – 'being in relationship' – as an ideal, ran through many spheres of life. Breathing exercises were concerned with an individual's relationship with his or her physical and social environment; in politics, the notion of *kokutai* (the 'national body') gained prominence both as a metaphor for connections of mutual interest and responsibility promoted by political leaders and as a 'larger self' in the context of which Japanese people could find their identity;[26] some of the earliest systems of psychotherapy focused on encouraging a restorative awareness of a person's relationships with and debts to family members; and finally, at a philosophical level, there was interest in elucidating a contrast between dichotomous (either/or) thinking and a more unitive and inter-relational vision – most notably in Nishida Kitarō and his disciples within the Kyoto School of philosophy.[27]

The extent to which this was a new phenomenon in Japan in the Meiji period is debatable. Masahisa Nishizono offers a nuanced approach to this question, willing on the one hand to invoke 'common threads' running through Chinese, Korean, and Japanese culture back across large expanses of historical time: 'harmony with nature', 'importance of family', and the socialization of children such that they grow up understanding themselves fundamentally as part of networks of 'interpersonal relationships'.[28] On the other hand, Nishizono notes that social and cultural pressures emerging during Japan's first period of modernization – which he dates from the Meiji era right through to 1945 – gave rise to particular forms of psychopathology, including conflict between self and family, and *taijinkyō fushō* (fear of interpersonal relations). These sorts of mental health problems, a combination of Japan's long-standing patriarchal arrangements with a transition to modernity that was experienced particularly acutely by urban middle-class Japanese men before 1945, influenced in turn the rise of psychotherapies (such as Morita therapy and Kosawa's style of psychoanalysis) that emphasized close attention to individuals' family and cultural circumstances. Indeed, many of Morita's early patients suffered forms of *taijinkyōfushō*, while Kosawa became known for his work on erythrophobia – the fear of blushing, particularly in front of others.

From both an ethical and a methodological perspective this analytical balancing of long-term cultural trends with fast-moving historical context and contingent political realities matters greatly: observations about 'common threads' may be of real therapeutic use – as advocates of 'cultural competence' in mental health would broadly argue[29] – but this has always to be weighed up against an awareness of their potential for abuse, not least in helping to legitimize authoritarian socio-political arrangements such as those in Japan in the immediate pre-war years.

## Early 'scientific' psychotherapies: 1910–1945

Recent work by Yoshinaga Shin'ichi, Shimazono Susumu, and others has shown that there existed by the 1910s as yet no fixed sense of precisely what constituted 'legitimate' psychotherapy or psychological therapy. Instead, shifts in professional and popular understandings were influenced by a combination of media-fuelled fad, governmental and institutional dynamics such as those explored above, the personal experiences and interests of pioneers and clients, and a pervasive sense that western psychotherapeutic ideas needed to be domesticated to fit the particular requirements of the Japanese context.[30] The earliest practices resembling psychotherapy in the modern era were various forms of hypnotism, popular interest in which boomed in the early 1900s – in part as a result of magico-religious healing practices from previous decades being squeezed out of new definitions of 'religion' and effectively banned by government.[31]

Medical and scientific professionals in Japan lost interest in hypnotism after a short period of experimentation, but amateur enthusiasts continued to practise and publish in large numbers. Perhaps the most influential proponent was Kuwabara Toshirō, who combined somewhat inflated claims for the healing powers of hypnotism – physical as well as psychological – with a quasi-religious account of how hypnotism worked: bringing the human psyche (*seishin*) into tune with the greater universal *seishin* of which it was a part.[32] Kuwabara's ideas, owing a great deal to modernized, pantheistic interpretations of Japanese Buddhism, and encapsulated in his three-volume *Seishin Reidō* (1903), proved enormously popular, and within a few years thousands of therapists – calling themselves *reijutsuka* (spiritual practitioners) or *seishinryōhōka* (psychotherapists) – were practising hypnotism across Japan.[33]

Fearing for the reputation of medical and scientific treatments, doctors, academics, and scientifically oriented hypnotists went on the offensive against these spiritualized forms of the technique, with some demanding legislation to limit the practice of hypnotism to the medically qualified – ostensibly on the basis that clients were being placed in vulnerable and dangerous situations, but with an eye too to the profitability of their own practices and the status of their professions. Limited anti-hypnotism legislation was duly passed in 1908, in line with the general direction of Japanese legislation at this time against non-western or religiously tinged medical interventions. But it was the spectacular fall from academic grace in 1913 of Fukurai Tomokichi, an associate professor of psychology at the University of Tokyo, which succeeded in bringing a final close to the hypnotism boom.[34] The idea of therapy remained popular, however, with therapists continuing to employ techniques akin to hypnotism while dropping the use of that term.

Crucially, many of these therapists took what Yu-chuan Wu, in his survey of 'mental therapies' in this period, has called a 'double approach': rooting their work in modern psychological theories, including those linked with hypnotism, while publicizing it in terms of theories of consciousness and terminology (including *musō* [no-thought] and *munen* [no-idea]) derived from Buddhism and other Japanese religious and self-cultivation traditions. Many asserted the reality of 'spirit', developed accounts of the workings of mind and body that blended traditional metaphysics with modern psychological and hydrodynamic theories, and insisted that mental states induced via hypnotic or breathing practices were not new or artificial states of mind but were instead a return to natural states from which clients had simply become estranged due to the patterns and pressures of modern western life.[35]

A second common factor in therapy around this time, both during and after the hypnotism boom, was the idea that a client's sense of belief in the practitioner was the key to success. Kondō Yoshizō, an influential hypnotist,[36] had claimed that for the practice to work the client ought to be intellectually and socially inferior to the practitioner – and many male hypnotists claimed to prefer women and children as their subjects, on this basis – while other therapists emphasized the basic importance of authority in a would-be practitioner.

Authority and orthodoxy were entrenched in many cases through the establishment of small local organizations dedicated to training people in using a particular therapy for themselves – training institutions with master therapists and disciples, short-term students, learning materials, and even correspondence courses, were more prevalent than single therapists seeking customers or clients.[37] The relationship between master therapists and their disciples, sometimes based on the traditional *Iemoto* system (whereby precious skills were passed down in a familial or quasi-familial lineage), was crucial to these psychotherapeutic organizations. As with many Japanese religious lineages, including those within Zen Buddhism, the difficulty of knowing and substantiating another person's inner attainments was addressed in part by using a person's rising status within the master's estimation and within the organization as a useful way of inferring this kind of progress. In broader terms, these organizations offered something of a surrogate family at a time when family structures were changing fast in urban Japan, and many young men in particular were living away from home for long periods. Therapies such as that of Kimura Tenshin, which was later likened to a primitive form of psychoanalysis because of the stress laid upon vocalizing conflicts and feelings hidden in one's latent consciousness (*senzai ishiki*), paid great attention to the role played by familial relationships both in people's distress and in their healing. For Kimura, whose therapy was heavily influenced by Buddhist ideas, including notions of sin and karma, family members both dead and alive could play a psychogenic role in a patient's mental illness. The task of therapy, then, was to resolve conflicts both within the client and with his or her family members – whom it was considered workable and legitimate to treat alongside the student him or herself.

Although therapists such as Kimura faced criticism for undermining filial piety by seeking to blame family members for people's distress – the relative lack of success of psychoanalysis in Japan in later years was frequently attributed to its reputation as a self-centred blame game – it was not uncommon for therapists to give central importance to a strong, functional family, sometimes setting this in the broader political context of Japan's drive to build a strong family state (see above). Fukurai Tomokichi himself emerged as an ardent nationalist, establishing the *Keishin Sūsokyō kai* (The Society for the Worship of Deities and Ancestors) and suggesting that the psychotherapeutic goal of no-self (*muga*) was one of the conditions of a genuine Japanese identity.[38] There was nothing inherently nationalistic or conservative about psychotherapy. Ohtsuki Kenji, a lay psychoanalyst discussed below, wrote extensively on left-wing and liberal issues, and was forced to flee Tokyo in the early 1940s when Japan's Special Higher Police, the *Tokkō*, came calling.[39] But therapies that emphasized the restoration of familial bonds, the tempering of 'pathogenic' individualism, and the good sense to be found in traditional Buddhist and Confucian values had the potential to dovetail conveniently with a conservative Japanese ethos that had been in evidence since the late 1880s, when reaction gathered pace against Japan's overzealous political and cultural turn to the West.[40]

Carrying through from the ethos of the previous generation and the metaphysical and social cosmologies invoked by hypnotists and post-hypnotists, relationship became a central theme in the first major psychotherapy to become known across Japan and later internationally: Morita therapy. Morita Masatake was a trained psychiatrist and student of Kure Shūzō, who made major revisions to current theories of neurasthenia as a result of his and colleagues' own personal experiences with the condition. Some of the latter he treated in his own home, and in 1921 he produced a systematization of his experiences and technique: *The Treatment of Neurasthenia and Shinkeishitsu*. Morita's was one of the first major theories in Japan to give psychogenesis a prominent place in understanding mental illness (as opposed to seeking or presuming organic causes), and at its core was the idea that suffering arises from a natural disposition towards neurosis (*shinkeishitsu* translates as 'constitutional neurasthenia') together with a mistaken popular and philosophical dualism that insists one part of the mind can be used to control the other to a significant degree. Morita suggested that a person relinquish these harmful attempts at cognitive control, and instead learn to live in relationship with reality as it is [*arugamama*]. Morita's arrival at his ideas via careful study of recent western psychotherapies and via his own personal and clinical experience led him to claim scientific status for his therapy, while at the same time advertising its rootedness in non-elite Japanese culture.[41]

This latter dimension to Morita therapy was crucial, since it reflected a trend in the psy disciplines that was characteristic of the intellectual life of the Taishō and early Shōwa periods (from 1912 into the 1930s) more broadly: increasing co-operation between individuals, based in different disciplines and traditions, who shared an interest in understanding and treating mental health problems. Morita's work was influenced in large part by his association with Nakamura Kokyō, a writer who had turned to the study of medicine and mental health after his brother, who suffered from schizophrenia, died in hospital. From 1917, Nakamura's *Hentai Shinri* (Abnormal Psychology) journal, and his *Nippon Seishin Igakkai* (Society for Japanese Psychiatry) became notable for their bringing together of a diverse group of people – from medicine, psychology, the law, sexology, anthropology, criminology, literature, and elsewhere – to consider in broad humanistic terms various contemporary experiences of psychological distress and mental illness. Alongside Morita, another prominent contributor to the new Society was Fukurai Tomokichi, whose lectures at the University of Tokyo Nakamura had attended. Nakamura and Morita opened the first dedicated facilities for psychotherapy in Japan within a year of one another, in 1917 and 1918 respectively.

Nakamura's journal ceased publication in 1926, when he went to medical school, but a similar journal and organization emerged in Tokyo just two years later, carrying on the cosmopolitan spirit, this time under the banner of psychoanalysis. There had been interest in Freud's ideas within Japanese psychology since Ohtsuki Kaison published 'The Psychology of Forgetting' in the journal *Shinri Kenkyū* (Psychological Research) in 1912, and within psychiatry since Professor Marui Kiyoyasu of Tohoku University returned from studying with Adolf Meyer in the US in 1919 and began to include psychoanalytic perspectives in his writing and teaching.[42] The new group meeting in Tokyo from 1928 was particularly significant, however, in its professional inclusiveness: of the four initial leaders of what came to be called the Tokyo Psychoanalytical Society, one was an experimental psychologist (Yabe Yaekichi), another a writer (Ohtsuki Kenji), and a third a former Waseda University professor (Hasegawa Seiya). Their large membership, publication of journal articles (from 1933), and consultancy work extended into literature, cultural commentary, sexual and left-wing politics, education, religion, the police, and the judicial system. Ohtsuki in particular was prolific in seeking to bring psychoanalytic ideas to bear on a wide range of contemporary social and political questions, aiming to do so in a way that attracted a mass audience – even if this occasionally required indulging in rather lowbrow writing on the Freudian associations of neckties and baseball bats.[43]

Rivalling both Ohtsuki and Morita in Tokyo from the early 1930s was Kosawa Heisaku, who had trained in psychiatry with Marui at Tohoku and followed this up with psychoanalytic training in Vienna in 1932–1933.[44] Returning to Japan in 1933, Kosawa set up his own private practice, insisting to colleagues back in Europe, and later in the US, that he was the only person truly practising psychoanalysis in Japan at this point – Marui was primarily a theoretician, while Ohtsuki lacked either medical or psychoanalytical training. Although all three individuals – Morita, Ohtsuki, and Kosawa – claimed to be engaged in a scientific enterprise, in the sense of a sustained, systematic attempt to understand the inner life based on clinical work with patients, there emerged in this period overlapping debates both within psychotherapy and within the religion–psy dialogue on three key points: qualifications, legitimacy, and efficacy. As far as Morita was concerned, his own medical and training credentials under Kure Shūzō were immaculate, while by the late 1920s he could offer numerous cases that proved the efficacy of his therapy. In contrast, so devastating was his attack on the pretentious inefficacy of psychoanalysis at an academic congress in 1927 that Takeda Makoto has suggested this was what finally persuaded Kosawa to pack his bags for Europe, to find out where his psychoanalytic training in Japan thus far had been flawed.[45] Within Japanese psychoanalysis there followed similar scraps over legitimacy and efficacy, into which Freud himself was dragged to try to bring rival psychoanalytic factions together – something not achieved until after the Second World War.[46]

The interest of all three individuals in religion, and in Buddhism in particular, further complicated these questions of qualifications, legitimacy, and efficacy. None could boast a dual professional competence that encompassed religious as well as psy matters, and instead they relied for their claims to legitimacy where the former were concerned by passing often rather imperious quasi-psychological judgement on what they saw as false religious ideas. Kosawa had strong links with traditional Japanese Buddhism (in particular the Jōdo Shinshū sect) and was particularly scathing about many of Japan's new religions, which he saw as offering false comfort and manipulating the masses. Ohtsuki criticized both the metaphysical and psychological inadequacy of Christianity relative to Japanese Buddhism – he even attempted to get a series of his writings on Buddhism and psychoanalysis published, without success.[47] And Morita homed in on the potential for religion to exacerbate *shinkeishitsu*, while drawing approvingly on Buddhism's critique of human desire as generative of suffering and suggesting links between 'true religion' and the settled state of mind at which Morita therapy aimed. All three were heir to the spirit of Inoue Enryō and other reformers in an earlier period, in that they were often inclined to discuss Buddhism specifically as a dimension of Japanese (occasionally Asian) culture, and as such a window into the Japanese psyche that predated the modern scientific disciplines and terminologies in which they had been schooled. This is a point worth underscoring, since discussions of religion and psychotherapy sometimes invoke 'Christianity' or 'Buddhism' as though there is some essential core to these religions that can be dealt with independently of the beliefs and practices of people in particular times and places: this risks dramatically underrating the extent to which most Japanese psychotherapeutic pioneers interested in religion in this period understood it as part and parcel of the culture, society, and problems around them, rather than transcendentally or in the abstract.[48]

A striking example of the close attention paid by these three individuals to the changing cultural climate around them, in seeking to create effective psychotherapies, is their creation of a familial atmosphere in treating their patients.[49] Morita's therapy began in his own home, and he continued to offer it there, in collaboration with his wife, long after he and his therapy were well established. Ohtsuki occasionally invited young clients (all male, as far as can be determined) to spend the weekend with himself and his wife at their country home, where away from the stresses of Tokyo life Ohtsuki would take long walks with them and fill temporarily the shoes of the compassionate, listening father that he suspected many of his clients had never had.[50] Kosawa invited some of his analysands to stay for tea after the session was over, and in at least one recorded case Kosawa took a patient to listen to Buddhist lectures. All three men to an extent encouraged clients to look upon them personally as the source of their salvation: one of Morita's clients compared him with Jesus Christ, while Doi Takeo later resented what he saw as the messianic dimension in Kosawa's therapeutic style.[51]

## Modernization, American psychology, and rediscovering 'the Japanese': 1950s to 1970s

Doi's criticism of Kosawa, made in the 1940s, was a sign of things to come in postwar Japan: personality, relationships, and shared culture would never again bind together the religious and the 'psy' in the way they did with Morita and Kosawa's generation. In part this was because of the whiff of 'feudalism' that their sort of therapeutic culture now had about it – use of the word 'feudal' being, in the early postwar years, a philosophically and emotionally charged means of rejecting the recent Japanese past, expressing contrition for it,[52] and drawing a boundary with the 'New Japan' that the Allied Occupation (1945–1952) was helping to forge.[53]

A form of therapy that revolved so obviously around an unequal paternalistic personal relationship, with the agency of the individual client effaced by the authority of the therapist, was far less acceptable in the new climate than in the old.[54] At the same time, new professional standards in psychiatric and psychotherapeutic care made it more difficult to invite clients into one's home – as opposed to a section of one's house separated off as a therapy room.

Japan's new Civil Law of 1947 did away with the old family system – in legal terms at least – while a new Mental Hygiene Law in 1950 offered a renewed focus on hospital care and the building, at last, of a comprehensive psychiatric infrastructure across Japan.[55] Hospital care did not necessarily mean good care, however, and Ohtsuki Kenji became just one of many critics of this new system, in which hurriedly constructed (and once again frequently private) facilities appeared too often to be run with an emphasis upon custody and profit over care and recovery.[56] This state of affairs was not helped when public and police reaction to an assault by a disturbed teenager on the American ambassador Edwin O. Reischauer succeeded in steering the focus of the planned 1965 Mental Hygiene Law away from attention to community care and back towards incarceration, with greater surveillance powers for the police.[57]

Despite a general embracing by Japanese thinkers and politicians of western liberal and left-wing values in the early years after 1945, the idea remained strong that psychotherapeutic theories originating in the West required some sort of domestication to the Japanese social and cultural situation. The rationale did change, however, reflecting new socio-political realities in Japan and the aspirations of the postwar generation.[58] An important dimension of this was a repudiation – in both constitutional and cultural terms – of the kind of religious outlook that was widely believed to have played a key part in the militarism of the 1930s and 1940s. State support for Shintō was done away with, and religious affairs in general were now to be kept separate from public life and the business of government. American psychological ideas began to flood into Japan, although those expecting a new dawn for psychoanalysis as a result were to be disappointed. Kosawa managed to attract promising young students from elite universities into psychoanalytic training, and to set up an influential new psychoanalytic organization, clarifying its links to the international movement. But Japan's psychiatric establishment remained wedded to Kraepelinian neuropsychiatry, with influential voices such as the University of Tokyo's Professor Uchimura Yūshi (son of Uchimura Kanzō) regarding psychoanalysis as a dead-end, at least in theoretical terms.[59] At the same time, the therapeutic advantages of psychoanalysis were overshadowed by the influx of American clinical psychology and counselling, into schools and mental health facilities in particular. Carl Rogers' non-directive counselling became influential – Rogers himself made a visit to Japan in 1960 – while general books on counselling by Karl

Menninger, in whose translation Kosawa Heisaku assisted, sold well amongst educators and the general public.

The major new psycho-religious therapy of this period reflected the secularizing mood.[60] Yoshimoto Ishin was a member of the same Japanese Buddhist sect, Jōdo Shinshū, as Kosawa Heisaku, and was linked with a particular sub-sect based at Teikan-an temple in Osaka. Here he came into contact with a practice called *mishirabe*, or 'looking into oneself', through which a practitioner spends days in ascetic semi-isolation, meditating on his or her life, sins, and death, aided by occasional visits from senior practitioners. Yoshimoto's early attempts at *mishirabe* ended in failure, but eventually he succeeded in attaining the conviction of his own salvation – somewhat akin to 'enlightenment', although this is a word with hotly contested meanings in Japanese Buddhism. He resolved to develop a form of *mishirabe* that could be made available to people outside his Buddhist sect, and even to those unmoved or put off by any sort of religious context. Yoshimoto opened his first dedicated 'Naikan' centre in 1953. It was a testament both to the value of the practice and to Yoshimoto's successful rebranding of it that Naikan was soon receiving the warm approval of clinicians and being offered in prisons and schools across Japan. In present-day Japan it is used in connection with neurotic disorders, drug dependency, terminal care, depression, and schizophrenia. Kawahara Ryuzo has noted that a major element in Naikan's success is that it addresses – as did Kosawa's and Doi's forms of psychoanalysis in their own ways (Kosawa via the Ajase Complex, Doi via *Amae*) – a cultural–familial situation in modern Japan whereby close interpersonal relationships, especially between mother and son, can give rise to overindulgence and unrealistic expectations about what and how the world at large will provide for people once they grow up. Naikan helps people 'relearn reality, develop the ability to see things from others' perspectives, and discard the self-obsessed mind'.[61]

Morita therapy continued to thrive through the efforts of Morita's former students, and in an age when western anthropologists and psychoanalysts were increasingly interested in the 'Japanese mind' – in part a hangover from strategic wartime interest with Japanese military conduct – Morita therapy was studied by American psychologists and analysts as the quintessential 'indigenous Japanese therapy'. One high-profile student of Morita therapy was the American neo-Freudian Karen Horney, whose interests spanned religion and philosophy as well as psychology and psychiatry: amongst her friends were the Japanese Buddhist reformer D.T. Suzuki and the Christian theologian Paul Tillich. She travelled to Japan not long before her death in 1952, in the company of Suzuki, Richard DeMartino, and her student (and Zen practitioner) Kondo Akihisa, amongst others, and visited both Zen temples and Morita therapy facilities. More generally in the 1950s and 1960s there was fresh interest in American and Japanese religious and psy circles in the potential complementarity of Asian religion and philosophy with western psychotherapy. The English philosopher Alan Watts, living and working in the US, did much in his writings to popularize Japanese, Chinese, and Indian philosophy both in their own right and for their therapeutic potential: in the same edition of the *American Journal of Psychoanalysis*, in 1953, Watts' overview of 'Asian psychology and modern psychiatry', which effectively rearticulated Inoue Enryō's old argument that Buddhism was both psychology *and* religion, appeared alongside an outline of Morita therapy written by Kondo. Erich Fromm later became interested in such questions, publishing *Zen Buddhism and Psychoanalysis* with Suzuki and De Martino in 1960.

This interest in cultural psychology and in the psychotherapeutic potential of Asian philosophies continued into the late 1960s and 1970s, as vilification of the pre-war era gave way to a fresh self-confidence – a dividend of rapid economic growth, symbolized in the success of the 1964 Tokyo Olympics and the running of the first *shinkansen* bullet trains the same year. There was now a willingness once again in Japan to consider questions of national identity, with *nihonjinron* – linguistic, sociological, and psychological theories about the Japanese – proliferating and ensuring, where psychoanalysis was concerned, that although clients remained in short supply there was recognition to be found in cultural and social commentary. Two former students of Kosawa, Doi Takeo and Okonogi Keigo, led the way, Okonogi with a reworking of Kosawa's 'Ajase Complex' and Doi with his '*Amae*' theory. Developed from the mid-1950s onwards, with a popular English translation of one of Doi's books published in the early 1970s as *The Anatomy of Dependence*, the *Amae* theory postulated a tendency for a child or social inferior to express in their behaviour a dependency and presumption upon the affection or good will of a parent or superior. *Amae* came to be regarded as a key concept in understanding the Japanese, receiving enormous attention both inside and outside Japan.

A common criticism of this *nihonjinron* boom has been the way in which Japanese scholars effectively colluded with naively romantic or postcolonial guilt-ridden non-Japanese counterparts (the latter living in fear of their preconceptions) in presenting Japanese society and culture as something to which standard western categories simply could not be applied.[62] The excesses of the *nihonjinron* literature should not, however, be allowed to detract from the very real social questions tackled by the likes of Doi through his exploration of cultural psychology. Amy Borovoy sees Doi as a 'bridging figure', attempting to reconcile Japanese communitarian ideals with the liberal democratic mood of the postwar era. He hoped to find ways – and here we return to the central Japanese psychotherapeutic theme of 'being in relationship' – in which human beings could live simultaneously as individuals and as members of social communities that necessarily made demands upon them.[63] In Doi, Freud's concerns about the compromises required for a civilized society to work – expressed in *Civilization and its Discontents*[64] – were made to speak to Japan's postwar dilemmas over individualism, democracy, and Marxist political thought. Morita's successors, along with Kawai Hayao (see below), tackled similar problems in their therapeutic work and popular publications. Doi and Kawai in particular sought to construe these problems of independence, dependence, and relationship as universal rather than uniquely Japanese, with both men's commentaries on the Japanese context containing strong implied criticisms of what they viewed as exaggerated and unrealistic western ideals of autonomous being and action. Doi's linking of *Amae* to western Christian humanism was part of this effort, very much in tune with the humanistic psychology of Carl Rogers and the theology of Paul Tillich.[65]

## From 'new new religions' and the spiritual world to Jung and disaster care: 1970s–the present day

Although the public mood in Japan after the war was generally one of ambivalence or outright hostility towards both Shintō and Buddhism (many of whose leaders had supported the war effort), Japan's more open postwar political and constitutional arrangements made it possible for so-called 'new religions' to flourish once again. New groups, alongside old ones that had refused to support the war, did particularly well. Sōka Gakkai was the prime example of the latter. Formed in 1930 and suffering the death of its leader Makiguchi Tsunesaburō in prison in 1944, it was able to rebuild after 1945, with a soaring membership, a softer rhetorical tone after 1960, and the formation of an allied political party – Kōmeito – which went on to become one of the largest in Japan.

The 1970s witnessed a new wave of religious organizations in Japan – so-called 'new new religions' – which adopted a notably more antagonistic attitude towards Japan's social and cultural status quo. Amongst them was Aum Shinrikyō. By 1984 there were thought to be around two or three thousand new and 'new new' religious organizations in Japan, with Shimazono Susumu estimating the total membership of such groups by the early twenty-first century at up to 20% of the Japanese population.[66] A common feature of these organizations was a focus on this-worldly salvation, incorporating an element of '*kokoro naoshi*':[67] transformation of the heart (back) to a pure, unclouded state. In part this was an inheritance from the vitalism of Shintō, as was a focus on family and ancestors. But these organizations drew too, for practical purposes, on psychological theories and techniques introduced into Japan from the Meiji period onwards.

The 1970s also saw the emergence of a 'Spiritual World' (*seishin sekai*) movement, encompassing interest in yoga, meditation, healing, psychological therapies, alchemy, near-death experiences, reincarnation, and self-enlightenment seminars, along with a strong publishing dimension. The label '*seishin sekai*' began to appear on bookshelves all across Japan.

Although the Spiritual World movement was not a direct analogue of the West's New Age, the two shared a deep scepticism about what they saw as the narrow vision of the world and of human potential arising out of modern science and rationalism.

The mixture of pessimism and desire for alternative models of living that these new religious and spiritual movements seemed to represent was complemented by a third development around the same time: popular scepticism about psychiatry, both as a body of theory and as a profession – not least as a result of the generally poor standards of hospital care after the war (see above), which were exposed in Japanese newspapers. The anti-psychiatry movement in Europe and the US became influential, with widespread criticism of controversial treatments such as lobotomy, over his use of which a Professor of Psychiatry at Tokyo University was eventually forced to retire. By the 1990s these social and medical convulsions had succeeded in opening up Japanese psychiatry, with greater interest paid to psychotherapy, to culture,[68] and to the establishment of community clinics – a move that brought psychiatrists into contact with the sorts of mood disorders previously addressed mainly via the non- or quasi-medical therapies discussed above. Complementing this shift in Japanese psychiatry was the expansion and professional accreditation of clinical psychology, aided in the 1980s by the emergence of new organizations and moves towards the creation of university Masters' courses.[69]

A key figure in securing institutional status for, and public interest in psychology in Japan was Kawai Hayao. Carl Jung had largely been ignored by Japan's pre-war psychoanalysts – dismissed as a deserter from Freud's movement – but thanks to Kawai, who studied in the early 1960s at the University of California and the C.G. Jung Institute in Zurich, Jung's ideas belatedly found a Japanese audience. In addition to Kawai's work in helping to establish the Association of Japanese Clinical Psychology (*Nihon Shinri Rinshō Gakkai*) in 1982 and training students at Kyoto University, his publications and television appearances raised the profile of psychology and psychotherapy and formed links in people's minds between the Japanese psyche and the nation's folk tales and Buddhist inheritance.[70]

Thanks to new religious and spiritual movements, community psychiatry, and the rise of Jungian psychology and psychotherapy, Japan's religion–psy dialogue from the 1970s onwards came to turn increasingly on the notion of *iyashi*, 'healing', understood in a sense that went beyond medical cure and incorporated the *kokoro naoshi* elements of the new new religions, alongside Jungian notions of individuation.[71] Two traumatic events in 1995 helped to accelerate this shift: Aum Shinrikyō's sarin attacks on the Tokyo subway system, and the Kobe earthquake. The Aum attacks advanced considerably the general postwar decline of 'religion' in popular estimation, helping to bring about a boom for all things '*supirichuaru*' ('spiritual') instead. As Horie Norichika has pointed out, *supirichuaru* is not so much about questions of 'spirit' or transcendence (seen in western

Christian or post-Christian usages of 'spiritual') as it is about this-worldly action and virtue.[72]

Japan's 'spiritual business' in the early twenty-first century has echoes of the hypnotists and post-hypnotists of a century earlier: a highly competitive environment, partly the creation of the media (including celebrities like Ehara Hiroyuki), in which people in need are ministered to by therapists acutely aware of how they should present themselves, their credentials, and their therapies – aware too of the need now and again to offer something new and exciting.[73] Ioannis Gaitinidis suggests that two separate processes are in operation here, 'the sacralization of the therapeutic and the commercialization of the sacred', while Chikako Ozawa-de Silva's work shows that established therapies such as Naikan have shifted the way they present themselves to accommodate these changing public tastes: Naikan, says Ozawa-de Silva, was firmly in a 'spiritual phase' at the turn of the twenty-first century.[74] The long-term significance of these trends is as yet unclear, however, and Ian Reader has been amongst those suggesting that the 'rise of the spiritual' is more a matter of scholarly hope or over-eager analysis than of any empirically verifiable social trend.[75]

The damage done to the reputation of traditional religion in the aftermath of the Kobe earthquake was primarily a matter of the aid response by religious organizations being deemed inadequate – especially when set alongside the efforts of clinical psychologists and psychotherapists, which were generally better received. In the wake of Japan's triple disasters in March 2011 – earthquake, tsunami, and nuclear crisis – religious organizations have been keen to avoid repeating the mistakes of Kobe. Aside from the clear humanitarian imperatives, it has been well recognized that the conduct of religious organizations at such times impacts powerfully upon public perceptions of religion for a considerable time afterwards. With religious care in medical contexts regularly coming up against legal and cultural opposition to the presence of religion in public spaces, despite a growing trend in religiously inflected hospital, hospice, and 'grief' care, there is a sense that doing the right thing at times of great crisis may help to soften public attitudes – perhaps smoothing the path for longer term projects.[76]

\* \* \*

The anthropologist Ueda Noriyuki has suggested that the broad notion of *iyashi*, or 'healing', which has been emerging since the 1970s, is bound up with concepts of relationship and relatedness that reach far back into Japan's Buddhist past but for many people no longer require the language of religion for their expression.[77] Michael J. Sherrill notes that Japanese Christian denominations have been relatively slow to tap into this mood, tending to focus instead upon political and social justice while remaining relatively orthodox in their theology and spirituality.[78] A key exception is Japan's small Pentecostalist movement, in which Christian ideas and practices are frequently blended with counterparts from Japanese folk religion.[79] For Shimazono Susumu, whose recent work has been much concerned with the emerging field of Death and Life Studies, the category of psycho-religious composite movement is useful in catering for practices that emphasize 'healing' broadly construed in bodily, spiritual, and communal terms, and which are not easily categorized as 'religion' or 'psychotherapy'.[80]

Questions of categorization were touched upon in the Introduction, and so too in this chapter's brief overview of religion and psychotherapy in Japan they have appeared regularly. Readers might usefully ask the question, as they make their way through the essays that follow, whether such questions may really only be a problem for scholars seeking narrowly coherent modes of analysis: for practitioners, clients, laities, readers and others with a personal involvement it may be that the rich ambiguity of mixed content and the stimulating tensions that emerge between imperfectly overlapping religious, therapeutic, and medical ideas is part of what makes early twenty-first century practices or affiliations 'work'. Readers may also want to consider that Japanese religion and philosophy have tended to be marked, in comparison at least with modern western counterparts, by an emphasis upon being rather than believing (in the propositional sense), upon the phenomenal world as the real, and upon manifesting truth in one's way of living rather than seeking encapsulation in formulae of one kind or another.[81] At critical moments from 1868 to the present day, the religion–psy dialogue in Japan seems to have been inspired and guided by these three key dynamics.

## Notes

1 On religious conflict in this period, see Ketelaar, *Of Heretics and Martyrs* and Thelle, *Buddhism and Christianity in Japan*. See also Yoshinaga, this volume, on government restrictions upon magico-religious healing practices.
2 Blocker and Starling, *Japanese Philosophy*, pp. 2–3.
3 On Inoue and Meiji Buddhism, see Staggs, '"Defend the nation and love the truth"'; Josephson, 'When Buddhism became a "religion"'; and Ketelaar, 'Strategic occidentalism'. On Kosawa and Japan's new religions, see Harding, 'The therapeutic method'; and 'Japanese psychoanalysis and Buddhism'.
4 On Christianity in Japan, see Mullins (ed.), *Handbook of Christianity in Japan*. On the relationship between Buddhism and Christianity in this period, see Thelle, 'Christianity encounters Buddhism in Japan'; and *Buddhism and Christianity in Japan*. Also Ballhatchet, 'The religion of the West'.
5 See Iwata, this volume. See also Washington, 'Fighting brick with brick'.
6 On Japan's emerging scientific culture see Low (ed.), *Building a Modern Japan*; and Mizuno, *Science for Empire*.
7 Thelle, *Buddhism and Christianity in Japan*; and 'Christianity encounters Buddhism in Japan'.
8 Ballhatchet, 'The religion of the West'.
9 In addition to the above, on Japanese science, see Bowers, *When the Twain Meet*.

A four-phase view   45

For links with the early modern Japanese context, see Jansen, 'Rangaku and Westernization'; and Gooday and Low, 'Technology transfer and cultural exchange'.
10 Suzuki, 'The state, family, and the insane'.
11 Hashimoto Akira has written of the 'Germanization' of psychiatry and of medicine in general in Japan in this period. Hashimoto, 'A "German world" shared among doctors'.
12 On Kure see Okada, *Kure Shūzō: Sono Shōgai to Gyōseki*; on the relationship between government and psychiatrists in Japan, see Matsumura, 'Mental health as public peace'; Suzuki, 'A brain hospital in Tokyo'; Hashimoto, 'A "German world" shared among doctors'.
13 Suzuki, 'The state, family, and the insane', p. 224.
14 The Japanese state made manic-depression, for example, a basis for legal incompetence. Kitanaka, *Depression in Japan*.
15 Sawada, *Practical Pursuits*.
16 Ibid., p. 3.
17 As Hashimoto shows in this volume, some of the temple and shrine treatments for mental ill health were derived from a particular form of *shugyō*: *shugendō*, or mountain asceticism.
18 Hardacre, 'Creating state Shinto', pp. 37–38.
19 Sawada, *Practical Pursuits*, p. 93.
20 See Yoshinaga, this volume.
21 See Lock, *East Asian Medicine*.
22 See Yoshinaga, this volume. See also Daidoji, 'Treating emotion-related disorders'. On *ki* in particular see Kamata, *Ki no Dentō*. In general the concept of *ki* went through a process of metaphorization from the late nineteenth century onwards, although it continued to be treated literally by some, in the context of revived forms of East Asian medicine (including 'Kampō baptized by science') and in experiments that sought to detect *ki* as a psychophysical phenomenon. See Daidoji, 'Treating emotion-related disorders'; Yuasa, *The Body, Self-Cultivation, and Ki-Energy*; and Kitanaka, *Depression in Japan*.
23 See Yoshinaga, this volume.
24 Wu, *A Disorder of Ki*.
25 Suzuki, 'The state, family, and the insane', pp. 204–220. On Okinawa, see Shiotsuki, this volume.
26 See Doak, *A History of Nationalism in Modern Japan*.
27 See Heisig, *Philosophers of Nothingness*; and Sharf, 'The Zen of Japanese nationalism'. See also Conclusion.
28 Tseng, Chang, and Nishizono, 'Asian culture and psychotherapy', pp. 3–6.
29 Kirmayer, 'Cultural competence'.
30 See in particular Yoshinaga, *Nihonjin no Shin-Shin Rei* and Shimazono, *Iyasu Chi no Keifu*.
31 See Yoshinaga, this volume.
32 See Yoshinaga, *Nihonjin no Shin-Shin Rei*, volume 4.
33 See Yoshinaga, this volume.
34 Sato, 'Rises and falls of clinical psychology'.
35 Wu, *A Disorder of Ki*, pp. 146–147 and p. 183.
36 See Yoshinaga, this volume.
37 Wu, *A Disorder of Ki*, p. 173. Wu notes that some of these organizations styled themselves as universities, offering Bachelor degrees. See also Hirotaka, *Saiminjutsu no Nihon Kindai*.
38 Wu, *A Disorder of Ki*, pp. 180–183.
39 Author interview with Nagai Nachiko, the grand-daughter of Ohtsuki Kenji, May 2013.

46  *Christopher Harding*

40 For a useful survey, see Chapter Three, on Meiji Conservatism, in Wakabayashi (ed.), *Modern Japanese Thought*.
41 See Kondo and Kitanishi, this volume.
42 See Blowers and Yang Hsueh Chi, 'Freud's deshi'. On sexology in Japan, see Frühstück, *Colonizing Sex*.
43 See Harding, *Japan's First Psychotherapists* (forthcoming). For a survey of Ohtsuki's work, and his clashes with the psychiatric establishment, see Blowers and Yang Hsueh Chi, 'Ohtsuki Kenji and the beginnings of lay analysis in Japan'.
44 See Harding, 'The therapeutic method'.
45 Takeda, *Seishinbunseki to Bukkyō*.
46 On the invocation of Freud's name and personal friendship in the internal politics of Japanese psychoanalysis, see Harding, 'Sigmund's Asian fan-club?'
47 Harding, *Japan's First Psychotherapists*.
48 On the 'essentialist fallacy', in regard to thinking and writing about Buddhism, see Silk, 'The Victorian creation of Buddhism', pp. 171–196.
49 On the family in Asian psychotherapies, see Section II of Tseng, Chang, and Nishizono, *Asian Culture and Psychotherapy*.
50 Joint interview conducted by the author with the grand-daughter and a former client of Ohtsuki Kenji, February 2013.
51 See Iwata and Ando, this volume.
52 Japan's great post-war political theorist, Maruyama Masao, who experienced the atomic bomb blast at Hiroshima first-hand, later wrote of a rare moment of 'collective contrition' on the part of Japanese intellectuals after the war (Maruyama Masao, 'Kindai Nihon no Chishikijin [Modern Japanese intellectuals]', in *Kōei no Ichi Kara*), while the Japanese Prime Minister in late August 1945 had urged the Japanese people as a whole to assume the moral burden of defeat.
53 For activity amongst Japanese intellectuals during this period, see Chapter Six in Wakabayashi, *Modern Japanese Thought*, on 'Postwar social and political thought'; and Koschmann, 'The debate on subjectivity in postwar Japan'.
54 See the brief post-war debate on 'subjectivity' and the search for a new basis for non- or post-nationalist ethics and action in Japan. Koschmann, ibid.
55 On the situation in Okinawa, see Shiotsuki Ryoko, this volume.
56 The World Health Organization's Clark Report of 1968 (cited in Kitanaka, *Depression in Japan*, p. 51), which criticized Japanese mental health facilities on precisely these grounds, was both a low and eventually a turning point for Japanese psychiatry.
57 Kitanaka, *Depression in Japan*, p. 50.
58 See Borovoy, 'Doi Takeo and the rehabilitation of particularism'.
59 See Kitanaka, *Depression in Japan*.
60 See Shimazono, this volume.
61 Ryuzo Kawahara, 'Japanese Buddhist thought and Naikan therapy', p. 190 and p. 197.
62 Dale, *The Myth of Japanese Uniqueness*, pp. 5–17.
63 Borovoy, 'Doi Takeo and the rehabilitation of particularism', p. 265.
64 Freud, *Civilization and its Discontents*.
65 See Cooper, *Paul Tillich and Psychology*.
66 Shimazono, *From Salvation to Spirituality*, p. 4.
67 '*Kokoro naoshi*' is a term used originally in the Japanese new religion, Tenrikyō, later taken up by Shimazono Susumu as a general term to refer to new religions' interest in psychological healing.
68 See Shiotsuki, this volume, on shifts in attitudes towards *yuta* and *kamidari* amongst Japanese psychiatrists.
69 See Sato Tatsuya, *Nihon ni Okeru Shinrigaku no Juyō to Tenkai*.
70 See Tarutani, this volume.

71 See Reader and Tanabe, *Practically Religious*.
72 See Horie, 'Spirituality and the spiritual in Japan'.
73 See Gaitanidis, 'Socio-economic aspects of the 'spiritual business' in Japan'.
74 Gaitinidis, 'At the forefront', p. 202. Chikako Ozawa-de Silva, *Psychotherapy and Religion in Japan*, pp. 160–161.
75 Reader, 'Secularisation, RIP?', pp. 29–31.
76 See Taniyama, this volume.
77 See Ueda, 'Iyashi'.
78 See Sherrill, 'Christian churches in the postwar period'. See also Yumiyama, 'Varieties of healing'. For a broader view of contemporary developments in Japanese religion, health, and well being, see Roemer, 'Religion and health'.
79 See Mark Mullins on *Iesu no Mitama Kyōkai* (Spirit of Jesus Church): Mullins, 'The social forms of Japanese Christianity'.
80 See Shimazono, *Iyashi Chi no Keifu*. On death and life studies see Shimazono, 'Foreword'.
81 Author interview with Dennis Hirota, 4th July 2013. See also Bloom, *Shinran's Gospel of Pure Grace* (1965), pp. 78–85; Hirota, 'The awareness of the natural world in Shinjin'; and Blocker and Starling, *Japanese Philosophy*, p. 31.

# References

Ballhatchet, Helen. 'The religion of the West versus the science of the West', in John Breen and Mark Williams (eds), *Japan and Christianity: Impacts and Responses* (London: Macmillan, 1996).

Blocker, H. Gene and Starling, Christopher L. *Japanese Philosophy* (Albany: State University of New York Press, 2001).

Bloom, Alfred. *Shinran's Gospel of Pure Grace* (Tucson: University of Arizona Press, 1965).

Blowers, Geoffrey H. and Yang Hsueh Chi, Serena. 'Freud's deshi: the coming of psychoanalysis to Japan', *Journal of the History of the Behavioral Sciences* 33, no. 2 (1997).

Blowers, Geoffrey H. and Yang Hsueh Chi, Serena. 'Ohtsuki Kenji and the beginnings of lay analysis in Japan', *The International Journal of Psycho-Analysis* 82, no. 1 (2001).

Borovoy, Amy. 'Doi Takeo and the rehabilitation of particularism in postwar Japan', *The Journal of Japanese Studies* 38, no. 2 (2012).

Bowers, John Z. *When the Twain Meet: The Rise of Western Medicine in Japan* (Baltimore: Johns Hopkins University Press, 1980).

Cooper, Terry. *Paul Tillich and Psychology: Historic and Contemporary Explorations in Theology, Psychotherapy, and Ethics* (Macon: Mercer University Press, 2006).

Daidoji Keiko. 'Treating emotion-related disorders in Japanese traditional medicine: language, patients and doctors', *Culture, Medicine and Psychiatry* 37, no. 1 (2013).

Dale, Peter N. *The Myth of Japanese Uniqueness* (New York: St Martin's Press, 1986).

Doak, Kevin M. *A History of Nationalism in Modern Japan: Placing the People* (Leiden: Brill, 2007).

Frühstück, Sabine. *Colonizing Sex: Sexology and Social Control in Modern Japan* (Berkeley: University of California Press, 2003).

Gaitanidis, Ioannis. 'Socio-economic aspects of the "spiritual business" in Japan', *Shūkyō to Shakai* [*Religion and Society*] 16 (2010).

Gaitanidis, Ioannis. 'At the forefront of a "spiritual business": independent professional spiritual therapists in Japan', *Japan Forum* 23, no. 2 (June 2011).

Gooday G. and Low M. 'Technology transfer and cultural exchange: western scientists and engineers encounter late Tokugawa and Meiji Japan', *Osiris*, 13 (1998).

Hardacre, Helen. 'Creating state Shinto: the great promulgation campaign and the new religions', *Journal of Japanese Studies* (1986).

Harding, Christopher. 'The therapeutic method of Kosawa Heisaku: "religion" and "the psy disciplines"', *Japanese Contributions to Psychoanalysis Volume 4* (2013).

Harding, Christopher. 'Japanese psychoanalysis and Buddhism: the making of a relationship', *History of Psychiatry* 25, no. 2 (June, 2014).

Harding, Christopher. *Japan's First Psychotherapists* (forthcoming).

Hashimoto Akira. 'A "German world" shared among doctors: a history of the relationship between Japanese and German psychiatry before World War II', *History of Psychiatry* 24, no. 2 (2013).

Heisig, James. *Philosophers of Nothingness: An Essay on the Kyoto School* (Honolulu: University of Hawai'i Press, 2001).

Hirota, Dennis. 'The awareness of the natural world in Shinjin: Shinran's concept of Jinen', *Buddhist–Christian Studies* 31 (2011).

Hirotaka Ichiyanagi. *Saiminjutsu no Nihon Kindai [Hypnotism in Modern Japan]* (Tokyo: Seikyusha, 1997).

Horie Norichika. 'Spirituality and the Spiritual in Japan', *Journal of Alternative Spiritualities and New Age Studies* 5 (2009).

Jansen, M.B. 'Rangaku and Westernization', *Modern Asian Studies* 18, no. 4 (1984).

Josephson, Jason Ananda. 'When Buddhism became a "religion": religion and superstition in the writings of Inoue Enryō', *Japanese Journal of Religious Studies* 33, no. 1 (2006).

Kamata Shigeo, *Ki no Dentō [The Tradition of Ki]* (Kyoto: Jinbun Shoin, 1996).

Kawahara, Ryuzo 'Japanese Buddhist thought and Naikan therapy', in Tseng, Chang, and Nishizono (eds), *Asian Culture and Psychotherapy: Implications for East and West* (Honolulu: University of Hawai'i Press, 2005).

Ketelaar, James E. 'Strategic occidentalism: Meiji Buddhists at the world's parliament of religions', *Buddhist–Christian Studies* 11 (1991).

Ketelaar, James E. *Of Heretics and Martyrs in Meiji Japan* (Princeton: Princeton University Press, 1993).

Junko Kitanaka. *Depression in Japan: Psychiatric Cures for a Society in Distress* (Princeton University Press, 2011).

Kirmayer, Laurence J. 'Cultural competence and evidence-based practice in mental health: epistemic communities and the politics of pluralism', *Social Science & Medicine* 75 (2012).

Koschmann, J. Victor. 'The debate on subjectivity in postwar Japan: foundations of modernism as a political critique', *Pacific Affairs* 54/4 (1981).

Lock, M.M. *East Asian Medicine in Urban Japan: Varieties of Medical Experience* (Berkeley: University of California Press, 1980).

Low, Morris (ed.). *Building a Modern Japan: Science, Technology, and Medicine in the Meiji Era and Beyond* (New York: Palgrave Macmillan, 2005).

Maruyama Masao. 'Kindai Nihon no Chishikijin [Modern Japanese intellectuals]', in *Kōei no Ichi Kara* (Tokyo: Miraisha, 1982).

Matsumura, Janice. 'Mental health as public peace: Kaneko Junji and the promotion of psychiatry in modern Japan', *Modern Asian Studies*, 2004 vol. 38 (4) pp. 899–930.

Mizuno, Hiromi. *Science for Empire: Scientific Nationalism in Modern Japan* (Stanford: Stanford University Press, 2009).

Mullins, Mark. 'The social forms of Japanese Christianity', in John Breen and Mark Williams (eds), *Japan and Christianity: Impacts and Responses* (London, Macmillan Press: 1996).

Mullins, Mark R. (ed.). *Handbook of Christianity in Japan* (Leiden: Brill, 2003).

Okada Yasuo. *Kure Shūzō: Sono Shōgai to Gyōseki [The Life and Works of Kure Shuzo]* (1982).

Ozawa-de Silva, Chikako. *Psychotherapy and Religion in Japan: The Japanese Introspection Practice of Naikan* (Abingdon: Routledge, 2006).

Reader, Ian and Tanabe, George. *Practically Religious: Worldly Benefits and the Common Religion of Japan* (Honolulu: University of Hawai'i Press, 1998).

Reader, Ian. 'Secularisation, RIP? Nonsense! The rush hour away from the gods and the decline of religion in contemporary Japan', *Journal of Religion in Japan* 1, no. 1 (2012).

Roemer, Michael K. 'Religion and health in Japan: Past research and future directions', in Anthony J. Blasi (ed.), *Toward a Sociological Theory of Religion and Health* (Leiden: Brill, 2011).

Sato, Tatsuya. 'Rises and falls of clinical psychology in Japan: a perspective on the status of Japanese clinical psychology', *Ritsumeikan Ningenkagaku Kenkyū* 13 (2007).

Sato Tatsuya. *Nihon ni Okeru Shinrigaku no Juyō to Tenkai [The Reception and Development of Psychology in Japan]* (Kyoto: Kitaoji Shobo, 2004).

Sawada, Janine Anderson. *Practical Pursuits: Religion, Politics, and Personal Cultivation in Nineteenth-Century Japan* (Honolulu: University of Hawai'i Press, 2004).

Sharf, R.H. 'The Zen of Japanese nationalism', *History of Religions* 33, no. 1 (1993).

Sherrill, Michael J. 'Christian churches in the postwar period', in Mark Mullins (ed.), *Handbook of Christianity in Japan* (2003).

Shimazono Susumu. *Iyasu Chi no Keifu [A Genealogy of Healing Knowledge]* (Tokyo: Yoshikawa Kobunkan, 2003).

Shimazono, Susumu. *From Salvation to Spirituality: Popular Religious Movements in Modern Japan* (Melbourne, Trans Pacific Press, 2004).

Shimazono, Susumu. 'Foreword', in 'Toward the construction of death and life studies', *Bulletin of Death and Life Studies*, Vol. 1 (2005).

Silk, Jonathan A. 'The Victorian creation of Buddhism', *Journal of Indian Philosophy*, 22/2 (1994).

Staggs, Kathleen M. '"Defend the nation and love the truth": Inoue Enryō and the revival of Meiji Buddhism', *Monumenta Nipponica* 38, no. 3 (1983).

Suzuki, Akihito. 'A brain hospital in Tokyo and its private and public patients, 1926-45', *History of Psychiatry* 14, no. 3 (2003).

Suzuki, Akihito. 'The state, family, and the insane in Japan, 1900–1945', in Roy Porter and David Wright (eds), *The Confinement of the Insane: International Perspectives, 1800–1965* (Cambridge: Cambridge University Press, 2003).

Takeda, M. *Seishinbunseki to Bukkyō [Psychoanalysis and Buddhism]*. (Tokyo: Shinchōsha, 1990).

Thelle, Notto R. *Buddhism and Christianity in Japan: From Conflict to Dialogue, 1854–1899* (Honolulu: University of Hawai'i Press, 1987).

Thelle, Notto R. 'Christianity encounters Buddhism in Japan: A historical perspective', in John Breen and Mark Williams (eds), *Japan and Christianity: Impacts and Responses* (1996).

Tseng, Wen-Shing, Chang, Suk Choo and Nishizono, Masahisa. 'Asian culture and psychotherapy: an overview', in Tseng, Chang, and Nishizono (eds), *Asian Culture and Psychotherapy: Implications for East and West* (2005).

Ueda Noriyuki, 'Iyashi [Healing]', in Aoki T., (ed.), *Iwanami Kōza Bunka Jinruigaku Vol. II: Shūkyō no Gendai [The Iwanami Lecture in Cultural Anthropology: Religion in the Present Age]* (Tokyo: Iwanami Shoten, 1997).

Wakabayashi, Bob Tadashi (ed.), *Modern Japanese Thought* (Cambridge: Cambridge University Press, 1998).

Washington, Garrett. 'Fighting brick with brick: Chikazumi Jōkan and Buddhism's response to Christian space in Imperial Japan', *Cross Currents: East Asian History and Culture Review*, 6 (March 2013).

Yu-chuan Wu. *A Disorder of Ki: Alternative Treatments for Neurasthenia in Japan, 1890–1945* (University College London, 2012).

Yoshinaga Shin'ichi. *Nihonjin no Shin-Shin Rei [Body, Mind, Spirit Amongst the Japanese]* (Tokyo: Kuresu Shuppan, 2004).

Yuasa, Yasuo. *The Body, Self-Cultivation, and Ki-Energy* (Albany: State University of New York Press, 1993).

Yumiyama, Tatsuya. 'Varieties of healing in present-day Japan', *Japanese Journal of Religious Studies* 22/3–4 (1995).

# 2 Psychiatry and religion in modern Japan
## Traditional temple and shrine therapies

*Hashimoto Akira*

In late eighteenth-century Western society, the rise of mental science was deeply intertwined with processes of industrialization and urbanization. Psychiatry as a discipline developed with the founding of a new type of asylum – therapeutic rather than custodial – that rapidly increased in number in the nineteenth century as an urbanizing society became more sensitive to the presence of psychotic individuals.[1] In the case of Japan, the modernization, or Westernization,[2] of society and the introduction of modern psychiatry from the West came together after the Meiji Restoration in 1868. The history of psychiatry in Japan, however, cannot be described simply as a developing process in which traditional therapies were replaced by Western medicine under the influence of 'enlightened' doctors.[3] In the course of the modernization of psychiatry, leading psychiatrists generally criticized traditional therapies for the mentally ill, which were widely practised in the form of bathing, incantations, and prayers at religious institutions all over the country. Yet psychiatrists occasionally acknowledged a traditional therapy if it was consistent with Western medical theories, and in some cases they attempted to combine modern medicine with traditional therapies. Moreover, the shortage in Japan of psychiatric institutions, together with increasing demands from patients, succeeded in giving renewed life and potential to traditional therapies.

When we look at ordinary people's theories on mental illness, traditional Japanese folk beliefs seem to be active still in modern society. Since ancient times people have attributed mental derangement to possession by an evil spirit of a living or dead person, or of an animal such as a fox, a tanuki (raccoon dog), a dog, a monkey, and so on. Among them the fox has a special meaning for the Japanese: it is believed to bewitch people, but at the same time it is worshipped as a messenger of the god of bumper crops.[4] Probably such folklore led people to believe that the fox had supernatural power and could possess people. According to Hiruta Genshirō, who has analysed various representations of possession depicted in Japanese classical literature, possession by *mononoke*, or evil spirits, is often to be found in literature from ancient times through to the medieval period, while *kitsune tsuki*, or fox possession, becomes more dominant from the pre-modern Edo period (1603–1868) onwards.[5]

Hayami Yasutaka has suggested that the spread of *kitsune tsuki* in the seventeenth century can be linked to socioeconomic change: a money-based economy came to the villages, changing human relationships and promoting new sorts of conflict between the poor and the rich.[6] After the Meiji Restoration people's belief in *kitsune tsuki* lived on despite attempts at 'enlightenment' in the newspapers. While psychiatrists began to try to understand *kitsune tsuki* and other forms of possession in medical terms,[7] traditional therapies continued to emphasize the exorcism of evil spirits. These latter therapies seem to have appeared more attractive and realistic to people suffering from mental illness than psychiatric treatments, at least in the early stages of modernization.

In this chapter I will explore the role of religion in the treatment of mental illness from the mid-nineteenth to the mid-twentieth century in Japan. I will look at conflict and harmony between traditional therapies and Western medicine in terms of therapeutic effectiveness and scientific rationale, and also at the historical and social context of religious therapists and institutions.

## The history of research on traditional therapies

The first article by a Japanese scholar to refer to traditional therapies in Japan was an 1886 piece on Japanese psychiatry written in German by Sakaki Hajime, the first professor of psychiatry at the University of Tokyo. He wrote:

> As far as the history of psychiatry [in Japan] is concerned, we know little about it. There have been no descriptions of it until now. (...) Treatment of the mentally ill was left in the hands of priests, fortune-tellers, or sometimes laymen. (...) Such treatments were practiced in a Buddhist temple or at home. This was the situation in the past, but even now some of it remains the same.[8]

In 1903 Sakaki's pupil Kure Shūzō, who at the time was a professor of psychiatry at the University of Tokyo, published an article on the history of Japanese psychiatry in an Austrian medical journal.[9] The article dealt with traditional therapies and ranged from ancient times to the early modern Edo period. There was little in these two articles, however, about traditional therapies practised from the beginning of the modern Meiji period onwards. Instead, an article written by Kure in 1912[10] described at length and for the first time the state of Japanese traditional therapies in his own day. He introduced twenty-one temples and shrines all over Japan where the mentally ill gathered and were treated by religious healers – Kure called them 'non-medical institutions for the mentally ill'. A 1918 article by Kure and his colleague Kashida Gorō[11] then reported the generally miserable situation of mental patients under home custody,[12] and looked specifically at six locations associated with traditional healing. While not a broad survey, Kure and Kashida described each in detail and offered case studies of particular mental patients who were staying and being treated at these institutions.

The Japanese government too was, at this time, seeking knowledge about the state of non-medical institutions for the treatment of mental illness. Influenced by policy in European countries, the government in the early twentieth century was very much interested in the Japanese nation's health and experience of disease: to this end, the *Hoken'eisei Chōsakai* (Health Inspection Committee) was established in 1916, as an advisory body to the Minister of Home Affairs.[13] The aim of the committee was to investigate the condition of the nation's health, including that of mental patients both at home and in various psychiatric institutions. The 1917 report of the committee (published by the Ministry of Home Affairs)[14] listed eighteen non-medical institutions ('temples and shrines, waterfalls, hot springs, and others') for the mentally ill, albeit containing only basic information such as the names and addresses of institutions, and the number of patients at each institution. After that until the 1940s, the Ministry of Home Affairs (from 1938 onwards the Ministry of Health and Welfare) published a similar list of 'temples and shrines, waterfalls, hot springs, and others' several times. The number of institutions seems actually to have increased as years went by: from eighteen in the 1917 report (by the Health Inspection Committee),[15] to twenty-nine in 1927,[16] thirty-four in 1937,[17] and fifty-five in 1940.[18] These reports are useful in statistical terms, but they do not give any details about the practice of traditional therapies. Of greater help to historians is a 1937 article by Kan Osamu,[19] a psychiatrist at Matsuzawa Mental Hospital in Tokyo, which lists forty-five non-medical institutions for the mentally ill and includes the name of the person in charge and the year of establishment for each institution, in addition to the basic information given above.

After the Second World War psychiatrists seemed to lose interest in monitoring traditional therapies for a while, until Kobayashi Yasuhiko, associate professor of psychiatry at Nagoya City University, published a monograph on the history of Japanese psychiatry in 1963.[20] Whereas articles published before the war were inclined to criticize the backwardness of traditional therapies, Kobayashi depicted them as unique and attractive.

In the 1970s and 1980s, probably using information contained in the articles by Kure (1912), Kure and Kashida (1918), and Kan (1937), he inspected dozens of temples, shrines, and hot springs, gathering information and publishing several articles.[21]

Psychiatrist Omata Waichirō's 1998 book on the history of mental hospitals in Japan,[22] which greatly contributed to attracting public interest to this field, was heavily influenced by Kobayashi's positive perspective on traditional therapies.

There are clear methodological limits to many of these surveys, since traditional therapies were almost always documented through the eyes of medical doctors – it was very rare for ordinary people to keep a record of such therapies. For my purposes here, I combine these medical surveys with fieldwork conducted with my colleagues over the past few years, visiting many religious institutions and collecting testimony from all those concerned.[23]

## Bathing under waterfalls and in hot springs

In 1918 Kure Shūzō and Kashida Gorō published a report on treatments for mental patients that were rooted in Buddhism, Shintoism, and various folk beliefs.[24] In general, they criticized these therapies as having no real effect, and as being rather harmful to patients from the viewpoint of modern medicine.

They referred to temples in various parts of Japan in which mental patients stayed with their family members while the patient underwent treatment. Bathing, incantations, and prayers were prevalent. Bathing under waterfalls was most popular, and is thought to have been influenced by the syncretistic belief known as Shugendō, or mountain asceticism, peculiar to Japan. Shugendō is derived from an early practice of worshipping the gods of a mountain, or the mountain itself as a god. Shugendō is said to have achieved the form of an organized religion by the twelfth century at the latest, under the influence of various imported religious systems, including shamanism, Taoism, and Buddhism. Practitioners of Shugendō stayed in the mountains and were trained in ascetic practices such as wandering, praying, or bathing under waterfalls. Through such training they were thought to gain healing powers. The most powerful trainees, who were called *shugenja*, were respected by the nobility at the time. In the early modern Edo period, however, the lifestyle of the *shugenja* – who were based in the mountains and were sometimes involved in espionage activities while freely wandering around the country, which might be detrimental to the shogunate[25] – was regarded as dangerous by the Tokugawa government, which attempted to settle them permanently in communities. *Satoshugenka*, or the settlement of *shugenja* in the villages, was promoted, and here *shugenja* prayed for local people's spiritual and material benefit in this world while conducting exorcisms and other treatments for the sick, including the mentally ill.[26] At the same time, from the middle of the Edo period, pilgrimage to holy mountains such as Fujisan (Mount Fuji) and Kiso Ontake became popular. Sometimes people organized pilgrimage groups known as *kō* and regularly visited holy mountains together.

In this way the original ideas and practices of *shugenja*, including bathing under waterfalls to obtain healing powers and to recover from illness, spread through the mutual interaction of *shugenja* coming down from the mountains and into the villages, and through people visiting the mountains.[27] Even when the Meiji government after 1868 sought to establish Shintoism as the national religion and put an end to Shugendō,[28] these treatments survived and appear in fact to have become more popular.

As an example of bathing under waterfalls, Kure and Kashida described the practices at Nissekiji Temple located in the mountainous area of Ōiwa, Toyama Prefecture, in central Japan.[29] Mount Tateyama in Toyama Prefecture was known as a centre of Shugendō. Tateyama is a general term for three peaks of *c*.3,000 metres above sea level. The cult of Tateyama probably began with the worship of the mountain itself, but its syncretistic character is obvious: Oyama Shrine, which stands on the summit of the mountain, is dedicated to the gods of Japanese mythology, while it is said that located at the top of Tateyama are a Buddhist paradise and Buddhist hell. In the Edo period from the seventeenth to the mid-nineteenth century, the cult of Tateyama became very popular among *shugenja* and ordinary people, with pilgrimages to Tateyama from across Japan. For the worship of this mountain a pilgrimage group, *Tateyama kō*, was organized nationally. A *Tateyama kō* from each region visited Tateyama, fostering the emergence of villages that specialized in supplying pilgrims' lodgings (*shukubō*) along the route to Tateyama.[30] At the foot of Mount Tateyama are sacred places connected to the cult of Tateyama,[31] including Nissekiji Temple in the Ōiwa district, where many of the sick used to stay to undergo treatment. According to legend, Nissekiji Temple in Ōiwa was established in 725, when the famous Buddhist monk Gyōki visited and carved an image of Fudō Myō Ō (a Buddhist deity) on a rock, one of the most important cultic objects of Shugendō.[32] But it was not until the mid-seventeenth century that the main buildings of the temple were fully developed. From around 1700, people came to the temple believing that holy water from the waterfalls around it were effective in healing eye diseases.[33] The waterfalls were also thought to be effective for treating mental illness.[34]

In 1868 this esoteric Buddhist temple completed the construction of a waterfall consisting of six streams: tradition says that people who bathe under these falls will form a connection with Buddha and purify the six human *kon* (roots of living energy).[35] At Nissekiji Temple, mental patients stayed with their families for a while in a small temple called a *sanrōjo* next to the main temple, or in inns run by the villagers in front of the temple.[36]

While accommodation in a *sanrōjo* was free of charge, the patient's family had to do their own cooking and borrowed bedclothes from the inns (wealthier patients lodged at the inns).

According to families' particular demands for incantations and prayers, a priest might burn *goma* (small pieces of wood, burned on an altar to invoke divine help) for the patients, but the falls were the most important aspect of the treatment. The temple did not force bathing on the patients and their families but let them do as they pleased. Patients generally bathed under the falls several times a day, five to ten minutes each time. At the family's request, the bathing was sometimes assisted by a part-time helper called a *gōriki* who brought reluctant patients to the falls by force and restrained them for the duration of the bath.

Kure and Kashida (1918) wrote that an eighteen-year-old schizophrenic farmer, who was lodging with his father in one of the inns, had his hands and feet bound with towels and was taken to the falls by two *gōriki*, since he was acting violently. After five minutes he went back to the inn, but his condition deteriorated badly. He complained of a pain in his head and ears and continued to mumble to himself. Two other patients reportedly also took a turn for the worse after bathing. Seeing for himself how the patients bathed, the inspector (Kashida) told them that they had misunderstood the effect of the falls and should discontinue the bathing.

*Figure 2.1* A waterfall therapeutic practice at Nissekiji Temple. Two *gōriki* hold a schizophrenic farmer (centre) for the duration of the bath (source: Kure and Kashida 1918, p. 98).

In the same report, Kure and Kashida also referred to the waterfall of Yakuōin Temple, an esoteric Buddhist temple, in Takao, Tokyo Prefecture. The system of bathing there was almost the same as at Nissekiji Temple. Kure and Kashida criticized Yakuōin Temple over eight patients who had died during the year as a result of bathing, and for its lack of medical control, for which the temple should have taken responsibility.[37]

In addition to bathing under waterfalls, Jōgi Onsen offered an example of bathing in *onsen*, or natural hot springs, as a therapy for the mentally ill.[38] Although Kure and Kashida did not describe this as a religious therapy, *onsen* were originally associated with religion: from ancient times people had worshipped *onsen* themselves as gods. Until the Middle Ages, access to *onsen* was limited to the nobility, priests, and the ruling class, becoming popular amongst ordinary people only from the Edo period onwards. To attract visitors, in addition to the effects of the *onsen* themselves, the power of religious guardian figures was invoked: some *onsen* were dedicated to gods of Japanese mythology such as Ōnamuchi no mikoto and Sukunabikona no mikoto, heroes of the national foundation myth of Japan, while others were dedicated to Buddhist gods such as Yakushi nyorai and Jizō bosatsu.[39]

The custom of *tōji*, or *onsen* cure, is said to have been established in the Edo period, consisting of three elements: the hot spring itself, a bathhouse, and accommodation. People stayed at an inn for some time (mainly during an off-season for farmers) and walked to a nearby bathhouse, where water was drawn from the source of a hot spring.[40] Jōgi Onsen, probably the most popular that we know of in the history of psychiatry in Japan, was located in the suburbs of Sendai in Miyagi Prefecture in northern Japan. When the inspector Shimoda Mitsuzō, a research assistant at the University of Tokyo, visited the *onsen* in the early twentieth century, there were about twenty patients there with their families. Most of them were suffering from schizophrenia, manic depression, neurasthenia, and similar conditions. Men and women would soak together in the 37°C bath almost all day long, believing that a shorter immersion would be ineffective. They were all staying at the only inn at Jōgi Onsen, run by the Ishigaki family.[41]

In terms of the origins and development of this *onsen* there are various views, but it seems certain that the Ishigaki family started the *onsen* business by the middle of the nineteenth century. The golden age of the hot spring was from the Taishō (1912–1926) to early Shōwa period before the start of the Pacific War. During this period 5,000 to 6,000 guests visited Jōgi Onsen every year.[42] Even so it must have been very difficult for the Ishigaki family to run the inn solely on the basis of the accommodation charge, which was relatively modest – unless the Ishigakis were a large landowning family.[43]

Legend has it that Yunoyama Onsen, in Hiroshima Prefecture, dates back to the ninth century, while Yunoyama Myōjinsha shrine, which is connected with Yunoyama Onsen, is protected by six guardian gods of Japanese mythology including Ōnamuchi no mikoto and Sukunabikona no mikoto. In 1707 the hot springs started to flow stronger than ever, drawing more and more people – a feat repeated in 1748, when the hot spring again became active, following a brief hiatus. Hiroshima Han, the local government, appointed village headmen as *onsen* officials, supervising visitors and keeping the bathing areas in good condition. In 1797 Oka Minzan, a retainer of Hiroshima Han, visited Yunoyama, bathed in the bathhouse, and stayed at the Iwataya, one of several inns for *onsen* guests, which continued to be used until the second half of the twentieth century. He wrote in his diary, *Tsushimi ōrai nikki*, that some people made full recoveries from illness as a result of spa treatment.[44] Yunoyama Onsen was especially well known as a spa for the treatment of mental illness,[45] and at the time of a report published in 1940 by the Ministry of Health and Welfare it was still listed as a facility capable of accommodating the mentally ill.[46]

Why were these bathing places specified for the treatment of mental illness? In Europe during the Middle Ages pilgrimage sites attracted people hoping for recovery from illness, and each destination had a patron saint connected with a particular area of health. St. Dimpna in Geel, Belgium, was regarded as a patron saint of mental illness because madness was a feature of her own life story.[47] However, as far as these places in Japan are concerned, the reason why mental patients in particular gathered there remains unclear.

## Incantations and prayers

Kure and Kashida reported on the saying of incantations and prayers at Nichirenshū (a sect of Buddhism) temples Hokekyōji and Myōgyōji in Chiba Prefecture, and at the (Shinto) Hozumi Shrine in Shizuoka Prefecture (originally linked to Shugendō).[48]

Established in 1260, Hokekyōji Temple in Nakayama is one of the head temples of the Nichirenshū sect. Within this temple was a *sanrōjo* in which twenty-five people, including fourteen mental patients, were boarding together when it was inspected in October 1917. The ritual of *shuhō*, a form of incantations and prayers, began at five o'clock every morning.

People moved from the *sanrōjo* through a corridor to another small temple, where they sat in front of the altar of Kishibojin (the goddess of childbirth and children) and loudly recited the phrase 'Nammyō hōren gekyō'[49] to the accompaniment of a drum, while the priest sat to the side overseeing the ritual. The prayers lasted for twenty minutes and started again after a break of thirty minutes. Aside from mealtimes, they continued to do this until nine o'clock in the evening. Kure and Kashida noted that four patients, whom they regarded as schizophrenic, did not recite the prayers and instead looked around and smiled blankly during the ritual. Another male patient, regarded as paretic, laid his breast and belly bare, hit himself around the navel, and smiled. Though the priest explained to the inspector Miyake Kōichi, a Tokyo University research assistant, that 70 per cent of the patients had been cured and that so far no scandals had occurred, the inspector heard from another person that quite a few mental patients had simply run away from the temple.

Myōgyōji Temple in Baraki was established in the sixteenth century and was restored at the end of the eighteenth century. The accommodation and practices were almost the same as those of Hokekyōji Temple. At the time of Miyake's visit thirty-two people were gathered in front of the altar in the place where *shuhō* was performed: ten were patients who were about to be treated. When it came to the turn of one middle-aged woman, who was not a mental patient, she complained of a severe pain in her side. The priest made a noise by beating his wooden clapper and asked her, 'How long have "you" hurt this woman, after "you" came into her body?' The sound of the clapper was so ear-splitting that some of the other patients trembled. The woman answered, 'For twenty-three years.' After a few questions and answers were exchanged, the priest declared, 'This woman will recover from her illness by tomorrow.' This was *shuhō* as it was practised in Myōgyōji Temple at the time. Whether or not the woman recovered by the next day is unfortunately not recorded.

The inspector of these two temples noted that their respective *sanrōjo*, where mental patients were housed, appeared to be pavilions styled after psychiatric wards in European countries. He further suggested that *shuhō*, where the cause of mental illness was thought to be possession or heresy, was in fact a form of psychotherapy or hypnotism. This was perhaps more than just a personal feeling for the similarities here between Japan and Europe: in general, Japanese psychiatrists at this time were inclined to look for elements of contemporary European therapies in Japanese traditional or religious ones (see below). The inspector had high hopes that Nakayama Ryōyōin (Nakayama Mental Hospital), established in 1917 by Hokekyōji Temple, would combine modern therapy with religious psychotherapy. Nakayama Ryōyōin is one of the oldest cases of a religious institution developing into a modern mental hospital.[50]

Kure and Kashida also reported on another type of prayer practised at this time at Hozumi Shrine in Shizuoka Prefecture, which had been converted from a Buddhist temple in the wake of Meiji religious policies that favoured Shintoism over Buddhism as a national religion. Hozumi Shrine had been known as a place where mental patients could find a cure in *yukitō* (hot water prayers). Every morning and evening the priest offered prayers to the patients, and at the same time sprayed hot water on their heads, which was boiled in a pot placed before the shrine. Patients and their families stayed and cooked in accommodation designed for pilgrims in the grounds of the shrine. When the inspector, Suizu Shinji, from Tokyo University, visited Hozumi Shrine in August 1911, there was only a single twenty-eight-year-old male patient staying there with his father.

60  *Hashimoto Akira*

Prior to coming to the shrine the patient had thrown an axe at his wife and injured her. Since then his health had deteriorated, and he had started *yukitō* from July of that year. His father took care of him, and in the daytime the patient tried to help his father do light work such as weeding or chopping wood, but he soon got bored. The inspector offered a generally negative account of the treatment at Hozumi, commenting on the relative lack of patients and the poor standard of the accommodation.[51]

## Religious therapist, philanthropist, swindler?

The type of therapy used at temples and shrines differed from one religious sect to another: in general, bathing under waterfalls tended to be practised at Mikkyō (esoteric Buddhism) temples, which were deeply influenced by Shugendō, while incantations and prayers were used more in Nichirenshū temples.[52] Shintō, Sōtōshū (a Zen sect), and Shinshū (True Pureland Buddhism) seem not to have offered a great deal of treatment for mental illness.[53] In many cases the difference in religious sect does not seem to have been crucial; however, at a single institution, priests of different sects could be found practising a range of therapies, depending on their personal inclinations – including their reasons for offering treatment and care to mental patients in the first place. The particular ways in which these priests arranged and controlled the daily lives of patients during their stays is also crucial, and were linked in important ways to the religious therapies themselves.

The work of the *shugenja* Yamamoto Shūsen (1786–1870) offers an example of the centrality of the priest and his personal experience. Yamamoto established Yamamoto Kyūgosho (Yamamoto Relief House) in the grounds of Tenjōji Temple, in Miyashiro Village (now Tarui chō, Gifu Prefecture) in 1840 after he succeeded in healing a member of his own family who had been mentally ill. As a *shugenja* he himself bathed under waterfalls with mental patients and performed prayers and incantations for the treatment of mental illness. He invented a form of *settoku*, or persuasion therapy: according to his own experiences, he was convinced that the symptoms of mental illness could be improved by the positive attitudes of family members toward a patient, and so he persuaded family members to change their behaviour.[54] Yamamoto died in 1870, apparently killed by a patient, and his son Yamamoto Shūdō (1827–1892) took over the family business.[55] In the same year, Shūdō's three-year-old daughter was carried off by a female patient, and neither were ever seen again. Regardless of these tragedies, the Yamamoto family continued to take care of the mentally ill, while Shūdō's own eccentricities prompted a local newspaper to publish an article about 'the mad cur[ing] the mad'.[56]

Shugendō, regarded as a syncretic blend of Shintoism and Buddhism, was abolished by government order in the Meiji period. As a result, in 1870 Yamamoto Shūdō had to change from a *shugenja* to a Shintoist and join Shintō Shūseiha, one of the new government-approved sects of Shintoism, which was established by Nitta Kunimitsu (1829–1902) in 1873. 'Shūrikosei Kōkameisai', the doctrine of Shintō Shūseiha, provided a system of ethics for daily living, and began to influence the treatment of patients looked after by the Yamamoto family. In keeping with the doctrine, patients engaged in daily activities such as light work and cleaning, which could be regarded in retrospect as a sort of occupational therapy.[57]

After Shūdō's death his son Yamamoto Ichiji (1873–?) took care of the patients, and the Yamamoto family business extended into a third generation. However, not long after the end of the Second World War,

*Figure 2.2* The building used for Yamamoto Kyūgosho, sometime before 1963 (source: Kobayashi Yasuhiko's personal photo albums).

Yamamoto Kyūgosho was finally closed, due either to food shortages[58] or to the new Mental Hygiene Act of 1950.[59] By this Act, two previous laws, the Mental Patients' Custody Act (1900) and the Mental Hospital Act (1919), were repealed and replaced. The 1900 Act had been criticized for allowing the confinement of mental patients at home (home custody), while the latter had failed to promote the construction of public mental hospitals. The new law stipulated the medical treatment and protection of mental patients, and required that their accommodation be limited to mental hospitals. Non-medical institutions were thereby forced to give up receiving mental patients.

The work of the Nichirenshū Buddhist priest Hasegawa Kanzen in the town of Minobu, in Yamanashi Prefecture, shows us something of the links between mental healthcare and general philanthropy in modern Japan.[60] Shocked to find, one winter's day, that an old, homeless woman had died in the grounds of Kuonji Temple, Hasegawa established Minobusan Kudokukai (hereafter referred to as Kudokukai) in 1906 to provide accommodation for the homeless, a number of whom were mentally ill. Hasegawa's Kudokukai was involved not so much in religious therapy per se as in Buddhist philanthropy, the nature of which gradually changed as the Japanese government sought to incorporate religious philanthropy into the strong nation-state that it was determined to build.[61] According to Kan Osamu's 1937 article, the number of mentally ill staying in Kudokukai was five.[62] When the Kudokukai buildings were extended in 1940, some confinement rooms for the mentally ill were constructed, accommodating six patients.[63] After the Second World War, Kudokukai was transformed into an institution for the aged. It seems that Kudokukai was unable to accommodate any more mental patients because accommodation was restricted to mental hospitals by the new Mental Hygiene Act in 1950.[64]

Meanwhile, religious therapies sometimes deteriorated into the abuse of mental patients. At a retreat centre called Ryōzen'an, which was built at the foot of Mount Ryōzen in Fukushima Prefecture in the 1920s, the founder and (probably Shugendō) trainee monk Ōe Ryōken recited a sutra as a remedy for mental patients. As his reputation grew, more and more patients visited Ryōzen'an. At its peak, thirty to forty patients lived at the retreat. In Kan's article, Ryozen'an was described as a Seishinbyōsha hoyōjo, or a sanatorium for mental patients.[65] In 1936, however, Ōe and his colleagues were arrested by the police, and the local authorities demanded the retreat be closed: a mental patient who had run away from Ryōzen'an had complained to the police about violent abuse in the name of therapy. A local newspaper reporting on Ryōzen'an wrote:

> While Ryōzen'an collected a lot of money from patients through charging for board, the patients were given meals poorer than those of beggars. So that the patients would sleep well at night, they were compelled to work, chained to one another like prisoners.[66]

The newspaper also reported that some patients seemed to have died under punishment, while others were raped. Ōe was eventually sentenced to eighteen months of penal servitude for the crime of illegal confinement and injury.[67]

Terayama Kōichi, a psychiatrist and local historian in Fukushima, analysed the case of Ryōzen'an in the following terms:

> Since some psychogenic-psychotic patients can be cured by praying or a change of air, some patients in Ryōzen'an were cured. That must have made Ryōzen'an popular, so people began to leave patients in its care. Although at first the institution must have been faithful to its patients' care, the increase in the number of patients changed its character, and it came to pursue profit and to treat troublesome patients badly.[68]

Nevertheless, because of the shortage of psychiatric beds in Fukushima Prefecture, where the first mental hospital was built with just thirty-nine beds in Kōriyama in 1933, people had little choice but to leave patients in the 'questionable' care of Ryōzen'an.[69]

## Doctors' views of traditional therapies

Leading medical doctors generally criticized traditional therapies practised at religious institutions. Kure and Kashida primarily criticized the lack of medical supervision in the treatment of the mentally ill, hoping to transform unscientific remedies into 'modern treatment' in the Western sense. Although they conceded that bathing under waterfalls could be a kind of hydrotherapy,[70] and that incantations and prayers could be a kind of psychotherapy, they worried about problems of hygiene and morality associated with these therapies: the degree of mental illness or the physical constitution of each patient was often ignored and patients were force-treated. Kure and Kashida also criticized local and central governments for failing to control traditional therapies, even though such therapies contravened the Mental Patients' Custody Act (1900), which prohibited the accommodation of patients at non-psychiatric institutions.[71]

However, in spite of the criticisms levelled at traditional therapies, they still seem to have prospered, not least because of the poor state of psychiatry at that time. Japan suffered from a chronic shortage of beds for psychiatric patients, and most patients who needed to be treated had to choose either home custody, under police observation and without sufficient medical care, or traditional remedies at religious institutions.[72]

At the same time, people were highly doubtful of the treatment in mental hospitals. Kodama Sakae, psychiatrist and director at Aichi Prefectural Mental Hospital, reported in 1934 that most of the families who confined their patients at home under the Mental Patients' Custody Act simply did not trust mental hospitals and did not want to leave their family members there. They responded (on questionnaires) that 'Nobody knows how patients are treated in mental hospitals', or 'Since we are relatives, I would like to take care of the person at home, even if admission into a mental hospital would cost little or nothing'.[73] Although religious institutions may also have gained some notoriety, the bad reputation of mental hospitals must have increased through the scandals reported regularly in the newspapers. From May 7 to June 20, 1903, the Yomiuri newspaper ran a series entitled 'Mental hospitals: the darkest world of mankind',[74] which revealed lurid details of ill treatment in public and private mental hospitals.[75]

Despite their criticisms, Kure and Kashida did not argue that traditional therapies should be abolished. They thought that it would be useful and appropriate if medical doctors were to supervise traditional therapies, or if such religious institutions were to be transformed into mental hospitals. Moreover, they suggested to the central government and the public that traditional therapies could be reorganized according to modern psychiatric theories accepted in Western countries.[76] In other words, traditional remedies were accepted and recommended only if they could be understood in terms of the methods or concepts of modern Western medicine. Traditional practices were reinterpreted and given the terminology of modern medicine, as seen in the examples of Nichirenshū temples in Chiba and other traditions described in Kure and Kashida's report: *shuhō*, for example, would be religious psychotherapy,[77] and bathing in the hot springs at Jōgi Onsen in Miyagi Prefecture would be duration bathing (Dauerbad),[78] which was practised in Europe as physical therapy for mental patients at the beginning of the twentieth century.

Some doctors tried to combine modern medicine with traditional remedies – for example, Matsumura Masami in Takizawa, Gumma Prefecture. The mountainous Takizawa district was originally a holy place for *shugenja*, and Kure's article of 1912 had reported the use of bathing under waterfalls for the treatment of mental illness in Takizawa. In 1930, Matsumura established a sanatorium for hydrotherapy near the waterfalls in Takizawa, because in his words 'hydrotherapy is highly regarded in Western countries.'[79] As a modernist doctor he introduced 'Dampfdusche', or steam showers, most likely from Germany, for which a special room and facilities were constructed. He also adopted traditional bathing under waterfalls, according to patients' symptoms.

In this way he did not simply interpret bathing under waterfalls as hydrotherapy, but rather he tried to combine modern and traditional treatment, making use of the natural and historical environment in Takizawa. This all came to an end when Matsumura, serving as an army surgeon, died on the battlefield in 1943.[80]

Awai Shrine at Naruto in Tokushima Prefecture serves as another example and was written about by Kure in 1912.[81] This Shinto shrine was known for its long tradition of *suigyō*, or bathing at the seaside. In 1927 Awaijima Mental Hospital was established beside the shrine by a Shinto priest and villagers. In planning the hospital, they had visited some modern institutions in Tokyo and Kyoto. Kure visited the hospital and evaluated its combination of modern Western hospitalization and Japanese tradition. The bathing of patients continued as part of the daily treatment until the postwar period. According to the daily schedule of the hospital, *suigyō* was conducted three times a day (at seven and at eleven in the morning each for thirty minutes, and at four in the afternoon for ninety minutes).[82] The institution was criticized, however, for making the practice of *suigyō* compulsory.[83] In 1948 a military official of the US occupation army, thought to have worked as a psychiatric social worker in a mental hospital in America, inspected Awaijima Mental Hospital and ordered that religious practice there should be abolished because it was inhumane.[84]

## Traditional therapies and the public in a changing context

By the 1940s traditional therapies seem to have entered a new phase. Mental hospitals were now constructed not only in urban areas but in the countryside as well. Until 1899 almost all mental hospitals existed only in three out of forty-seven prefectures (Tokyo, Kyoto, and Osaka), but by 1918 at least one mental hospital had been built in each of fourteen further prefectures; by 1935 every prefecture except for Aomori and Okinawa Prefectures had at least one mental hospital (see Shiotsuki, this volume).[85] With this emergence of institutionalism, the number of mental patients who were admitted into mental hospitals gradually increased, although sometimes it took many hours to convince their families that they should be hospitalized, since many people still attributed mental illness to possession by foxes or other beings and so relied on incantations and prayers.[86] In addition, under the influence of the Regulation for Control of Hospitals and Clinics in 1933, each prefecture controlled medical and medicine-related institutions more and more strictly. It became more difficult than before for traditional therapies to survive: in 1933 Kanagawa Prefecture prohibited traditional treatment at Shōmyōji Temple in Kamakura. Since 1915 the temple had run a special house called Konsenzan Seiyōjo (Konsenzan Sanatorium) for mental patients who stayed there for incantations, prayers, and to bathe in the falls. A newspaper article at the time reported that the founder of the institution, a Buddhist by the name of Narumi Zuiō (1881–1954) planned to turn it into a mental hospital by hiring the necessary medical staff – he was apparently ready to apply to the local government office for the required permission.[87]

For some reason, however, the mental hospital idea was not realized – possibly Narumi's plan was rejected by the local government. Instead the temple seems to have introduced regular consultations by a doctor in order to keep Konsenzan Seiyōjo going.[88] As for the inn run by the Satō family located near the waterfall of Yakuōin Temple in Takao, Tokyo, it was unable to continue to accommodate mental patients as a result of control by Tokyo Prefecture. But it did, however, succeed in establishing a mental hospital, Takao Hoyōin, in 1936.[89]

The movements of the emperor of Japan had a powerful influence on the evolution of hospitalization amongst mental patients. As the Sino-Japanese war broke out in the 1930s, the emperor frequently visited places where army manoeuvres were held, and prior to his visits police strictly controlled mental patients who lived outside psychiatric institutions – if necessary confining them in mental hospitals, and even going so far as to construct new mental hospitals in areas in which there were none.[90] Similarly, Ganryūji Temple in Hyōgo Prefecture, a Shingonshū (a sect of esoteric Buddhism) temple established in the ninth century, attracted the attention of the police just prior to the emperor's visit to Kobe. The head of the police department and a policeman from a substation visited Ganryūji Temple and requested that the priest no longer accommodate any patients in the temple.[91]

After the Second World War, the accommodation of mental patients anywhere outside psychiatric institutions was prohibited by the Mental Hygiene Act of 1950, and the number of mental patients staying at religious institutions for treatment went into decisive decline. Even before the Act, however, religious treatment was already waning. As more and more patients were hospitalized in the 1930s and 1940s, people gradually came to think of treatment at temples and shrines as a kind of 'occult' practice. It is not easy to detect a clear moment of change in people's view of traditional therapies, but probably by the 1930s the public began to keep a distance from traditional practices. Whereas from the 1950s onwards the numbers of psychiatric inpatients in Western countries decreased, against a background of deinstitutionalization policies, the promotion of community mental health, and the introduction of antipsychotics, in Japan the trend ran in the opposite direction. Numbers of mental hospitals and psychiatric beds continued to increase right through to the 1990s: in 1950 the number of the beds was just less than 18,000; in 1970, around 250,000; and in 1980, the number exceeded 300,000. The peak number of the beds was 363,010, in 1993.[92]

The following quote, from a sarcastic newspaper article of 1950, illustrates the lost prestige of religious treatments by this time:

> In the time of penicillin and X-rays, rural customs persist. Several mental patients seem to be staying at Ryūfukuji Temple in Iwai, Chiba Prefecture, and bathing in the waterfalls there. When I visited in mid summer, I saw a naked woman bathing under the falls with a grin on her face. The sight sent chills down my spine.[93]

While bathing in the falls became an object of ridicule, the temple degenerated into a place of abuse. Mental patients accommodated at Ryūfukuji Temple were ill treated until the Mental Hygiene Act in 1950, according to an article by Satō Ichizō, a psychiatrist at Chiba University.[94] Satō came to learn of traditional therapy for the first time through his experience with patients whose hands and feet were badly scarred by chains. They all came from Iwai. He visited Ryūfukuji Temple in May 1949 and found that a dozen patients were accommodated in some of the temple buildings, chained at the ankle and connected to pillars such that they could move only within a range of one metre. They were chained even when eating, relieving themselves, and bathing under the waterfall.[95]

## Conclusion

In the course of the modernization of psychiatry in Japan, leading psychiatrists generally criticized traditional therapies. Occasionally, however, doctors acknowledged a traditional remedy if it was consistent with Western medical theories. The fact that people believed in the effectiveness of traditional therapy might, in itself, have given rise to cures in some cases. Crucially, people had a great suspicion that patients would not be cured in mental hospitals and, even worse, might be badly treated there. Nevertheless the 1930s saw the construction of mental hospitals even in rural areas and the hospitalization of mental patients increasing nationwide. Under Japan's wartime regime more and more 'dangerous' patients in the community were confined in psychiatric institutions. The use of traditional therapies, long supported by public belief, began to decline. It was in this period in prewar Japan, when the hospitalization of mental patients was still behind that of Europe and North America, that the ground was laid for the drastic institutionalization seen in postwar Japan.

This institutional trend did not, however, reflect a general shift in public attitudes away from religious therapies and towards understanding mental illness entirely as a medical problem. As the philosopher Uchiyama Takashi has pointed out, the long-standing Japanese view that man belongs to – is a component of – nature helped to produce ideas such as Shugendō, in which mountains were worshipped as gods, and fox possession. This reflected a close relationship between people, gods, and nature, which lasted for hundreds of years until a period of unprecedented economic growth in the 1960s, when social and industrial structures drastically changed in Japan.[96] Still today traditional understandings seem to be alive in places. A few years ago at a group meeting held to decide upon activities for mental health patients at a public health centre in Yamaguchi Prefecture, one patient proposed Taikodani Inari Shrine in Tsuwano,

68  *Hashimoto Akira*

Shimane Prefecture, only for another patient to object that if they went they might be possessed by a fox.[97]

Let us return, finally, to Ōiwa in Toyama Prefecture, where Nissekiji Temple is located, a place blessed with beautiful natural surroundings. On the occasion of the Panama–Pacific International Exposition held in San Francisco in 1915 it was hailed as one of the most pleasant summer retreats in the province, where 'even now bathing in the waterfalls is popularly believed to be efficacious for curing mental derangement and also eye diseases, and thus the place is visited by sick people all the year round.'[98] Infrastructural conditions for accepting mentally ill people and their accompanying family members were also in place. As Ōiwa had been developed as a destination for pilgrimages, it had sufficient capacity to accommodate guests, as mentioned above, in a small temple next to the main building of Nissekiji Temple and in several inns across from the temple. The opening of a railway in 1913 made access to Ōiwa easier. The care of the mentally ill was supported not only by family members but also by the entire community, including priests, innkeepers, helpers for waterfall bathing, a resident police officer, and villagers. In the context of twenty-first-century psychiatry, this would be highly regarded as an example of community mental health – of a sort with a short record in Japan, only introduced in these terms in the 1960s, but a very long history.[99]

## Notes

1 Shorter, *A Historical Dictionary of Psychiatry*, pp. 3–4.
2 For a critical discussion of the relationship between modernization and Westernization in Japan, see Suzuki, *Nyūmon nihon kingendai bungeishi*.
3 For a discussion of the limitations of the modernization paradigm, see Geyer, 'Deutschland und Japan im Zeitalter der Globalisierung'.
4 Komatsu, *Hyōrei shinkō ron*, p. 22.
5 Hiruta, 'Nihon no seishin iryōshi'.
6 Hayami, *Tsukimono mochi meishin*. The prominent folklorist Yanagita Kunio wrote an introduction for this book (the first edition in 1953), but he criticized Hayami's socioeconomic analysis of fox possession. cf. Itoh, *Yanagita Kunio to Umesao Tadao*, pp. 38–41.
7 Okada, *Nihon seishinka iryōshi*, pp. 113–122.
8 Sakaki, 'Ueber das Irrenwesen in Japan'.
9 Kure, 'Geschichte der Psychiatrie in Japan'.
10 Kure, *Wagakuni ni okeru seishinbyō ni kansuru saikin no shisetsu*.
11 Kure and Kashida, *Seishinbyōsha shitakukanchi no jikkyō oyobi sono tōkeiteki kansatsu*. This article was also published in the medical journal *Tokyo igakukai zasshi*, vol. 32 (no. 10–13) in 1918. It dealt not only with mental patients under home custody, but also folk therapies, folk medicine, and transportation of mental patients (from home to mental hospitals). Field research for the article was undertaken between 1910 and 1916, by twelve assistants at the University of Tokyo.
12 'Home custody' was a form of confinement of mental patients at home under the control of the police, which was regulated by the Mental Patients' Custody

Act in 1900. Most of the home custody patients were confined in a small cage built inside or outside their own house.
13 Hoken'eisei chōsakai [Health Inspection Committee], *Hoken'eisei chōsakai dai ikkai hōkokusho*.
14 Naimushō [Ministry of Home Affairs], *Seishinbyōsha chihōbetsuhyō*.
15 Ibid.
16 Naimushō [Ministry of Home Affairs], *Seishinbyōsha shūyōshisetsu chōsa*.
17 Naimushō [Ministry of Home Affairs], *Seishinbyōsha shūyōshisetsu chōsa* (at 1 January 1937).
18 Kōseishō [Ministry of Health and Welfare], *Seishinbyōsha shūyōshisetsu chōsa* (as 1 January 1940).
19 Kan, 'Honpō ni okeru seishinbyōsha narabini koreni kinsetsu seru seishin'ijōsha ni kansuru chōsa'.
20 Kobayashi, *Nihon seishin'igaku shōshi*.
21 For a typical article of his from this period, see Kobayashi, 'Nihon seishin'igaku no rekishi'.
22 Omata, *Seishinbyōin no kigen*.
23 For more on this fieldwork, see Hashimoto (ed.), *Chiryō no basho to seishin'iryōshi*.
24 Kure and Kashida , *Seishinbyōsha shitakukanchi no jikkyō oyobi sono tōkeiteki kansatsu*.
25 Japan's political system of the time, incorporating a ruling elite of regional leaders (daimyō) with a shōgun at the top.
26 Miyake, *Shugendō*.
27 Sakurai, *Kō shūdan seiritsukatei no kenkyū*, pp. 572–582.
28 Miyake, *Shugendō*, pp. 120–121.
29 Kure and Kashida, *Seishinbyōsha shitakukanchi no jikkyō oyobi sono tōkeiteki kansatsu*, pp. 97–99.
30 *Toyama dai hyakkajiten gekan*, pp. 120–123.
31 Tanego (ed.), *Shugenja no michi*, p. 4.
32 The story that tells of Gyōki carving the image in the eighth century must be an invention. Based on the style of the carving, it seems instead to have been completed in the late Heian period (794–1185/1192). cf. *Toyama dai hyakkajiten gekan*, p. 122.
33 Nojima (ed.), *Ōiwasan Nissekiji*, pp. 25–26.
34 Kure and Kashida, *Seishinbyōsha shitakukanchi no jikkyō oyobi sono tōkeiteki kansatsu*, pp. 97–99.
35 According to the tradition of Nissekiji Temple, the six roots are: eye, ear, nose, tongue, body, and will.
36 After the Second World War the *sanrōjo* at Nissekiji Temple was destroyed. However, some of the inns continue to be used today. According to Takigawa Iwao, the innkeeper of Dangoya Inn, whom we interviewed in September 2005, the former main building of Nissekiji Temple burned down in 1967. But before that time the *sanrōjo*, which had adjoined the main building, had already disappeared. It seems that Nissekiji Temple stopped accommodating the mentally ill in the *sanrōjo* after the Mental Hygiene Act of 1950.
37 Kure and Kashida, *Seishinbyōsha shitakukanchi no jikkyō oyobi sono tōkeiteki kansatsu*, pp. 89–91. According to Kure and Kashida, the internal rules of Yakuōin Temple stipulated that a person planning to bathe in the falls should first consult a doctor and obtain medical permission. However, the inspector Ishikawa Teikichi, a research assistant at the University of Tokyo, heard that many patients came to the temple without having had any medical consultation, and that some other patients went to the temple after undergoing ineffective medical treatment.

38 Kure and Kashida, *Seishinbyōsha shitakukanchi no jikkyō oyobi sono tōkeiteki kansatsu*, p. 99.
39 Onsen bunka kenkyūkai, *Onsen wo yomu*.
40 Ibid.
41 Kure and Kashida, *Seishinbyōsha shitakukanchi no jikkyō oyobi sono tōkeiteki kansatsu*, p. 99.
42 Hiruta, ' "Kichigai no yu": Jōgi Onsen no rekishi kikigaki'.
43 Kondō, 'Tōjiba ni okeru seishinbyō chiryō: Miyagiken Jōgi no "sanchū no tenkyō'in"'.
44 Hiroshimaken kyōiku iinkai, *Hiroshimaken bunkazai chōsahōkoku dai ni shū*.
45 Asada, 'Nihon seishin'igaku fudoki Hiroshimaken'.
46 Kōseishō, *Seishinbyōsha shūyōshisetsu chōsa*.
47 Hashimoto, 'Geel no seishin'iryōshi: denshō to junrei ni tsuite'.
48 Kure and Kashida, *Seishinbyōsha shitakukanchi no jikkyō oyobi sono tōkeiteki kansatsu*, pp. 91–93.
49 The phrase comes originally from Sanskrit: 'I embrace the teachings of the Hokekyō (the Lotus Sutra).'
50 The number of modern mental hospitals originating from a religious institution is limited. Honda Byōin (Osaka Prefecture) is thought to be the oldest, originating from Jōkenji Temple, which was established in the sixteenth century and became a hospital in 1882. See Tokyo seishinbyōin kyōkai, *Tokyo no shiritsu seishinbyōinshi*; Okada, *Nihon seishinka iryōshi*, pp. 46–48.
51 Kure and Kashida, *Seishinbyōsha shitakukanchi no jikkyō oyobi sono tōkeiteki kansatsu*, p. 97.
52 Omata, *Seishinbyōin no kigen*.
53 Kure and Kashida, *Seishinbyōsha shitakukanchi no jikkyō oyobi sono tōkeiteki kansatsu*, p. 87.
54 Umemura, 'Yamamoto Kyūgosho no rekishi'.
55 Kure, *Wagakuni ni okeru seishinbyō ni kansuru saikin no shisetsu*, pp. 125–126.
56 Umemura, 'Yamamoto Kyūgosho no rekishi'.
57 Ibid.
58 Ibid.
59 Kobayashi, *Nihon seishin'igaku shōshi*, p. 51.
60 Hashimoto, 'Yamanashiken Minobu no seishinbyōsha'.
61 See Yoshida and Hasegawa, *Nihon bukkyō fukushi shisōshi*, pp. 147–195. National control of psychiatric institutions in the run-up to, and during, wartime included a fixed distribution system for rice and other food, which led to many patients' deaths from malnutrition across Japan. See Okada, *Shisetsu Matsuzawa Byōin shi*, pp. 529–559; and Okada, *Nihon seishinka iryōshi*, pp. 198–199.
62 Kan, 'Honpō ni okeru seishinbyōsha narabini koreni kinsetsu seru seishin'ijōsha ni kansuru chōsa'.
63 *The Minobu Kyōhō*, on September 3rd, 1940.
64 Hashimoto, *Chiryō no basho to seishin'iryōshi*.
65 Kan, 'Honpō ni okeru seishinbyōsha narabini koreni kinsetsu seru seishin'ijōsha ni kansuru chōsa'.
66 *The Fukushima Mimpo*, on 10 December 1936.
67 *The Fukushima Mimpo*, on 20 December 1936.
68 Terayama, 'Ryōzen'an oboegaki'.
69 Terayama, 'Nihon seishin'igaku fudoki Fukushimaken'.
70 In his 1916 textbook Kure introduced contemporary hydrotherapy as it was being practised in Europe: warm and cold baths aimed at refreshing the mind and body. See Kure, *Seishinbyōgaku shūyō dai 2 han zenpen*, pp. 885–894.
71 Kure and Kashida, *Seishinbyōsha shitakukanchi no jikkyō oyobi sono tōkeiteki kansatsu*, pp. 136–137.

Psychiatry and religion in modern Japan 71

72 According to Ministry of Health and Welfare statistics, at least until 1928 the number of patients who were cared for in non-medical institutions (mostly home custody) was larger than that in mental hospitals. As for the patients who stayed at religious institutions, there are no accurate statistics. See Kōseisho (Ministry of Health and Welfare), *Isei 80 nenshi*, pp. 802–803.
73 Kodama, 'Aichiken ni okeru seishinbyōsha, seishinhakujakusha chōsahōkoku'.
74 See Minami, Okada, and Sakai, *Kindai shomin seikatsushi 20: Byōki eisei*, pp. 183–223.
75 The predominance of private mental hospitals over public ones was (and remains) a notable feature in Japan. According to Kure and Kashida, around the year 1918 public mental hospitals (including university and medical school psychiatric wards, public general hospitals, military and naval hospitals, etc.) offered around 1,000 beds between them, whereas a total of thirty-seven private mental hospitals together provided about 4,000 beds. The Japanese government enacted the Mental Hospital Act in 1919 with the aim of establishing a public mental hospital in all forty-seven prefectures, with poorer patients to be admitted at public expense. However, only eight prefectural mental hospitals (Tokyo, Kanagawa, Aichi, Kyoto, Osaka, Hyōgo, Fukuoka, and Kagoshima Prefecture) were actually built under the auspices of this law (1919–1950). On the other hand, private mental hospitals continued to increase right up to the beginning of the Second World War. The leading private mental hospitals were recognized by the local government as a substitute for public mental hospitals (*daiyō seishinbyōin*) and received poor mental patients at public expense. See Kure and Kashida, *Seishinbyōsha shitakukanchi no jikkyō oyobi sono tōkeiteki kansatsu*, pp. 4–5, and Okada, *Nihon seishinka iryōshi*, pp. 180–181.
76 Kure and Kashida, *Seishinbyōsha shitakukanchi no jikkyō oyobi sono tōkeiteki kansatsu*, p. 137.
77 Ibid, p. 94.
78 Ibid, p. 99.
79 Matsumura, 'Suichi ryōhō ni tsuite', p. 117.
80 *Kasukawa mura hyakunenshi*.
81 Kure, *Wagakuni ni okeru seishinbyō ni kansuru saikin no shisetsu*, pp. 127–128.
82 Tokushimaken seisin'eisei kyōkai, *Tokushimaken seishin'eiseishi*, p. 18.
83 Ibid, p. 22.
84 Ibid, p. 26.
85 Okada, '*Senzen no nihon ni okeru seishinkabyōin seishinkabyōshō no hattatsu*'.
86 For an example in Yamanashi Prefecture, see Matsuno, 'Nihon seishin'igaku fudoki Yamanashiken'.
87 *The Chugai Nippō*, on 17 March 1934.
88 Nakanishi, *Bukkyō to iryōfukushi no kindaishi*, pp. 179–180.
89 Hiruta, 'Takaosan takichiryō: Kikigaki'.
90 For instance Miyazaki Nōbyōin (Miyazaki Mental Hospital) was established as the first mental hospital in Miyazaki Prefecture in 1935 shortly before the emperor visited this area. cf. Miyazaki kenritsu Fuyōen, *50 shūnen kinenshi 1952–2002*, p. 103.
91 Sakata *et al.*, 'Ganryūji ni okeru "sanrō" ni tsuite: Seishinbyōin seiritsu zengo no minkanryōho no ichi jirei', pp. 110–117.
92 See Okada, *Nihon seishinka iryōshi*, pp. 198–205; and *Wagakunino seishinhokenfukushi heisei 22 nendo ban*, p. 789.
93 *The Chiba Shimbun*, 31 July 1950.
94 Satō, ''Iwai no taki' kenbunki.
95 In 2007 the current chief priest, whose father was Hijikawa Kampō, the former chief priest, was interviewed about former conditions there. He said:

In the temple patients were chained at the ankle and connected to pillars, whose corners were rounded off from the chains. They had infected wounds on their ankles, which were sometimes infested with maggots. Patients in good health were not chained and worked in the garden. Local people were hired as helpers and took patients to the falls, prodding them with bamboo sticks as they went. After my father was demobilized in 1946 following the war, a newspaper criticized the treatment of patients here. We then tried to have the patients go back to their homes.

cf. *Kindai nihon seishin iryōshi kenkyūkai tsūshin*: 15–20

96 Uchiyama, *Nihonjin wa naze kitsune ni damasarenaku nattanoka*; Uchiyama, 'Nihon no dentōtekina shizenkan ni tsuite', pp. 20–40.
97 Account given by public health nurse to the author. Shrines in this area are famous for being at the centre of the *Inari* faith, which worships the fox as a messenger of the god of good harvests. See Hyōdō, *Seishinbyō no Nihon Kindai: Tsuku Shinshin kara Yamu Shinshin e*.
98 Ishizu, *The Mineral Springs of Japan*, p. III–47.
99 The revised Mental Hygiene Law of 1965 provided for the first time the promotion of community mental health services through public health centres.

# References

Asada S., 'Nihon seishin'igaku fudoki Hiroshimaken [The History of Psychiatry in Hiroshima Prefecture]', *Rinshō seishin'igaku* 15(8) (1986): 1419–1424.
Geyer, M., 'Deutschland und Japan im Zeitalter der Globalisierung. Überlegungen zu einer komparativen Geschichte jenseits des Modernisierungs-Paradigmas', in S. Conrad and J. Osterhammel (Hg.), *Das Kaiserreich transnational. Deutschland in der Welt 1871-1914* (Göttingen: Vandenhoeck & Ruprecht, 2004).
Hashimoto A., 'Geel no seishin'iryōshi: denshō to junrei ni tsuite [A History of Psychiatry in Geel, Belgium: Legend and Pilgrimage]', *Seishin'igakushi kenkyū* 5(2) (2001): 19–28.
Hashimoto A., (ed.), *Chiryō no basho to seishin'iryōshi* [*Place of Treatment and the History of Psychiatry*] (Tokyo: Nihon hyōron sha, 2010).
Hashimoto A., 'Yamanashiken Minobu no seishinbyōsha [The mentally ill in Minobu, Yamanashi Prefecture]', *Bulletin of The Graduate School of Human Development, Aichi Prefectural University* 1 (2010): 19–26.
Hayami Y., *Tsukimono mochi meishin* [*Superstition of Tsukimono mochi*] (Tokyo: Akashi shoten, 1999).
Hiroshimaken kyōiku iinkai, *Hiroshimaken bunkazai chōsahōkoku, dai ni shū* [*Hiroshima cultural assets investigation report vol.2*] (Hiroshima: Hiroshimaken kyōiku iinkai, 1962).
Hiruta G., '"Kichigai no yu": Jōgi Onsen no rekishi kikigaki ["Hot Spring for the Mad": Oral History at Jōgi Onsen]', *Nihon ishigaku zasshi* 23(3) (1977): 370–380.
Hiruta G., 'Nihon no seishin iryōshi [History of psychiatry in Japan]', in Matsushita M. (ed.), *Rinshō seishinigaku kōza S1* [*Clinical Psychiatry Course*] (Tokyo: Nakayama shoten, 1999).
Hiruta G., 'Takaosan takichiryō: Kikigaki [Bathing in the falls at Mount Takao: A verbatim note]', *Presentation at the 8th Annual Meeting of the Japanese Society of the History of Psychiatry on October 30th, 2004, at Keio University, Tokyo*.
Hoken'eisei chōsakai [Health Inspection Committee], *Hoken'eisei chōsakai dai ikkai*

hōkokusho [*First Report by Health Inspection Committee*] (Tokyo: Hoken'eisei chōsakai, 1917).
Hyōdō A., *Seishinbyō no Nihon Kindai: Tsuku Shinshin kara Yamu Shinshin e [Mental Disease and Japanese Modernity: From the Possessed Mind/Body to the Diseased Mind/ Body]* (Tokyo: Seikyūsha, 2008).
Ishizu R., *The Mineral Springs of Japan with Tables of Analyses, Radio-Activity, Notes on Prominent Spas and List of Seaside Resorts and Summer retreats* (Tokyo: Sankyo Kabushiki Kaisha, 1915).
Itoh M., *Yanagita Kunio to Umesao Tadao [Yanagita Kunio and Umesao Tadao]* (Tokyo: Iwanami shoten, 2011).
Kan O., 'Honpō ni okeru seishinbyōsha narabini koreni kinsetsu seru seishin'ijōsha ni kansuru chōsa [Report on Psychiatric Patients and Psychopaths in Japan]', *Seishinshinkeigaku zasshi* 41(10) (1937): 793–884.
*Kasukawa mura hyakunenshi [100 Years of Kasukawa Village]* (Gumma: Kasukawa mura, 1994).
*Kindai nihon seishin iryōshi kenkyūkai tsūshin* 11 (Aichi: 2007): 15–20.
Kobayashi Y., *Nihon seishin'igaku shōshi [A Short History of Psychiatry in Japan]* (Tokyo: Chūgai igaku sha, 1963).
Kobayashi Y., 'Nihon seishin'igaku no rekishi [A history of psychiatry in Japan]', in Kaketa K., Ōkuma T., Okonogi K., Miyamoto T. and Yasunaga H. (eds), *Gendainihon seishin'igaku taikei 1A seishinigaku sōron I* (Tokyo: Nakayama shoten, 1979), pp. 125–161.
Kodama S., 'Aichiken ni okeru seishinbyōsha, seishinhakujakusha chōsahōkoku [Research report of mental patients and mentally retarded people in Aichi Prefecture]'. *Seishin'eisei* 1(6) (1934): 6–14.
Komatsu K., *Hyōrei shinkō ron [Possession and Belief]* (Tokyo: Kōdansha, 1994).
Kondō H., 'Tōjiba ni okeru seishinbyō chiryō: Miyagiken Jōgi no "sanchū no tenkyō'in" [The treatment of mental illness in hot springs: "an asylum in the mountain" at Jōgi in Miyagi Prefecture]', in Hashimoto A. (ed.), *Chiryō no basho to seishin'iryōshi [Place of Treatment and the History of Psychiatry]* (Tokyo: Nihon hyōron sha, 2010), pp. 51–82.
Kōseishō (Ministry of Health and Welfare), *Seishinbyōsha shūyōshisetsu chōsa [The Statistics of Institutions for Mental Patients (as 1 January 1940)]* (Tokyo, 1941).
Kōseisho (Ministry of Health and Welfare), *Isei 80 nenshi [80 Years' History of the Medical System]* (Tokyo, 1955).
Kure S., 'Geschichte der Psychiatrie in Japan', *Jahrbücher für Psychiatrie und Neurologie* 23 (1903): 1–17.
Kure S., *Wagakuni ni okeru seishinbyō ni kansuru saikin no shisetsu [Recent Psychiatric Institutions in Japan]* (Tokyo: Tokyo igakukai jumusho, 1912).
Kure S., *Seishinbyōgaku shūyō dai 2 han zenpen [The Compendium of Psychiatry, The first part of the second edition]* (Tokyo: Tohōdō shoten, 1916).
Kure S. and Kashida G., *Seishinbyōsha shitakukanchi no jikkyō oyobi sono tōkeiteki kansatsu [The Present State and the Statistical Observation of Home Custody Mental Patients]* (Tokyo: Naimushō, 1918).
Matsumura M., 'Suichi ryōhō ni tsuite [On hydrotherapy]', *Kenu* 3 (1932): 117–127.
Matsuno M., 'Nihon seishin'igaku fudoki Yamanashiken [The history of psychiatry in Yamanashi Prefecture]', *Rinshō seishin'igaku* 27(10) (1998): 1293–1300.
Miyake H., *Shugendō* (Tokyo: Kōdansha, 2001).

Miyazaki kenritsu Fuyōen, *50 shūnen kinenshi 1952-2002* [*50 Years of Fuyōen: 1952-2002*] (Miyazaki: Miyazaki kenritsu Fuyōen, 2003).

Naimushō [Ministry of Home Affairs], *Seishinbyōsha chihōbetsuhyō* [*Statistics of Mental Patients According to Prefectures (at 30 June 1917)*] (Tokyo, 1918).

Naimushō [Ministry of Home Affairs], *Seishinbyōsha shūyōshisetsu chōsa* [*Statistics of Institutions for Mental Patients (at 30 June 1927)*] (Tokyo, 1928).

Naimushō [Ministry of Home Affairs], *Seishinbyōsha shūyōshisetsu chōsa* [*Statistics of Institutions for Mental Patients (at 1 January 1937)*] (Tokyo, 1937).

Nakanishi N., *Bukkyō to iryōfukushi no kindaishi* [*Modern History of Buddhism, Medicine and Welfare*] (Kyoto: Hōzōkan, 2004).

Nojima K. (ed.), *Ōiwasan Nissekiji* [*Nissekiji Temple*] (Kurobe: Ecchū bunkazai kenkyūjo, 1962).

Okada Y., *Shisetsu Matsuzawa Byōin shi* [*The History of Matsuzawa Mental Hospital*] (Tokyo: Iwasaki gakujutsu shuppansha, 1981).

Okada Y., 'Senzen no nihon ni okeru seishinkabyōin seishinkabyōshō no hattatsu [The development of psychiatric services in prewar Japan]', *Nihon ishigaku zasshi* 31(1) (1985): 93–107.

Okada Y., *Nihon seishinka iryōshi* [*History of Psychiatry in Japan*] (Tokyo: Igaku Shoin, 2002).

Omata W., *Seishinbyōin no kigen* [*A History of Mental Hospitals in Japan*] (Tokyo: Ōta shuppan, 1998).

Onsen bunka kenkyūkai, *Onsen wo yomu* (Tokyo: Kōdansha, 2011).

Sakaki H., 'Ueber das Irrenwesen in Japan', *Allgemeine Zeitschrift für Psychiatrie und psychisch-gerichtliche Medizin* 42 (1886): 144–153.

Sakata K., Ikumura G., Iwao S. and Yoshida T., 'Ganryūji ni okeru "sanrō" ni tsuite: Seishinbyōin seiritsu zengo no minkanryōho no ichi jirei [On "Sanrō" in Ganryūji Temple: A Case of Folk Therapy in the Time of the Rise of Mental Hospitals]', in Minami H., Okada Y. and Sakai S. (eds): *Kindai shomin seikatsushi 20: Byōki eisei* [*The Life of Ordinary Folks in the Modern Period: Illness and Hygiene. Vol. 20*] (Tokyo: San'ichi shobō, 1995).

Sakurai T., *Kō shūdan seiritsukatei no kenkyū* [*Study on Formation Process of Kō*] (Tokyo: Yoshikawa kōbundō, 1962).

Satō I., '"Iwai no taki" kenbunki [A record of personal experiences of the Iwai falls]', *Chibaken seishin'eisei* 5 (1962): 1–5.

Shorter, E., *A Historical Dictionary of Psychiatry* (Oxford: Oxford University Press, 2005).

Suzuki S., *Nyūmon nihon kingendai bungeishi* [*An Introduction to Modern and Current History of Literature in Japan*] (Tokyo: Heibonsha, 2013).

Tanego T. (ed.), *Shugenja no michi* [*The Roads of Shugenja*] (Kamiichi: Ōiwa shidan sākuru, 1991).

Terayama K., 'Ryōzen'an oboegaki [A Memorandum of Ryōzen'an]', *Kyōen* 27 (1982): 6–10.

Terayama K., 'Nihon seishin'igaku fudoki Fukushimaken [The history of psychiatry in Fukushima Prefecture]', *Rinshō seishin'igaku* 14(10) (1985): 1535–1544.

Tokushimaken seisin'eisei kyōkai, *Tokushimaken seishin'eiseishi* [*The History of Mental Hygiene in Tokushima Prefecture*] (Tokushima: Tokushimaken seisin'eisei kyōkai, 1986).

Tokyo seishinbyōin kyōkai, *Tokyo no shiritsu seishinbyōinshi* [*The History of Private Mental Hospitals in Tokyo*] (Tokyo: Makino shuppan, 1978).

*Toyama dai hyakkajiten gekan* [*Encyclopedia of Toyama Vol. 2*] (Toyama: Kitanihon shinbunsha, 1994).

Uchiyama T., *Nihonjin wa naze kitsune ni damasarenaku nattanoka* [*Why Are Japanese People No Longer Bewitched by the Fox?*] (Tokyo: Kōdansha, 2007).

Uchiyama T., 'Nihon no dentōtekina shizenkan ni tsuite [On Japanese traditional view of nature]', in Ikuta S. *et al.* (eds), *'Basho' no shigaku* (Tokyo: Fujiwara shoten, 2008).

Umemura S., 'Yamamoto Kyūgosho no rekishi [The history of Yamamoto Kyūgosho]', *Gifuken kyōdoshiryō kenkyū kyōgikai kaihō* 14 (1976): 13–17.

*Wagakunino seishinhokenfukushi heisei 22 nendo ban* [*Mental Health Welfare in Japan, The version in the Heisei 22 fiscal year*] (Tokyo: Taiyo bijutsu shuppanbu, 2010).

Yoshida K. and Hasegawa M., *Nihon bukkyō fukushi shisōshi* [*The History of Ideas of Buddhist Welfare*] (Kyoto: Hōzōkan, 2001).

# 3 The birth of Japanese mind cure methods

*Yoshinaga Shin'ichi*

## Introduction

The Japanese language has multiple words meaning 'mind', including *kokoro, shinri,* and *seishin*. Among them, *seishin* still today has special implications. *Seishin* sounds more masculine than *kokoro, seishin teki* sometimes means 'spiritual', and *seishin ryoku* is a mental power that one cultivates. Today, *seishin ryōhō* refers specifically to psychotherapy carried out at medical institutions or researched at universities. *Seishin ryōhō* and *shinri ryōhō* are both translations of psychotherapy. It was after the Second World War that the practice of psychotherapy as a way to support 'normal' people was imported from America.[1]

There were two kinds of *seishin ryōhō* before the Second World War. One is the lineage of scientific psychotherapy,[2] which started with Inoue Enryō and Kure Shūzō, and ran through to Ishikawa Sadakichi, Nakamura Kokyō and others. This stream was rather narrow compared with the other group. This second group referred to *seishin ryōhō* as *reijutsu* (excellent art).[3] According to one book there were more than 30,000 therapists of this sort.[4] This form of *seishin ryōhō* covered a variety of practices, including spiritual healing, psychic healing, hypnotism, and osteopathy. Typically, its therapists practised preparatory physical exercises like abdominal breathing to enhance their healing powers, which they transmitted to their patients using their hands. Sometimes therapists or patients experienced automatic movements like the trembling of their bodies, which was interpreted as evidence of this healing power. A boom for this type of *seishin ryōhō* lasted from 1908, when the use of the earlier term *saiminjutsu* (hypnotism) came under legal control, to 1930, when the term *ryōjutsu* (healing method) was introduced by the police as a means of controlling alternative medicine. In this paper, the term *seishin ryōhō* is used to refer to therapies in this wider second grouping. Before going further, however, we must reconsider the meaning of *seishin*.

*Seishin* is different from the mind in the Cartesian sense, in that it is a more relational term. When the term *seishin ryōhō* came to be used by therapists after 1903, there had been a heated debate about the existence of 'soul' or 'mind'. The debate was started by a book, *Zoku Ichinen Yū-han, ichimei mushin museishin* (A Year and a Half Left, Volume 2: In Other Words, No Gods and No Minds), written by Nakae Tokususuke (Chōmin) (1847–1901).[5] Nakae was a journalist and a radical political thinker who had been diagnosed with a malignant cancer and been given eighteen months to live. In this book, he put forward a theory of materialistic monism. He denied the existence of God, life after death, or the mind's existence independent of matter. Nakae's book sold well[6] and his materialistic views caused a sensation and criticism among general readers, philosophers, Christians, and Buddhists. Nakae's thought was easy to criticize from the standpoint of Christians, but it was difficult for philosophers to handle.

Inoue Tetsujirō (1856–1944), one of the period's leading philosophers, and famous for his arguments against Christianity, criticized Nakae, defending the existence of mind using the law of the conservation of energy. But this criticism seemed to resort to the same type of materialism, in framing the mind as essentially energy. Inoue had already proposed a monistic theory of *genshō-soku-jituzai* (reality as phenomena), so he could not admit the dualism of soul and body.[7] Buddhists were also troubled, since while popular Buddhism allows for a theoretical future life in heaven or hell, the idea of an individual soul surviving death is not admitted. For example, Suzuki Daisetsu (1870–1966) denied the existence of 'soul' and stressed the importance of faith,[8] while Inoue Enryō (1858–1919) defended the survival of the individual soul against materialism.[9] Such confusion in the variety of responses to Nakae shows the difficulty this problem presented to thinkers at the time.

There had been other conflicts between scientific and Buddhist worldviews before this. Inoue Enryō had claimed that there was a harmonious relationship between science and Buddhism in his arguments regarding the inferiority of Christianity. But when it came to the problem of the soul, he seemed to return to traditional Buddhism. Here, the soul or mind plays a central role in enlightenment in two ways. One is subjective faith in the Absolute, and the other is the objective manipulation of the mind. Either way, the mind need not be substantial, in the sense of a soul in opposition to matter. But if the mind is completely associated with mechanistic materialism, the mind loses its independence and, as a result, loses its will to attain enlightenment. When confronted with the materialism of Nakae, Buddhists were frightened because this materialism looked dangerously similar to Buddhism. They came to be aware that the existence of the mind was not an *a priori* proposition but something that had to be theorized as part of their monistic worldview.

In 1903 a journalist named Kuroiwa Shūroku (Ruikō) (1862–1920) published *Ten-nin Ron* (A discourse on the universe and human beings), which presented a monistic worldview that preserved the existence of mind. His monism can be called a kind of vitalism or pan-psychism, as every being, animate or inanimate, has mind in so far as it moves. Everything is at the same time both material and spiritual depending on the point of view. 'Movement, seen by itself, appears as the mind to itself. The mind, seen by others, appears as movement to others.'[10] He referred to the mind in the first sense as '*jikan*' (self-reflection). For Kuroiwa, the universe itself possesses what might be called 'the great spirit' (*tairei*). What is called 'soul' (*reikon*) is the 'spirituality' (*reisei*) or 'true self' (*shinga*) at the root of every life, which is linked to this great spirit. This true self is a kind of life principle that organizes material. In Kuroiwa's system the 'soul' does not have a solid and individual existence, but rather it is more of an ethereal image. At death, the true self returns to the great spirit, though the memory of this life continues because the vibrations emitted from the brain during life will be stored in the universe.

Kuroiwa presented a solution here to the Buddhist materialist dilemma, but the mind he presented was not substance but rather movement or process. If such a mind stops moving, it will lose its existence. Moreover, the mind's power was necessary for being. This last point became central for the worlds of hypnotism and *seishin ryōhō*, and Kuroiwa's book was frequently used by these therapists – although his name was not always mentioned.

Also, the 'mind' has traditionally played an important role in Buddhism, and there are broadly two ways to deliverance or enlightenment, namely *jiriki* and *tariki*. The former emphasizes one's own efforts in attaining enlightenment, while the latter involves relying completely on the power of Amida. This division is also effective outside Buddhism. As Janine Sawada points out, citing Kobayashi Junji, there were:

> two poles in Tokugawa discourse about the mind or heart (*kokoro no gensetsu*): *shinpō*, a method of actively cultivating one's inner states; and *shinjin*, placing one's faith entirely in the power of an Other (and becoming purified through identification with that other).[11]

These two poles would continue in Meiji. At one extreme was Kuwabara Toshiro, who claimed the mind could move independently, and at the other extreme were Pure Land Buddhist philosophers like Kiyozawa Manshi (1863–1903) who stressed an absolute dependence on Other Power.[12]

If we construct a spectrum of techniques of manipulation of mind and body in Japanese religion, they range from self-cultivation methods like Zen or *Shingaku* (heart learning), an eclectic practice consisting of Confucianism and Zen Buddhism, to magico-religious practices like *Shingon* or *Shugen*. Some nineteenth-century methods of self-cultivation continued into the Meiji era, not least in the work of Hara Tanzan, explored below as the first example of this type of exercise making use of a modern psychological framework. After 1910 a range of breathing techniques emerged, called *shūyō* or *kenkōhō* (health methods). A book on breathing, titled *Yasen Kanna*, written by Hakuin (1686–1769), a Rinzai Zen monk, was popularly revived, while Okada-shiki-seizaho (Way of still-sitting by Okada), a method of still-sitting with abdominal breathing invented by Okada Torajiro (1872–1920), also became popular, attracting thousands of followers, including teachers, artists, writers, and university students.[13]

These methods of *shūyō* were accepted as 'decent', but magical practices were not. The government sought to control the latter techniques, which produced altered states of consciousness such as causing possession by spirits or gods. In 1873, possession by fox spirits or spirits of the dead was prohibited. The largest body of magical religion was *Shugen*,[14] which found itself attacked during the Meiji period in the context of the separation of Shinto and Buddhism.[15] In 1868, Shugendō was ordered to become part either of Shinto groups or the esoteric Buddhist sects of Shingon and Tendai – a near-fatal blow, to which was added government prohibition of possession rituals in 1874 and of healing prayer rites in 1875. This was aimed at suppressing non-institutional charisms, but it also supported the monopolization of healing by the medical profession.[16] Imura Kōji has pointed out that hypnotism came into vogue to fill a space left by the disappearance of magical healers from traditional religions.[17] As we will see later, it is plausible that hypnotic healers were, in some senses, 'successors' of Shugen practitioners, as hypnotists imitated their miraculous feats. But in the same way that Tanzan absorbed Dutch medicine of the Edo era, so *seishin ryōhō* therapists offered forms of hypnotism transformed to match a Japanese monistic worldview.

*Seishin ryōhō* was born in Japan as a successor of this imported and integrated hypnotism and through the transformation of physical practices in Japanese religions, especially Buddhism. The purpose of this paper is to show how this occurred, tracing its history from Tanzan to Inoue Enryō to Kuwabara Toshiro.

## Forerunner of *Seishin Ryōhō*: the Zen practice of Hara Tanzan

Hara Tanzan (1819–1892), a Soto Zen monk, was famous as a scholar of Buddhism and a high-ranking priest.[18] One might call him a pioneer of modern Buddhist scholarship since he was the first lecturer on Buddhism at the University of Tokyo. Tanzan started as a student of Confucianism, then studied Chinese medicine, and after being defeated in a debate with a Zen monk, he himself became a monk. While in Kyoto, he debated with Komori Sōji, a professor of Dutch medicine (which was the only western medicine permitted during the Edo era at Kyūridō medical school) over the location of the mind. Tanzan, believing the mind was in the heart (*kokoro*), lost the debate. Tanzan started to study Dutch medicine and constructed an original method and theory of Zen.

Tanzan's lifelong concern was how to ease distress and acquire stability of mind. For him Buddhism was both a theoretical and a clinical psychology.[19] His *Mumyō-ron* (*On Ignorance*, 1847) had explained the source of distress in the traditional way, but he expounded his new physical system of Zen in *Shinshiki-ron* (*On Mind-Consciousness*, 1860), *Nō-Seki-Itai-Ron* (*On the Difference between Brain and Spinal Cord*, 1869), *Waku-Byō-Dōgen-Ron* (*Theory on the Shared Source of Distress and Illness*, 1869), *Shinsei-Jikken-Roku* (*On the Experience of Mind*, 1873), and other works. Tanzan's ideas bear the imprint of the Daoist and Dutch anatomical systems available to him, alongside Buddhist *Yuishiki* (vijñapti-mātratā or Consciousness-only) theories and the major Buddhist text, *The Awakening of Faith in the Mahayana* (dai-jōkishin-ron).

His was a psychosomatic theory.[20] First, Tanzan distinguishes between two sorts of consciousness, each of which is linked to a physiological structure. The first is *kaku*, the pure and enlightened mind or Buddha-nature, which resides in the brain or the cerebrum. *Kaku* is an illustration of the idea of original enlightenment (*hongaku*) in biological terms. Popular in Japanese Buddhism, original enlightenment is the idea that every being possesses Buddha-nature innately and is, in that sense, 'originally' enlightened. The second sort of consciousness is *adana-shiki*, or simply *dana*. This is a kind of life-force, which takes the form of a viscous liquid in the spinal cord. It is necessary to maintain life, but at the same time it causes the defilements and worldly passions that lead to worries in the mind and illness in the body.

These two forms of consciousness come together to give rise to a state of consciousness called *wagō-shiki*: 'mixed consciousness'. *Wagō-shiki* is the basic state of the mind in everyday life. *Dana* travels up to the brain, mixes with *kaku*, and the resulting *wagō-shiki* then circulates throughout the body. Using *Yuishiki* terminology, Tanzan referred to *wagō-shiki* travelling down to the abdomen as *dai roku shiki*, 'sixth consciousness', and *wagō-shiki* travelling to the breast as *dai nana shiki*, 'seventh consciousness'. As long as wagō-shiki circulates unimpeded, the person remains healthy. Occasionally, however, wagō-shiki coagulates and stops moving: this is known as a state of *mumyō* (ignorance, or avidya), involving distress to both mind and body. The idea that stagnation causes illness is common to the traditional *kanpō* (Chinese medicine) theory of *ki* (*qi*). In addition to this fluid model of health, Tanzan added the idea that psychological troubles can cause physical disease, and vice versa. He called this '*Wakubyō-Dō-gen-Ron*', or 'the theory of the same source of distress and illness'.

According to the theory of enlightenment that emerged from this theory of consciousness, if the flow of *dana* into the brain could be stopped, *kaku* would be cleaned of this impure substance and the state of original enlightenment could be regained. Tanzan insisted that the brain and spinal cord were two independent organs, hence the realistic possibility of separation – he later viewed the two as continuous, but still insisted

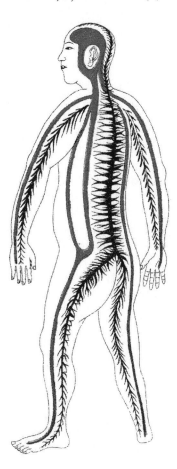

*Figure 3.1* Hara Tanzan's system of psychology: *kaku* appears as shaded, *fukaku* in black (source: Araki (1907).

that their functions differed. By means of special techniques, *dana* would be turned back at the neck, and rather than entering the brain would flow down into the body, maintaining its vital processes. *Wagō-shiki* in the brain would then become pure *kaku*. In this way, perfect peace of mind and perfect health of body would be achieved.

Tanzan claimed to have 'cut' the '*suji*' (veins or a kind of nerve fibre) of his own *dana* at three points: in the abdomen, in the pit of stomach, and at the nape of the neck. How exactly he thought he had managed this, controlling the pseudo-physiological state of *mumyō*, is difficult to understand as he left little account of it in his writings except for saying that he used Zen '*jōriki*' – a kind of willpower, but a rather ambiguous word. From Araki Giten (1907) we know also that Tanzan used methods of introspection and visualization of his own body. While sitting in zazen, Tanzan inspected his mind and body, located the passage of coagulated *dana* (*mumyō*) moving up from his back and removed it with *jōriki*. In his writing, Araki advised practitioners to aid the willpower element of *jōriki* by using Hakuin's method of breathing through the abdomen. In this way the veins of *dana* could be completely cut: first in the abdomen, and then in the pit of the stomach and at the neck. Once completed, the person would become able to see the world as it is and would gain freedom of mind.

Tanzan believed that he had proved his theory by means of his own experimentation (*jikken*) – risking his life three times in the process. In *Wakubyō dōgen no jikken* (*Experiences of the Shared Source of Distress and Illness*), he recalls his near-fatal experiences in his Zen exercises. He focused on the development of *jōriki*, causing the growth of what was considered to be a fatal tumour in his abdomen. Tanzan put this down to the stopping of the normal flow of *dana*. Then, when he directed *jōriki* towards the pit of his stomach for a few years, he became thin and went mad by the age of forty-two. At sixty-five he became paralysed for around 100 days. All of these things were the side effects of cleaning up his *dana*. Whatever the causes of these afflictions might have been, Tanzan survived them all and lived to be seventy-three – a long life in the Meiji era.

He propagated his methods to lay Buddhists through a group called *Bussensha*, which was organized in 1878. It promoted health in mind and body: *bussen* consists of *bu* which means Buddha, and *sen* which means an adept in Daoism. The former is related to the health of the mind, and the latter to that of the body. The group published its own journal, *Bussen-kai zasshi*, from July 1888 until at least May 1889. This was the first modernized *seishin ryōhō* group born out of Buddhism, although that word had not yet emerged.

While the terminology of Tanzan's enlightenment theory could reasonably be called Buddhist, his notion of a pulsating flow of *dana* running throughout the body and his anatomical understanding of cranial nerves may have been shaped by non-Buddhist influences. First, Daoism and

Chinese medicine were key. According to Neijing medicine, a traditional Chinese medical system based on the *Huangdi neijing* (The Yellow Emperor's Internal Canon), there is a *du-mai* (governing vessel) that flows through people's backs. It is said to go up the spine from the perineum, enter the head through the occiput, pass through the vertex, and arrive at the inner part of the upper lip. One of the therapeutic methods that makes use of this flow is called *xiao zhou-tian* (the small circuit of the heavens). Using a breathing method in tandem with one's imagination, one draws *qi* (*ki*; life energy) up through the *du-mai* in the back, and then, after passing it through the face and chest, brings it down again to a point below the navel.[21]

While in this 'small circuit of the heavens' technique health is improved by circulating *ki*, in Tanzan's method the flow of life energy is not considered positive in itself: rather, enlightenment (the highest form of health) is obtained instead by cutting this flow. Moreover, in Tanzan's physiology, the correspondence of the body as microcosmos to the universe as macrocosmos, characteristic of Daoist physiology, disappears. Nevertheless, the *du-mai* channel and *dana* flow are similar in that both are conceived of as vessels that flow from the back to the front of the body.

Another, more important influence came from Dutch anatomy, which helped Tanzan localize the essence of salvation in the brain and illustrate (using Dutch anatomical charts) the method of deliverance. This 'Dutch medicine' was not, however, a purely western product, but had itself been transformed by Japanese medical doctors. When Tanzan learned it, the standard textbook on Dutch medicine was Udagawa Genshin's (1769–1834) *Seisetsu ihan teimō shakugi* (*An Outline Explanation of Western Medical Examples*), commonly referred to as *Ihan teimō*.[22] Since this text was used at Kyūridō school, it is likely that it would have been one of the first consulted by Tanzan when he began to learn about western medicine. Genshin had been creative in adding his own interpretations to western medicine. For example, his explanation of nerves is three times longer than his chapter on blood vessels, despite the fact that the Dutch-language anatomical text that served as his basis devotes slightly more pages to the latter. In addition, there are more passages on neurohumours than on anatomical knowledge relating to the structure of the brain: Genshin translated neurohumour as *reieki* ('liquid with excellent power'), and understood it as the essence of consciousness.

According to Genshin, *reieki* is a thin, blue substance that comes out of the brain and spinal cord. It is more than pure matter: it also has an energetic component (*shinki*), which is the basis of mind (*seishin*). Genshin claimed that though *reieki* is widely distributed throughout the body, it always fills its source, the brain: this shows that the brain is the location of the mind. He argued too that *reieki* presides over the body's self-nourishing activities, the workings of the vital organs, the control of blood and muscles, and so on. While *reieki* is actively moving, one is healthy. Clearly, Genshin conceded to *reieki* a far wider role than that of mechanistic nerve fluids. Frederik Cryns points out that Genshin's ideas here are similar to those of *yingqi* (nutrient qi) in Chinese medicine.[23] This theory of *reieki* is close to Tanzan's theory of *dana* as a life principle and consciousness. So it seems that Tanzan owes at least some of his ideas to a Japanized version of Dutch medicine.

Tanzan's method of Zen seems to have been practised for a while in temples of the Soto sect, though it was discontinued after his death in 1892, as was his group of lay Buddhists, *Bussensha*. His medical 'discoveries' were neglected by medical doctors at the University of Tokyo.[24] This was natural, since Japanized Dutch medicine had fallen rapidly out of date after contemporary German medicine was introduced. However, Tanzan's method would be revived more than a decade after his death, and would bring a new dimension into *seishin ryōhō* (see below).

Tanzan's understanding of Buddhism may have influenced young students at the University of Tokyo, where he was a lecturer. Inoue Enryō was one of these, and may have inherited elements of Tanzan's Buddhist thought. Tanzan and Inoue had clear points in common: both of them were Buddhist priests, pioneers of psychotherapy; both regarded Buddhism as a rationalistic philosophy and the mind as the most important element in Buddhism. But there is one important difference: Tanzan thought of Buddhism as a theory about Buddha-nature (*Busshō*) and the way to let that *Busshō* shine from inside, while Inoue regarded Buddhism as a philosophy and as faith in the Absolute, which for him sometimes meant the Universe as the absolute reality. In short, the difference between Tanzan and Inoue here was between *jiriki* and *tariki*. This might be one reason why Inoue rarely mentioned Tanzan's name in his writings.

## Mid-Meiji hypnotism: fluid, pathological, and psychological theories

Compared to Tanzan's attempt to re-imagine Japanese Buddhism in a psycho-physiological framework, the history of the trajectory from hypnotism to *seishin ryōhō* could be thought of as creating Japanized psycho-physiological therapies out of imported methods. After the Meiji Restoration, knowledge of hypnotism was imported from the West.[25] The terms 'mesmerism', 'hypnotic', and 'spiritualism' were included in one of the earliest English–Japanese dictionaries, *Eiwa Jii* (*English–Japanese Dictionary*), published in 1873. *Tetsugaku Jii* (*Dictionary of Philosophy*) (1881) also contained entries for these words. 'Abnormal psychology' (including mesmerism) was taught at the University of Tokyo's Faculty of Letters. Hypnotism was initially introduced by way of novels and stage entertainers, but after 1885 its theories and practices began to take a more solid root.

To understand the history of hypnotism in the Meiji era, it is useful to divide it into two periods according to the number of publications on the topic. The first period runs from 1885 to 1902. 1885 saw the first translation of the phrase 'animal magnetism' and the establishment of hypnotherapeutic practices and theories. Majima Tōhaku opened what may have been the first hypnotherapy clinic. Inoue Enryō published articles related to hypnotism and abnormal psychology in *Tetsugakukai Zasshi* (*Journal of the Society of Philosophy*). During this period, hypnotism was imported without major re-interpretation. An important exception, however, was Kondō Yoshizō's *Majutsu to Saiminjutsu* (1892), described below, which tried to explain the magical phenomena of religion in terms of the power of mind. The second period runs from 1903 to 1908: the period of a hypnotism 'craze', and the year that Kuroiwa published *Ten-nin Ron*. We see an increase in the number of books published whose titles included the word *saimin* (hypnotic). While there was only one such book in 1902, there were thirteen in 1903, twenty-two in 1904, and thirteen in 1905. This boom contributed to the development of *seishin ryōhō*, which became the dominant terminology after anti-hypnotism legislation was passed in 1908. One of the innovators of hypnotism, Kuwabara Toshirō, called his technique *Seishin-Reidō-Jutsu* (the art of the excellent movement of the mind), because he thought that his method testified to the supernatural power of *seishin*. One of Kuwabara's disciples, Takuma Iwao, published a book entitled *Jikken Seishin ryōhō* (1905), the first entitled '*seishin ryōhō*' in Japan's National Diet Library catalogue.

The introduction of methods and theories of hypnotism to Japan during the first period was the work of a number of pioneering intellectuals. Some were individuals who had happened to learn it from hypnotists while abroad. Others were medical practitioners who took an interest in hypnotism as a new therapeutic method. Scholars at the University of Tokyo's medical school soon followed, but took critical attitudes toward it. Scholars related to the University's Faculty of Letters, on the other hand, conceded hypnotism's therapeutic value.

Influential in the spreading of knowledge about hypnotism was Kawada Ryukichi (1856–1951), a shipbuilding engineer and entrepreneur. He was sent to Scotland to study shipbuilding in Glasgow from 1877 to 1884, and during this time he learned about hypnotism. It appears that Kawada held at least one public demonstration of hypnotism at his house in Tokyo, on 13 June 1885. He hypnotized two maids, one about fourteen years old and the other around twenty-four. He stared at their faces, called their names, and rubbed their foreheads with his thumbs to put them into a hypnotic trance. He then suggested various things to them, such as that the water in the room was rice wine. The demonstration was successful, but he discontinued his activity as a hypnotist. He taught hypnotism to the medical doctor Suzuki Manjiro (1860–1930), who translated into Japanese what became the first book on hypnotism (or, more precisely, animal magnetism) to be published in Japan. Suzuki may also have been among the earliest practitioners of hypnotism.[26]

Suzuki's book was *Dobustu Denki Gairon* (*Outlines of Animal Electricity*), and it claimed to be based on work by Franz Mesmer. The real author of the book, however, was the American John Bovee Dods (1795–1872), one of the most famous magnetists of the mid-nineteenth century. The first eleven pages of Suzuki's book were a translation of Dods' *Six Lectures on the Philosophy of Mesmerism* (1843) and the rest was taken from Dods' *The Philosophy of Electrical Psychology in a Course of Twelve Lectures* (1852). Dods was a Universalist pastor turned hypnotist. His theory was a variation on Mesmer's fluid theory, in which the vital energy fluid of magnetism connects everything in this universe. He introduced the concept of electricity into the fluid theory because the existence of neuroelectricity was already an established scientific fact by the middle of the nineteenth century. Dods posited electricity instead of magnetism as an energy that fills the brain, serves as a link between mind and body, and explains hypnotism. Dods wrote that when the hypnotist empties the subject's brain and fills it with his own electricity, he can control the subject at his will. The method used to induce trance involved no spoken suggestions, and instead involved concentration by staring at coins, pushing the subject's elbows or pushing between the eyes with a thumb, as well as the famous 'passes' used by Mesmer.

Dods' theory used electricity as a way to bridge the relationship between both mind and body and Creator and Creation. As Edward S. Reed has written: 'Much of nineteenth-century psychological thought emerged from religious apologists' efforts to justify specific views of the deity or the soul. Dods's lectures offer an excellent example of this kind of creative apologetics.'[27] Dods claimed that electrical fluid has the power to move, organize and transform all matter, and that it arose from the mind of the universe, namely the Creator.[28] Suzuki did not directly translate all of Dods' concepts. He omitted talk of a 'Creator', and made do with the 'universe'[29] – a small but significant change: Dods' mechanical-theistic cosmology was turned into a vitalistic model of a universe without a God, a picture more harmonious with both natural science and Buddhism.

In 1887, Ōsawa Kenji (1852–1927), a professor of physiology at the University of Tokyo,[30] gave a lecture on hypnotism at the request of the university's president, Kato Hiroyuki. Published in *Chugai Iji Shinpō* (*Journal of Medical News Home and Abroad*) and later reprinted as *Masui Jutsu* (*The art of hypnotism*)[31] this lecture featured the new coinage, *masui jutsu*. '*Ma*' means magical or demonical, while '*sui*' means sleeping, reflecting Ōsawa's critical attitude. In the printed version of his lecture Ōsawa, who had studied medical science in Germany and had witnessed performances by the stage hypnotist Carl Hansen (1833–1897) in Strasbourg, summarized the history of hypnotism and its research, from Mesmer's animal magnetism through Reichenbach's odic force and Braid's psycho-physiological theory to Charcot's theory of three stages of hypnotic trance. He took a pathological view of hypnotism and attributed the cause of hypnotic trance to the brain's instability, which in turn is a result of the weakness of its structure. Ōsawa himself hypnotized women with success but failed with male students, reinforcing his prejudices about women's fragility.

Ōsawa's biggest concern about hypnotism was that hypnotists had perfect control of their subjects. He warned readers that women might be raped in hypnotic trance, and concluded that 'hypnotism can be of benefit when it is in the hands of people with a bachelor's degree, but it should not be used by ordinary people.'[32] Ōsawa's antagonistic attitude here emerged in the context of the legal regulation of the medical professions in Japan. In 1874 the medical practitioners' qualifying examination was initiated, based on institutions in the West, and in 1879 graduates of the University of Tokyo's medical faculty were made exempt from the examination.[33] Clearly Ōsawa wanted to model hypnotism on this exclusive system, perhaps fearing otherwise that the monopoly of medical doctors over hypnotism would be threatened.

Even before Suzuki's translation, students of the University of Tokyo's Faculty of Letters knew of hypnotism. Toyama Masakazu (1848–1900), who taught several courses at the university, was a pioneer in the fields of both sociology and psychology. He had studied chemistry and philosophy at the University of Michigan from 1872 to 1876, and upon his return to Japan became the first Japanese professor at the University of Tokyo (at this time still Tokyo Kaisei School), whose faculty up until that point had been composed entirely of non-Japanese. Toyama's favourite theme was Spencerian philosophy, which reached its height of influence during the late 1870s and 1880s in Japan. Toyama's knowledge of psychology came mainly from the writings of William Benjamin Carpenter, Alexander Bain, and Herbert Spencer,[34] and it seems that his use of Carpenter's *Principles of Mental Physiology*[35] will have meant students being introduced to hypnotism. Carpenter's psychology seemed to interest Buddhists studying at the university. His secular approach to psychological phenomena was an inspiration for Inoue Enryō in his *Yōkai Gaku*.

Inoue Enryō was born to a Buddhist priest of the Jōdo Shin sect (Higashi Honganji) in Niigata prefecture.[36] Financially supported by Higashi Honganji temple (the sect's main temple), he entered the preparatory school of the University of Tokyo in 1878, and enrolled at the university in 1881, where he studied philosophy and gained an interest in psychology through Professor Toyama. At this time, Higashi Honganji was sending promising young students to the university, amongst whom were later Buddhist reformers including Tokunaga Manshi (later Kiyozawa, 1863–1903) and Chikazumi Jōkan (1870–1941).[37]

Inoue's books *Bukkyō Katsuron joron* (*Introduction to Active Discussion on Buddhism*) (1887) and *Shinri Konjin* (*Golden Needle of Truth*) (1886–1887) were read widely by Buddhist activists at the time, and helped a weakened

Buddhism recover by framing the religion in nationalist and anti-Christian terms.[38] Inoue was not, however, a naive revivalist. He attacked Christianity for its unscientific characteristics, dismissing the idea of a Creator outside the Universe and a 'creatio ex nihilo' as absurd. He saw Buddhism as rational in the sense that it regarded every being in the universe as *shin'nyo* (tathata), 'suchness'.[39] It needed only to rid itself of its superstitious elements in order to become a religion for intellectuals.[40] Inoue's fundamental philosophy was, simply put, that the world is as it is, and nothing else. This monistic theory is called *genshō-soku-jituzai* (the phenomenal is the real),[41] which was popular among philosophers in Meiji era such as Tokyo University's Inoue Tetsujirō. It is said that this theory was based on Mahayana Buddhism, as taught by Hara Tanzan at the university.

After graduating from the department of philosophy in 1885, Inoue did not go on to work as a priest (though he had been ordained) as the Higashi Honganji had expected. Instead, he started various groups and institutions to propagate philosophy and enlighten people. As Inoue's motto, *gokoku airi* (defend the nation, love reason)[42] indicates, his aim in popularizing philosophy was to create citizens for the Japanese nation-state. While still a student in 1884 Inoue joined with leading scholars to form *Tetsugakukai* (Society of Philosophy). Three years later, in 1887, he started publishing *Tetsugakukai Zasshi* (*Journal of the Society of Philosophy*) and opened *Tetsugakukan* (Philosophy Hall) in Tokyo, which is now Tōyō University. This school opened its doors wide with correspondence courses, and frequently published records of the lectures given there.

In his writings, Inoue popularized philosophical thinking and debunked superstitions. He brought these themes together in his applied psychology, which he called *Yōkai Gaku* (*yōkai* means monster, and *gaku* means scholarship), for which he is well known.[43] He had been interested in paranormal phenomena since childhood, and in January 1886 organized a group called *Fushigi Kenkyukai* (Strangeness Research Group) with other graduates of the University of Tokyo. This group lasted for only three months, but his interest continued. From 1887 to 1892, almost forty articles or translations about hypnotism, psychical research, and abnormal psychology were published in *Tetsugakukai Zasshi*. Many of these are thought to have been penned by Inoue, reflecting both personal interest and trends in psychology at the time. Over time, Inoue developed his critiques of *kokkuri-san* (a practice similar to table-turning) into a systematized field called *Yōkai Gaku*, which he considered part of applied psychology. In the preface of *Ōyō Shinrigaku* (*Applied Psychology*) (approx. 1888) by Tokunaga Manshi, Inoue wrote, 'Psychology can be divided into a theoretical department and an applied one; the latter should deal with and explain *yōkai*.'[44] Here, he extended the meaning of *yōkai*, which usually means monstrous beings, to include abnormal or supernormal phenomena in general. Starting in 1893, he published six volumes on *Yōkai Gaku* and tried to establish it as an academic discipline at

Tetsugakukan. His fellow scholars did not, however, see the academic merit of these writings on *Yōkai Gaku*.

Inoue did not intend to propagate materialist rationalism through *Yōkai Gaku*. Rather, he wanted to purify 'true religion', specifically true Buddhism, by eliminating its superstitious elements. He did not, however, want to exclude all of what a true materialist might consider the superstitious elements of religion because he saw value in faith and in faith healing.

Inoue's views on hypnotism are most clearly expressed in his Introduction to Majima Tōhaku's *Saiminjutsu Chiryōhō* (*Hypnotherapy*) (1888).[45] Majima is thought to have been the first medical practitioner to open a hypnotism clinic. He had been a practitioner of Dutch medicine before starting hypnotherapy in 1885. In 1888, he met Inoue Enryō and talked with him about hypnotherapy. Inoue became interested in the idea and invited him to his school, Tetsugakukan, where Majima gave a demonstration and lecture in May of that year. In his booklet, Majima summarized briefly the history of hypnotism, referenced Kawada's demonstration, and quoted the medical records of his patients. He succeeded in treating about 120 patients overall. His booklet was presumably the first medical report on hypnotic therapy in Japan.

Inoue's introduction, titled *Chiryōhō no Shin Hatsumei* (A new invention in therapy), is important because it was the first theoretical discussion in Japanese of the significance of psychotherapy. In this essay, Inoue divided therapy into physiological and psychological. He stressed the importance of psychotherapy and the necessity for medical doctors to learn philosophy or psychology to complement their physiological therapies. According to Inoue, hypnotism was a way to remove pain – and once pain is removed, natural healing power arises from the body. Inoue claimed too that this therapy had been practised since ancient times as faith healing, linking it with the healing potential of religious faith (faith being a key characteristic of his Jōdo Shin sect). Later, in *Shinri Ryoho* (1904), Inoue claimed that the best psychotherapy is faith in the universe as *tathatā* (*shin'nyo*, the Buddhist concept of 'suchness').[46]

Thus, for Inoue, there were two buffer zones between science and religion. One was the zone of superstition in which there are seemingly mysterious things that can in fact be explained away by psychology. The other was the zone of psychotherapy, in which religious healing miracles can be translated into psychologically authenticated therapy.

By the late 1880s, three theories about hypnotism had been imported into Japan: the fluid theory, the pathological theory, and the psychological theory. In 1892 Kondō Yoshizō published a book entitled *Majutsu to Saiminjutsu* (*Magic and Hypnotism*),[47] written for general readers, including young students. Containing information on the history and methods of hypnotism, alongside explanations of religious miracles in terms of hypnotism, it sold well and was reprinted for an exceptionally long time.[48]

Little is known about Kondō, but he seems to have had some relationship with Shintōism. He distinguished 'magic' from 'hypnotism', which he described as a way to induce a sleep-like trance. He argued that magic is not superstitious thing, but a natural ability common to ordinary people. According to him, magic is 'a method to control the minds and bodies of human beings and animals or to transform matter through mental effects, namely the power of correspondence between minds'.[49] While Inoue said that illness could be cured thanks to the pain reduction effects of hypnotism, Kondō asserted that magical powers must be the cause of hypnosis-based healing. 'The therapist hopes for the illness to be cured so earnestly that his mind-power concentrates and leads to an effective cure through *kantsū* between minds'.[50] *Kantsū*, and the similar term *kan'nō*, can be translated as 'correspondence', in the religious context of *kami* (deities) responding to people's prayers. Kondō, however, tried to explain *kantsū* and *kan'nō* as effects between people, and gave a quasi-physiological explanation. Brain functions vibrate the molecules of the nervous system, he argued. This vibration is transmitted to the site of the patient's illness through the gases that fill the space between therapist and patient.

Like Inoue, Kondō tried to explain supernatural phenomena via the scientific worldview. However, Kondō admitted the direct effects of the mind on far away things and minds, which Inoue did not. Inoue criticized Kondō's book as a fantasy that tried to explain the strange stories of the past in terms of *reiki* (mysterious atmosphere) in the universe. For Inoue, such supernatural phenomena were no more than hallucinations during hypnotic trances.[51] The important thing here is that although Kondō rejected the existence of animal electricity as a superstition,[52] he believed in correspondence between the mind and distant objects. He represents a process whereby the fluid model in hypnotism was Japanized: in place of terms like 'animal magnetism' or 'electricity', traditional Japanese religious concepts such as '*reiki*', '*kantsū*' and '*kannō*' were used to explain influence at a distance.

## The birth of *Seishin Ryōhō*

1903 saw a sudden rise of interest in hypnotism in Japan, for a number of possible reasons. Rapid industrialization and urbanization was causing health problems such as tuberculosis and neurasthenia, which were not effectively treated by medical doctors.[53] Anxiety surrounded a looming war with Russia. '*Hanmon*' (existential distress) was on the rise amongst students after a University of Tokyo student committed suicide at Kegon Falls and left an influentially philosophical suicide note.[54] Books on *shinpi shugi* (mysticism) were being published, with Tsunashima Ryōsen's *Byōkan Roku* (*Records of Illness*, 1905) especially popular. At the same time, psychical research was in the midst of a revival, linked to its popularity in Europe and America.[55]

The 1903 hypnotism craze was ignited by two authors in particular, Takeuchi Nanzō and Kuwabara Toshirō. Takeuchi first studied at a school run by Unitarians and later took philosophy as an elective course at the University of Tokyo, where he majored in ethics and psychology. He later became principal of Narita Middle School. He published *Saiminjutsu Jizai* (1903),[56] for the most part a translation of Albert Moll's *Der Hypnotismus* (1889), which sold so well that Takeuchi kept writing about hypnotism for another two years despite not being a hypnotism expert. Later, he switched his position and warned against hypnotism. During this boom, Fukurai Tomokichi (1869–1947) wrote the first doctoral dissertation on hypnotism at the University of Tokyo in 1906, published as *Saimin Shinri-gaku* (1906).[57] Ono Fukuhei (1867–1911) and Fukurai co-operated in hypnotism research, with Fukurai siding with Ono in criticizing Kuwabara's extraordinary healing. Fukurai had been a student of Motora Yūjirō (1858–1912), the founding father of experimental psychology in Japan, who had studied hypnotism in America and was prepared to let his student, Fukurai, address this theme. It may be that Motora hoped Fukurai would develop hypnotherapy in Japan.[58]

Fukurai became further interested in psychical research when he became one of the early members of the *Shinshō kai* (Society for Psychical Phenomena), founded by the ex-Unitarian and lay Buddhist, Hirai Kinza.[59] The group only lasted for a few years, but had a great impact on the trajectory of Fukurai's career. His initial interest may have been in William James, the renowned American psychologist and psychical researcher. In 1910, Fukurai, then an assistant professor at the University of Tokyo, started a series of experiments on mediums. Fukurai's research on *senrigan* (clairvoyance) caused a great sensation in the media.[60] One could say that the *zeitgeist* in Japan became more 'spiritual' around 1910, with the hypnotism boom helping lead up to it. Unfortunately, Fukurai became so absorbed in researching two women clairvoyants that he became involved in scandal, made worse after they both died in early 1911, one by suicide. Fukurai was forced to leave the university in October 1913, and the academic study of psychic phenomena, including hypnotherapy, in Japan came to an end. Instead, in the 1910s thousands of *seishin ryōhō*, or Japanese-style mind cure therapists, appeared outside of medical and academic institutions. The originator of this movement was the hypnotist Kuwabara Toshirō.

Kuwabara Toshirō (Ten-nen) (1873–1906) was born to a farming family in Gifu prefecture, his mother a pious Buddhist of the Jōdo Shin sect.[61] Kuwabara studied Chinese literature at the Higher School of Education (Koto Shihan Gakko) and became a teacher at the Shizuoka School of Education (now Shizuoka University) in 1899. On 12 September 1901, he happened to begin reading *Majutsu to Saiminjutsu*, which he had bought two years earlier. Based on its content, he successfully hypnotized one of his maids who was thirteen years old. He continued this every night thereafter, over 100 times. The maid was easily hypnotized and turned out to be a clairvoyant medium. Kuwabara then started healing patients, using both verbal and non-verbal suggestion, becoming convinced of the mind's supernatural powers, which he discovered also in himself.

Kuwabara wrote a series of essays on his experiments for the journal *Kyōiku Jiron* (*Review of Education*), in which he distinguished between hypnotism and *seishin sayō* (mental effects). He claimed that the former only induces sleeping while the latter can produce supernormal phenomena. The first volume of his book *Seishin Reidō*[62] was filled with supernatural episodes, classified into: (1) healing illnesses with hypnotic trance; (2) healing illnesses without hypnotic trance; (3) failed cases; and (4) supernatural powers. Kuwabara claimed to have cured a seven-year-old child with a skin disease using hypnotism, and, without using hypnotism, a seventeen-year-old whose body was bent by spinal disease. Kuwabara managed the latter over the course of three treatments, causing the boy's body to become straight and healthy. Kuwabara's non-hypnotic treatments took the form of touching the site of disease and willing the patient to recover. The first subject, namely the maid, he hypnotized demonstrated extrasensory powers, able to see distant places while she was in hypnotic trance. Kuwabara next experimented with the wonders said to be worked by religious people, including the monks of Shingon Buddhism. He repeated those miracles using only his will, without the help of rituals.

Of course, these writings of Kuwabara's were severely criticized. However, their first-person narrative leant credibility to their content, and they received many favourable responses from readers, most of whom were teachers of elementary schools. There were so many letters of inquiry that Kuwabara quit Shizuoka School and moved to Azabu Middle School in Tokyo, where he organized his own group *Seishin Kenkyu Kai* (Society for the research of mind), and wrote about his system of what he now called '*seishin ryōhō*' in a three-volume work entitled *Seishin Reidō* (1903, 1904).[63] His group published a monthly journal, *Seishin*, beginning in 1905. Kuwabara died young in 1906, but his followers organized another group, *Seihin gakuin* (School of mind) that published its journal, *Kokoro no tomo*, from 1906 to at least 1912.

Kuwabara called his system *Seishin-Reidō-Jutsu* (excellent movement of mind), which he explained in the three volumes of *Seishin Reidō*. The first volume was about hypnotism, consisting of articles initially published in *Kyōiku Jiron*. Kuwabara's own theories feature in the second volume, based on the lectures given at *Seishin Kenkyu Kai* and centring around the following four propositions.

1 Mind is energy, a moving agent inherent in things. So everything, living or not, has a mind.
2 Each mind can affect other minds with or without the aid of mediums, which may be invisible or visible, and audible or inaudible. This is

because mind is not a solid soul but a force. The therapist's will is able to heal patients. Therefore, therapists need not have a rapport with patients. Therapists may use verbal suggestion, but willing alone is enough.

3   This understanding of mind can be applied to the universe. Just as a human being has a mind, a small self, the universe has its own mind, the large self. This large self is called by various names: Brahma, Tathatā, Heaven, God, Taichi, Truth, Nirvana, and so on. 'This force exists in all of space. It exists in any place where there is no air. It exists in anything even if it is the smallest or the largest, the hardest or the softest.... Everything is powered by this excellent thing. Nothing, whether it is the hardest or the strongest, can beat this force. Living or non-living things depend on this force.'

4   If we stop worrying and become free from all distracting thoughts, the stable mind will appear in us. This stable mind is an offshoot of the great mind of the universe. When we enter this state, we can work wonders. 'There are neither esoteric ways nor secrets. We just need to be single-minded, maintain concentration, and be intent on one thing. There is no other way.'[64]

Although Kuwabara seemed to borrow some of his basic ideas from Kondō Yoshizo's theories on magic, the pan-psychism of Kuroiwa's *Ten-nin Ron*, and possibly also Inoue Tetsujiro's theory of the large ego,[65] he helped him to develop these into a unique psychology or cosmology, consisting of Chinese philosophy, Buddhism, Christianity, and comparative religion. This volume can be called the first original Japanese piece of thought born of the influence of hypnotism. Kuwabara's vocabulary was more eclectic than Tanzan's, and his method more simple. His uniqueness lay also in that his narrative was based on his own experiences, related to his religious faith. He repeatedly confessed in his books that he revived his religious faith after he started experimenting with hypnotism. *Seishin-Reidō-Jutsu* was not only the way to manipulate the mind but also the doorway to faith, because he thought the miraculous phenomena of hypnotism indicated the existence of Great Mind.

In the third volume of his work Kuwabara wrote about his view of religion, about the altruistic character of the larger self and a desire to combine the Jōdo Shin sect with Christianity. For Kuwabara, the Universe is the Great Mind, which makes religion the cosmic psychology. This volume can be called an attempt to re-create 'religion' using psychological terms, based on Kuwabara's understanding of the Jōdo Shin sect.

Kuwabara's books are a result of historical changes surrounding Japanese religion in two ways. First, the demise of Shugendō (see above) had left medical, psychological and religious roles open to be filled. Second, Kuwabara tried to answer the question of what shape *shūkyō* should have, if it is to be constructed on faith. He resolved these problems by using terms borrowed from western thought and from Chinese philosophy and Buddhism, combining these with his own experiences (Kuwabara stressed the importance of *jikken*, as Tanzan had).[66] Third, and most importantly, Kuwabara wanted to combat materialism, asserting the existence of *seishin* without resorting to dualism. He sought to solve this dilemma by understanding the objective world in terms of an emanation of mind. Ultimately, Kuwabara based his discussion on his own experiences, rooted in his conversion from materialism to religion through hypnotism. The influence of Kuwabara's theory of *seishin*, especially the relationship between small self and large self, can be found in many of the therapists of *seishin ryōhō* who appeared in the Taishō period (1912–1926).

Hypnotic therapists multiplied rapidly during the hypnotism craze. In 1906, an officer of the Ministry of Interior reported that there was at least one practitioner of hypnotism in thirty-two of the forty-four prefectures in the country. Hypnotism was in vogue briefly among medical professionals. In 1902, the Japanese Society of Neurology (now the Japanese Society of Psychiatry and Neurology) was established, and according to its annual reports in 1903 and 1904 more than ten articles about hypnotism were published in those years by the organization. But as hypnotism became popular, tensions between therapists and medical practitioners came to the surface. A good example was the case of the hypnotic therapist Yamauchi Tokuma.[67] In 1903, the local medical association of Miyazaki prefecture took him to court for violating medical practitioners' law. He had been a principal of an elementary school and, after learning about hypnotism in 1903 had created a new method of therapy. After he cured his mother of her rheumatism, many patients visited him for cures. He was found guilty at his first trial for violating the medical practitioners' law, but was found not guilty at a second trial. The given reason for the latter judgment was that Yamauchi's psychological therapy went beyond what was covered in the medical licence exam, and therefore could not be thought of as medical activity. As this episode shows, hypnotism did not come under the control of medicine in the way that people in the field had hoped.

In general, medical professionals saw hypnotism as a medical activity, and sought to monopolize it. Some hypnotists and psychologists, like Ono Fukuhei, Yamaguchi Sannosuke, and Fukurai Tomokichi proposed instead to introduce a hypnotists' licence. Others, such as Kuwabara Toshirō, did not want hypnotism limited to either physicians or psychologists. *Kokka Igaku kai* (the Society of State Medicine, which dealt with public healthcare and forensic medicine) took an antagonistic stance. They invited Koga Renzō (1858–1942) and Ōsawa Kenji to give lectures on the subject at their annual meeting in October 1903.[68] At this point a new system of criminal law was being prepared and Koga was influential in its planning, as a justice of the Supreme Court and a jurist. In his lecture, Ōsawa repeated the same criticisms he had levelled in 1886, concluding that hypnotism should be regulated. Koga put forward the opposite view, however. He turned out to be sympathetic to Kuwabara's *Seishin Reidō*, and claimed that legal controls should not be applied to hypnotism. He remarked sarcastically to Ōsawa, at the end of his lecture, that 'the harm done by a physiologist constrained by his own prejudices, and trying to handle arbitrarily the law of the state, is much more severe than the harm done by hypnotism.'[69]

With Koga strongly against hypnotism's legal control, the struggle between the three parties continued for some years.[70] In 1908, the *Keisatsuhan Shobatsu Rei* (now the Minor Offenses Act) was issued, under which those who use hypnotism 'without due cause' were deemed punishable. *Keisatsuhan* means light crimes, which do not need to be brought before a court. The police are able to deal with such crimes quite freely, and since no definition was given for 'without due cause', in practice the police were able to arrest any hypnotist if they so desired. The Act dissuaded many medical doctors or the psychologists from experimenting in hypnotism. In their place, therapists – mostly male, although numbers of women increased from the 1920s – began to use the term *seishin ryōhō* instead of *saimin jutsu*, in order to avoid police interference. '*Seishin ryōhō*' or 'mind cure' – in the sense not of 'curing the mind' but 'curing *using* the mind' – is an appropriate descriptor for their practices.

It was in this period that we see what eventually became of Tanzan's Zen. The last monk to teach it was the Sōtō Zen monk Harada Genryū (1838–1928), who had first become Tanzan's pupil back in 1867. He edited and simplified Tanzan's method, and called his new method *Jikon-Entsū-Hō* (The way of perfect freedom via the bases of ears), which he tried to propagate outside the monasteries. Amongst the laypeople who practised Harada's method was a hypnotist/psychotherapist named Kihara Kibutsu (Tsūtoku) (1873–?). He first became an entrepreneur and then a newspaper man, after which he opened hypnotism clinics in several cities. He boasted that he cured more than 1,000 Chinese patients while in Kobe. From 1906 to 1918 he stayed in Matsue, where he practised *seishin ryōhō*. He organized the *Shinrei Tetsugaku kai* (Society for Psychical Philosophy), with more than 1,000 members, before converting to the new religion *Ōmoto-kyō* and moving to Ayabe where *Ōmoto-kyō* had their headquarters.[71]

Kihara developed the new method *Yōki-Hō* (The way of nourishing *ki*), a kind of energy healing. He also started to practise *Jikon-Entsū-Hō* in 1905, and was given a licence by Harada in 1916. He then went on to unite *Yōki-Hō* and *Jikon-Entsū-Hō* into *Jikon-Entsū-Myōchi-Ryōhō* (*myōchi ryōhō* means the 'therapy of excellent wisdom'), in which the therapist is expected to develop supernatural healing powers through *Jikon-Entsū-Hō* and then transmit that through his hands to patients.

Both the method and theory of Tanzan's Zen were significantly secularized by Kihara, with the mysterious *Jōriki* turned into a simple contraction of muscles. Kihara advised people to bite their teeth gently and then direct

*Jōriki* into their ears with full force from their roots of their teeth. In doing so, they could expect to experience a 'tremor at the back of the brain', as the brain became empty and clean. Kihara promised that practitioners would experience the effects of this method within five days, or two weeks at the most. Kihara introduced into Harada's *Jikon-Entsu-Hō* easy training, simplified procedures, and near-instant effects.

While Kuwabara wrote that he had achieved miraculous healing powers, he never discussed how to develop that power. His golden rule for healers and patients alike was simply to 'concentrate your will'. In fact various physical methods were practised with the patients in Kuwabara's clinic,[72] but the means of acquiring supernatural healer's powers had not been known. The introduction of Tanzan's Zen was a good solution as it was sufficiently psychologized and secularized for therapists to use.

By the 1910s various methods of self-cultivation such as sitting and deep breathing had become popular in Japan. Most *seishin ryōhō* therapists used or invented methods of breathing or exercises, like those of Kihara. They mainly used these physical exercises to manipulate *seishin* in a way that would lead to healing. Over time, the meaning of *seishin* widened and it came to be regarded as an agent for explaining all sorts of supernormal phenomena. Spiritual or psychic healers began competing, with all sorts of mind cures going under the banner of *seishin ryōhō*.

## Conclusion

*Seishin ryōhō* went on to prosper in the Taishō era (1912–1926), absorbing various methods imported from contemporary America. Therapists advertised short-term programmes for developing healing powers as a way of recruiting more members to their groups. A great many books and journals were published on *seishin ryōhō*, promising easy methods and miraculous healings. A trend towards the occult emerged, with the journal of *Taireido* filled with reports on psychical phenomena gleaned from its members.[73] Sometimes the police tried to use the above-mentioned Act to accuse therapists of using hypnotism, but neither the police nor the medical profession were particularly strict in applying the law.

Ironically, the most severe critic of *seishin ryōhō* during the Taishō era was Nakamura Kokyō (1881–1952),[74] himself a pioneer of psychotherapy as well as a collaborator with Morita Masatake.[75] Nakamura published the journal *Hentai Shinri (Abnormal Psychology)* (1917–1926), which attacked the new religious movement, *ōmoto-kyō*, to which Kihara had been attracted, as well as other spiritual and psychical healers. Nakamura had been the editor (1907–1910) of a journal called *Shin Bukkyō (New Buddhism)* (1900–1915), which had played an important role in modernizing Buddhism and extirpating superstitions. Nakamura was here continuing the interests of Inoue Enryō in psychotherapy and rationalistic religion, eager to debunk superstitions and to pursue 'true' psychotherapy.

*The birth of Japanese mind cure methods* 97

Whether or not one regards Nakamura as having succeeded, two trends emerged following the Taisho *seishin ryōhō* boom. First, alternative therapies gradually became less metaphysical and more physical and practical in response to the needs of a new generation of consumers. This tendency became especially conspicuous with the entering into vogue of *ōteate ryōji* (healing by laying of hands) in 1930. Second, a 'cultic milieu' of therapists continued to exist in the space between religion and natural science in spite of Nakamura's efforts. In the 1980s the *seishin sekai* movement saw a boom of publications and workshops corresponding to New Age in the western world.[76] The term covered UFOs, occultism, psychic healing, and other phenomena. *Seishin* had not lost its aura even after 80 years.

## Notes

1 Koyano, 'Nippon no haisen to shinrigaku no sai shuppatsu'.
2 On this lineage, see Shimazono, *Iyasu chi no keifu: kagaku to shūkyō no hazama*.
3 For research on *reijutsu* and *seishin ryōhō* see Imura, *Reijutsu-ka no Kyōen*; Nishiyama, 'Reijutsu kei shin shukyo no taito to huatsu no "kindaikka"'; Tanabe, *Yamai to shakai: hīring no tankyū*; and Yoshinaga, *Minkan seishin ryoho no jidai*. Imura (*Reijutsu-ka no Kyōen*) was the first to notice the forgotten healers of *reijutsu*, especially Hamaguchi Yūgaku (a modernized Shugen practitioner), as well as Kuwabara Toshiro, as the founding fathers of *reijutsu*. Nishiyama tried to conceptualize the term 'reijutsu', from the viewpoint of the sociology of religion. In *Yamai to shakai: hīring no tankyū* Tanabe deals mainly with the latter years of *reijutsu* and its transformation into *ryojutsu*. In *Minkan seishin ryōhō no jidai*, Yoshinaga proposed to use *seihin ryōhō* instead of *reijutsu*. *Seishin ryōhō* and *reijutsu* were interchangeable in the Meiji and Taisho eras, but *seishin ryōhō* appeared more frequently than *reijutsu* in the media from the end of Meiji into the early years of Taisho. *Reijutsu* and *seishin ryōhō* should be distinguished from the *reigaku* (spiritual research) or chinkon-kishin-hō (settling the soul and being possessed) of Ōmoto-kyō, which seeks to control the departed spirit of kami (deities) or animal spirits or monsters.
4 Reikai kakusei dōshikai, *Reijutsu to reijutsuka*. This book is a directory of hundreds of *reijutsu* therapists.
5 Nakae, *Zoku Ichinen Yū-han*.
6 According to Asukai in *Nakae Chōmin*, 27,000 copies of this book were sold in a month.
7 See Mineshima, 'Meijiki ni okeru seiyou tetsugaku no juyou to tenkai (8)'.
8 Suzuki, 'Reikon no umu to shinko no tai-huten'.
9 See sections 7 and 8 of Inoue Enryō, *Yōkai Gaku kogi* vol. 5.
10 Kuroiwa, *Ten-nin Ron*, p. 25.
11 Sawada, *Practical Pursuits*, p. 78. Also see Kobayashi, 'Kinsei ni okeru "kokoro no gensetsu"'.
12 Kiyozawa's modernized version of Buddhist thought is called *Seishin shugi*, stressing subjective faith in Amida. It is still valued highly inside and outside of Jōdo Shinshū Buddhism (Higashi Honganji).
13 For further information, see Kobori, 'Za: Okada Torajirō to Okadashiki-Seiza-Hō'.
14 See Hashimoto, this volume.
15 See Harding (Chapter One), this volume.
16 See the section 'Taming Demons' in Josephson, *The Invention of Religion in Japan*.

17 Imura, *Reijutsu-ka no Kyōen*.
18 I owe Tanzan's biographical information to Ōuchi Seiran, 'Tanzan Rōshi no rireki', pp, 1–39. As for the historical significance of Tanzan in modern Buddhism, see Klautau, 'Nihon bukkyō' izen: Hara Tanzan to Bukkyō no Fuhenka'.
19 Kimura, 'Hara Tanzan to "Indo tetsugaku" no tanjō', p. 32.
20 This summary of the theory is based on Yoshinaga, 'Hara Tanzan no shinrigaku-teki Zen'; and Hara, *Tanzan Oshō Zenshū*.
21 This description of *xiao zhou-tian* is from the item 'shou shu ten', in Noguchi *et al.*, *Dōkyo Jiten*, p. 275.
22 Cryns, *Edo jidai ni okeru kikaironteki shintaikan no Juyo*.
23 Ibid.
24 Furuta, 'Hara Tanzan to jikken Bukkyō gaku', p. 153.
25 See Ichiyanagi, *Saiminjutsu no nihon kindai*, for the further details about the early history of hypnotism.
26 Sakaki (1890), p. 48.
27 Reed, *From Soul to Mind*, p. 3.
28 Dods, *The Philosophy of Electrical Psychology*, pp. 18 and 19.
29 Suzuki, *Dobustu denki gairon*, p. 11.
30 The University of Tokyo changed its name several times in the Meiji era. In 1877, the University of Tokyo was born when Tokyo Kaisei School and Tokyo Medical School merged. In 1886 it became an imperial university consisting of five colleges. In 1897, its name changed to the Imperial University of Tokyo. In this paper the current name, 'University of Tokyo', is used.
31 Ōsawa Kenji, *Masui Jutsu* (The art of hypnotism) (1887).
32 Ōsawa, *Masui Jutsu*, p. 47. A Bachelor's degree was, at this time, only available at one place in Japan: the University of Tokyo, where Ōsawa taught.
33 Sakai, *Nihon no iryoshi*, pp. 425 and 426.
34 Sato and Mizoguchi, *Tsūshi Nihon no shinrigaku*, pp. 44 and 45.
35 Carpenter, *Principles of Mental Physiology*, 1875.
36 I owe the biographical information here mainly to Kikuchi, *Yōkai gaku no so Inoue Enryo*.
37 On Chikazumi, see Iwata, this volume.
38 See Harding (Chapter One), this volume.
39 Inoue, *Shinri konjin shohen*, pp. 74 and 75.
40 Inoue wrote that the majority of Buddhist priests were imbeciles. See Inoue, *Shinri konjin shohen*, p. 165.
41 As for more detailed discussion about philosophy, see Hariu, 'Inoue Enryo no tetsugaku'.
42 Inoue, *Bukkyō Katsuron joron*, p. 5.
43 On the birth of *Yōkai Gaku*, see Miura, 'Kaisetsu; Inoue Enryō to Yōkai Gaku no tanjo'.
44 Tokunaga Manshi, *Ōyō Shinrigaku*, p. 1.
45 Majima, *Saiminjutsu Chiryōhō*.
46 See Inoue, *Shinri Ryōhō*. Though this book was published in the middle of the hypnotism boom, Inoue did not mention hypnotism in it.
47 Kondō, *Majutsu to Saiminjutsu*.
48 The last edition was Chōshunen shujin, *Majutsu oyobi saiminjutsu jizai* (1936).
49 Kondō, *Majutsu to Saiminjutsu*, p. 5.
50 Kondō, *Majutsu to Saiminjutsu*, p. 52.
51 Inoue, *Yokaigaku Kogi vol. 4*, pp. 366 and 367.
52 'To explain the effects of hypnotism by something like electricity or magnetism through fingers ... is a kind of foolish superstition.' Kondō, *Saiminjutsu dokushu*, p. 23.
53 See Harding (Chapter One), this volume.

*The birth of Japanese mind cure methods* 99

54 My analysis of the relationship between 'hanmon' and hypnotism is based on Ichiyanagi, *Saiminjutsu no nihon kindai.*
55 Ichiyanagi, *Kokkuri san to senri gan,* pp. 79–84.
56 Takeuchi Nanzo, *Saiminjutsu Jizai.*
57 Fukurai Tomokichi, *Saimin Shinrigaku.*
58 Sato and Mizoguchi, *Tsūshi Nihon no shinrigaku,* pp. 138–140.
59 See Yoshinaga, *Minkan seishin ryoho no jidai.*
60 For further information, see chapter 3 of Ichiyanagi, <*Kokkuri san*> *to* <*senri gan*>, and the first section of chapter 2 of Sato and Mizoguchi, *Tsūshi Nihon no shinrigaku.*
61 For biographical data, see chapter 3 of Imura, *Reijutsu-ka no Kyōen.*
62 Kuwabara, *Seishin Reidō* vol. 1.
63 Kuwabara, *Seishin Reidō* vols 1–3.
64 Kuwabara, *Seishin Reidō* vol. 2, pp. 252–253, 287.
65 On Inoue Tetsujirō's theory of the large ego, see Yoshinaga, 'Tairei to kokka'.
66 'I lack learning and ability…I am only an experimentalist'. Kuwabara, *Seishin Reidō* vol. 1, p. 1.
67 Kokka Igakukai, *Saiminjutsu oyobi zuggesution ronshū ge,* pp. 127–146, and *Saiminjutsu oyobi zuggesution ronshū jō*; Yamauchi, *Rei to kenkō.*
68 The struggle between hypnotists and medical doctors is recorded in Ono, *Ono Saimin gaku,* pp. 43–73.
69 Kokka Igakukai, *Saiminjutsu oyobi zuggesution ronshū ge,* p. 102.
70 Ono wrote about the debates on the regulation of hypnotism. See Ono, *Ono Saimin gaku.*
71 For further information on Kihara's method, see Kihara, *Shinshin kyōken Yōki-Hō, Jikon-Entsū-Hō hiroku* and *Jikon-Entsū Myōchi-Ryōhō hiroku*. Katagiri Masao took over Kihara's activities on the propagation of *Jikon-Entsū-Hō*. See Katagiri, *Jikon entsū hō kaisetsu,* pp. 1–4.
72 See Takuma, *Jikken Seishin ryōhō.* Takuma used most of the techniques used by *seishin ryōhō* therapists.
73 Taireido was the largest *seishin ryōhō* group, started by Tanaka Morihei (1884–1929) in 1916. It explained mental and physical phenomena in terms of the workings of Tairei (Great Spirit) and Reishi (spirit-particles). It promised that anyone could acquire psychical power by taking a ten-day course. See Yoshinaga, 'Tairei to kokka'.
74 Sone, 'Nakamura Kokyō to "Shin Bukkyō"'. See Harding (Chapter 1), this volume.
75 See Kondo and Kitanishi, this volume.
76 See Horie Norichika, this volume.

# References

Araki Giten, *Zen gaku shinshō jikken roku (The Record of the Buddha-nature in Zen)* (Tokyo: Seiretsudo, 1907).
Asukai Masamichi, *Nakae Chōmin* (Tokyo: Yoshikawa Kōbunkan, 1999).
Carpenter, William B., *Principles of Mental Physiology Second Edition* (London: Henry S. King, 1875).
Cryns, Frederik, *Edo jidai ni okeru kikaironteki shintaikan no Juyo (The Reception of the Mechanistic View of the Body in the Edo Era)* (Kyōto: Rinsen Shoten, 2006).
Dods, John Bovee, *The Philosophy of Electrical Psychology in a Course of Twelve Lectures* (New York: Fowlers and Wells, 1852).
Fukurai Tomokichi, *Saimin Shinrigaku (Hypnotic Psychology)* (Tokyo: Seibido, 1906).

Furuta Shōkin, 'Hara Tanzan to jikken Bukkyō gaku (Hara Tanzan and his experimental Buddhism study)', in *Nihon Daigaku Seishin Bunka Kenkyujo Kyōiku Seido Kenkyūjo Kiyō* (Tokyo: Nihon University, 1980), pp. 145–167.

Hara Tanzan, *Tanzan Oshō Zenshū (Complete Works of Rev. Tanzan)* (edited by Shaku Goan) (Tokyo: Kōyūkan, 1909).

Hariu Kiyoto, 'Inoue Enryō no tetsugaku (The philosophy of Inoue Enryō)', in *Inoue Enryō kenkyū no.1* (Tokyo: Tōyō University, 1981), pp. 81–111.

Ichiyanagi Hirotaka, *Kokkuri san to senri gan (Kokkuri san and Clairvoyance)* (Tokyo: Kōdansha, 1994).

Ichiyanagi Hirotaka, *Saiminjutsu no nihon kindai (Modern Japan Seen from the Perspective of Hypnotism)* (Tokyo: Seikyūsha, 1997).

Imura Kōji, *Reijutsu-ka no Kyōen (The Festival of Reijutsu Therapists)* (Tokyo: Shinkōsha, 1984).

Inoue Enryō, *Shinri konjin shohen (The Golden Needle of the Truth: First Series)* (Tokyo: Hōzōkan, 1886).

Inoue Enryō, *Bukkyō Katsuron joron (Introduction to an Active Discussion on Buddhism* (Tokyo: Tetsugaku shoin, 1887).

Inoue Enryō, *Yōkai gaku kogi dai4 satsu (Yōkai gaku vol. 4)* (Tokyo: Tetsugakukan, 1896 [revised and enlarged edition]).

Inoue Enryō, *Yōkai gaku kōgi dai5 satsu (Yōkai gaku vol. 5)* (Tokyo: Tetsugakukan, 1896 [revised and enlarged edition]).

Inoue Enryō, *Shinri Ryōhō (On Psychotherapy)* (Tokyo: Nankōdō, 1904).

Josephson, Jason Ananda, *The Invention of Religion in Japan* (Chicago: University of Chicago Press, 2012).

Katagiri Masao, *Jikon-Entsū-Hō kaisetsu (Explanation of Jikon-Entsū-Hō), Kenju shūyō kai* (Kyōtō: Kenju Shūyōkai, 1919).

Kihara Tsūtoku, *Shinshin kyōken Yōki-Hō (The Method of Nurturing Ki for the Health of Mind and Body)* (Matsue: Yōki Ryōin, 1910).

Kihara Tsūtoku, (Kihara Kibutsu), *Jikon-Entsū-Hō hiroku (Secret of Jikon-Entsū-Hō)* (Matsue: Sinrei Tetsugaku kai, 1917).

Kihara Tsūtoku, (Kihara Kibutsu), *Jikon-Entsū Myōchi-Ryōhō hiroku (Secret of Jikon-Entsū Myōchi-Ryōhō)* (Matsue: Sinrei Tetsugaku kai, 1917).

Kikuchi Noritaka, *Yōkai gaku no so Inoue Enryo (Inoue Enryō, the Founder of Yōkai Gaku)* (Tokyo: Kadokawa Gakugei Shuppan, 2013).

Kimura Kiyotaka, 'Hara Tanzan to "Indo tetsugaku" no tanjō (Hara Tanzan and the birth of "Indian philosophy")', *Indogaku Bukkyōgaku Kenkyū vol. 49 no. 2*, pp. 27–35 (The Janapese Association of Indian and Buddhist Studies, 2001).

Klautau, Orion, '"Nihon bukkyō" izen: Hara Tanzan to Bukkyō no Fuhenka' (The historical studies of Buddhism as a thought of modern Japan), in *Kindai Nihon shisō to shite no Bukkyō Shigaku* (Kyōtō: Hōzōkan, 2012), pp. 55–81.

Kobayashi Junji, 'Kinsei ni okeru "kokoro no gensetsu" (Disourse of "kokoro" in early modern period)', Koyasu Nobukuni (ed.), *Edo no Shisō (Thoughts in Edo era) no. 6* (Tokyo: Pelican sha, 1997), pp. 158–178.

Kobori Tetsuro, 'Za: Okada Torajirō to Okadashiki-Seiza-Hō (Sitting: Okada Torajirō and Okada's way of still-sitting)', in Tanabe Shintarō, Shimazono Suzumu, & Yumiyama Tatsuya, *Iyashi wo ikita hitobito: kindaichi no orutanatibu (Those Who Lived to Heal: Alternatives to Modern Knowledge)* (Tokyo: Senshū Daigaku Syuppankyoku, 1999), pp. 47–86.

Kokka Igakukai (ed.), *Saiminjutsu oyobi zuggesution ronshū jō (Reports on Suggestion and Hypnotism vol. 1)* (Tokyo: Nankōdō, 1904).

Kokka Igakukai (ed.), *Saiminjutsu oyobi zuggesution ronshū ge (Reports on Suggestion and Hypnotism vol. 2)* (Tokyo: Nankōdō, 1904).

Kondō Yoshizō, *Majutsu to Saiminjutsu (Magic and Hypnotism)* (Tokyo: Eisai shinshi sha, 1892).

Kondō Yoshizō, *Saiminjutsu doku-shu (Hypnotism Self-Taught)* (Tokyo: Daigakukan, 1904).

Koyano Kuniko, 'Nippon no haisen to shinrigaku no sai shuppatsu (The defeat of Japan and the restart of psychology)', *Nippon shinrigakushi no kenkyu* (Hōsei shuppan kabushiki gaisha, 1998), pp. 72–98.

Kuroiwa Shūroku, *Ten-nin Ron (A Discourse of the Universe and Human Beings)* (Tokyo: Chōhōsha, 1903).

Kuwabara Toshirō, *Seishin reidō dai1 hen, saiminjutsu (The Excellent Work of the Mind vol.1; on Hypnotism)* (Tokyo: Kaihatsusha, 1903).

Kuwabara Toshirō, *Seishin reidō dai2 hen, seishinron (The Excellent Work of the Mind vol. 2; on Mind)* (Tokyo: Seishin reidō vol. 2; on seishin) (Kaihatsusha, 1904).

Majima Tōhaku, *Saiminjutsu Chiryōhō (Hypnotherapy)* (Tokyo: Tetsugakukan, 1888).

Mineshima Hideo, 'Meijiki ni okeru seiyou tetsugaku no juyou to tenkai (8)—Inoue Tetsujirō, sono tetsugaku no sai-ginmi (The reception and development of the Western philosophy no. 8: Re-examination of Inoue Tetsujirō's philosophy)', *The Waseda commercial review no. 229* (Tokyo: Waseda University, July, 1972), pp. 61–80.

Miura Setsuo, 'Kaisetsu; Inoue Enryō to Yōkai Gaku no tanjō (Commentary: Inoue Enryō and the birth of Yōkai Studies)', *Inoue Enryo Senshū vol.21* (Tokyo: Tōyō University, 2001), pp. 464–493.

Nakae Tokusuke (Chōmin), *Zoku Ichinen Yū-han, ichimei mushin museishin (A Year and a Half Left, Volume 2: Or No Gods and No Minds)* (Tokyo: Hakubunkan, 1901).

Nishiyama Shigeru, 'Reijutsu kei shin shukyo no taito to huatsu no "kindaikka" (The rise of reijutsu new religions and two forms of "modernization")', *Kokugakuin Daigaku Nihonbunka Kenkyujo Kiyo no. 61* (Tokyo: Kokugakuin University, 1988), pp. 85–115.

Noguchi et al. ed., *Dōkyo Jiten (Encyclopedia of Daoism)* (Tokyo: Hirakawa shuppansha, 1994).

Ono Fukuhei, *Ono Saimin gaku (Ono's Study on Hypnotism)* (Tokyo: Dai Nippon Saimin Gakkai, 1909).

Ōsawa Kenji, *Masui Jutsu (The Art of Hypnotism)* (1887).

Ōuchi Seiran, 'Tanzan Rōshi no rireki (Biography of Rev. Tanzan)', Shaku Goan (ed.), *Tanzan Oshō Zenshū* (Tokyo: Kōyūkan, 1909).

Reed, Edward S., *From Soul to Mind* (New Haven: Yale University Press, 1997).

Reikai kakusei dōshikai, *Reijutsu to reijutsuka (Reijutsu and its Therapists)* (Tokyo: Nishōdō, 1928).

Sakai Shizu, *Nihon no iryoshi (History of Medical Care in Japan)* (Tokyo: Tōkyō shoseki, 1982).

Sakaki Tokitoshi, *Fukushima ken meishi retsuden (Who's Who in Fukushima prefecture)* (Fukushima: Fukushima-kappansha, 1890).

Satō Tatsuya and Mizoguchi Hajime (eds), *Tsūshi Nihon no shinrigaku (History of Japanese Psychology)* (Kyōto: Kitaōji Shobō, 1997).

Sawada, Janine Tasca, *Practical Pursuits: Religion, Politics, and Personal Cultivation in Nineteenth-Century Japan* (Honolulu: University of Hawai'i Press, 2004).

Shimazono Suzumu, *Iyasu chi no keifu: kagaku to shūkyō no hazama (A Genealogy of 'Healing Knowledge': Between Science and Religion)* (Tokyo: Yoshikawa Kōbunkan, 2003).

Sone Hiroyoshi, 'Nakamura Kokyō to "Shin Bukkyō" (Nakamura Kokyō and "Shin Bukkyō")', in *'Hentai Shinri' to Nakamura Kokyō* (Tokyo: Fuji Shuppan, 2001), pp. 162–179.

Suzuki Daisetsu, 'Reikon no umu to shinko no tai-huten (The existence of the soul and faith)', *Beikoku Bukkyō vol. 4 no. 10* (San Francisco: Beikoku Bukkyō Seinenkai, Oct. 1903). pp. 6–8.

Suzuki Manjirō, *Dobustu denki gairon (Outlines of Animal Electricity)* (Tokyo: Jūjiya, 1885).

Takeuchi Nanzo, *Saiminjutsu Jizai (Complete Guide to the Use of Hypnotism)* (Tokyo: Daigakukan, 1903).

Takuma Iwao, *Jikken Seishin ryōhō (Experimental Psychotherapy)* (Tokyo: Kaihatsusha, 1905).

Tanabe Shintaro, *Yamai to shakai: hīring no tankyū (Illness and Society: The Quest for Healing)* (Tokyo: Kōbundōshoten, 1989).

Tokunaga Manshi, *Ōyō Shinrigaku (Applied Psychology)* (Tokyo: Tetsugakukan, n.d. [approx. 1888]).

Yamauchi Tokuma, *Rei to kenkō (Spirit and Health)* (Tokyo: Tokyō hōrei gakudō, 1929).

Yoshinaga Shin'ichi, 'Minkan seishin ryoho no jidai (The age of seishin ryōhō)', *Nihonjin no shin shin rei vol. 8* (Tokyo: Kress Shuppan, 2004).

Yoshinaga Shin'ichi, 'Hara Tanzan no shinrigaku-teki Zen (The psychologized Zen of Hara Tanzan: His thought and historical Influences)', *Jintai Kagaku vol. 15 no. 2* (Society for Mind-Body Science, 2006), pp. 5–13.

Yoshinaga Shin'ichi, 'Tairei to kokka (Great spirit and the nation)', *Jintai Kagaku vol. 17 no. 1* (Society for Mind-Body Science, 2008), pp. 35–51.

# 4 The mind and healing in Morita therapy

Kondo Kyoichi and Kitanishi Kenji[1]

*Because a person innately has a strong 'desire for life', the fear of that which obstructs its actualization, namely the fear of death, is also strong. The desire for life and fear of death are two sides of a coin, so to speak. In this sense, a fear of death is, for humans, a natural emotion. Recognizing this 'innateness of human emotion' – 'just as it is' – and living with the fear of death is none other than the truth of our human lives.*

## The history of Morita therapy

Morita therapy, an original form of psychotherapy created in Japan by Morita Masatake (1874–1938), has become well known not only within its country of origin, but also abroad. It has achieved unparalleled recognition for its treatment of various neuroses that stem from *shinkeishitsu*, or 'nervous character or temperament', especially the fear of interpersonal relations (*taijin kyōfu*), hypochondria, anxiety, and compulsiveness. In recent years, its application has extended into areas as varied as terminal care, mental health care provided in family, school, and corporate settings, and even problems associated with lifestyle choices and perspectives on life. Like Freud, the founder of psychoanalysis, Morita himself suffered from neurosis. One could say that Morita therapy was the result of systematizing the experience of treating his own neurosis. In the case of psychoanalysis, there has been a considerable degree of systematic theorization and formalization. Morita therapy, by contrast, while not lacking systematization, has not built up as elaborate a theory as its Freudian counterpart. Instead, in Morita's concepts, techniques, and theory of *shinkeishitsu*, one can discern the influence both of Morita's view of humanity and the spirit of the times in which he was living.

This chapter considers the relationship between psychotherapies and the cultural settings that produced them. Euro-American treatments, with psychoanalysis as their representative form, emerged for the most part in the twentieth century. Their main unique feature is that they are formalized by means of adaptation to a model of scientific and objectivist medicine. One can see reflected here the scientific worldview that is one of the unique features of modern, Western societies. Needless to say, the methodologies of Western, scientific psychotherapy are rooted in the kind of specialized knowledge aimed at a universally applicable epistemology of nature. In locating the cause of illness and the condition that needs to be eliminated, or in targeting an abnormality, this kind of knowledge (and the methodologies based upon it) is undoubtedly effective. However, in terms of comprehensively understanding the life or way of living of a person with psychological worries in the real world, and providing realistic, concrete support, this kind of knowledge might be seen as insufficient. As Seneca said, 'it takes a lifetime to learn how to live.'[2]

To live as a person is certainly difficult, and problems arise when this obvious fact is neglected in favour of a focus on making a particular diagnosis of illness. In other words, it is a serious problem if the target of treatment becomes objectified into something cut off from either human existence or the reality of life. In comparison to psychotherapies established along the lines of medical science, psychoanalysis being the most obvious example, the theory of neurosis advocated by Morita is more commonsensical and therefore easier to understand. According to Morita, the emotions that move human beings are not originally all that complicated; in fact, an individual's emotions all resemble one another. To avoid the heart being held captive, and to attain peace of mind, it is important that one respond gently to the reality of human life just as it is.

In order to resolve the endless troubles and hardships of people living in the world, every conceivable idea and method has been suggested and practised. Amongst these, a small selection have been methodically purified and backed by theories about the client–clinician relationship – primarily in the context of artificial human relationships. One can say that this is the essence of psychotherapy: the abstraction and formalization of relationships between one person and another in the world of everyday life, or the life techniques that become necessary within the context of those relationships.

Currently, most psychotherapists practising in Japan, even if their theories and techniques differ, are working while sharing in the everyday life experiences of patients. On this point, in comparison with specialists in Europe and the U.S., psychotherapists in Japan tend to compromise more in their treatments and approach. A therapist is not so much a theorist as an ordinary person who lives life, relying on his or her own experiences and understandings of human beings. Morita therapy does not leave struggles with neuroses closed up in the interior of the mind, but addresses them within the context of the wider life environment. On this point it takes a different position from those of leading therapists in Europe and the U.S. The efficacy of Morita therapy has not only been verified in clinical settings, but has gone further to produce a theory about human beings that is now commonly invoked in Japanese society. This has led to it becoming arguably the representative thought of Japanese psychiatry.

In all societies, various means of support are available for people who suffer from ailments of the mind and body. Some people take home remedies, while others ask for advice from relatives and friends or visit folk healers, religious figures, and doctors. Depending on which methods can be accessed and whether one can pay for them, some people opt for still different approaches, using a combination either simultaneously or one after another. As a society expands and becomes more complex, the degree of freedom to choose between different treatment methods increases: over time medical care tends to become more complex and pluralized.[3] Arthur Kleinman divided health care into three categories: popular, folk, and specialist.[4] In the case of popular health care in Japan, families carry most of the burden of provision. For folk health care, there are osteopaths, midwives, *kanpō* doctors, spiritual healers, and shamans. Specialist health care is carried out by those trained in contemporary scientific medical science. Morita viewed himself as a disciple of Emil Kraepelin, the founder of modern psychiatry (though he never met Kraepelin), and he claimed that Morita therapy was a form of modern, scientific treatment.

If we use Kleinman's categorization of health care, then, Morita therapy would obviously fall into the third category as a specialist medical treatment method. And yet Morita therapy cannot be understood only in this way. While it may not be apparent in the theorized and formalized parts of Morita therapy, in its *clinical* applications the cultural value and efficacy of the other two fields of health care discussed by Kleinman (popular and folk health care) have been fully recognized and utilized. Underlying this recognition of the value of non-specialist care is the fact that Morita psychotherapy itself is firmly rooted in fields of health care closely tied to non-elite culture. One could say, then, that Morita therapy is a specialized, scientific treatment method built with non-elite culture as its foundation.

Morita Masatake was born in 1874 in present-day Noichichō, ten kilometres east of Kōchi in the region of Shikoku. Contemporaries of Morita included the botanist Masano Tomitarō (1862), writer and poet Ōmachi Keigetsu (1869), and anarchist Kōtoku Shusui (1871), who was involved in the 'High Treason Incident', a 1910 plot to assassinate the Meiji Emperor. According to Irokawa Daikichi, such figures made up the second generation of 'Meiji youth', living at a time when Japan's democratic movement experienced its first setbacks and Westernization was both promoted and opposed. This generation is said to have felt various kinds of doubts about the value of prioritizing politics in life, becoming interested instead in a variety of concerns linked to cultural nationalism.[5] Thinking about Morita's work, sayings and deeds, and accounts of his life given by people who knew him, the extent to which he was a product of these times in Japan becomes clear.

What were the particular trends of the time in international psychiatry and mental health care? Following the movement for humanitarian treatment, rooted in eighteenth-century Enlightenment thought, the era of nineteenth-century natural science dawned. Kraepelin, the last major biological psychiatrist of the pre-Dynamism era, and Freud, the first creator of a theory of neurosis, were both born in 1856 and were thus of the same generation. The first attempts to elucidate scientifically the anxieties and struggles that arose in the hearts of the people born in this era produced treatment methods such as Morita therapy in Asia and psychoanalysis in the West. Although they both had as their designated target the pathology of neuroses, they chose different objects: in Japan it was *shinkeishitsu* and in the West it was hysteria.

Morita's father, Morita Masafumi, belonged to a social group known as *gōshi*, or landed samurai. He worked as a temporary instructor at an elementary school, and introduced his son to the spirit of sincerity that was supposed to be the mark of landed samurai. He taught also a means of pursuing one's full abilities without flattery or fawning, and the cultivation of a happiness that came from taking an active interest in the outside world. And yet the young Morita Masatake came to dislike studying because his father's passion for education made for much strictness – he often cried because he did not like going to school.

When Morita was born, his father was twenty-two years old and his mother twenty-six years old. Morita had an elder sister, Michime, five years his senior, with two younger siblings: a brother, Tokuya, and a sister, Isoji. He became especially close to his brother Tokuya, but at times favoured a female cousin who was a year younger than him: this was his mother's younger sister's child Hisai, who would later become Morita's wife.

Morita entered Kōchi's prefectural middle school in 1888 when he was fourteen years old, but since his grades were not very good it took him eight years to graduate from the fifth-year level. During this time he experienced two setbacks. The first was during his second year when he complained of discomfort of the heart and was under the care of a doctor for two years. This was one reason for him having to stay in the same class for a year. Later he would come to understand that the discomfort of this time had to do with neurosis. It was at the age of fifteen, however, an age when the symptoms of *shinkeishitsu* often appear, that Morita's own trials with *shinkeishitsu* began.

Then, when he was eighteen years old, Morita defied his father by leaving home and going to Tokyo. There he tried and failed to work his way through school. One might interpret this as typical adolescent behaviour, but in his own records Morita writes: 'I became angry that my father restricted my education expenses and so I decided to go to Tokyo to try to pay my own way through my education. Together with Ike, a fellow student, I left home without warning.'[6] During the fifth year of middle school, Morita suffered a serious case of typhoid fever and ended up having to be treated for over two months. At that time, cholera, typhus, and smallpox epidemics were raging: more than 800,000 people died over a twenty-year period. Morita was able narrowly to escape death thanks to the devoted care shown to him by his brother Tokuya, but soon after recovery he fell into a state of anxiety neurosis. People also made fun of the way Morita looked when he smiled, saying it was idiotic, giving rise to great sensitivity on Morita's part: he developed a so-called 'fear of smiling', suffering for a while a compulsive tendency to try to not show a smile. Also, around this time Morita began deliberately to dress oddly and to participate in drinking contests – open to interpretation as a kind of compensatory behaviour. Like many adolescents of the time, Morita kept a diary, a practice he continued throughout his life. Today the diary offers us important clues as to his thoughts, his lifestyle, and by extension, his therapy.

Morita's early years were the source of his interest in a broad range of subjects encompassing psychology, philosophy, and religion. As he writes in his personal papers:

> I remember when I was around nine or ten years old, I was taken to the village temple, where I saw a richly coloured wall-hanging illustrating hell. Based on my experience of seeing this illustration, I couldn't help but become worried about what happened after death, wondering if I would fall into a hell of mountains made of needles and blood-filled ponds. These scenes appeared even in my dreams and so I couldn't help but become scared when night fell, and I would be unable to sleep. Even while in middle school, my interest continued to be piqued by miracles and superstitious things. I became engrossed in telling fortunes by examining the shape of skulls, inspecting facial features, and consulting the I Ching. I also happily told other people their fortunes by means of oracle sticks. I would predict the next day's weather with 50 percent accuracy. My father scolded me, saying that I wasn't going to become a fortune teller and that I should put more of an effort into my studies.[7]

Saitō Mokichi, a psychiatrist who, along with Morita, became a student of Kure Shūzō,[8] was also deeply affected by an illustration of hell that he saw as a child in his hometown temple. He wrote about it in a collection of poetry called *Shakkō* (*Red Rays*). The psychologist Minami Hiroshi has indicated that this kind of emotional childhood experience related to the fear of death has been experienced historically by many Japanese and continues to be the case.

Morita's extraordinary interest and concern for problems associated with religion and healing in the broadest sense did not come to an end in childhood. Even as an adult, he eagerly experimented with exorcism prayers (*kaji kitō*), *Kiai-jutsu*, *Taireidō*, diaphragm breathing techniques, Hakuin Ekaku's Naikan therapy,[9] and Zen meditation, in addition to taking an interest in various kinds of folk beliefs and popular therapy.

Morita does not seem ever to have become a believer in a particular religion, but there was a time when he was heavily absorbed in reading about Buddhism and Christianity. The following comments by Morita hint at how the therapy he developed as a psychiatrist connected to his interest in religious topics:

> The so-called problem of life and death is never far from my mind [...]. I never miss a chance at inquiring into this problem.[10]
>
> The fear of birth, aging, sickness, and death is the origin of religion. Moreover, religion is by no means the thing that will satisfy one's desires. First there is deliverance and peace of mind in the garden of one's self-effacement and then comes true religion.[11]

In 1895, the year after the beginning of the Sino-Japanese War, Morita graduated from middle school and entered Kumamoto Fifth High School. At first his father did not approve of his son, so prone to illness, continuing with school, but his agreement was secured on the condition that the Osaka doctor Ōguro Tatatsu would provide a scholarship. Discovering that this condition meant that his son would be adopted by the Osaka doctor, Morita's father agreed to pay the school fees himself and broke off relations with Ōguro. Wary of his son's reckless ways, he said that he would provide the money on the condition that he marry his cousin Hisai. So in July 1895, the wedding between the two took place. At first they lived together only when Morita returned home for summer vacations; during the rest of the year, the new bride Hisai worked as a spinning teacher.

Students in Japan's high school system at the time were all elite men looking forward to bright futures. Morita, as a young man in his late teens and early twenties, enjoyed their company but his predisposition to *shinkeishitsu* continued to dog him. To treat his heart problem, chronic headaches, and back pain he tried injections, hot springs therapy, and acupuncture, amongst other things, but nothing had the slightest effect. Instead, since each of these ailments healed naturally over time, Morita later looked back and said they had probably all been neurogenic conditions (*shinkeisei*).

While in high school, Morita continued to be interested in religion and philosophy, but in his third year he decided to become a psychiatrist. In 1898 he entered the College of Medical Sciences at Tokyo Imperial University – going to Tokyo this time with his father's full support. He was twenty-two years old. Life in the big city with its high cost of living was by no means easy, however. Morita became angry when living expenses sent by his father arrived late, and there were times when he would spend day after day fretting. Various kinds of anxiety built up, and discomforts of mind and body returned. He was diagnosed at the university hospital with neurasthenia and vitamin B deficiency. As his final exams approached, Morita, who found himself in a difficult situation and sensitive to exhaustion, started to cram and was prepared to blame his father and his unfulfilled promises if things went wrong. As it turned out, however, not only did Morita receive grades so high that he surprised himself and his friends, but the symptoms of neurasthenia that had previously raged so fiercely – difficulty concentrating and paying attention, being quick to tire, numbness of feet, and feelings of fogginess and pain in the head – vanished. Morita realized that the then-current treatment therapy for neurasthenia, which involved resting the body, was not correct because the cause of neurasthenia (*shinkeisuijaku*) was not in fact, as the term would lead one to believe, exhaustion of the nerves.

Morita's bodily ailments were not yet fully cured, however, and his mother had to come to Tokyo to look after him. Later, his wife Hisai came to Tokyo and began to run the household in his mother's place. Morita's symptoms finally improved once he graduated from university and set out to practise psychiatry.

## The birth of Morita therapy

In 1903, Morita was hired as an assistant in the psychiatric research group at Tokyo Imperial University and became a student of Kure Shūzō. Kure was at the time busy implementing innovative policies based on the knowledge and experiences he had gained while abroad in Europe. The department of psychiatry during this time was located in Sugamo and housed inside the prefectural Sugamo Hospital. Kure attached great importance to occupational therapy and created twenty-two principles to govern its practice. Together with Morita's designation the previous year as chief of occupational therapy this is said to constitute the beginning of occupational therapy in Japan. Morita hoped to specialize in psychotherapy, but this was a truly unique desire, considering the dominance of the biological approach in psychiatric medicine at the time in Japan (although Kure probably approved of Morita's ambition here). While Morita was engaged in this work, his neurosis was cured before he realized it.

One of the projects Morita worked on while affiliated with the university was a survey report of dog-spirit possession in the Tosa region. This kind of possession phenomenon, along with the fox possession of the San'in region, was well known at the time. Morita, who had long been interested in abnormal psychology, spent a month conducting the survey in his hometown. One of the insights to emerge from it was what Morita would later term 'invocation psychosis' (*kitōsei seishinbyō*): a form of psychogenic mental illness, born out of superstitions or folk beliefs. Listening to the experiences of those who prayed, and conducting experiments related to 'stone breaking' and 'fire prevention prayers', became foundational for making this new diagnosis.

Around this time Nagamatsu-san, head nurse at Sugamo Hospital and a close friend of Morita, became neurasthenic and approached him for help. It is never easy to treat the illness of a friend, but Morita invited her to live on the second floor of his house, asking in return that she help him with housework. Though he never seemed to be giving her any kind of treatment, in less than a month her neurasthenia improved. From then on, Morita accommodated and treated in his own home several people suffering from neuroses. One after another their conditions improved. A patient suffering from fear of blushing (erythrophobia), whom Morita had had difficulties treating before, also recovered around this time. This deepened Morita's sense of confidence, and one can perhaps locate some of the origins of Morita therapy in these accumulated experiences.

After three years of conducting research at Sugamo, Morita assumed the position of adviser and head doctor at an old prefectural psychiatric institution called Negishi Hospital. Around the same time he also held the post of professor at Jikei Medical School, the predecessor to Jikei College of Medicine. He turned down, however, a professorship at the National School of Medicine – a position that in those days would have promised future promotion and success.

In 1917 Morita met Nakamura Kokyō, a writer and literary critic who had been moved to train as a doctor and to open his own hospital in Chiba by his brother's death in hospital while suffering from schizophrenia. Nakamura came to be involved with the Mental Health Preservation Movement, while taking a research interest in abnormal psychological phenomena. With a few other researchers he established the Society for Japanese Psychiatry, notable for its members' experience in law and literature, in contrast to the primarily medical membership of what is today known as the Society for Psychiatry and Neurology. Nakamura's group aimed to address public hygiene issues relating to mental health, and Morita along with two other doctors, Kurosawa Yoshitami and Saitō Mokichi, were asked to participate. In those days, university-based doctors who collaborated with people from other fields in efforts to enlighten and improve society were often criticized. But Morita recognized the importance of addressing the problem of mental health in its broad social context, and agreed wholeheartedly to take part in the activities that Nakamura had initiated. Together with other participants, Morita went to Shinshū (present-day Nagano) to conduct experiments on thoughtography (*nensha*)[12] and to attend lectures on the practice of Taireidō. Getting to know Nakamura became a significant turning point in Morita's life.

In 1920, Morita was struck with an illness that began with hematochezia and fever. He spent day after day in pain without a definitive diagnosis, and was starting to prepare for death when signs of recovery finally appeared. The things he read and contemplated in his recovery bed gave Morita a chance to analyse and systematize his clinical experience up until that point. The result was *The Treatment of Neurasthenia and Shinkeishitsu* (published in 1921) and the birth of Morita therapy. Morita recognized a natural disposition that placed people at risk of outbreaks of *shinkeishitsu*, and termed this 'hypochondriacal temperament' (*hipocondoriisei kichō*). An outbreak of neurosis could occur as a result of acquired or environmental factors, but Morita attached great importance right from the start to the question of disposition, perhaps a legacy of his training in Kraepelinian psychiatry. This biological approach in Japanese psychiatry was, however, beginning to be augmented around this time with a search for psychological causes of illness. Morita made his debut as a psychiatrist just at the time when people at academic conferences were starting to show interest in the pathology and treatment of psychogenic mental illness and neuroses. According to Henri Ellenberger the period, internationally, between 1880 to 1890 was decisive in two ways: magnetism, hypnosis, and the like 'were recognized finally for the first time as "official medical science" by a new dynamic psychiatry, and were widely disseminated', while largely thanks to Freud this new dynamic psychiatry got firmly underway.[13]

Although it is not possible here to delve into the relationship between Morita and Freud, it is well known that Morita was critical of Freudian psychoanalysis, perhaps because of strong antagonisms in the world of psychiatry at the time and because the clinical point of departure for the two differed: Morita started with compulsive neuroses and Freud with hysteria. A third reason might be the difference in Morita's and Freud's views on humanity and the world, as well as on methods of treatment: Morita emphasized the present circumstances of the patient and believed in the natural curative power and the desire to live that lies inside humans in general, while *The Future of an Illusion* amply illustrates Freud's pessimism about human beings' deeply rooted irrationality and unwillingness to know the truth of their own selves. The two men's outlooks were diametrically opposed.

While Morita had been taking his first steps as a psychiatrist under the guidance of Kure Shūzō, the term 'neurasthenia' (*shinkeisuijaku*), first proposed by the American psychiatrist George Miller Beard, was in popular use. However, the precise meaning of the concept was unclear. In Beard's view, the cause of illness was a weakening of the stimulation of the central nervous system, but Morita argued against this explanation based on his own clinical experience. Morita insisted instead that in order for physiological exhaustion to develop into so-called chronic neurasthenia, something extra was required. There had also to be specific conditions in place at the level of underlying personality and psychology. For this reason Morita decided to use a new word, *shinkeishitsu*, in place of *shinkeisuijaku*, to describe the form of illness in which he was interested.

At the same time, Morita had been interested in the new method of hypnotic induction, and was using it to treat neuroses. Morita later turned his interest from hypnosis to isolated bed rest therapy (*gajyoku ryōhō*), while Freud turned his from hypnosis to free association. Morita's experiences of treating neuroses with hypnotherapy seem to have shown him differences between the personality structure or psychological apparatus associated with *shinkeishitsu* on the one hand and hysteria on the other – based on the differential effects of (hypnotic) suggestion. In a related vein, his experience of conducting occupational therapy with schizophrenic patients suggested to him the existence of a 'desire for life' that appeared in cases of *shinkeishitsu*. One might regard Morita as rather unusual and even courageous in locating the cause of neurotic symptoms in the psyche at a time when treatment for neuroses relied on scientific materialist approaches.

Morita was also exploring the bases and practical value of a range of other imported Western therapies, from isolation therapy to the rest cure (a method in which patients rest in a controlled environment, one that resembled Morita therapy's 'isolated bed rest' component), and from Paul Dubois's persuasion therapy to Binswanger's obesity therapy – this last aimed at preserving the mind and body as well as supplying nourishment by prescribing a life of regularity for the patient. After twenty years of trial and error, Morita reached the conclusion that rather than adopt any one of these therapies *in toto* it made sense to discard any method that did not demonstrate clinical efficiency and to revise and combine methods that showed greater clinical promise. So although Morita therapy was, in the end, Morita's own original creation, it was nevertheless the result of contact with a great many treatment techniques originating in Europe and the U.S. Morita's true worth lies in his combinative approach and his re-discovery of the curative value of traditional Japanese therapies, to which we now turn.

## The mind and the problem of suffering in Morita therapy

Morita therapy was first developed during a period of conflict in Japan, as the country's values were shaken by the introduction of Western culture, value systems, and technologies. According to the philosopher Nakamura Yūjirō, when Western philosophy was introduced to Japan in the Meiji period as the essential element of Western civilization, a certain questioning began as to whether something worthy of the name 'philosophy' existed in Japan.[14] Philosophy was considered to have two components: first, it was a form of knowledge derived from theoretical scholarship; and second, it offered perspectives on the world and on humanity. Western philosophy had gained universality as a theoretical form of knowledge, through strictly defined concepts and the system of knowledge that was built from those concepts. This was seen as the foundation of much of modern Western industrial and popular culture, science, technology, and law. Japanese and Asian philosophical thought more generally had a noticeable inclination towards the second component of philosophy: a world perspective, and a perspective on humanity – but there remained the question of whether this could really be called philosophy.[15]

An appreciation of this historical context is essential to an understanding of the fundamental philosophy underlying Morita therapy. Morita had been trying the various Western therapies mentioned above in tackling neurasthenia, whose shared characteristic was their focus on the body and the environment. Morita was familiar with Asian thought, which does not separate the mind from the workings of the body in the way that Cartesian philosophy tends to do, and so was receptive to these body-focused ideas and treatment methods. Morita's innovation was to systematize and combine the rest cure, occupational therapy, and life regulation therapy under the terms of an original worldview and understanding of human beings, grounded in Asian psychology and philosophy. Dubois' persuasion therapy was excluded from Morita's new system (see below), as was Freudian psychoanalysis. Of the latter, Morita wrote:

> For me, the fact that people think that the body and spirit are separate, and in particular that one's own mind can only be known to oneself, and can be controlled to serve the purposes of one's own goals, is the source of the contradiction between ideas and reality in the world. The part of oneself that one can control at will, whether body or mind, is an extremely limited portion of oneself, only a small part of the periphery. Things such as forgetfulness or having a sudden idea are not within our control; they are *phenomena of nature*.[16]

Herein lies the essence of the thinking behind Morita's psychotherapy. Can we really, by knowing ourselves, relieve or control our anxiety? Can we direct the movements of our minds at our convenience? Morita believed that our attempts to control and use our minds like this are the reason why worries and suffering arise. In truth, we can at best only ever control a tiny, relatively unimportant part of our minds' activities. And since forgetting and remembering are natural workings of the mind, painful episodes – past wounds of the heart – cannot alone be the source of neurosis. Instead, since the important thing is disposition, that with which we are born, Morita could not agree with Freud that suffering has purely psychological causes or that the mind has special mechanisms of defence.

Morita's explanation here was perhaps a touch simplistic, but it is nonetheless very clear: deliberately to try to forget and remove the unpleasant memories and desires of the past, which are no more than natural reactions, was to contradict reality and to risk increased attachment to those memories and desires. Neurosis itself was produced by just such contradiction. Finding no therapeutic meaning, therefore, in searching for a certain (traumatic) incident and bringing it to consciousness (as psychoanalysis sought to do), Morita hypothesized that the source of neurosis was first one's natural disposition, and second an excessively acute awareness of the reactions of one's own mind and body.[17]

Morita directed his new critique not just at psychoanalysis but also at Dubois' persuasion therapy. Dubois was a very well known psychotherapist of the early twentieth century, who believed that neuroses occurred because of errors in our ways of thinking and that those errors could be resolved by means of rational persuasion and correct education. Dubois' theory, particularly the linking of anxiety to the predominance of a certain way of thinking, was deeply grounded in Western culture, and gave rise to one of the major trends in Western psychotherapy: cognitive psychotherapy. But Morita criticized this kind of persuasion therapy, emphasizing bodily experience instead. For Morita, the use of intellectual persuasion to control emotions seemed like a contradiction in terms, although Morita's own therapy did give a place to perception and cognition.

Morita argued that the group of neuroses he called Morita *shinkeishitsu* was made up of three components: hypochondriacal temperament; opportunity; and proximate cause of illness (a particular episode of 'psychic interaction'). He suggested that disposition was the original source of neuroses, even while he acknowledged the limited influence of environment. A person with a natural tendency to fall easily into anxious states brought about through internal or external stimulation (the latter is what he means by 'opportunity') experiences emotional reactions that could occur in anyone. But by deciding that this natural emotional reaction is somehow negative in the context of one's life and adaptation to circumstances ('contradiction by ideas') the person goes on to focus his attention far too powerfully on his reaction. This intensifies the emotional reaction, attracting the person's attention to it even more acutely ('psychic interaction'), creating a vicious cycle of sensations and attention. In Morita therapy, this process is called 'obsession' (*toraware*).[18]

Building on his critique of Dubois and Freud, Morita started to see psychic phenomena – such as anxiety – not in terms of direct cause and effect, but as arising in relationship to multiple causes. This has parallels in Buddhist philosophy, where a single cause does not produce an effect solely by itself, but only when an assisting cause is present – this second cause is known as an 'indirect condition'.[19] What this means for Morita therapy is that rather than search for a single cause, the focus should be upon the destruction of a *vicious cycle* of the arising of causes and conditions.

Morita drew also on Buddhist ideas about the centrality of desire and its non-fulfilment in the genesis of human suffering and fear.[20] In Morita's understanding, the desire for life produces fear of death, or pain, and he hoped to harmonize desire and fear (suffering) – both of which he regarded as natural phenomena. Conflict between nature and thinking (logocentrism) is, he thought, the fundamental structure of humanity's conflicts.[21] By 'nature', he meant:

1  Physicality, sensation, and sensitivity: a person's bodily feelings and senses.

2 Desire: the desires necessary in order to keep living, and the further desires to which these give rise.
3 Emotion: the universal emotions that we all feel, including unpleasant emotions such as fear.
4 The activities of the mind in general.

Ideas stand in opposition to nature: the narcissistic self tries to make things work in exactly the way it wants by means of thinking mediated by words, or through an attitude of attachment. The man-made ideas involved here have the following characteristics:

1 Thinking that the self and the world 'are our possessions'.
2 Theories built up on this basis.
3 Consciousness of an enlarged ego.
4 The predominance of theories that are substantiated by means of language, and a concomitant downgrading of physicality and emotion.

In this way we try to control everything in our heads, using our own concepts. In trying to make everything our own we lose the original harmony of nature and emphasize negative, self-destructive aspects of ourselves instead – we then respond to this negativity by redoubling our efforts to control nature via our ideas. Desire at this point loses its original homeostasis and ends up creating a bloated self or ego.[22] The solution to this problem does not lie with the creation of an orderly world with language at the centre. Instead, it means having as the goal of therapy an awareness of the causes of one's own suffering – an awareness that does not seek to control anxiety or other forms of suffering. It involves recovering the power to harmonize with nature, by experiencing and expressing one's own nature – one's desires and emotions – just as it is, and making adjustments, through bodily experience, to the desires that have created an inflated sense of self. This aspiration forms the core of Morita's critique of Western psychotherapy and is the main focus of his own form of psychotherapy.

## Nature, mind, body, and (no-)self in Asia

This kind of perspective on nature is not unique to Morita or to Japan. The philosopher of ancient China, Lao-tzu, pointed out that when one discards artificiality, nature asserts itself. Nature contains within it a correct order to which human knowledge has no access, but which appears to us as a state of self-lessness (*mushi*) or no-self (*muga*).[23] In Morita therapy this is referred to as following nature, or *arugamama*: accepting reality as it is. Making nature and a theory of no-self the foundation of psychotherapy was therefore something that psychiatrists in China could readily understand and accept, and most Morita therapists in China point out that the views of nature found in Japan and China have major points in common. Xu Kangsheng *et al.* have focused on and discussed similarities between the thinking behind Morita therapy and Lao-tzu's idea of 'the Tao follows nature'.[24] Laozi says in the *Daodejing* that 'humans follow the Earth, the Earth follows Heaven, Heaven follows the Tao, and the Tao follows nature.'[25] So in order for a person to grow and develop in his or her life, he or she must adapt to and learn from nature. This is precisely what Morita meant by *arugamama* and by the need for people to recognize the truth of an objective reality (*jijitsu yuishin*). Furthermore, the idea in Morita therapy of 'doing what must be done' is nearly the same as what Lao-tzu called behaving in accordance with the law of nature, through *mui* – which literally means 'non-action' but also signifies doing things by following reason.

The Chinese philosopher Chuang-tzu said that it is not possible to communicate truth to another person through letters or words, nor therefore can truth be transmitted in the form of teachings. Truth does not come across in letters or words, but rather is to be understood through direct bodily intuition. We can already discover in the thought of Chuang-tzu what Morita described as the importance of bodily experience and a certain kind of limitation by, or even distrust of, words – and distrust of theories created by means of those words.[26] Herein lies the fundamental meaning of Morita therapy's non-questioning approach, or the act of not asking or searching for the meanings behind symptoms.

Morita therapy is, then, based in an affirmation of nature in all its aspects, and in an optimistic affirmation of humans who harbour desires. There is a sense in which it negates Western dualistic thinking and logocentrism by taking a unitary view of mind and body.

Morita himself described the relationship between the body and spirit through the example of an incense stick and the small ring of fire that appears when it is moved in a circular fashion: the incense stick is the material thing, while the active changes, the ring of fire, is the spirit. The incense stick and the ring of fire are by no means separate things, and when the incense goes out, the 'spirit' is also extinguished: 'the spirit is the very essence of our life's activities, and if those activities are taken away then we have nothing left to recognize [as spirit].'[27] From this stems a theory of bodily behaviour: in order to bring about change in the spirit, changes in bodily behaviour are required. This is the theoretical foundation of the treatment system in Morita therapy, relating to everything from isolation bed rest to occupational therapy. It is a position that posits the spirit and body to be one, and on the basis of that unity the therapy considers the movements, awareness, emotions, and workings of the spirit.

According to traditional ways of thinking in Japan, in order to master, learn, or attain enlightenment in regard to something, mastering some bodily comportment, some active, bodily pattern, is considered important. A craftsman learning his or her craft, more so than knowing the content of the work, must learn with their bodies the pattern of that work. Or, when practising Zen meditation, the sitting form is emphasized. This kind of understanding of spirit and body is, of course, connected to an emphasis on bodily behaviour and a concept of self that includes fundamentally a sense of the body.

## Conclusion

Asian psychology and philosophy are notable for their serious questioning of the way the self is when it is obsessed with narcissistic desires. This is what characterizes both Buddhism and Lao-tzu's and Chuang-tzu's Taoism. Morita therapy takes up this Asian understanding of human beings, while drawing also on a Japanese theory of nature described by Sagara Tōru as *onozukara*, meaning 'of itself'. As Sagara suggests, when nature is seen 'of itself', it includes in its meaning the Western conception of nature as the essence of the thing itself, in addition to what is called 'order' in Chinese thought.[28] Central here is a sense of spontaneous formation or becoming (*onozukara naru*); putting aside intellectual interpretation in favour of receiving and identifying with nature just as it is. Sagara saw the foundation of the modern Japanese person's inner struggles in the opposition between intending to be 'self' and intending to be 'no-self'. As modern self-consciousness developed, Japanese became attached to 'self' and could not easily discard it. Natsume Sōseki's pronouncement to 'follow Heaven, forsake the self' emerged as his solution to the sufferings he had endured through his attachment to self. People like him, who became aware of the self and its desires and then became attached to those desires, suffered intensely, and were calling in Morita's day for the expertise of Asian psychology and philosophy to resolve their conflicts.

## Notes

1 Translated by Yumi Kim. This essay is a modified translation of Kondo Kyoichi and Kitanishi Kenji, 'Kokoro: Morita ryōhō no Kokoro to Iyashi' [The heart and healing of morita therapy], in Shintaro Tanabe *et al.* (eds), *Iyashi wo Ikita Hitobito: Kindaichi no Orutanatibu* (Senshu University Press, 1990).
2 Seneca, *On the Shortness of Life*.
3 Helman, *Culture, Health and Illness*.
4 Kleinman, *Patients and Healers in the Context of Culture*.
5 Daikichi, *Nihon no rekishi*.
6 Morita, 'Wagaya no Kiroku'.
7 Ibid.
8 See Harding (Chapter 1) and Hashimoto, this volume.
9 Not to be confused with Yoshimoto Ishin's twentieth-century therapy of the same name – see Shimazono, this volume.
10 Morita, 'Furoku'.
11 Morita, 'Shinkeishitsu no hontai oyobi ryōhō'. Emphasis added.
12 The ability to project one's thoughts, burning them into a given material or into the minds of other people.

13 Ellenberger, *The Discovery of the Unconscious*, p. 254.
14 Nakamura, 'Nishida tetsugaku'. See also Godart, ' "Philosophy" or "religion"?'
15 See the discussion in Blocker and Starling, *Japanese Philosophy*, 'Introduction'.
16 Morita, 'Seishin ryōhō kōgi'.
17 Ibid.
18 Morita, 'Sinkeisuijaku oyobi kyōhakukannen no konchihō'.
19 See Yokoyama, *Yuishiki towa nanika*.
20 Nakamura, *Gensho bukkyō: sono shisō to seikatsu*.
21 Morita, 'Seishin ryōhō kōgi', 'Sinkeisuijaku oyobi kyōhakukannen no konchihō'.
22 Kitanishi, 'Morita ryōhō no konnichiteki kadai: hikakuteki kenchi kara'.
23 Mori, *Rōshi sōshi*.
24 Xu and Wang, *Morita shinri ryōhō to rōshi: 'Dōhō shizen' no shisō*.
25 Laozi, *Daodejing*.
26 Mori, *Rōshi sōshi*.
27 Morita, 'Seishin ryōhō kōgi'.
28 Sagara, *Nihon no shisō*.

# References

Blocker, H Gene and Starling, Christopher L, *Japanese Philosophy* (Albany: State University of New York Press, 2001), Introduction.

Ellenberger, Henri F., *The Discovery of the Unconscious: The History and Evolution of Dynamic Psychiatry* (New York: Basic Books, 1970).

Godart, Gerard Clinton, ' "Philosophy" or "religion"? the confrontation with foreign categories in late nineteenth century Japan', *Journal of the History of Ideas* 69, no. 1 (2008).

Helman, Cecil G., *Culture, Health and Illness* (Bristol: John Wright & Sons, 1990).

Irokawa Daikichi, *Nihon no rekishi*. Volume 21 (Tokyo: Yomiuri Shinbunsha, 1965).

Kitanishi Kenji., 'Morita ryōhō no konnichiteki kadai: hikakuteki kenchi kara [Modern themes in Morita therapy from a comparative perspective]' in Matsushita Masaaki *et al.* (eds), *Rinshō seishin igaku kōza, Volume 23* [Clinical Psychiatry Course] (1998).

Kleinman, Arthur, *Patients and Healers in the Context of Culture* (Berkeley: University of California Press, 1980).

Kondo Kyoichi and Kitanishi Kenji, 'Kokoro: Morita ryōhō no Kokoro to Iyashi [The Heart and Healing of Morita Therapy]', in Shintaro Tanabe *et al.* (eds), *Iyashi wo Ikita Hitobito: Kindaichi no Orutanatibu* (Tokyo: Senshu University Press, 1990).

Laozi, *Daodejing* (translated by Edmund Ryden); (Oxford: Oxford University Press, 2008).

Mori Mikisaburō, *Rōshi sōshi [Lao-tzu and Chuang-tzu]* (Tokyo: Kodansha, 1994).

Morita Masatake, 'Seishin ryōhō kōgi [Lecture on Psychotherapy]', in *Morita Masatake Zenshu Vol. 1*, pp. 509–638 (1922/1974).

Morita Masatake, 'Sinkeisuijaku oyobi kyōhakukannen no konchihō [The treatment of neurasthenia and obsession]', in *Morita Masatake Zenshu Vol. 2*, pp. 71–287 (1926/1974).

Morita Masatake, 'Furoku [Addendum]', *Morita Masatake Zenshu Vol. 2*, pp. 395–413 (1928/1974).

Morita Masatake, 'Shinkeishitsu no hontai oyobi ryōhō [The nature of Shinkeishitsu and its treatment] in *Morita Masatake Zenshu Vol. 2* pp. 238–394 (1928/1974).

Morita Masatake, 'Wagaya no Kiroku' [My personal record], *Morita Masatake Zenshu Vol. 7*, pp. 755–841 (1934/1974).

Nakamura Yūjirō, 'Nishida tetsugaku [The philosophy of Nishida]', in *Nakamura Yūjirō chosakushū* (Tokyo: Iwanami Shoten, 1993).

Sagara Tōru, *Nihon no shisō [Japanese Thought]* (Tokyo: Perikansha, 1989).

Seneca, Lucius Annaeus, *On the Shortness of Life* (translated by John W. Basore) (London: William Heinemann, 1932).

Xu Kangsheng and Wang Jianhua, *Morita shinri ryōhō to rōshi: 'Dōhō shizen' no shisō [Morita Therapy and Lao-tzu: The Idea of 'The Tao Follows Nature']* (Osaka: Okamoto Kinen Zaidan, 1991).

Yokoyama Kōitsu, *Yuishiki towa nanika [What is Vijnapti-matrata?]* (Tokyo: Shunjusha, 1986).

# 5 The dawning of Japanese psychoanalysis
## Kosawa Heisaku's therapy and faith

*Iwata Fumiaki*[1]

The first President of the Japan Psychoanalytical Association, Kosawa Heisaku (1897–1968), was instrumental in importing Freudian psychoanalytical techniques into Japan. This was not, however, a simple relocation of Freud's technique: Kosawa revised and adapted what he had learnt from Freud in order to suit what he regarded as a Japanese mentality. Kosawa taught the resulting techniques to major figures who would later represent Japanese psychoanalysis internationally: Okonogi Keigo (1930–2003), Doi Takeo (1920–2009), Nishizono Masahisa (1928–), Maeda Shigeharu (1928–), and Takeda Makoto (1923–). These individuals succeeded in attracting a great many Japanese readers for psychoanalytical works, while speaking out about the modern psychological condition of the Japanese. Kosawa's relationship with his students was intimate and sometimes difficult, with a strong bond established during supervisions and training analyses. Supervisions, also called 'directed training' (*kantoku kyōiku*), involved the trainee reporting to the supervisor the details of his or her conversations with patients, and receiving advice and guidance in response. In Kosawa's case, the bond between him and his students often gave rise to emotional struggle: Okonogi and Doi in particular did not simply replicate Kosawa's technique but instead developed their own ideas through critical engagement with Kosawa's.[2]

There were two sides to Kosawa and his theory. On the one hand, he was a devout follower of the True Pure Land sect of Buddhism (often referred to simply as 'Shin Buddhism'), and thus something of Japan's traditional religiosity was deeply ingrained in him. On the other hand, Kosawa had travelled to Vienna to train directly with Freud and his circle, making him a pioneering figure who imported and helped to Westernise psychiatry in Japan.[3] This chapter will focus on the coexistence of traditional religiosity and innovative psychiatric methods in Kosawa's life and work, the mediatory function that his religious ideas played in his own understanding of psychoanalysis, and the influence of Kosawa's ideas upon the later character of psychoanalysis in Japan. The account pays particular attention to the religious influence upon Kosawa of Chikazumi Jōkan (1870–1941), as well as the important revision of Kosawa's ideas in later years by Okonogi Keigo. Chikazumi was a Shin Buddhist monk of the Ōtani-ha school based at the Higashi Hongan-ji temple in Kyoto. After graduating from Tokyo Imperial University (Department of Philosophy), he was ordered by the Higashi Hongan-ji to go to the United States to learn about Christian social activities and missionary methods. On returning to Japan in 1902 he founded the Kyūdōgakusha hall of residence near Tokyo Imperial University, taking as his inspiration YMCA student accommodation. He followed this up in 1915 with the Kyūdōkaikan lecture hall just next door. Modelled on the architecture of Christian churches, Chikazumi used this as a base for his missionary work. Through these sorts of means Chikazumi influenced a number of young intellectuals around the turn of the twentieth century, including the philosophers Miki Kiyoshi and Tanikawa Tetsuzō, and the writer Kamura Isota, along with Kosawa Heisaku.

\* \* \*

A letter was recently discovered at the Kyūdōkaikan, addressed to Chikazumi Jōkan and sent by Kosawa Heisaku on 24 June 1936. It included five handwritten pages copied from a newspaper article written in German, taken from the 9 May 1936 edition of the newspaper, *Neues Wiener Tagblatt*. The article, entitled 'Thomas Mann, on Freud' (*Thomas Mann über Freud*), was based on a lecture delivered by Thomas Mann the previous day, in celebration of Freud's 80th birthday. The lecture, which had been a great success (tickets sold out the day they became available), paid respect to Freud and explored the significance of his work by comparing it with that of Novalis, Nietzsche, Kierkegaard and Schopenhauer. But why did Kosawa take the time to copy this article, and send it to Chikazumi?

The letter was sent three years after Kosawa's return to Japan from Vienna, following his studies with Freud and his circle. Immediately after his return, Kosawa had rented a house in the suburbs of Tokyo and opened a clinic. He soon began building a house in Denenchōfu, Ota-ku, and while living there he practised his psychoanalytic treatment. For these reasons, 1936 was an important year in Kosawa's life, full of hope in a new environment. Kosawa's son, the psychologist, Kosawa Yorio, when once asked about the letter, speculated that his father must have been so moved by the newspaper article that he wanted to share it with his Buddhist mentor, Chikazumi – a man whom he respected as much as Freud. Kosawa wanted to convey to Chikazumi the importance of his opening up a new psychoanalytic clinic. As such, the letter to Chikazumi was an affirmation of the coexistence of religion and psychoanalysis in Kosawa, which found particularly revealing expression in his 'Ajase Complex' theory, a modification of Freud's Oedipus theory.

## Kosawa's early life and education: from Chikazumi to Freud

Kosawa Heisaku was born in Funako, present-day Atsugi City (Kanagawa prefecture), in 1897, to a wealthy family with a traceable history of more than 400 years. The family belonged to the Pure Land sect of Buddhism but were not particularly devout followers, and many of Kosawa's relatives belonged to another Buddhist group, the Nichiren sect. Kosawa was the ninth of ten children, and the youngest son. There was a twenty-year gap between him and his elder brother, the fourth child. His mother being busy with housekeeping Kosawa was, in accordance with local tradition at the time, mostly left in the care of a nanny. The nanny was a ten-year-old girl, who used to play with other children and leave baby Kosawa tied to a tree. Kosawa used to tell this story even towards the end of his life, and his former student Takeda Makoto has speculated that 'this emotional damage left a scar deep in his unconscious, which later developed into his longing for the maternal.'[4]

In 1918, Kosawa entered the Second High School in Sendai to study science, and was placed in the Dōkōkai Jichi Hall of Residence, closely associated with the Shin Buddhist sect. Many of the students staying there were interested in Buddhism, and there was a tradition of reciting the Heart Sutra every morning before breakfast. In addition, prominent Buddhist figures were invited to deliver special lectures on Gautama Buddha's birthday and on the day of his Enlightenment. It was at one of these lectures that Kosawa first met Chikazumi Jōkan. There were also student debates, with common themes including the virtues of different Buddhist schools of thought in Japan (Shōdōmon versus Jōdomon, for example) and the importance of personal effort in the religious life (*jiriki*, or 'self-power') versus reliance upon the Other (*tariki*, or 'other-power'). Kosawa, it seems, was an enthusiastic advocate of *tariki* at this time. By the time of his graduation in 1921, Kosawa was suffering from serious eye problems: cataracts, plus an unsuccessful course of treatment that lasted for two-and-a-half years, left him blind in his right eye, with a mild strabismus affecting his left eye.

A voracious reader, there is no doubt that this turn of events caused Kosawa great pain, and had a significant impact on his later life – well beyond the immediate inconvenience of delayed admission to Tohoku Imperial University to study medicine.[5] Kosawa did, however, successfully graduate from Tohoku as a doctor, in 1926, and it was at this point that he decided to study psychiatry under Professor Marui Kiyoyasu.[6]

Kosawa was astonished by Freud's theory when he encountered it in Marui's lectures. He continued to find spiritual support in Shin Buddhism, and its head-on approach to the problems of human desire, but Kosawa also developed great hope for treatment based on new scientific methods and on psychoanalytic theories concerning the human psyche. At the time, Freud's ideas were gradually becoming accessible in Japan through translated works, but Marui was the only person who included Freud in university-level research in the field of psychiatry.[7] He had studied psychiatry under Adolf Meyer at Johns Hopkins University, including lectures on psychoanalysis. Although he was crucial to the establishment of psychoanalysis in Japan, Marui's import of it to Japan was indirect – via America – and this fact seemed to limit its prospects in Japan, somewhat to Kosawa's disappointment.

The close relationship between Kosawa and Chikazumi had continued after Kosawa moved out of Dōkōkai Jichi Hall of Residence. Yamamura Michio, Kosawa's junior on Marui's research team, remembers that as students in 1921 he shared a room with Kosawa and his friend Kurokawa Toshio. Chikazumi visited two or three times to talk about Buddhism. And when, after graduation, Kosawa became a research assistant for Marui and Yamamura entered the Medical Department at Tohoku, Yamamura was all but ordered by Kosawa to attend a lecture of Chikazumi's in Sendai.[8]

It was around this time, in June 1931, that Kosawa published his first essay on the Ajase Complex. He presented Freud with a German translation of the piece when he met him for the first time the following year, in Vienna. Takeda Makoto has written that 1931 was the biggest turning point in Kosawa's life.[9] Marui, who studied under Meyer, understood psychoanalysis intellectually but lacked experiential knowledge in using the technique to treat patients. Studying the *Complete Works* of Freud and realizing that study of the free-association technique was the fundamental basis for psychoanalysis, Kosawa saw Marui's divergence from Freud and made the decision to leave him and to travel to meet Freud himself.

Kosawa left for the Vienna Psychoanalytical Research Institute in late December 1931, and met Freud in January 1932. Freud gave him some academic direction and advice but suggested that Kosawa receive his training analysis from his student, Richard Sterba. Subsequently, Kosawa was supervised by Paul Federn. Kosawa stayed in Vienna for a year-and-a-half, but during that time Freud seems not to have shown great interest in Kosawa's 1931 essay.[10] In Freud's diary, written in his twilight years,[11] there are a few sections relating to Japanese people but no mention of the Ajase Complex.

After his return to Japan in 1933, Kosawa left Tohoku Imperial University to become the first person in Japan to open his own psychoanalytic clinic. He wrote to Freud in 1935, 'Everyday, I am using your technique and trying to devise ways to treat my patients.'[12] On the occasion of Freud's death in September 1939, Kosawa wrote an article of remembrance in which commented: 'I cannot help but to compare Dr. Freud's mindset with that of St. Shinran.'[13] Two years later, Chikazumi, with whom Kosawa had kept in touch following his return from Europe,[14] also passed away. Kosawa had lost his two great teachers, one after the other.

## The Ajase Complex Theory and the influence of Chikazumi Jōkan

After the war, many psychiatrists who were interested in psychoanalysis went to Kosawa for advice and training, drawing both on his extensive pre-war knowledge of the discipline and on his rare clinical experience. In 1953, Kosawa translated Freud's *Introduction to Psychoanalysis – Continued* [*Zoku seishin bunseki nyūmon*], which included in the translator's postscript an explanation of the Ajase Complex theory.[15] Two years later, the Japan Psychoanalytical Association was established, with Kosawa elected as its first President. For someone outside the university system, who was primarily a clinician, to become the leader of an academic association was an exceptional and rare event in Japan at the time. Three years later, however, in the summer of 1958, Kosawa fainted from encephalomalacia during a session of free association. After that he never again appeared in public, and he passed away ten years later in October 1968.

One of Kosawa's greatest legacies has been his theory of the Ajase Complex. Ajase was a contemporary of Gautama Buddha, who became King of Magadha in present-day India. His father was called Bimbisara, and his mother Vaidehi. Famously, Ajase killed his father in order to become the king, but learned repentance through the teachings of Buddha and became a protector of Buddhism thereafter. This story of salvation, of a son who murdered his own father, stimulated many writers to leave behind legends and sutras. Kosawa's Ajase Complex deviated, however, from the traditional Buddhist understanding of the legend, and Okonogi Keigo, who popularised the Ajase Complex theory after Kosawa's death, pointed out on a couple of occasions the problems with Kosawa's modification. However, both Okonogi and his critics amongst Buddhist academics made errors in their own analyses of the legend.

Below is a quotation from Okonogi's useful introductory article 'Ajase complex' in the *Iwanami Dictionary of Philosophy and Ideology* (1998), with his crucial misunderstanding underlined:

> Ajase Complex: A representative theory of Japanese Psychoanalysis formulated by Kosawa Heisaku.
>
> During his study in Vienna, Kosawa submitted a thesis entitled 'Two Types of Guilt – Ajase Complex' (1932) to Sigmund Freud. <u>At first, the theory was based on the Mahayana Mahaparinirvana Sutra: the story of Bimbisara, Vaidehi, and their son Ajase. However, the focus gradually shifted to the Contemplation Sutra, with its emphasis on the mother-son relationship between Vaidehi and Ajase.</u>
>
> In contrast to Freud's Oedipus Complex, based on a father–mother–son tripartite theory and focusing on 'father killing', Kosawa shifted the focus to the mother–son relationship and 'mother killing'. This is a uniquely Japanese psychoanalytic idea that is beginning to

gain international recognition. The theory has been promoted and developed by Kosawa's student, Okonogi, and is becoming internationalised.

According to Okonogi, an Ajase complex arises from the mother's yearning for her child, on the one hand, and, on the other, a wish to abort or to neglect, which creates an internal conflict within the mother. This unconscious distress is then transmitted to her child, causing him to hold a grudge against his mother. The Ajase complex is a sequence of psychological processes through which the son experiences an impulse to kill his mother; guilt then arises in relation to this desire, but in the end he is forgiven.[16]

Okonogi claims here that Kosawa took the Ajase story directly from Buddhist scriptures, such as the Mahayana Mahaparinirvana Sutra. In fact, although there are many reasons for Kosawa's modification of the legend of Ajase,[17] his own clinical experience and the influence of Chikazumi were key. Kosawa's essay on the Ajase Complex was first published in Tohoku Imperial University Medical Department's journal, *Gonryō*, Vol. 8 (15 June 1931). The title of this essay was later changed to 'Two types of guilt: the Ajase complex' and it was republished a number of times without its original introductory section: in *The Japanese Journal of Psycho-Analysis* [*Seishinbunseki Kenkyū*] Vol. 1, No. 4 (1954); in *Modern Spirit* [*Gendai no Esupuri*] Vol. 148 (1979); and finally in *Ajase Complex*, edited by Okonogi Keigo and Kitayama Osamu (2001).[18] These republished versions, which have become the basis for current understandings of the Ajase Complex, mix Kosawa's psychoanalytic theory with his religious belief in a way that seems not to make sense. However, with the deleted introductory section reinserted, it becomes clear that in fact this essay was originally a religious theory, which incorporated psychoanalysis. Here is the deleted section:

> The emergence and development of anti-religious movements has been influencing the way newspapers write about religious matters. Gonryō, which aspires to be a leading academic journal, has asked me to write on this topic. At first I refused this offer, since I had no time. This was a big problem for me: I had wanted to write and I was thinking of writing on this matter, but the offer was unexpected and they did not give me enough time to complete the article. Yet this was partly my own fault. I am happy now if I can contribute in different ways for you young readers. So: is religion really the opium of the people?

The rest of the original essay is almost the same as 'Two types of guilt: the Ajase complex', as published in *Psychoanalytic Research* Vol. 1, No. 4. First, Kosawa introduces Freud's totem theory: 'In theorising religion, Freud first pictured the killing and devouring of totem animals (something like the Bear Festival of the Ainu) ...' Kosawa goes on to suggest that Freud is not dealing with a truly religious state of mind here.

At this point, Kosawa is mainly interested in the idea of a 'completed/ unified religious mentality' [kansei saretaru shūkyōteki shinri] rather than psychoanalytical theory per se. What Kosawa means by a 'unified religious mentality' is a sense of 'heartfelt repentance' [zangeshin] that arises in a child when he or she witnesses their parents' self-sacrifice. The legend of Ajase is one specific example he uses to explain this very particular form of religiosity.

A long-running debate over the real closeness of the legend of Ajase to Kosawa's psychoanalytic theory has for the most part omitted one simple fact: Kosawa's essay, as it appeared in Okonogi and Kitayama's *Ajase Complex* volume contains a section that is more or less a paraphrase of material in Chikazumi Jokan's autobiographical *Zangeroku* [*Record of Repentance*].[19] In other words, the major part of Kosawa's reference to the legend of Ajase is in fact a quotation from his mentor Chikazumi. In the next section of his essay, Kosawa describes the legend of Ajase, quoting from a different source and placing more emphasis on the tension between Vaidehi and Ajase.[20] In doing so, Kosawa makes Freud's oral-stage sadism theory the basis for his Ajase Complex theory. In Kosawa's words, 'the desire to murder one's own mother because of love' lies at the foundation of the religious mentality. Kosawa illustrates this claim with the example of one of his patients:

> His worldview changed drastically, just like silver transforming into gold. And from the viewpoint of the most advanced scientific psychoanalysis, this change in his mentality represents the most harmonious and stable condition that a man is capable of achieving. So, is religion the opium of the people? I offer this ultimate question to anyone with a heart.[21]

It is now clear that Kosawa's essay was intended to answer the question of 'whether religion is really the opium of the people'. The legend of Ajase, and Freud's psychoanalytic theory, were used by Kosawa as tools in presenting his view that religion is not the opium of the people. This view of the Ajase Complex theory, as essentially a religious theory, has tended to be rejected by those who endeavour to practise psychoanalysis as a branch of science.[22] But seen from the point of view of Japan's intellectual history and spirituality, this is an interesting and important case that merits a little further exploration.

Until recently, when researchers discussed the basis of Kosawa's interpretation of the legend of Ajase, the emphasis was always upon how Kosawa himself shifted the focus onto the 'mother–son' relationship.[23] In other words, the Pure Land Buddhist interpretation of the legend of Ajase had traditionally focused on the tension and conflict between father and son, and it seemed that Kosawa had modified it to a struggle between mother and son.

What has generally been missed, however, is his reason for having done so: his desire to bring to people's attention the fundamental difference between Christianity and Buddhism, and to demonstrate the difference in their religious mentalities – using psychoanalysis. According to Kosawa, Freud considered religion to be rooted in 'the son's guilt, connected with emotional urges to murder his own father and with a "posthumous submission" that is an attempt at reconciliation with his father'.[24] For Kosawa, on the other hand, 'the son's desire to murder is melted [*torokasare*] by his realisation of his parents' self-sacrifice; this then turns into a kind of guilt'.[25] In his ideas about the child's religious conversion after being melted, it is clear that Kosawa was heavily influenced by Chikazumi Jōkan.

The concept of salvation through family relationship lay at the heart of Chikazumi's teaching, based on his own personal experience of religious conversion. Chikazumi had a metanoic experience in his hometown, Shiga, in 1897, which he saw as having parallels with Ajase's own conversion. During his student years at Tokyo Imperial University, Chikazumi had relationship problems with his peers and as a result suffered emotionally and spiritually, and even thought of committing suicide. On top of this, he was diagnosed with an intractable disease, which caused him a great degree of physical pain.

The decisive event happened after an operation at Nagahama Hospital in Shiga:

> When I was suffering, my father said to me: 'I am an old man now. I wish I could take on your suffering.' These words, I thought, sounded like King Bimbisara talking to King Ajase from Heaven. Likewise, my mother was worried and nursed me all night long when I had a high fever. This was identical with Vaidehi applying liniment to Ajase's scar. (...) In my heart, I felt the desire to identify with Ajase's wrongdoing.[26]

In this way, Chikazumi connected his own experience of guilt with what he knew of Ajase's, and assimilated family relationship into his understanding of salvation in Pure Land Buddhism. Such an interpretation does not, in itself, deviate from the Pure Land Buddhist tradition. The founder of Shin Buddhism, Shinran, had a profound interest in the conversion of Ajase, evident in his work *Kyōgyōshinshō*, where he quotes from the Mahayana Mahaparinirvana Sutra on the subject of Ajase's conversion. However, Shinran never compared his own parents to Bimbisara and Vaidehi. Moreover, he never discussed the complex emotions and desires that Vaidehi experienced in relation to her son Ajase. In contrast to Shinran, Chikazumi compared his own sinfulness with that of Ajase, writing in depth about the latter's indebtedness towards his parents and about their likely internal struggles, especially those of Ajase's mother. He alluded in particular to Vaidehi's anger/hatred towards her son, which he saw her expressing in such powerful terms as 'my son is not really my son, he is my sworn enemy'.[27] In this way Chikazumi provided the materials for an interpretation of the Ajase legend in which the mother–son relationship was central, making him an influential factor in shifting the focus from the father–son to mother–son relationship in the legend of Ajase.[28]

So Chikazumi remained within the boundaries of his Buddhist tradition while teaching Shin Buddhism in a way that corresponded with the modern psychological condition. Where the Ajase Complex is concerned, Chikazumi served a mediatory function for traditional religion and prepared the ground for the development of Ajase Complex theory. Through Chikazumi, this traditional concept of religious salvation became deeply entrenched in Kosawa.

As Chikazumi's idea was adopted by Kosawa, the legend of Ajase morphed from a religious story into a psychoanalytical theory. One concept in particular, which exemplifies this process, is *ruchū*, a severe skin disease. In 1953, more than twenty years after Kosawa first wrote about Ajase, he reintroduced the theory in the translator's postscript to *Introduction to Psychoanalysis – Continued*. This version was clearer than the 1931 original in terms of its psychoanalytical theorization, and was significant for Kosawa's revealing use of the word *ruchū* to describe Ajase's illness. The Mahayana Mahaparinirvana Sutra used the word '*kasa*' for Ajase's illness, as did Shinran's *Kyōgyōshinshō*. And Chikazumi never used the word '*ruchū*' to describe Ajase's illness. Kosawa instead seems to have drawn a link between Ajase's illness, and the illness he understood Chikazumi as having suffered.[29] This would suggest that the influence of Chikazumi upon Kosawa's understanding of the legend of Ajase was not something brief and transient, confined to an early period of Kosawa's thinking, but rather it had a more thoroughgoing effect. This postscript offered the salvation story of Ajase as a model for psychoanalytic theory, for patients who escape their mother's clutches to 'develop and mature … [to] adapt to society, and achieve a personality with a capacity to love others'.[30] This, Kosawa wrote, is the essential purpose of psychoanalysis.

## The torokashi technique

Kosawa's treatment is often summed up as 'torokashi', or 'melting'. His technique aimed to melt his patients' hatred towards him via his unconditional love for them. The word 'torokasu' originated from Chikazumi's teaching: Chikazumi often used the term, and he recalled his own conversion experience as being one in which his 'heart was melted by [Amida] Buddha's heart'.[31] At the foundation of his belief, it was ultimately Amida's mercy that melts an ordinary person's tendency to cling to himself. Parental love is a representation of, and a vehicle for, Amida's 'torokashi'.[32]

Chikazumi often compared the mentality of parents to Amida's mercy. In one of his sermons he made use of the Japanese folktale, 'Obasuteyama':

> For whom did the mother break twigs deep in the mountain? To help the descent of her child, who was planning to abandon her there.

Chikazumi's father used to tell him this story when he was very young.[33] An undutiful son carried his elderly mother deep into a mountain in a basket, with the intention of leaving her there. Without complaint, the mother started breaking off twigs from nearby trees, tying them with grass, and laying a trail of markers. The son watched her scornfully, thinking his mother would try to save herself by following the twigs back home. When they reached Mount Obasute, and as the son was about to leave his mother, she pulled his sleeve to tell him her final wish: 'This is our farewell, take care of yourself. You have come far into this mountain and it is difficult to get back home. I've laid a trail of twigs. Follow it to get home safely.' The son was astonished by these unexpected words and at last realized the true nobility of his mother. He collapsed onto the ground and could not stop crying. He begged, 'please get back into this basket, I will take you home and serve you as long as I can.'

For Chikazumi this folk tale expressed the very essence of parenthood, which moves the child to seek for forgiveness. The tale functioned allegorically, expressing the mercy of the Buddha. Even though the mother is portrayed as an 'ideal mother', her role is symbolic: more important than the restoration of the mother–son relationship is progress in one's faith. Chikazumi taught that the son, here, represents every sentient being, and that we should seek for forgiveness via this merciful melting.

Kosawa's psychoanalytic treatment embraced Chikazumi's teaching that Buddha's mercy melts every living thing. Through Kosawa, the focal point shifted to the mother's love melting the hatred within the child, but when actually conducting psychoanalysis Kosawa sought to fulfill the function of the Buddha. So while tension and reconciliation in the parent–child relationship were at the heart of the Ajase Complex theory, in practice Kosawa as a psychoanalyst provided the patient with something that was akin to the Buddha's sympathy, compassion, and salvation. Even if there was no explicit transcendent element in what Kosawa portrayed as an ideal mother, treatment itself provided a practical Buddhist transcendence.

Kosawa was both a theorist in the psychoanalytic vein and at the same time a devoutly religious man. All his students, who received training analysis from him, said that his personality as a religious person was the stronger. Doi Takeo has stated that, ultimately, what motivated Kosawa was his religiosity and strong 'self-perception as a saviour figure'. As a result, Doi criticized Kosawa for 'consuming' his patients – 'drink[ing]' them [*nomikomi*].[34] Another student of Kosawa, Maeda Shigeharu, received 105 training analyses from Kosawa between 18 May 1957 and 19 April 1958. He later wrote a detailed account of his experience of Kosawa's free-association method in his book *Record of Free Association* [*Jiyūrensōhō oboegaki*].[35] Of Kosawa's 'torokashi' technique, Maeda wrote:

> It is different from forcing patients to regress back to a state of dependency, seen in the oral stage of psychosexual development; [Kosawa] neither molly-coddled [*amayakashi*] nor attempted to enrapture his patients. Instead, his therapeutic motherly attitude – his fundamentally maternal approach – facilitated positive transformation and restoration of a basic level of internal unity. It was a profound interpersonal experience where both *amae* and hatred were dissolved/melted.[36]

Kosawa's technique required the analyst to assert his own personality, and to enter subjectively into the dialogue. When Maeda asked Kosawa about this, he candidly admitted the counter-transference involved: 'I certainly do assert myself too much.'[37]

Although it is possible that Kosawa's psychoanalytic treatment differed depending on the patient and the period, it seems likely that he applied a generally similar technique in most cases.[38]

## From Kosawa Heisaku to Okonogi Keigo

Most of Kosawa's students rejected the 'torokashi' technique, while nevertheless building on Kosawa's ideas and methods. Okonogi Keigo, regarded within the Japan Psychoanalytical Association as the successor of Kosawa, is a representative figure in this process. Okonogi did not use the word 'torokashi' – criticising it as lacking 'neutrality' – and he rejected Kosawa's religious approach altogether in his treatment in favour of engaging with the problems of the parent–child relationship by placing an emphasis on personal autonomy. For Okonogi, Kosawa's treatment required 'the analyst to direct a transference of the superego [in the process of which] the analyst becomes the superego'[39] and forgives his sins, whereas in fact the analyst ought to maintain his impartiality at all times. In this way, the patient will not risk being 'drunk' [*nomikomareru*] by the analyst and will not lose himself; instead he will be able to reach greater maturity. The relationship between Kosawa and Okonogi signifies somewhat the development of psychoanalysis in Japan: initially, psychoanalysis was imported from the West, and established upon deeply rooted Buddhist spiritual culture; this foundation was then rejected by the succeeding generation.

Okonogi, as a practising psychoanalyst and leader of the Psychoanalytical Association, wrote a great deal on the topic of Japanese culture. In the course of this he popularised the Ajase Complex based on his own interpretation of Kosawa's original theory, as in his article 'The Ajase

Complex of the Japanese' in *Chūōkōron* (1978).⁴⁰ Along with Doi Takeo's *The Structure of 'Amae'* (1971) and Kawai Hayao's *Pathology of Japan as a Maternal Society* (1976), Okonogi's idea created a sensation within Japanese society.⁴¹ Where the legend of Ajase was concerned, unlike Kosawa, Okonogi did not recognize religious salvation or the worldview that went with it. Instead, he focused on 'the basic structure of mother-son experience in Japan' and the 'Japanese frame of mind',⁴² proposing three stages to the mother–son relationship in the legend of Ajase. First, there is the 'idealized mother figure', and the son's 'amae' in his desire to identify this figure with his real mother. Second, the son's realization that the idealized mother figure was a fantasy; this prompts 'disillusionment' and subsequently 'hatred'. Finally, there is mutual 'forgiveness' and a 'sense of guilt' between mother and son. Okonogi places this in the context of a broader argument that after the war Japanese people accepted Western rationalism and as such rejected, on a conscious level, Japanese regulatory principles. Yet on a subconscious level they continued to desire the 'maternal', and as a result have not been able truly to achieve Western style individuality: the Japanese mentality ends up torn between an Ajase Complex and Westernized consciousness.

Okonogi suggests a third way: neither a return to Japaneseness nor simple identification with the West but rather an integration of the two in the 'search for a new Japanese ego'.⁴³ This requires Japanese to 'systematically trace the methods employed by people who have sought to unify [these two] elements',⁴⁴ of which Kosawa's Ajase Complex theory is a kind of prototype: superficially engaging with traditionally Japanese ideas and appearing to promote a return to an older Japan, and yet delving beneath the surface of everyday experience in order to draw up and conceptualize what it finds there. Just as Kosawa's encounter with Freud assisted the former in the conscious realization of his unconscious mental states, so, Okonogi believed, Kosawa's theory was an attempt at achieving an inner unity for Japanese people within the framework of a Westernized consciousness.

This argument of Okonogi's received a certain amount of support in the late 1970s, perhaps because many people begrudged the prevailing mood in favour of individual autonomy and rights. However, might there not be a problem in understanding the legend of Ajase in this way, not as a religious story but as a general story of the mother–son relationship in Japan? Okonogi agreed with Kosawa that 'forgiveness-based guilt is, prior to any religious or ethical interpretation, the natural state of Japanese mentality.'⁴⁵ However, this agreement was based on Okonogi's own personal understanding of Japanese religiosity, to which we must work to add further research and discussion.

## Conclusion

In forging a modern nation, Japan, like the West, had to alter and recreate its family structure. The pre-modern Japanese family was not only about kinship or local community, but was founded upon a broader ethical and traditional religious view. With the creation of a modern nation, local communities were dismantled and reorganized, and families divided into smaller, nuclear units. Members of these new families naturally developed a strong emotional bond with one another, giving rise to an intimacy that sometimes worked positively as an appropriate support mechanism but which also promoted excessive dependence. Chikazumi provided a Buddhist interpretation of this new type of family, seeing both conflict and reconciliation in the mother–son relationship. However, for Chikazumi this mother–son relationship was not just a place of human connection but also a place for salvation via the Buddha. Even though extensive discussion of the Buddha was missing from Kosawa's Ajase Complex theory, in practice Kosawa himself sought to perform the Buddha's function.

It is this crucial dimension that Okonogi missed when he claimed that Kosawa's notion of guilt had merely to do with the natural mentality of the Japanese. He suggested that a traditional maternal principle has existed in Japanese society and ways of thinking independent of any notion of religious transcendence: an 'idealized mother figure', which creates disillusionment and hatred, as well as mutual forgiveness and awareness of guilt between mother and son. However, in the legend of Ajase, these concepts are all founded upon a Buddhist worldview. The problem within Okonogi's understanding of the legend of Ajase is epitomized in his strong emphasis, which departs from Kosawa's theory, on the importance of hatred: the mother's conflict between her longing for, and the impulse to murder, her son, and the son's struggles with his hatred towards his mother upon realizing that his sense of unity with her was a mere illusion. In explaining this hatred, Okonogi uses an expression from the legend of Ajase, which he calls *mishōon*. He explains that '*mishōon* is an existential grudge held against one's origins',[46] which can be transmitted across generations.[47] Okonogi avoids the Pure Land Buddhist connotation of *mishōon*, which is connected with receiving salvation from an absolute being. In doing so, he exchanges religious salvation for a stronger emphasis on frustration and discouragement. In the traditional Buddhist interpretation this frustration is natural, since Ajase's mother, Vaidehi, is portrayed in the legend not as an ideal mother but an ordinary woman with her own weaknesses [*kleshas*, in Buddhist terminology]: even if the son becomes disillusioned and as a result hates his 'real mother', the Buddha's mercy will melt both mother and son, creating in the process a mutual sense of guilt and forgiveness. Only after experiencing this forgiveness does the son identify his real mother with the ideal mother figure. In other words, the origin of the ideal mother figure lies within the transcendental power of the Buddha.

Without this transcendence, the ideal mother figure loses its grounding. Though Okonogi rejects such a basis for the ideal mother figure, his arguments suggest an admiration of religious feeling – this could be interpreted as a wistfulness for the 'absent': 'something which should be there, but is not'.

From this point of view, the difficulty of achieving personal autonomy in modern Japanese society becomes clear: beyond Okonogi's particular understanding of human mentality, the question of the intimacy between mother and son and Japanese admiration of an 'idealized mother figure' is a common challenge for all in Japan. We cannot restore this idealized mother figure, and people suffer as a consequence. Okonogi stated that by learning about Freud, Kosawa 'became distressfully aware of a Japanese ethnic 'unconscious', and attempted to effect an inner unity with a Westernised form of consciousness'.[48] Kosawa's distress continues to haunt Japanese people whose aim is to achieve personal autonomy. Looking closely at the development of the Ajase Complex theory, as we have done here, shows us the problems and challenges not just within Japanese psychoanalysis but within Japanese society as a whole.

## Notes

1 Translated by Inoue Yoshinobu and Christopher Harding.
2 See Ando, this volume.
3 On Kosawa's time in Vienna, see Harding, 'The therapeutic method of Kosawa Heisaku'.
4 Takeda, *Seishinbunseki to Bukkyō*, p. 126.
5 Kosawa, 'Chichi, Kosawa Heisaku to Ajase Konpurekkusu'.
6 On Marui, and on Kosawa's relationship with him, see Blowers and Yang Hsueh Chi, 'Freud's deshi: the coming of psychoanalysis to Japan'.
7 Kitami, 'Senzen ni okeru Nihon no Seishinbunsekigaku Hattatsushi'.
8 Yamamura, 'Nihon Seishinbunseki Gakkai Nijūgonen no Ayumi wo Kaikoshite'.
9 Takeda, *Psychoanalysis and Buddhism*, p. 139.
10 Nishizono, 'Tōron: Ajase Konpurekkusu' p. 62.
11 Kobayashi (trans.) *Furoito Saigo no Nikki*.
12 Takeda, *Psychoanalysis and Buddhism*, p. 155.
13 First published as 'Freud', *Tōkyō Iji Shinshi* [Tokyo Medical New Journal] Vol. 3155 (1939); and in *Seishinbunseki Kenkyū* [The Japanese Journal of Psycho-Analysis] Vol. 1, No. 6 (1954).
14 Kosawa's son, Yorio, was sent on errands to Chikazumi's house on a couple of occasions.
15 The Ajase Complex continues to be recognized in the West as one of Japan's most prominent psychoanalytic theories. See, for example, Chikako Ozawa-de Silva, 'Demystifying Japanese Therapy: an Analysis of Naikan and the Ajase Complex Through Buddhist Thought', *Ethos* 35, no. 4 (December 2007).
16 Okonogi, 'Ajase Complex', p. 16.
17 See Iwata, 'Rekishi to Monogatari – Ajase Konpurekkusu no Seisei'.
18 Okonogi and Kitayama (eds), *The Ajase Complex*.
19 Chikazumi, *Zangeroku*. Sakurai has also pointed this out in his essay 'Zaiaku Ishiki no Nishu no Bukkyōteki Haikei'.

20 The emphasis on the mother–son relationship derives mainly from the Pāli Jātaka 338: 'Thusajātakaṃ'. It is very possible that Kosawa used Yasui Kōdo's *Idaike Hujin* [Queen Vaidehi] (1920), which draws upon Thusajātakaṃ, as a source of reference. On the possible origins of Kosawa's modification, see Michael Radich, *How Ajatasatru Was Reformed*; Daigūji and Moriguchi, 'Ajaseō Setsuwa no Higekika ni tsuite'; Moriguchi, 'Idaike no Hensen to Ajase Konpurekkusu'; and Sueki, *Kindai Nippon to Bukkyō*.
21 Kosawa, 'Zaiaku Ishiki no Nishu: Ajase Kompurekkusu', p. 83.
22 See, for example, Okonogi, *Nihonjin no Ajase Konpurekkusu*.
23 See, for example, Kawai, *Yungu Shinrigaku to Bukkyō*, especially pp. 99–106. Also, 'Kosawa-ban Ajase Monogatari no Shutten to sono Saikōsei Katei' [The reconstruction process and the source of Kosawa's version of the legend of Ajase] in Okonogi, *The Ajase Complex of the Japanese*.
24 Kosawa, 'Zaiaku Ishiki no Nishu: Ajase Kompurekkusu', pp. 75–76.
25 Kosawa, Ibid., p 76.
26 Chikazumi, *Zangeroku*.
27 Chikazumi Jōkan, *Jinsei to Shinkō*, p. 157.
28 For more on this shift from the father–son relationship to the mother–son relationship, see Yasui Kōdo's *Idaike Hujin*, and Fuji Shūkō's *Ajase ō*. I have argued this point elsewhere, in Iwata, 'Rekishi to Monogatari', while Michael Radich has provided valuable new details in Radich, *How Ajatasatru Was Reformed*, pp. 88–104.
29 Radich, *How Ajatasatru Was Reformed*, p. 89.
30 Kosawa Heisaku, 'The translator's postscript to The Freud Collection Vol. 3: Introduction to Psychoanalysis – Continued', in Okonogi and Kitayama (eds), *The Ajase Complex*, p. 86.
31 Chikazumi Jōkan, *Shinkō no Yoreki*, p. 14.
32 Chikazumi himself never specifically stated the situation in this way, but his written work strongly suggests it, for example 'Obasuteyama'.
33 Chikazumi, *Jiai to Shinjitsu*, pp. 30–33.
34 Doi, 'Kosawa Sensei to Nihonteki Seishinbunseki', p. 18. For detailed accounts of the relationship between Doi and Kosawa, see Ando's essay in this volume and Kumakura and Itō, *'Amae' riron no kenkyū* [Study of the 'Amae' Theory].
35 Maeda, *Jiyūrensōhō Oboegaki*.
36 Ibid, p. 220.
37 Ibid, p. 187.
38 For an account of Kosawa's final analytic sessions, with the novelist (and later Buddhist nun) Setouchi Harumi, see Harding, 'The therapeutic method'.
39 Okonogi, 'Ajase Konpurekkusuron no Tenkai', p. 47.
40 Okonogi, 'Nihonjin no Ajase Konpurekkusu'.
41 Doi, *'Amae' no Kōzō*; and Kawai, *Boseishakai Nihon no Byōri*.
42 Okonogi, *Nihonjin no Ajase Konpurekkusu*, p. 17.
43 Ibid. p. 69.
44 Ibid. p. 71.
45 Ibid. pp. 23–24.
46 Ibid. p. 39.
47 Okonogi, *Edipusu to Ajase*. Here, Okonogi discusses 'intergenerational transmission' in detail.
48 Okonogi, *Nihonjin no Ajase Konpurekkusu*, p. 71.

# References

Blowers, Geoffrey H and Yang Hsueh Chi, Serena, 'Freud's deshi: the coming of psychoanalysis to Japan', *Journal of the History of the Behavioral Sciences* 33, number 2 (1997).
Chikazumi Jōkan, *Jinsei to Shinkō [Life and Faith]* (Tokyo: Moriehonten, 1908).
Chikazumi Jōkan, *Zangeroku [Record of Repentance]* (19th edn) (Tokyo: Morieshoten, 1941).
Chikazumi Jōkan, *Jiai to Shinjitsu [Compassion and Truth]* (Kyoto: Teijiyashoten, 1954).
Chikazumi Jōkan, *Shinkō no Yoreki [Residue of Faith]* (Kyoto: Bunmeidō, 1974).
Daigūji Makoto and Moriguchi Mai, 'Ajaseō Setsuwa no Higekika ni tsuite' [On tragedizing the legend of Ajase], in *Indo Tetsugaku Bukkyōgaku [Indian Philosophy, Buddhist Studies]* Volume 20 (Sapporo, 2005).
Doi Takeo, '*Amae*' *no Kōzō [The Structure of 'Amae']* (Tokyo: Kōbundō, 1971).
Doi Takeo, 'Kosawa Sensei to Nihonteki Seishinbunseki [Kosawa and Japanese psychoanalysis]', *Seishinbunseki Kenkyū [The Japanese Journal of Psycho-Aanalysis]* Volume 24, Number 4 (1980).
Fuji Shūkō *Ajase ō [King Ajase]* (Kyoto: Zōkyōshoin, 1922).
Harding, Christopher, 'The therapeutic method of Kosawa Heisaku: "Religion" and "the psy disciplines"', *Japanese Contributions to Psychoanalysis Volume 4* (2013).
Iwata Fumiaki, 'Rekishi to Monogatari – Ajase Konpurekkusu no Seisei [History and stories: the formation of the Ajase complex]', in Hase Shōtō and Hosoya Masashi (eds) *Shūkyō no Kongensei to Gendai Dai Ikkan [Modernity and the Fundamentality of Religion, Volume One]* (Kyoto: Kōyōshobō, 2001).
Kawai Hayao, *Boseishakai Nihon no Byōri [Pathology of Japan as a Maternal Society]* (Tokyo: Chūōkōronsha, 1976).
Kawai Hayao, *Yungu Shinrigaku to Bukkyō [Jungian Psychology and Buddhism]* (Tokyo: Iwanamishoten, 1995).
Kitami Yoshio, 'Senzen ni okeru Nihon no Seishinbunsekigaku Hattatsushi [The history of the development of psychoanalysis in pre-war Japan]', *Seishinbunseki Kenkyū [The Japanese Journal of Psycho-Aanalysis]* Volume 3, Numbers 9–10 (1954).
Kobayashi Tsukasa (trans.) *Furoito Saigo no Nikki [The Diary of Sigmund Freud 1929-1939]* (Tokyo: Nihonkyōbunsha, 2004).
Kosawa Heisaku, 'Freud', in *Tōkyō Iji Zasshi [Tokyo Medical Journal]* Volume 3155 (1939).
Kosawa Heisaku, 'Freud', in *Seishinbunseki Kenkyū [The Japanese Journal of Psycho-Analysis]* Volume 1, Number 6 (1954).
Kosawa Heisaku, 'The translator's postscript to The Freud Collection Vol. 3: Introduction to Psychoanalysis – Continued', in *Ajase Konpurekkusu [The Ajase Complex]*, Okonogi Keigo and Kitayama Osamu (eds), (Osaka: Sōgensha, 2001).
Kosawa Heisaku, 'Zaiaku Ishiki no Nishu: Ajase Kompurekkusu [Two kinds of guilt feelings: the Ajase complex]', in Okonogi Keigo and Kitayama Osamu (eds), *Ajase Kompurekkusu [The Ajase Complex]* (Osaka: Sōgensha, 2001).
Kosawa Yorio, 'Chichi, Kosawa Heisaku to Ajase Konpurekkusu [Father: Kosawa Heisaku and the Ajase complex]', in Okonogi Keigo and Kitayama Osamu (eds), *Ajase Konpurekkusu [The Ajase Complex]* (Osaka: Sōgensha, 2001).
Kumakura Nobuhiro and Itō Masahiro, *'Amae' riron no kenkyū [Study of the 'Amae' Theory]* (Tokyo: Seiwashoten, 1984).

Maeda Shigeharu, *Jiyūrensōhō Oboegaki [Record of Free Association]* (Tokyo: Iwasakigakujyutsushuppansha, 1984).
Moriguchi Mai, 'Idaike no Hensen to Ajase Konpurekkusu [Vaidehi's transition and the Ajase complex]', in *Indo Tetsugaku Bukkyōgaku [Indian Philosophy, Buddhist Studies]* Volume 22 (Sapporo, 2007).
Nishizono Masahisa, 'Tōron: Ajase Konpurekkusu [Debate: The Ajase complex]', in Okonogi Keigo and Kitayama Osamu (eds), *Ajase Konpurekkusu [The Ajase Complex]* (Osaka: Sōgensha, 2001).
Okonogi Keigo, 'Nihonjin no Ajase Konpurekkusu [The Ajase complex of the Japanese]', *Chūō Kōron [Central Review]* (1978).
Okonogi Keigo, *Nihonjin no Ajase Konpurekkusu [The Ajase Complex of the Japanese]* (Tokyo: Chūōkōronsha, 1982).
Okonogi Keigo, 'Ajase complex', in *Iwanami tetugaku-shiso jiten [Iwanami Dictionary of Philosophy and Ideology]* (Tokyo: Iwanami Shoten, 1998).
Okonogi Keigo, *Edipusu to Ajase [Oedipus and Ajase]* (Tokyo: Seidosha, 1991).
Okonogi Keigo, 'Ajase Konpurekkusuron no Tenkai [Expansion of the Ajase complex theory]', in Okonogi Keigo and Kitayama Osamu (eds), *Ajase Konpurekkusu [The Ajase Complex]* (Osaka: Sōgensha, 2001).
Ozawa-de Silva, Chikako, 'Demystifying Japanese therapy: an analysis of Naikan and the Ajase complex through Buddhist thought', *Ethos* 35, number 4 (December 2007).
Radich, Michael, *How Ajatasatru Was Reformed* (Tokyo: The International Institute for Buddhist Studies, 2011).
Sakurai Akihiko, 'Zaiaku Ishiki no Nishu no Bukkyōteki Haikei [The Buddhist context of two types of guilt]', in Okonogi Keigo and Kitayama Osamu (eds), *Ajase Konpurekkusu [The Ajase Complex]* (Osaka: Sōgensha, 2001).
Sueki Humihiko, *Kindai Nippon to Bukkyō [Modern Japan and Buddhism]* (Tokyo: Toransubyū, 2004).
Takeda Makoto, *Seishinbunseki to Bukkyō [Psychoanalysis and Buddhism]* (Tokyo: Shinchōsha, 1990).
Yamamura Michio, 'Nihon Seishinbunseki Gakkai Nijūgonen no Ayumi wo Kaikoshite [Looking back at twenty-five years of the Japan Psychoanalytical Association]', *Seishinbunseki Kenkyū [The Japanese Journal of Psycho-Aanalysis]* Volume 24, Number 4 (1980).
Yasui Kōdo, *Idaike Hujin [Queen Vaidehi]* (Kyoto: Teijiyashoten, 1920).

# 6 Doi Takeo and the development of the 'Amae' theory

*Ando Yasunori*[1]

This chapter attempts to recapture the thought of the psychiatrist and psychoanalyst Doi Takeo (1920–2009),[2] assessing it from the point of view both of psycho-religious thought and Doi's own conflicts of identity: as a Japanese man, a Christian, and a part of the western tradition of psychoanalysis. The name of Doi Takeo is associated both inside and outside Japan with his first book for general readers, '*Amae' no Kōzō (Anatomy of Dependence*, 1971).[3] The term '*amae*' is often translated as 'emotional dependence', but this does not adequately convey its meaning. '*Amae*' is the noun form of the verb *amaeru*, and Doi himself explains the term in English as follows:

> Amaeru, can be translated as 'to depend and presume upon another's love.' This word has the same root as amai, an adjective which corresponds to 'sweet.' This amaeru has a distinct feeling of sweetness, and is generally used to express a child's attitude toward an adult, especially his parents. I can think of no English word equivalent to amaeru except for 'spoil,' which, however, is a transitive verb and definitely has a bad connotation; whereas the Japanese amaeru does not necessarily have a bad connotation, although we say we should not let a youngster amaeru too much. I think most Japanese adults have a dear memory of the taste of sweet dependency as a child and, consciously or unconsciously, carry a life-long nostalgia for it.[4]

Amongst dynamic psychiatrists and psychotherapists in modern Japan, particularly influential in recent years, through their research, clinical, and general publications (spanning society, culture, literature, history and religion), have been Okonogi Keigo (1930–2003), and Jung-school analyst Kawai Hayao (1928–2007).[5] Neither Okonogi nor Kawai, however, gained recognition for a particular book or concept in the way that Doi did with '*Amae' no Kōzō* and *amae*. '*Amae*' is a uniquely Japanese psychoanalytic theory: psychoanalyst Fujiyama Naoki praised it as the greatest contribution of the Japanese psychoanalytic community to psychoanalysis in the world, and indicated the commonality and parallelism between Doi's theory and some important psychoanalytic theories in the West in the latter half of the twentieth century such as those of Michael Balint, Wilfred Bion, and Donald Winnicott.[6]

It is widely known that the founders of psychoanalysis and analytical psychology, Freud and Jung, developed their theories and thoughts as a result of analyzing their own psychological conflicts, which were closely bound up with contemporary socio-cultural problems. The historian of psychiatry Henri Ellenberger developed the concept of 'creative illness' to refer to situations where these kinds of conflicts give rise to new theories and thoughts.[7] In the case of Freud, his period of self-analysis after his father Jacob's death and his interaction with Wilhelm Fließ[8] were crucial; in the case of Jung, his period of spiritual crisis after the break with Freud[9] was central to his development. This chapter argues that Doi's '*amae*' theory was also developed as a result of 'creative illness' and its overcoming, moving from a consideration of the *amae* theory and its reception in Japan to an analysis of how Doi's thought developed in the context of his life experiences.

## 'Amae' no Kōzō

Doi Takeo's book *'Amae' no Kōzō* has sold well ever since its initial publication in 1971, and it continues to be reprinted over forty years later. Of the various definitions used by Doi for the core concept of '*amae*', the two major ones are as follows:

1   Psychologically to deny the facts of separation, which are an intrinsic part of being human; to somehow sublate the pain of separation and obtain a sense of unity.
2   To depend and presume upon another's love. Doi considers that '*amae*' is both an infantile disposition to be overcome, and at the same time the source of healthy mental life. This duality is well expressed in his words, 'if it is unrealistic to cover your eye to the fact of separation, it is equally unrealistic to be overwhelmed by the fact of separation and isolated, out of depression, from the possibility of building human relationships.'[10]

After the English translation of *'Amae' no Kōzō* was published in 1973,[11] it was translated into seven other languages: French, German, Italian, Korean, Chinese, Indonesian and Thai. In the previous year, *Nihonjin to Yudayajin (The Japanese and the Jewish)* by Isaiah Ben-Dasan[12] was published, helping to create a fad for theories about the Japanese. Doi's book rode the crest of this wave, accepted as a kind of theory of the Japanese or Japanese culture. Cultural anthropologist Aoki Tamotsu discusses in his *'Nihon Bunka-ron' no Henyō (Transformation of 'Japanese Cultural Theories')* shifts in the Japanese sense of identity by tracing changes in theories about

Japanese culture and people in post-WWII Japan. Aoki cites *'Amae' no Kōzō* as an example of Japanese cultural theories he classifies as 'recognition of affirmative specificity' (typical of the period from 1964 to 1983).[13] During this period, Japanese people believed their nation to have become one of the major powers after achieving rapid economic growth, and so began positively to assess aspects of their characters or behaviour that had been viewed negatively in the past. Fujiyama Naoki, however, sees it as inappropriate to group *'amae'* with theories about the Japanese and Japanese culture: instead, Doi had expanded a specific Japanese term into a psychoanalytic concept while maintaining its implication as an ordinary word used in daily life; based on this concept he then interpreted various phenomena in everyday Japanese life. Thus, *'amae'* is a unique *psychoanalytical theory*, albeit with a broad range. Whether or not one agrees with Fujiyama, the *'amae'* theory should not be underestimated as a theory about the Japanese or Japanese culture.

Doi was torn apart by three conflicting identities: being Japanese, being a Christian and a Catholic, and being part of a discipline – psychoanalysis – rooted in western culture. He accepted the reality of conflict, and in the process of seeking integration his psychoanalytical ideas emerged. For Doi, being Japanese did not simply mean the natural fact of his birth and upbringing in Japan, his use of Japanese in daily life, and his possession of Japanese nationality. Rather, it involved a psychological challenge to 'confirm himself to be Japanese, consciously become Japanese and live as Japanese' while coping with the inconsistencies or conflicts inherent in also being a Christian and a psychoanalyst.

Many psychiatrists who have had contact with Doi agree that the attitude 'to think in Japanese – linguistically and conceptually – in a clinical office in Japan'[14] was a consistent feature in his psychological theory and its practice. Although psychoanalysis has only a small role in psychiatry and clinical psychology in Japan, Doi's publication *Hōhō toshiteno Mensetsu (Interviews as a method)*,[15] which can be said to be his therapeutic structure theory, has been strongly endorsed by psychiatrists, clinical psychologists, and students in these specialties and printed in a number of editions since its first publication in 1997. This is largely because the book was the first Japanese work systematically to discuss the structure and fundamentals of psychotherapy – remembering that despite the minority status of psychoanalytic *therapy*, as a form of cognition and view of the world it has been incorporated into many subsequent psychotherapeutic techniques and theories.[16] Doi's ability to describe this broader form of psychoanalytic cognition was inextricably linked with his ability to think reflectively and objectively about what it meant to be Japanese and use the Japanese language.

The *'amae'* theory dates, in embryonic form, from the 1950s – long before the publication of *'Amae' no Kōzō* for the general public. Fujiyama has noted that the *'amae'* theory appears clearly in Doi's thesis 'Shinkeishitsu no Seishin Byōri (The psychopathology of nervousness)' (1958)[17] and in his doctoral dissertation ' "Jibun" to "Amae" no Seishin Byōri ('the psychopathology of "myself" and "amae" ') (1960).[18]

In some of his publications, Doi revealed determinant experiences and encounters in his life up to that time. These included his youthful ideological explorations; conflicts and anguish over his Christian belief, followed by faith in Catholicism and his meeting with Father Heuvers, who became his life-time mentor; meeting and breaking with Kosawa Heisaku;[19] and three trips to the United States for study. Experiences during his time studying in the United States, and the culture shock he suffered while there, inspired him in developing his '*amae*' theory – readily described by Doi himself in a paper written in English in 1962, 'Amae',[20] and in '*Amae' no Kōzō* itself in 1971. In contrast, it was only in 1980, twelve years after the death of Kosawa Heisaku, that he described his relationship with Kosawa for the first time.[21] As for Father Heuvers, Doi wrote that 'I am too closely associated with him; I cannot take the necessary distance to write about him'. He finally put together an essay on the topic only in 1986.[22] Similarly, he was only able to talk about his childhood, youth, and early Christian life around 1990.[23]

## The early life of Doi Takeo

Doi Takeo was born the son of Suesaburo, a dentist, and his wife Midori in 1920. He spent his childhood under the strong influence of his mother who was an enthusiastic Protestant Christian.[24] From around the time he entered junior high school, Doi began to read the Bible and books about Christianity – especially, in his late teenage years, those by Uchimura Kanzō (1861–1930), an evangelist of Christianity in Japan, who led a Nonchurch Movement based on a combination of Evangelicalism and social criticism. Doi once said that 'Uchimura is always aware of being Japanese ... a witness of the age in which he lived'.[25] Although attracted by the spirit of Uchimura, Doi was disappointed that his Church failed to resist the ongoing inclination to war in the 1930s and 1940s. He was deeply disappointed, and began to be sceptical about his faith in Protestantism. He left the Church, and joined a group run by Yanaihara Tadao, another advocate of the Nonchurch Movement. But Doi soon became critical about the way that Yanaihara was promoted as the founder of a new sect, and he left the group after a year or so. Kügelgen's *Ichi Rōjin no Yōji no Tsuioku (An old man's recollection of childhood)*[26] opened Doi's eyes to Catholicism, after which time he began to empathize with a theological thesis offered by Sōichi Iwashita (1889–1940), a Catholic theologian well known for his devotion to the welfare of leprosy patients as the director of Kōyama Fukusei Hospital. Doi later dated his Catholicism back to this point.

But it was when Doi met Father Heuvers in 1942 that his firm lifelong Catholic belief began to emerge. He later wrote about being baptized by Father Heuvers: 'I thought that with this baptism, all the work I have to do has been completed. I even thought I could die now.'[27] Hermann Heuvers (1890–1977) was a German priest who came to Japan in 1923 as a Jesuit missionary. He served as a professor and chancellor of Sophia University, Tokyo, and as priest of Kōjimachi Catholic Church, and others. Doi gave two main points on which he agreed with, and respected, Heuvers' thought or attitudes. First, Heuvers had attempted to understand the characteristics of Japanese culture and the Japanese, and he clearly differentiated the essence of Christianity and European culture. Second, Heuvers saw deep 'religiosity' in everyday Japanese life. When he noticed that this religiosity was no different to the religiosity that defined the essence of Christianity, he became confident about the possibility of propagating Christianity in Japan.[28] Doi found this attitude of Heuvers a great support. For Doi, being Japanese and Christian was not a matter of the 'inculturation' or 'Japanization' of Christianity, as a western religion. Rather, it meant that he questioned how to live both as a Japanese person and as a follower of Christianity – as a universal religion essentially separate from western culture. It was Father Heuvers who provided him with the confidence to live in such a way. When Heuvers passed away in 1977, Doi wanted to cry out of deep emotion – happiness at having met someone like Father Heuvers. He recalled having a similar experience twenty-two years before, while he was in the US. He had been talking to someone about his first meeting with Father Heuvers back in 1942, and all of a sudden had begun to sob.[29] This episode may have occurred during a training analysis with Norman Leider in San Francisco (see below), in which case the coming together of memories of Father Heuvers with feelings of togetherness may have helped Doi in his formulation of his '*amae*' theory at this critical juncture in the development of his thought.

Doi's religious crisis and its resolution certainly became important in the formation of the '*amae*' theory in at least two ways. First, the attitude that he took trying to set psychoanalysis solidly in place in Japan closely resembled Heuvers' attitude in propagating Christianity.[30] Doi did not seek either to import psychoanalysis as a western scientific method and theory or to 'Japanize' it to fit the Japanese.[31] Instead, considering psychoanalysis to be universal he used the '*amae*' theory to show how psychoanalysis could be expressed in the language of everyday Japanese, and that psychoanalytic knowledge was already present, albeit hidden, in ordinary Japanese expressions. This brought him back to the roots of psychoanalysis: clinical attention to patients' narratives, and seeking psychoanalytic insights in literature[32] – in Doi's case this meant devotion to works by Japan's famed novelist Natsume Sōseki (1867–1916).[33] Doi sought, at the same time, to separate the knowledge of psychoanalysis from the context of western culture and to relativize it. Eventually, he shed light from a new direction on what Freud and other western psychoanalysts were vaguely aware of but for which they had not been able to provide clear explanations.

Second, Doi's religious and existential interest in the values by which humans can live was placed at the heart of his thought beyond his scientific interests. He was always conscious of this driving interest, and having graduated from medical school almost at the same time as he converted to Catholicism Doi later revealed that he had struggled to make up his mind about becoming a medical doctor because of the natural science-centrism where he studied and what he saw as the coldness of medical doctors in the university. When he did finally decide to become a medical doctor, the well-respected doctor Hashimoto Hirotoshi recommended that Doi join the class of Kakinuma Kōsaku of the first internal medicine department, but Doi turned this down, and joined the department of dermatology under Ōta Masao (1885–1945), who had been a student of Natsume Sōseki and who had himself worked as a writer using the pen name Kinoshita Mokutarō.[34]

## Meeting and breaking with Kosawa Heisaku

After WWII, while working as an internist, Doi developed an interest in the psychosomatic medicine that was gaining force at the time, and through this came across psychoanalysis and Kosawa Heisaku in 1949. This was the year that Kosawa formed the Japan Psychoanalytic Study Group, which later developed into the Japan Psychoanalytic Society (1955). Doi came to know him when Kosawa initiated the building of an organized foundation for psychoanalysis in Japan. On Kosawa's recommendation, Doi made his first visit to the United States in 1950–1952 to study at the influential Menninger Clinic.[35] After returning to Japan, he underwent a training analysis with Kosawa.

As early as the second year of his training analysis, Doi came to harbour strong doubts about Kosawa's approach to psychoanalysis. He left Kosawa in 1954, and the following year returned to the United States to study psychoanalysis in earnest. Doi's criticisms of Kosawa focused first on Kosawa's 'very Japanese method known as the melting technique':[36] melting the hatred that patients (analysands) direct towards therapists (analysts) using a kind of selfless love. This technique, in Kosawa's case, involved the blending of psychoanalytic knowledge with faith in Buddhism, and Doi felt that Kosawa's 'therapist' consciousness was swallowed by a religiously inspired 'saviour' consciousness – Kosawa seemed unable to separate one from the other.[37] This basic stance prevented Kosawa from remaining present to what patients said during analytic sessions; instead, Kosawa was concerned primarily with 'saving' these patients. As Doi observed, 'It is more accurate to say that the way he treated his patients was inspired more by Buddhism than by the information provided by patients. As a result, his treatment seemed to act suggestively on patients'.[38] Given the roots of psychoanalysis in patients' free association, Doi doubted that Kosawa's method could be considered genuine psychoanalysis.

Around this time Doi began to notice the particular implications of the Japanese word '*amae*' for the first time. He wrote his thesis 'Fuan Shinkeishō no Bunseki Rei (A psychoanalytic case study of anxiety neurosis)'[39] in 1953. It has been claimed that Kosawa commented to Doi that he should not use the word '*amae*' because it suggested an 'unfavourable' attitude. This may have been the reason why Doi did not use the term in his Japanese theses until he broke with Kosawa.

## America and the '*amae*' theory

During his second period of study in the United States (1955–1956) Doi was enrolled in the San Francisco Psychoanalytic Institute, where he received a training analysis from Norman Leider. Doi later said that this training analysis was full of 'frustration', and that 'an earnest self-analysis of the reason for the frustration' resulted in his conceptualization of '*amae*'.[40] Having left behind Kosawa's Japanized psychoanalysis, and striving to keep a distance from a (religious) saviour consciousness that he may have detected within himself, Doi appeared to have tried to learn psychoanalysis as a science at the best place he could find. He was surprised to find, however, that with only a small number of exceptions such as Leider, American analysts were insensitive towards patients' 'helplessness', and their feelings of loneliness and anxiety with no one to depend on. This led Doi to question the excessive scientific orientation of American psychoanalysis, a kind of faith in science that he found in it. While Kosawa's Japanese-style psychoanalysis did not separate psychotherapy from religious and cultural values, and thus, could not objectivize and analyze '*amae*', American psychoanalysis severed psychotherapy and religious and cultural values to the extent that it was oblivious of '*amae*' as a fundamental emotion. One could say that Doi developed the theory of '*amae*' as a means of overcoming these two styles of psychoanalysis at the same time. Doi sought a theory of psychotherapy that would be free of integration with specific religious and cultural values, yet would remain open to them.

One element of Doi's developing thought here can be seen in 'Some thoughts on helplessness and the desire to be loved', published in English in 1963.[41] In this thesis, Doi referred to the word 'helplessness' as it was used in Freud's *The Future of an Illusion*.[42] Doi discussed the apparent insensitivity of western people to the desire to be loved, relating it to their cultural values emphasizing independence and self-help. Freud defined religion, in *The Future of an Illusion*, as a remnant in adulthood of infantile narcissism: underlying this were feelings of helplessness in infants and the desire for or illusion of protection by an almighty father – God. Doi argued that Freud himself was dissatisfied with *The Future of an Illusion*, and the helplessness that he had identified in that book "was still too keen to be replaced by a belief in the progress of science".[43] For Doi, the essence of psychoanalysis lay not in negating such helplessness or powerlessness, but continuing to face it. Doi repeatedly emphasizes that although the sentiment of '*amae*' (and the expression of that sentiment using the term '*amae*') is specific to the Japanese, the desire to depend and presume upon another's love is universal. The sentiment of '*amae*' as the Japanese experience it becomes available to westerners, Doi thought, only with the aid of psychoanalysis. Otherwise, they may experience it as a kind of religious sentiment towards, for example, the Blessed Virgin Mary.[44]

Doi also argued that whereas in the West psychoanalysis' emergence as an alternative to religion, together with its ideal of itself as separated from religious tradition, resulted in a quasi-religious movement, in Japan links with religion were never denied and so there was no such negative effect on the Japanese movement.[45] Later in life Doi affirmed that 'practicing psychoanalysis does not mean that I believe in psychoanalysis.'[46] His disappointment in American psychoanalysis had taught him that he had a tendency to idealize psychoanalysis as it was practised in the United States and other western countries – depending on it, with a kind of '*amae*'. He seems to have found that in order to study genuine psychoanalysis and to be able freely to administer it as a therapy, he needed first to recognize his own '*amae*' – his own 'helplessness' – and to continue to confront it. His theory of '*amae*' came from precisely this realization.

A further significant insight into how Doi understood the relationship between religion and psychoanalysis comes in his short article 'Seishin Ryōhō to Shinkō (Psychoanalysis and faith)'[47] written in 1971 – the same year as '*Amae' no Kōzō*. He was inspired to write the article when one of his patients, who recovered after a difficult therapeutic process, said to him: 'Maybe you have not noticed, but I learned to pray from you'.[48] Doi was struck by this comment, because unlike Kosawa he was strict about not bringing his religious faith into the treatment room. Why did this patient feel that he had learned to 'pray' from Doi? Doi interpreted this comment by way of a concept of 'hidden faith'. In order to concentrate fully on his clients without falling into their despair, Doi held to the idea that light could somehow be cast on their situation. That light could not come from Doi himself, since that would make him too much like Kosawa – as a bearer of religious light. Instead, Doi was confident that this light would come of its own accord, as though from outside. This is what he meant by 'hidden faith', and it was in this sense that he could say: 'My faith as a psychiatrist casts light on every dark aspect that a patient shows me'.[49] Although Doi does not refer to the relationship between this 'hidden faith' and his own Catholic faith, the implication is that for Doi his religious self and his professional therapist self were not integrated (unlike in Kosawa's case), but rather these selves were contiguous.

## Conclusion

The theory of 'amae' was formulated in the context of Doi's efforts to integrate his triple identities: being Japanese, being a Christian and a Catholic follower, and being part of a psychoanalytic tradition rooted in western culture. Throughout his life, these three elements functioned as a catalyst for his ideas, as he sought to relativize them and look at each of them objectively. As a Christian and a psychoanalyst he was in a minority in at least two senses, and this encouraged him to live his Japaneseness not as something self-evident but via self-conscious, even existential efforts. Likewise, being both Japanese and Christian provided him with a means of grasping and verbalizing the essence of psychoanalysis that was unavailable to western psychoanalysts. Finally, being Japanese and having studied psychoanalysis seems to have helped Doi's Catholic faith to be a 'living faith' – without dependence upon or subordination to any specific cultural concept. Doi's theory of 'amae' and his work in general are examples of first-rate psycho-religious thought developed by struggling with and overcoming his 'creative illness'.[50]

## Notes

1 Translated by Hayashi Chine.
2 Doi's professional positions included Head Doctor of Neuropsychiatry, St. Luke's International Hospital (1957–1971), Professor of Medicine, the University of Tokyo (1971–1980), Professor, International Christian University (1980–1982), and Director, National Institute of Mental Health (1983–1985).
3 Doi, 'Amae' no Kozo.
4 Doi, 'Japanese language as an expression of Japanese psychology' p. 92.
5 See Tarutani, this volume.
6 Fujiyama, '"Amae" Riron no Taisho Kankeiron-teki Ganchiku'.
7 Ellenberger, *The Discovery of the Unconscious*.
8 Shertok and de Saussure, *The Therapeutic Revolution*.
9 Homans, *Jung in Context*.
10 Doi, 'Amae' no Kōzō.
11 Doi, *The Anatomy of Dependence*.
12 Ben-Dasan (translated by Yamamoto, Shichihei), *Nihonjin to Yudayajin*. It was later revealed that the author, Isaiah Ben-Dasan, was fictitious, and the real author was the translator, Yamamoto, who was the president of the publisher of the first edition as well as a critic.
13 Aoki, '*Nihon Bunka-ron' no Henyo: Sengo Nihon no Bunka to Identity*, p. 81.
14 Kano, 'Rikidō Seishin Igaku to Doi no Shigoto', p. 331.
15 Doi, *Hōhō toshiteno Mensetsu*. Reproduced in *Doi Takeo Senshu*.
16 Ando, 'Seishin Bunseki to Spirituality.
17 Doi, 'Shinkeishitsu no Seishin Byōri – tokuni "toraware" no Seishin Rikigaku ni tsuite'. (Reproduced in *Doi Takeo Senshu* 1).
18 Doi, '"Jibun" to "Amae" no Seishin Byōri'. (Reproduced in *Doi Takeo Senshu* 1.
19 See Iwata, this volume.
20 Doi, 'Amae: A key concept for understanding Japanese personality structure'. (Japanese version '"Amae" – Nihonjin no Personality Kōzō wo Rikaisuru tameno Kagi Gainen', in *Doi Takeo Senshu* 2.)

21. Doi, 'Kosawa Heisaku Sensei to Nihonteki Seishin Bunseki'. Reproduced in *Doi Takeo Senshu* 8.
22. Doi and Togawa (eds), *Heuvers Shinpu no Kotoba.*
23. Doi, *Shinkō to 'amae'.*
24. Later Doi's father Suesaburo met Father Heuvers, introduced by Takeo, and became a follower of the Catholic Church in 1943.
25. Doi, 'Uchimura Kanzō ni okeru Ningen Keisei to Christianity'. Later reproduced in *Shinko to 'Amae'.*
26. Kügelgen, *Ichi Rōjin no Yōji no Tsuioku (An old man's recollection of childhood)* translated by Ihara Motoji et al.
27. Doi, *Shinko to 'Amae'*, p. 198.
28. Doi, 'Heuvers Shimpu ni okeru Christianity to Nippon'.
29. Doi, 'Death of Father Heuvers'. Later reproduced in Doi, *Shinko to 'Amae'.*
30. Psychoanalyst Kitayama Osamu sees Doi as having 'considered Christian propagation and the import of psychoanalysis in the same context.' He also points out that 'when Doi was talking late in life about Father Heuvers, it seemed that he was talking about himself'. Kitayama, 'Freud Seishin Bunseki-gaku to Doi Takeo no "Kakutō" aruiwa "Teikō" ni tsuite', pp. 337–344.
31. More than 30 years after the establishment of his '*amae*' theory, Doi said 'the reason I developed the "amae" theory was not that I intended to Japanize psychoanalysis, rather, I wanted to make it more universal'. Doi, 'Sōseki to Seishin Bunseki'. Reproduced in *Doi Takeo Senshu* 7.
32. His attention to everyday expressions and seeing pioneers of psychoanalytic knowledge in literary people seem to follow Freud's process of creating psychoanalysis. When the English edition of the collection of Freud's works was promoted, Bruno Bettelheim made the criticism that the American style of 'specialized, medicalized psychoanalysis' was a distortion of Freud's thought. Cf. Bettelheim, *Freud and Man's Soul.* Doi seems to have been ahead of Bettelheim in making this point.
33. Doi, *Sōseki no Shinteki Sekai.* Reproduced in *Doi Takeo Senshu* 7.
34. Cf. Kumakura, 'Comment'.
35. Karl Menninger (1893–1990) was a renowned psychoanalyst in the United States, and the Menninger Clinic was one of the major organizations in the 1950s via which psychoanalysis exerted an influence on US psychiatry. See Fine, *A History of Psychoanalysis.* Doi studied psychoanalytic psychiatry there, rather than receiving a full-fledged training analysis. On Kosawa Heisaku's work with Karl Menninger, see Harding, 'The therapeutic method of Kosawa Heisaku: "Religion" and "the psy disciplines"'.
36. See Iwata, this volume.
37. Doi, 'Kosawa Heisaku sensei to Nihonteki Seishin Bunseki'.
38. Ibid, p. 230.
39. Doi, 'Fuan Shinkeishō no Bunseki Rei – Taikō Ten-i no Mondai'.
40. Doi, *Seishin Bunseki.*
41. Doi, 'Some thoughts on helplessness and the desire to be loved'. Reproduced in Doi, *Seishin Igaku to Seishin Bunseki.* In chapter 1 of '*Amae' no Kōzō* (1971) (p. 21), Doi touched upon this thesis and summarized it as follows: 'I started with psychiatric facts, and discussed differences in cultural background between the west and Japan. The standard of independence which is considered as the basic condition for psychoanalysis or psychotherapy is appropriate as a goal for patients to reach. However, it does not serve as a guiding principle in the process of treatment. If a therapist merely adheres to the standard, he may cause his patients to be left in a helpless condition, and he may not be able to understand patients' feelings. In short, I considered the American situation of

psychotherapy critically from the perspective of "amae," and at the same time I threw a question at contemporary western civilization'.
42 Freud, *The Future of an Illusion*.
43 *Doi Takeo Senshu* 8, p. 290.
44 Cf. Doi 'Amae: A key concept for understanding Japanese personality structure'.
45 Doi, 'Seishin Bunseki Ryōhō to Bunkateki Haikei (Psychoanalytic Therapies and their Cultural Background),' in *Japanese Journal of Psychotherapy*, 21 (1), pp. 6–11, (reproduced in *Doi Takeo Senshu* 8).
46 Doi, *Seishin Bunseki*, p. 9.
47 Doi, 'Seishin Ryōhō to Shinkō'. Reproduced in *Doi Takeo Senshu* 8.
48 Doi, *Doi Takeo Senshu* 8, p. 39.
49 Doi, *Doi Takeo Senshu* 8, p. 45.
50 For further reading in English, see Doi, 'The concept of *amae* and its psychoanalytic implications'; 'The cultural assumptions of psychoanalysis'; 'Psychotherapy: A cross-cultural perspective from Japan'; and Johnson, *Dependency and Japanese Socialization, Psychoanalytic and Anthropological Investigations into 'Amae'*.

## References

Ando Yasunori, 'Seishin Bunseki to Spirituality (Psychoanalysis and spirituality)', in Tsuruoka Yoshio and Fukazawa Hidetaka (eds), *Spirituality no Shukyō-shi Jōkan (Religious History of Spirituality Volume 1)* (Tokyo: Lithon, 2010), pp. 373–397.

Aoki Tamotsu, *'Nihon Bunka-ron' no Henyo: Sengo Nihon no Bunka to Identity (Transformation of 'Japanese Culture Theories': Japanese Culture and Identity in postwar days)* (Tokyo: Chuō Kōron-sha, 1990).

Ben-Dasan, Isaiah, (translated by Yamamoto, Shichihei), *Nihonjin to Yudayajin (The Japanese and the Jewish)* (Tokyo: Yamamoto Shoten, 1970).

Bettelheim, Bruno, *Freud and Man's Soul* (New York: Alfred A. Knopf, 1982).

Doi Takeo, 'Fuan Shinkeishō no Bunseki Rei – Taikō Ten-i no Mondai (A psychoanalytic case study of anxiety neurosis: problems of counter-transference)', *Seishin Bunseki Kenkyūkai Kaihō* (Psychoanalytic Study Group Bulletin), Vol. 2 No.2 (1953). pp. 1–6.

Doi Takeo, 'Japanese language as an expression of Japanese psychology', *Western Speech* 20(2) (1956).

Doi Takeo, 'Shinkeishitsu no Seishin Byōri – tokuni "toraware" no Seishin Rikigaku ni tsuite (Psychopathology of nervousness, especially psychological dynamics of "obsession")', in *Seishin Shinkei-gaku Zasshi (Psychiatria et Neurologia Japonica)* 60 (1958), pp. 733–744.

Doi Takeo, 'Amae: A key concept for understanding Japanese personality structure', in R.J. Smith and R.K. Beardsley (eds), *Japanese Culture: Its Development and Characteristics* (Chicago: Aldine Pub Co, 1962).

Doi Takeo, 'Some thoughts on helplessness and the desire to be loved,' *Psychiatry*, 26 (1963), pp. 266–272.

Doi Takeo, *Sōseki no Shinteki Sekai (Sōseki's Mental World)* (Tokyo: Shibundo, 1969).

Doi Takeo, *'Amae' no Kōzō* (Tokyo: Kōbundō, 1971).

Doi Takeo, 'Seishin Ryōhō to Shinkō (Psychoanalysis and faith)', in *Kokoro to Shakai (Mind and Society)*, 4 (1971).

Doi Takeo, *The Anatomy of Dependence: The Key Analysis of Japanese Behavior* (J. Bester, trans.) (Tokyo: Kodansha International, 1973).

Doi Takeo, 'Death of Father Heuvers', *Catholic Weekly of Japan,* July 10, 1977.
Doi Takeo, *Hōhō toshiteno Mensetsu (Interviews as a Method)* (Tokyo: Igaku-shoin, 1977).
Doi Takeo, 'Kosawa Heisaku Sensei to Nihonteki Seishin Bunseki (Prof. H. Kosawa and Japanese-style psychoanalysis)', in *Seishin Bunseki Kenkyū (Japanese Journal of Psychoanalysis)* 24 (4) (1980).
Doi Takeo, 'Uchimura Kanzō ni okeru Ningen Keisei to Christianity (Character formation and Christianity in Kanzō Uchimura)', in *Gendai no Esprit No. 117 Tensai no Seishin Byōri (Psychopathology in Geniuses)* (Tokyo: Shibundo, 1982).
Doi Takeo, 'Psychotherapy: A cross-cultural perspective from Japan', P.B. Pederson, N. Satorius, A.J. Marsella (eds), *Mental Health Services, The Cross-Cultural Context* (New York: Sage Publications, 1984).
Doi, 'Heuvers Shimpu ni okeru Christianity to Nippon (Christianity in Father Heuvers and Japan),' in Doi and Togawa (eds), *Heuvers Shinpu no Kotoba (Words by Heuvers)* pp. 108–153 (Tokyo: Kōbundō, 1986).
Doi Takeo, *Seishin Bunseki (Psychoanalysis)* (Tokyo: Kōdansha Gakujutsu Bunko, 1988).
Doi Takeo, 'The concept of *amae* and its psychoanalytic implications', *International Review of Psychoanalysis*, 16(3) (1989).
Doi Takeo, '"Jibun" to "Amae" no Seishin Byōri (Psychopathology of "myself" and "Amae")' in *Seishin Shinkeigaku Zasshi (Psychiatria et Neurologia Japonica)* 62 (1990).
Doi Takeo, *Shinkō to 'amae' (Faith and 'Amae')* (Tokyo: Shunjusha, 1990).
Doi Takeo, 'The cultural assumptions of psychoanalysis', in J.W. Stigler, R.A. Schweder and G. Herdt (eds), *Cultural Psychology, Essays on Comparative Human Development* (Cambridge: Cambridge University Press, 1990).
Doi Takeo, '"Amae" – Nihonjin no Personality Kōzō wo Rikaisuru tameno Kagi Gainen', in *Takeo Doi Selection* 2 (Tokyo: Iwanami Shoten, 2000), pp. 9–29.
Doi Takeo, *Doi Takeo Senshu* 8, Iwanami Shoten, 2000.
Ellenberger, Henri F., *The Discovery of the Unconscious, The History and Evolution of Dynamic Psychiatry* (New York: Basic Books, 1970).
Fine, Reuben, *A History of Psychoanalysis* (New York: Columbia University Press, 1979).
Freud, Sigmund, *The Future of an Illusion* (London: Hogarth Press, 1927).
Fujiyama Naoki, '"Amae" Riron no Taisho Kankeiron-teki Ganchiku (Object relations theoretical implication of the amae theory)', in *Seishin Bunseki Kenkyū (Japanese Journal of Psycho-analysis)* 54 (4) (2010).
Harding, Christopher, 'The therapeutic method of Kosawa Heisaku: "Religion" and "the Psy Disciplines"', in Ogawa Toyoaki (ed.), *Japanese Contributions to Psychoanalysis Volume 4* (Tokyo: Japan Psychoanalytical Society, December 2013).
Homans, Peter, *Jung in Context* (Chicago: University of Chicago Press, 1979).
Johnson, F.A., *Dependency and Japanese Socialization, Psychoanalytic and Anthropological Investigations into 'Amae'* (New York: New York University Press, 1993).
Kano Rikihachirō, 'Rikidō Seishin Igaku to Doi no Shigoto (Dynamic psychiatry and Doi's work)' in *Seishin Bunseki Kenkyū (Japanese Journal of Psycho-Analysis)*, 54 (4) (2010), pp. 331–336.
Kitayama Osamu, 'Freud Seishin Bunseki-gaku to Doi Takeo no "Kakutō" aruiwa "Teikō" ni tsuite (Freud's psychoanalysis and Takeo Doi's "struggles" or "resistance")', in *Japanese Journal of Psychoanalysis*, 54 (4) (2010).

Kügelgen, *Ichi Rōjin no Yōji no Tsuioku (An Old Man's Recollection of Childhood)* translated by Ihara Motoji et al (Tokyo: Iwanami Shoten, 1938).

Kumakura Nobuhiro, 'Comment', *Doi Takeo Senshu* 8 (Tokyo: Iwanami Shoten, 2000).

Shertok, Leon and de Saussure, Raymond, *The Therapeutic Revolution, From Mesmer to Freud* (New York: Brunner/Mazel, 1979).

# 7 From salvation to healing
## Yoshimoto Naikan therapy and its religious origins

*Shimazono Susumu*[1]

### Introduction: between religion and psychotherapy

Psychotherapy is a way of healing mental illness and distress by applying techniques rooted in rational understandings of the mind's structure and dynamic state. It occupies an important position in modern psychiatric medicine and clinical psychology. So what is the original source of its development? It may seem that scientific psychological therapy developed in tandem with the systematic accumulation of knowledge about the mind by modern science, but in fact the history of psychotherapy can be traced back many centuries beforehand. A classic book on the history of psychotherapy in the West is *The Discovery of the Unconscious*, by Henri Ellenberger.[2] Its subtitle – *The History and Evolution of Dynamic Psychiatry* – refers to a method of psychological therapy that uses the concept of 'unconsciousness', and which seeks a scientific understanding of the mind by directing attention to its hidden depths and to the dynamic relations that exist between unconsciousness and consciousness. It is largely associated with Sigmund Freud, but around the same time Pierre Janet, Alfred Adler and Carl Gustav Jung also established their own forms of dynamic psychiatry. Even these four scholars, however, were preceded by 'primary dynamic psychiatry'.

Chapter One of *The Discovery of the Unconscious*, entitled 'The ancestry of psychotherapy', discusses 'primitive psychotherapy' or 'primitive therapy'. Ellenberger gives the example of a shamanic therapy that returns the soul to the body of a person whose sickness was rooted in the soul's departure. Other examples of primitive therapy include a person whose illness was caused by the invasion of a certain substance, and another who was possessed by a demon – healing in these cases involved the use of a rite to clear away the foreign substance or the demon. There are many other such examples of primitive therapy, which do not have the separation of mind and body as a precondition. Clearly, psychological approaches perform a very important role in healing not only mental diseases but also physical diseases.

Postulating the separation of mind and body, modern medicine attempted to apply purely natural-scientific therapies in medical care, largely excluding psychological approaches. It sought to specify physiological causes, and to rely on chemical and physical treatments, even for mental illness. The development of dynamic psychiatry represented a restoration of psychological approaches, with links to 'primitive therapy', although primitive therapy and dynamic psychiatry are not, of course, identical. The difference between the two can be clarified by looking into the background of the establishment of the 'first dynamic psychiatry' in 1775. Chapter Two of Ellenberger's account, 'The emergence of dynamic psychiatry', recalls an incident that occurred in southern Germany in 1779. At that time, a Catholic priest named Johann Joseph Gassner attracted people's attention as an exorcist who, through prayer, had ordered a demon to depart from a person in whom it was causing illness.

An increasing number of people at this time viewed such things with scepticism and in June 1779 the liege lord and priest of Regensburg ordered an inquisition. Although the decision went in favour of Gassner, a subsequent inquisition ordered by the electoral prince of Bavaria decided against him. Dr Franz Anton Mesmer was called to give evidence, a man known for his discovery of a new principle called 'animal magnetism'. Mesmer conducted an open experiment: he had a patient go into convulsions and explained that since these were caused by animal magnetism they could also be cured by animal magnetism. He said that what Gassner considered a disease caused by the action of the devil and curable by exorcists was in fact caused by the action of animal magnetism. According to Mesmer, Gassner is not a bluffer: he cured his patients with animal magnetism without knowing it. Partially because of the result of this open experiment, the Court in Vienna requested the liege lord and priest of Legensberg to expel Gassner. An inquisition at the Holy See concluded that although exorcising evil spirits could be allowed, caution was required in its practice.

Ellenberger saw these incidents as marking the emergence of dynamic psychiatry. Catholic exorcism as represented by Gassner had been the continuance of primitive therapy in a different style: people in these traditions believed in the power of mysterious or supernatural beings such as God, demons and evil spirits, and understood disease and treatment in terms of interaction between humans and these beings. In fact, they were working on patients psychologically, but they perceived their work in terms of mysterious beings. In contrast, the 'animal magnetism' postulated by Mesmer was difficult to detect directly with the five senses, but it was of a type with other phenomena in the natural world and was a force without independent personality or will. By assuming an impersonal force in this way, Mesmer predicted that humans would become subjects able to control our own minds and bodies, through the application of psychological approaches based on rational knowledge. In this way, dynamic psychiatry was brought into being. Mesmer's victory over Gassner was the victory of dynamic psychiatry over 'primitive therapy'.

According to Ellenberger, psychological therapy in dynamic psychiatry emerged by giving religious 'primitive therapy' a rationalist, psychological make-over – a process initiated by Mesmer in 1775, carried on through New Mesmerism by Marquis de Puységur (who considered hypnotism to have therapeutic potential), and into the work of psychiatrists such as J.M. Charcot and H. Berheim. Finally, around 1900, the 'New Dynamic Psychiatry' of Freud and others began to flourish.

This line of development from Mesmer to Freud was not, however, the only one running from religion into modern psychotherapy. Mesmerism was introduced into the United States, where it brought forth a healer called Phineas Parkhurst Quimby. Quimby believed in the 'cure of disease by changing one's thoughts', and he became the father of the New Thought and Christian Science movements, which continue today both as psychotherapeutic and religious healing movements.[3] As healing movements, they have gained strong popular support, equalling that of purely rationalistic psychological therapy. Still other, newer religious movements gained popular support in the 1960s in the United States, and in the 1970s in Japan: 'New Age' in the United States and the 'Spiritual World' in Japan.[4] They are aggregates of amorphous movements and networks with no clearly stated doctrines or specifically religious forms of organization. Even so, they share common ideas and attitudes, emerging in major cities around the world almost simultaneously: let us call them 'New Spirituality Movements'.[5]

A characteristic of these New Spirituality Movements is that they do not consider science and religion to be truly in conflict with each other, but rather as capable of integration into a single entity from which new cosmic views or worldviews will emerge. In these Movements, the ideas and practices of psychotherapy and religious healing play major roles. *Seishin Ryōhō to Meisō* [Psychotherapy and Meditation] (1991), listed seventy-seven types of 'therapy and meditation'.[6] They included psychotherapies recognized scientifically ('academism') including family therapy, client-centred counselling and logical therapy; those usually considered to belong to the world of religion such as Tibetan Tantric Buddhism, Cabala, Steiner; and finally, methods that cannot readily be classified as either religion or science such as manipulative treatment, Holotropic Breathwork, and biosynthesis. Those who were attracted by the New Spirituality Movements – mainly young people – considered that these elements altogether structure a single world.

For our purposes here we shall refer to these psychotherapeutic and religious healing movements collectively as a 'psycho-religious composite movement'. By taking this broad view of the psycho-religious composite movement, a deeper understanding of the meaning of transformations in thought and attitude widely observable in modern society – in other words, from religion to psychotherapy, or from salvation to healing – can be achieved.

Some Japanese new religions exhibit characteristics of the psycho-religious composite movement. Hito-no-michi, founded in 1925 by Miki Tokuharu (1871–1938), and Seichō-no-ie, founded in 1930 by Taniguchi Masaharu (1893–1985), are typical.[7] A remarkable characteristic observed in both is their teaching on changing one's way of thinking. The core of their teachings is that evil and unhappiness arise because people have a negative way of thinking, and if they would only change their way of thinking, their fates would change and they would become happier. Most new religions in Japan have a strong interest in helping people to change their fates in this world. Measures employed to this end include magic, prayer, rites, ethical practice in daily life, missionary work, and voluntary activities. In addition, Hito-no-michi and Seichō-no-ie emphasize the importance of individual members changing their way of thinking. As changing one's way of thinking, deepening faith, and carrying out various practices are often closely related, changing one's way of thinking can be said to be important too even in religions that differ from Hito-no-michi and Seichō-no-ie.[8]

This faith that one's fate can be improved by changing one's way of thinking came into being to replace the belief in intervention by a transcendent power which had been a feature of much traditional religion. Instead of praying to bring about healing through God's power, as practised in the past, New Religions in Japan attempt to bring healing by encouraging their followers to 'change their ways of thinking', here and now. In addition to a waning of belief in the intervention of a divine power, there are social dynamics at work here: in complicated human relations in urban society, for example, there is a higher risk that anxiety or fear of strangers might prevent people from successfully adapting to their surroundings. 'Changing one's way of thinking', then, is associated with the practical effects of improving people's social interactions through the skilful control of their psychological processes in certain contexts. One might argue that religions of this type are simply adopting techniques and modes of thought common to rational thinking and to the pragmatic understanding of human psychological functioning. The shared territory with scientific psychotherapy here, in deploying pragmatic and technical approaches to the mind, is in part a legacy of the inroads into Japanese religion made by psychotherapeutic elements in the context of the broader New Spirituality Movement since the 1970s.

Some scholars view this change from the perspective of societal mores: in modern society, transcendental legislators such as God or absolute ethical norms become less and less acceptable. Instead, ethical attitudes that attach value to peace of mind and to adaptation to the environment occupy a superior position – Philip Rieff and Robert Bellah call this a 'psychotherapeutic attitude'.[9] They argue that a process of transition in the symbolic system that solves ethical conflicts from religion to psychotherapy has been ongoing through modern times down to the present day.

154  *Shimazono Susumu*

New Religions in Japan tend to possess the psychotherapeutic characteristics referred to by Rieff and Bellah – particularly so organizations such as Seichō-no-ie and Hito-no-michi.

Religious movements incorporating significant psychotherapeutic elements constitute a part of our category of the psycho-religious composite movement. Within the psycho-religious composite movement one can observe activities that are much closer to secular scientific psychotherapy than to religious activities, traditionally understood. Indicative movements established by the mid-twentieth century include Morita Masatake's Morita Therapy[10] and Yoshimoto Ishin's (1916–88) Yoshimoto Naikan therapy. These two therapies are generally regarded as unique to the cultural climate of Japan; both are recognized as rational psychotherapies in the world of psychiatry and psychology and generally enjoy acceptance in academic circles. However, there has been little attempt to understand them as psycho-religious movements or as a phenomenon close to religious movements, with the important exception of Chikako Ozawa-de Silva's recent anthropological work.[11] In this chapter Yoshimoto Naikan will be explored as an exemplar of the psycho-religious composite movement. Through this case study, keys will be found to understand how the changes in society have caused the evolution from religion to psychotherapy, and from salvation to healing, clarifying what has happened in the relationship between religion and the mind in Japanese society in the late modern period and since.

## Yoshimoto Naikan

Yoshimoto Naikan is noted by psychologists and psychiatrists in Japan as a technique of psychotherapy that has developed out of Japanese culture.[12] Yoshimoto Ishin, the founder of this technique, called it simply 'Naikan', but as the term 'Naikan' is used in various other ways besides, this therapy is generally called Yoshimoto Naikan to avoid confusion. Its essence is that a participant stays in a one-metre square space created by screen partitions for one week, engaged in focused introspection on the subject of his or her past relationships with others. The participant sits and meditates in this small space from 5:30 a.m. to 9:00 p.m., with breaks for meals, baths, and interviews with a guide. This meditation activity is called 'Naikan', literally 'looking inwards'. The style of sitting is not regulated, allowing each person to adopt a posture that they find relaxing.

The principal purpose of Naikan in looking back upon one's relationships with others is to ask 'What he/she did for me', 'What I did for him/her in return', and 'What troubles I caused him/her'. A standard time distribution is for about 20 per cent of the overall meditation to be spent on each of the first two subjects, with the remaining 60 per cent dedicated to 'troubles that I caused others'. Most participants begin with their relationship with their mother. Starting with the early years of their elementary school days, they divide their life into sets of three years until they arrive at the present day. After reviewing their relationship with their mother, they proceed to their relationship with their father, siblings, senior work colleagues, teachers and friends, and so on. Sometimes they are asked to reflect on their past misconduct, recalling times they told a lie or stole something, calculating how much their parents have spent to raise them, or totalling up the amount of money they have spent on alcohol.

A guide usually visits each participant once every ninety minutes or two hours, asking what he or she has recalled during that time. If it appears that introspection is not going smoothly, the participant is instructed to reflect on his or her life using simple words. Otherwise, the guide gives participants a nod and directs them to the next stage of introspection. A typical interview lasts from three to five minutes. Recordings of model reflections are played during meal times and at waking and sleeping. Since several meditation spaces tend to be located in the same room, when a participant is telling a guide about his or her reflections or realizations, other participants get a sense of the mood of that reflection, even though the words themselves cannot be clearly heard. When Naikan goes well, participants realize that they 'have received so much from others' but 'have returned too little to them', and 'have further caused great trouble to others'. They come to entertain a sense of wrongdoing and to be filled with thankfulness to others – they are often moved to tears. On the final day, participants gather together for a roundtable talk for about an hour.

There are about forty-five Naikan Training Centres in Japan, as of 2013, with clients visiting for an average of one week. At the Yamato Koriyama Naikan Training Centre in Nara, where the founder Yoshimoto Ishin himself interviewed participants, figures from 1982 showed around 1,300 persons in total practising concentrated introspection in a single year.

A number of hospitals, prisons, juvenile reformatories, senior high schools, and other educational facilities across Japan have incorporated Naikan practice into their routine activities. However, a single concentrated or group Naikan session alone does not bring forth the long-lasting effect of Naikan, and benefits may only be short-term.

To sustain the effect of Naikan, each person is advised to practise Naikan every day at home – this is called 'daily Naikan' or 'dispersed Naikan'. Concentrated Naikan is to be regarded only as an initiation leading to daily Naikan. However, it seems quite difficult, for many people, to sustain a practice of daily Naikan.

In one of his books Yoshimoto Ishin reproduced postcards sent to him by a woman describing what she had found through daily Naikan, practised over a period of twenty-three years. Her reflections included the following:

> I am reflecting on my relationship with my mother. My elder brother and sister quit school to find jobs as live-in workers. My mother went

to work every day leaving my younger brother and sister with my grandmother. I hated to be with my grandmother, and followed my mother to her workplace, where she prepared meals for many craftspeople. I understand now that she was hesitant about bringing me with her to her workplace. I have done nothing to express my thankfulness to her. I caused her so much trouble. While she was working, I used to go out to play quite a long way away, and returned very late. I don't know how much she worried about me. I feel very sorry for it now.[13]

Yoshimoto Naikan has been an object of study for many psychologists and psychiatrists, with a large number of academic papers exploring the practice as a form of psychotherapy. A Naikan Academic Society was formed in 1978. Much of this scholarship understood Yoshimoto Naikan as therapy or a redress for neurosis, for psychiatric disease and for social deviance. Yoshimoto himself died in 1988, but Yoshimoto Naikan is set to carry on through the lives and work of psychologists, psychiatrists, and people who have experienced fundamental self-transformation by means of this therapy.

## The establishment of Yoshimoto Naikan and its development as a psychotherapy

Yoshimoto Ishin was born in 1916, the third son of a wealthy family running a fertilizer business and an agricultural farm in Yamoto Koriyama city, in Nara prefecture. His younger sister died when he was a second year pupil at elementary school, and from this point onwards his mother began listening enthusiastically to sermons and teachings at a local Jōdo Shinshū ('Shin') Buddhist temple. The young Ishin followed her and listened to the preaching, and the two recited sutras together. Upon graduating from Koriyama Horticulture High School, at around seventeen years old, Yoshimoto began frequently to visit the temple and to study the teachings of Jōdo Shinshū, while working as a teacher of Japanese calligraphy. At the age of nineteen, he was introduced to Morikawa Kinuko as his future wife. In the Morikawa family, there were many eager supporters of a religious group based at the Taikan-an temple in Fuse, Osaka, which had a unique brand of faith within Shin Buddhism. Under the influence of this group, Yoshimoto had a religious experience that shaped his future life profoundly.

Jōdo Shinshū is the largest Buddhist group in Japan. Along with Jōdoshū it believes in salvation via rebirth in Amida Buddha's Pure Land Paradise. Shinran (1173–1262) gave a new direction to this faith in salvation after death and established Jōdo Shinshū.

In Shin teachings, ordinary people are so innately weak that they are unable to achieve salvation by themselves. They rely instead on a pledge made by Amida Buddha to save human beings. Generous in his mercy, Amida would save anyone who conducted sincerely the basic practice of reciting the nembutsu: 'namu amidabutsu (Hail to Amida Buddha)', and would help them to be reborn in Amida's Pure Land.

In other words, according to Shin Buddhism people can be saved only by depending upon the power of Amida Buddha (reliance on religious power, or 'other power': *tariki*), and not by training themselves in any particular form of knowledge or ascetic practice ('self power': *jiriki*).[14] Shinran further strengthened this belief in salvation by Amida Buddha's power by insisting that so fundamentally weak and tainted are human beings that even reciting the nembutsu or believing in Amida Buddha cannot be accomplished by human power, but only through the power of Amida Buddha. Once people fully understand their weakness, faith that Amida Buddha will save them wells up from the bottom of their hearts. And with this faith, humans find assurance that they will be reborn in the Pure Land paradise.

There have been followers of both Jōdoshū and Jōdoshinshū who were uncertain about whether they would be reborn in the Pure Land after death, and occasionally groups of people emerged who tried to achieve salvation from Amida Buddha through esoteric training. Considered heretical, these practices were suppressed in the Edo period, and members of these groups were known as 'clandestine nembutsu' groups. From the Meiji period onwards, however, they were accepted to some extent within the mainstream. Taikan-an temple in Fuse, Osaka, was established by the monk Taikan Nishimoto, who belonged to one of these groups that emphasized the importance for salvation of esoteric practices.

In the Taikan-an context, the practice of shutting oneself in a room to reflect thoroughly on one's sins, to realize the inevitability of death, and to learn to fear falling into hell, was called *mishirabe* (looking into oneself). While undertaking this practice, one is forbidden from contact with anyone from the outside. The person undergoing *mishirabe* (who is referred to as a 'sick person') lives in basic conditions, without food, water, or sleep. Persons already confident of their own salvation ('enlightened persons', or training centre leaders) visit, one after another, pushing the 'sick person' constantly to raise their awareness. Eventually, the sick person undergoes a religious experience in which they gain the conviction of being saved by Amida Buddha, such that their rebirth in the Pure Land is secure (*shukuzen kaihotsu*). The experience is referred to as 'encounter with the Buddha'.

Yoshimoto thought himself a dedicated follower of Shin Buddhism, and even preached Buddhist teachings to others. But when he met Kinuko's uncle and other followers of the Taikan-an temple, his confidence was shattered and he realized that he had done no more than accumulate knowledge, without undergoing any real religious experience. In 1936, he undertook his initial *mishirabe* at the age of twenty. Possessed by strong suspicions about himself, he failed to achieve confidence about his salvation. He repeated *mishirabe* a number of times – in secret, because of his father's disapproval of the temple's activities – but to no avail. Finally, more than a year after his first *mishirabe*, he attained the sought-after state of realizing his own salvation.

In 1938, Yoshimoto began to run a leather cloth wholesale business in Osaka. He worked hard at it by day, and propagated the teachings of Taikan-an temple in the evenings, paying visits to local households. His business grew to twelve separate branches, employing a large number of people, and Yoshimoto continued to work at it even after he was struck by tuberculosis in 1945 and was confined to bed for eight years. Yoshimoto had thought from the beginning that his business was not the true purpose of his life but rather a means of building up the assets required for him to be able to propagate his religious beliefs. Leaving the business in 1953, Yoshimoto opened a Naikan Training Centre in Yamoto Koriyama in Nara, and threw himself into the extension of Naikan while living off his accumulated assets.

Yoshimoto reformed the practices of Taikan-an temple in a number of respects. Already around 1940, a conflict had begun between two groups of followers. One insisted upon a once-and-for-all experience of salvation, while the other emphasized the depth of self-introspection through *mishirabe*.

The former invited people to an ecstatic experience, attracting great numbers of people – who tended not, however, to sustain their faith. The latter group recognized only a few people as having had the experience of true salvation, but the faith of its members was generally sustained for longer. Yoshimoto took the position of the latter group, and made changes in the way *mishirabe* was practised. In 1943 he began to have the employees of his company practise Naikan, and from then onwards the religion's ecstatic, esoteric elements were weakened. This in turn helped the practice to earn favourable evaluations from non-religious professionals such as psychologists and psychiatrists.

## From religion to psychotherapy

Between approximately 1940 and 1953, *mishirabe* rooted in esoteric Shin Buddhist practice was transformed into a practice almost equivalent to the Naikan of today: a quasi-psychotherapeutic activity of self-reflection. Reforms made during this period can be summarized as follows:

1   Instead of a once-and-for-all experience of salvation, the continuation of self-searching is emphasized. In the early days of Naikan, participants on a course were encouraged to continue reflecting on their past conduct without hurrying to gain a mystical experience of salvation by Amida Buddha, and later on the experience of salvation was no longer

pursued at all. Emphasis came to be placed on the process of self-reflection itself rather than on any outcome – courses were timed to last one week, as opposed to continuing until an experience of salvation. Where in the past no organized meditation was required after gaining the salvation experience, now continuous meditation on a daily basis was encouraged.
2   Mysterious and ascetic practices, along with specifically religious terminology, were jettisoned. Participants were permitted sufficient food and sleep, and were allowed to meet people from the outside. Secularized terms were used: *mishirabe* became *naikan*; *kaigonin* (a term referring to those believed to have experienced salvation) became *shidōsha* (guide).
3   The introspection process was organized in a methodical and rational way: specific points for reflection were set, such as one's moral debt to various people, and specific timings were laid down. The same guide would meet a participant regularly during the course, instead of various different *kaigonin* going in succession to meet the same participant.
4   An emphasis on a sense of transience was shifted to a sense of guilt. In the past, the aspiration for salvation was heightened by fears about death and hell (hence feelings concerning transience), but now one's moral debt to others was more of a focus.
5   The goal of Naikan was changed from meeting or relating to a transcendental being to the improvement of one's daily life. Noticeable changes in one's relations with others in actual life were considered a more important goal than meeting the Buddha in an experience of salvation.[15]

Yoshimoto Ishin's own ideas about the relationship between Naikan and religion are rather subtle. He certainly believed in rebirth in the Pure Land after death, with the aid of Amida Buddha. And he thought that a person who successfully went through introspection would attain religious faith.

He obtained certification as a Buddhist monk around 1950, and turned his own home in Yamato Koriyama, which had been used as a centre for Naikan, into Naikan Temple in 1955. The Naikan Institute became an annex facility belonging to the temple. On the other hand, he emphasized that Naikan is not religion. Behind this statement perhaps lies his ambition and activity in extending Naikan to prisons, juvenile reformatories, and senior high schools. According to Japan's post-war constitution, activities by religious organizations are strictly limited where public institutions are concerned; if Naikan were defined as a secular psychotherapy, however, staff members of a prison would be allowed to use it as part of their routine activities.

Yoshimoto became less insistent on the ideas of salvation by Amida Budda and rebirth in the Pure Land as a result of his experience of guiding his employees through Naikan. Workers who went through *mishirabe* (or Naikan) at the instruction of Yoshimoto began to feel a greater sense of gratitude for their working life. They tended to grumble less, and interpersonal relations improved. Witnessing such practical effects, Yoshimoto seemed to realize that he no longer needed to preach salvation by Amida Buddha and faith in rebirth in the Pure Land. In addition, he considered that Naikan ought to be spread widely amongst people and not be practised only by a special group. Perhaps Yoshimoto thought that, in order to achieve this, Naikan ought no longer to be a religious activity. In these terms, secularization seems to have been a success, since Naikan came to be well known and practised, with the help of psychologists and psychiatrists who were willing to consider it a form of psychotherapy. Scholars and the media too, who in general have taken strict positions in opposition to New Religions,[16] have been supportive of Yoshimoto Naikan.[17]

It cannot be said that Yoshimoto himself considered Naikan a form of secular psychotherapy. He called his method 'looking into the inner self', or 'self-insight method', and he saw Naikan as a means of learning the deepest truth about human beings, and as something that universalized the truth of traditional religions on a higher level beyond their differences and conflicts.[18] It may be legitimate to see Naikan as a new type of religion for people who are familiar with scientific thinking and who respect the claims of the sciences.

## Conclusion: Yoshimoto Naikan as a psycho-religious composite method

Yoshimoto Naikan differs from New Religions in its organization and practice. Since it does not mention physical healing or the manifestation of mystical power, it ought not to be categorized as belonging to the New Religion Movement. Nevertheless, it can be defined as a psycho-religious composite method in the sense outlined at the beginning of this chapter. There are some differences between Naikan and other parts of the psycho-religious composite movement, such as Seichō-no-ie and Hito-no-michi. While the latter two are clearly religious, Yoshimoto Naikan is religious only in a somewhat broader sense: the practice of deep introspection; a concern with evil deeds; an interest in gratitude, directed not just towards other human beings but also towards something beyond; the valuing of a feeling of emotional freedom, which is very close to an experience of religious conversion; and a particular set of ethics and way of living, inculcated via a fixed practice.

There is, however, no organization of followers: people who have undertaken intensive introspection do not afterwards continue to interact. This clearly places Naikan closer to psychotherapy than to religious organizations. However, there are also an increasing number of religious movements today in Japan that do not attach great value to followers' organizations. This tendency is particularly strong in the Spirituality Movement, and is close to what Thomas Luckman has described as 'invisible religion'.[19]

Another notable difference with Seichō-no-ie and Hito-no-michi is that Naikan encourages people to develop a sense of guilt while the other two organizations tend to encourage positive thinking among their members, so that bright feelings may drive out anxieties and fears. Naikan takes a more pessimistic stance towards people – to the point where some of those who have undergone introspection have considered suicide. This major difference may be explained as follows. Both Seichō-no-ie and Hito-no-michi focus their attention on impersonal interpersonal relations in urban society, encouraging members to let go of psychological conflicts. In contrast, Yoshimoto Naikan directs people's attention towards the close personal relations still existent in urban society, and aims to reform interpersonal attitudes. This latter stance is common to a number of New Religion organizations: Reiyū-kai, for example, strongly recommends their members to repent of sins, and even Seichō-no-ie and Hito-no-michi adopt ethical reflection and attention to sins to some extent. Many New Religion organizations adopt both a sense of guilt and positive thinking in their practice. However, the three representative organizations of the psycho-religious composite movement – Seichō-no-ie, Hito-no-michi and Yoshimoto Naikan – divide into extremes in their primary emphasis upon either a sense of guilt or positive thinking.

The concept of a psycho-religious composite movement is based on the presupposition that a change in thinking from religion towards psychotherapy occurs widely in highly urbanized societies where the hegemony of institutional science has been established. If this presupposition is right, there is a higher probability of the growth of psycho-religious composite movements in societies, such as Japan, where older cultural traditions survive alongside the expansion of sciences and urbanization. Together with movements offering physical healing based on non-western scientific ways of thinking, and ecological movements, a psycho-religious composite movement can be understood as part of a major cultural trend in pursuit of combination rather than conflict where science and religion are concerned.[20]

## Notes

1 Translated by Hayashi Chine. This essay is an updated translation of Shimazono, 'Sukui kara Iyashi e'.
2 Ellenberger, *The Discovery of the Unconscious*.
3 Larson, *New Thought Religion*. Sydney E. Ahlstrom describes this trend as one of 'harmonial religion': Ahlstrom, *A Religious History of the American People*.
4 See Harding (Introduction), this volume.
5 See Shimazono, *Gendai Kyūsai Shūkyō ron*, and *Shin Shin Shūkyō to Shūkyō Būmu*.

6 Takarajima Editorial Staff (ed.), *Seishin Ryōhō to Meisō*.
7 On the psycho-therapeutic characteristics of Seichō-no-ie and Hito-no-michi, see: Shimazono, 'Seichō-no-ie to Shinri-ryōhō-teki Sukui no Shisō'; 'Toshigata Shin Shūkyō no Kokoro Naoshi'; and 'Kami to Hotoke wo Koete'.
8 'Changing one's way of thinking' has been considered in the following publications: Shimazono (ed.), *Sukui to Toku*; Shimazono, 'Kokoro Naoshi to Kotoba'; 'Kokoro Naoshi to wa Nani ka'.
9 Rieff, *The Triumph of the Therapeutic*; Bellah *et al.*, *Habits of the Heart*. Prior to the therapeutic concept, Philip Rieff used the concept of 'psychological man'. See: Rieff, *Freud: The Mind of the Moralist*; Homans, *Jung in Context*.
10 See Kondo and Kitanishi, this volume.
11 Ozawa-de Silva, *Psychotherapy and Religion in Japan*.
12 On Yoshimoto Naikan, see: Miki, *Naikan Ryōhō Nyūmon*; Yoshimoto, *Naikan no Michi*; *Naikan 40 nen*; *Naikan he no Shōtai*; and *Gendai no Esupri 202*; and Ozawa-de Silva, *Psychotherapy and Religion in Japan*.
13 Yoshimoto, *Invitation to Naikan*, pp. 99–100.
14 See also Iwata, this volume.
15 See also Yoshimoto, *Invitation to Naikan*, pp. 47–66.
16 A number of New Religion organizations such as Honbushin and Risō-kyō incorporate Naikan practice into their activities.
17 Koriyama Naikan Institute published Yoshimoto Ishin (ed.), *Naikan 25 nen no Ayumi* [25 Years of Naikan] in 1980: a collection of articles about Yoshimoto Naikan gathered from newspapers, magazines, encyclopaedias, books, etc.
18 On pp. 44–45 of *Invitation to Naikan*, Yoshimoto writes that Naikan can be a path to different kinds of religion. Similarly, within Seichō-no-ie and Hito-no-michi there were claims, now and again, that they were not religions, or that their teachings were common to all kinds of religion.
19 Luckman, *The Invisible Religion*.
20 Cultural trends such as these developed as society sought out knowledge that would be an alternative to the modern knowledge associated with sciences and systems. This trend evolved into new religious and cultural movements, which together can be thought of as an alternative knowledge movement. The psycho-religious composite movement referred to in this chapter is a typical case of an alternative knowledge movement. See Shimazono, 'Views of the environment', pp. 37–47.

# References

Ahlstrom, Sydney E., *A Religious History of the American People* (New Haven: Yale University, 1972).
Bellah, Robert; Madsen, Richard; Sullivan, William M.; Swidler, Ann and Tipton, Steven M., *Habits of the Heart: Individualism and Commitment in American Life* (Berkeley: University of California Press, 1985).
Ellenberger, H.F., *The Discovery of the Unconscious: The History and Evolution of Dynamic Psychiatry* (New York: Basic Books, 1972; 2nd printing 1980).
Homans, Peter, *Jung in Context: Modernity and the Making of a Psychology* (Chicago: University of Chicago Press, 1979).
Larson, Martin A., *New Thought Religion: A Philosophy for Health, Happiness and Prosperity* (Allied Books Ltd, 1989; 2nd revised edition, 1987).
Luckman, Thomas, *The Invisible Religion* (London: Macmillan, 1967).
Miki Yoshihiko, *Naikan Ryōhō Nyūmon: Nihonteki Jiko Tankyū no Sekai [Introduction to Naikan Therapy: a Japanese Style of Inner Exploration]* (Tokyo: Sogensha, 1976).

Ozawa-de Silva, Chikako, *Psychotherapy and Religion in Japan: The Japanese Introspection Practice of Naikan* (Abingdon: Routledge, 2006).
Rieff, Philip, *Freud: The Mind of the Moralist* (New York: Doubleday, 1959).
Rieff, Philip, *The Triumph of the Therapeutic* (New York: Harper & Row, 1966).
Shimazono Susumu, 'Seichō-no-ie to Shinri-ryōhō-teki Sukui no Shisō: Taniguchi Masaharu no Shisō Keisei Katei wo megutte [Seichō-no-ie and its thought in regard to psychotherapeutic salvation: founder Taniguchi Masaharu's process of thought formation]', in Sakurai and Tokutaro (eds), *Nihon Shūkyō no Seitō to Itan [Orthodoxy and Heresy in Japanese Religion]* (Tokyo: Kobundo, 1988).
Shimazono Susumu, 'Toshigata Shin Shūkyō no Kokoro Naoshi: Hito-no-michi Kyōdan no Shinriryōhō-teki Kyūsai Shinkō [Changing one's way of thinking through an urban new religion: psychotherapeutic salvation beliefs]', in Yuasa Yasuo (ed.), *Taikei Bukkyō to Nihonjin 3 Mitsugi to Shugyō [Buddhist Systems and the Japanese, Vol. 3: Secret Ceremonies and Training]* (Tokyo: Shunjusha, 1989).
Shimazono Susumu, *Gendai Kyūsai Shūkyō ron [Contemporary Salvation Religion]* (Tokyo: Seikyusha, 1992).
Shimazono Susumu, *Shin Shin Shūkyō to Shūkyō Būmu [New New Religions and the Religion Boom]* (Tokyo: Iwanami Shoten, 1992).
Shimazono Susumu (ed.), *Sukui to Toku: Shin Shūkyō Shinkōsha no Seikatsu to Shisō [Salvation and virtue: the life and thought of new religion believers]* (Tokyo: Kobundo, 1992).
Shimazono Susumu, 'Kami to Hotoke wo Koete: Seichō-no-ie no Kyūsai Shisō no Seisei [Beyond gods and Buddha: the formation of salvation thought in Seichō-no-ie]', in Ueda Kansho *et al.* (eds), *Iwanami Koza Nihon Bungaku to Bukkyō, No. 8 Kami to Hotoke* [Iwanami Lecture: Japanese Literature and Buddhism, No. 8: Gods and Buddha] (Tokyo: Iwanami Shoten, 1994).
Shimazono Susumu, 'Kokoro Naoshi to Kotoba: Shin Shūkyō ni okeru Goroawase no Kinō wo megutte [Changing one's way of thinking, and words: the function of puns in new religions]', in: International Communication Institute, Kanda University of International Studies, Chiba, *Ibunka Communication Kenkyū [Studies in Inter-Cultural Communication]* No. 6 (Chiba: International Communication Institute, Kanda University of International Studies, 1994).
Shimazono Susumu, 'Kokoro Naoshi to wa Nani ka: Shin Shūkyō no Nichijōteki Rinri Jissen to Nippon no "kokoro" kan no Dentō [What does changing one's way of thinking mean? The practice of everyday ethics in new religion and the Japanese tradition of the view on "mindset"]', in Komazawa University, *Shūkyō gaku ronshu [Collection of Theses of Religious Studies]* vol. 17 (1995).
Shimazono Susumu, 'Sukui kara Iyashi e: Yoshimoto Naikan to sono Shūkyōteki Kigen [From salvation to healing: Yoshimoto Naikan therapy and its religious origins]', in Shigehiko Araya *et al.* (eds), *Iyashi to Wakai: Gendai ni okeru Kea no Shosō* (Tokyo: Harvest–sha, 1995).
Shimazono Susumu, 'Views of the environment as reflected in alternative knowledge movements in Japan', in Yamaori Tetsuo (ed.), *Views of the Environment in Asian Countries: The Relationship to Sustainable Development* (Tokyo: Asian Pacific Center and The United Nations University, 1999).
Takarajima Editorial Staff (ed.), *Seishin Ryōhō to Meisō [Psychotherapy and Meditation]* (Tokyo: JICC Press, 1991).
Yoshimoto Ishin, *Naikan 40 nen [40 years of Naikan]* (Tokyo: Shunjūsha, 1965).
Yoshimoto Ishin, *Naikan no Michi [The Path of Naikan]* (Nara: Naikan Institute, 1977).

Yoshimoto Ishin (ed.), *Naikan 25 nen no Ayumi [25 Years of Naikan]* (Nara: Naikan Institute, 1980).

Yoshimoto Ishin, *Naikan he no Shōtai [Invitation to Naikan]* (Tokyo: Tokishobo, 1983).

Yoshimoto Ishin, *Gendai no Esupri 202 – Meisō no Seishin Ryōhō: Naikan Ryōhō no Riron to Jissen [Contemporary Esprit vol. 202, Mental Therapy: Theory and Practice of Naikan Therapy]* (Tokyo: Shibundo, 1984).

# 8 Naikan and mourning

## A Catholic attempt at Naikan meditation

*Terao Kazuyoshi*[1]

Although Christians account for no more than a scant 1 per cent of the entire Japanese population, this does not relieve the Catholic Church in Japan of the need to address problems of the mind or soul, or such difficult issues as that of spiritual care. Long ridiculed as 'more Roman than Rome', the Japanese Catholic Church in recent years has been making strenuous efforts toward inculturation. So far it has struggled to move beyond an academic theology of religions and reach Japanese believers in more practical terms, but that is not to say that there have been no trial-and-error attempts worthy of note. Catholic Naikan meditation as developed by Fujiwara Naosato is one such. In what follows I offer an outline of Fujiwara's project as it relates to 'mourning work' – one aspect of the spiritual care project and an important issue for contemporary 'death and life studies' in Japan. I preface this with a brief survey of Christian psychotherapy in modern Japan.

Psychotherapy has made few if any advances in the world of Japanese Christianity from pre-Second World War years through the postwar period and up to the present. Japanese Protestants of various denominations have shown theirs to be what one might call religions of 'faith' founded on Bible-centrism and strict dogma. There has also been a strong tendency toward abstemious, intellectual non-denominationalism. For these reasons, Japanese Protestantism for the most part has not taken much interest in psychological matters. Nonetheless one finds here and there within Japanese Protestantism psychologically oriented innovations relating to metaphysics, spiritual exercises, and non-mainstream psychotherapy.[2] Muramatsu Kaiseki and Kawai Shinsui, for example, both established unique systems of spiritual exercises that drew on Asian methods – legitimizing this by claiming that ancient Asian teachings represent an additional 'old testament' for Christianity. However, wartime religious controls and the postwar flowering of Barthianism, with a concurrent influx of foreign missionaries, left little room for any attempt to fuse religion with the culture of psychotherapy. The closest that Japanese Protestantism has come to engaging with psychotherapy at the present time is the application of English or American-style pastoral care.

Japanese Catholicism, likewise, has confined itself to the adoption of Western-style spiritual care and has relied to a high degree on the sacraments. Psychological dimensions of life have been catered for by visits to monasteries and retreat centres. Again, there has been relatively little interest in psychotherapy.

## The anthropological dimension of Catholic spirituality

'Spiritual care' is a topic that has been coming up frequently of late in Japanese society. As one might imagine from the expression 'spiritual, not religious', use of the word 'spiritual' in many modern contexts constitutes a rejection of established religions. And yet its Latin root word *spiritualis* has functioned, historically, as an important theological concept in the Christian world, rendering it familiar to contemporary Christianity and other established religions. Deriving as it does from *pneuma* ($\pi\nu\varepsilon\hat{v}\mu\alpha$) – 'air in motion' – it has the further advantage of suggesting an unimpeded bridge between God and man.[3] The term 'spiritual', then, manages to maintain rich, helpful connotations while circumventing the rigidity of traditional theology – and this is how it is used in present-day Japanese Catholicism. The approach is of great value for churches and other communities engaged in work with the ageing and dying. 'Spirituality' tends to drive this work more than 'theology' in contemporary Catholicism.[4]

There is a certain inevitable vagueness to this 'spirituality'. Inoue Yōji, a Catholic priest who was a close friend of the Japanese Catholic novelist Endō Shūsaku, has said: 'As a person lives his life, the sweat of life drips down and turns into words. The matter of that experience turning into each and every word is the "spirit."'[5] According to the Jesuit systematic theologian Momose Fumiaki:

> Spirituality is how each Christian receives the good news of Jesus Christ, and how each goes about putting their way of living their faith into practice. It is the way they actually perform their faith, the patterns by which they make their faith real.

Theology, meanwhile, is more a matter of 'reflecting on the practice of faith, ascertaining those elements that are central, and then assigning new directions to the ways in which someone lives their faith'.[6] On this basis, without spirituality there can be no theology, and both become bound up with anthropology.

The Department of Philosophical Anthropology at Sophia University, in Tokyo, observes on its website that anthropology is grounded in Christian humanism. As a discipline it directs its attention towards 'being persons for others', 'being persons who are with others', and 'being persons conscious of promoting justice'.[7] Clearly, anthropology aims for that breadth that comes from directing one's attention towards other people rather than deeply investigating the self. Anthropology is not a monologue, but rather a shared project of thinking and seeking to understand. This breadth does not require a sacrifice of depth: the human self has a natural depth to it, which prevents anthropology from lapsing into solipsistic superficiality. In its natural interdisciplinarity and striving to develop a wide-angle field of vision, anthropology differs significantly from orthodox theology, with its top-down pattern of assumptions premised upon a transcendent being. Anthropology, which makes practical use of areas of scholarship that historically have stood in opposition to theology – such as religious studies and psychology – is capable of pointing out the unavoidable distortions of orthodoxy and of fostering a holism that incorporates the marginal, the hypothetical, and from time to time even the irrational.[8]

Thus, when seeking out Catholic spirituality in present-day Japan, from an anthropological perspective that combines breadth with depth, one should seek to incorporate human elements at the margins of orthodox theology and especially practical engagements with real issues of life and death.[9] Catholic Naikan meditation can be presented as the quintessential example of this.

## What is Catholic Naikan meditation?

Catholic Naikan meditation is a psychotherapeutic mental training activity that was inaugurated by Fujiwara Naosato, a parish priest attached to the Archdiocese of Osaka. Currently, it is practised by Fujiwara together with a small number of collaborators. Fujiwara was born in 1944 in Osaka to devoutly Catholic parents. The family had been Catholic since his Akita-born father's generation. Fujiwara entered divinity school at the age of nineteen in 1964, at the time of the first Tokyo Olympics and the Second Vatican Council. Education policies at these divinity schools were influenced by the on-going church reforms and changed dramatically almost on an annual basis. Amidst all this Fujiwara came to believe that systems necessarily change.[10] Rather than limiting himself to Scholastic theology Fujiwara chose a highly unconventional topic for his master's thesis: a comparative study of the theories of evolution developed by the Japanese anthropologist Imanishi Kinji and the Jesuit palaeontologist Pierre Teilhard de Chardin. He was supervised by Peter Nemeshegyi, a Jesuit professor of systematic theology at Sophia University.

Conflicted in his quest for a spirituality rooted in culture, Fujiwara learned about the Naikan method devised by Yoshimoto Ishin through a book by Miki Yoshihiko (*Naikan ryōhō nyūmon*, 1976). He went to experience Naikan firsthand from Yoshimoto himself and later from Yoshimoto's disciples at a Naikan *dōjō* ('exercise hall'). He also took sabbatical leave under the guidance of Okumura Ichirō, a Carmelite friar who was actively involved in the international dialogue between Catholicism and other religions, including Zen Buddhism in particular. Fujiwara also developed contacts with groups for those with intellectual disabilities through Sawada Kazuo, a Tokyo parish priest doing missionary work on the streets of the city's largest day-labourer district, San'ya. Subsequently, at the age of forty-nine, Fujiwara received the permission of then-Archbishop Yasuda Hisao to be excused from his duties as a parish priest, whereupon he established the 'Kokoro no ihori' [Hermitage of the Heart] Naikan Meditation Centre. Currently located in Neyagawa City, Osaka Prefecture, the land and buildings are treated as a branch of the Kōri Catholic church but they are operated for all intents and purposes by Fujiwara himself. Fujiwara's system is implicitly independent of the Catholic Church hierarchy as a result. Fujiwara leaves the Centre around fifteen times a year, touring Japan and serving as a Naikan guide. He has claimed that around 1,300 people have taken part in his retreat over the last eighteen years, though he does not keep specific records.[11]

The essential point of Naikan method (see Shimazono, this volume) lies in becoming conscious of one's sins, and entails scrutiny of one's memories – 'memories of the root' of oneself in relation to one's own mother and others close at hand. One asks three key questions: 'what has that person done for me?', 'what have I done for them in return?' and 'what troubles have I caused them?' The method of Catholic Naikan is basically the same as this, differing only in that a Mass is held on the final day of a Naikan retreat and the breathing techniques are slightly modified (see below).[12] Fujiwara leads participants in his unique method of Yoga-like exercise on tatami mats. Crucial to this development of Naikan into a Catholic 'mystic-spiritual' practice has been Tanaka Teruyoshi, a Carmelite priest and hermit who drew, in his work, on Japan's Buddhist spirituality. This helped preserve the religious contemplative dimensions of the practice, where modern Naikan is generally non-religious.[13] But Naikan method generally has no relationship to ancestor worship, focusing instead on the practitioner's personal history.

Yoshimoto Naikan is characterized by a strict methodology when it comes to the three aforementioned questions and the practice environment. This leaves little room for spontaneous alterations by the guide (*dō kōsha*, lit. 'fellow traveller'). Thus, no counselling of any sort is offered to practitioners: Naikan meditation is free, in principle at least, from subjective control by the guides. This is a virtue in that if one takes into account the current situation wherein the guide does not receive any exceptional training in psychiatry or psychology, then one can empirically avoid dangerous psychological interventions as they see fit. On the other hand, there is also the danger that an investigation of sin may sometimes lead to the repression of emotions such as sadness, resulting in turn in some form of psychological violence. This potential shortcoming is one that Fujiwara's Catholic Naikan meditation shares.

## Catholic Naikan meditation as 'mourning work'

Although the Resurrection constitutes the core of the Christian faith and occupies a central position in the religion's doctrines, the immense weight that the event carries has meant that the development of theology around it has differed to that developed around other problems in Christian thought. For example, the theological understanding in the Western Church of a Descent into Hades preceding the Resurrection has been developed only minimally, even though it appears in the Apostles' Creed. The Eastern Church avoided turning it into dogma, instead leveraging its dramatic potential. Fujiwara's version of Naikan meditation made the most of this relative lack of theological development where the Resurrection is concerned, linking theological speculation with psychotherapy and developing the two in a reciprocal fashion. Nowhere is this clearer than in what is called 'mourning work'.

New Testament scholar Satō Migaku interprets the Resurrection story in the Gospels as a tragic narrative; that is, an example of mourning work performed by Jesus' disciples, building on the thinking of early church historian and fellow New Testament scholar Dale C. Allison in this area. Satō argues that there are seven aspects to mourning work, which one can see are shared in common amongst various kinds of grief work. These are: a sense of presence, pain arising from an awareness of guilt, feelings of anger, the idealization of the dead, remembrance of the dead, seeing one's fate as something shared with the dead, and having visions of being reunited.[14] One could compact this list into (1) a sense of the dead being real, (2) a feeling of anger, (3) seeing one's fate as something shared with the dead, and (4) having visions of being reunited. These are the hallmarks both of mourning work within spiritual care and theological understandings of the Resurrection.

Before looking at how mourning work and Naikan meditation come together, it is important to pay attention to two major orientations in Fujiwara's thought. First, in his intellectual contemplations he highlights two means by which he hopes to get away from the excesses of Western rationalism: Buddhist spirituality and the spirituality of the Eastern Church. Fujiwara's theology is rooted in the Gospel of John and influenced heavily by the work of Tanaka Teruyoshi, who has sought to 'de-Westernize' Catholic theology in Japan through his deep understanding of Buddhism in general and Pure Land Buddhism in particular. As with many others who have sought out a new Catholic theology in dialogue with Buddhism, Tanaka and Fujiwara arrived at a 'kenotic theology' – that is to say, a theology of 'self-emptying'.[15] Fujiwara quotes Tanaka in one of his works: 'The substance of the vow [made by the Fazang bodhisattva] coincides with the "self-emptying" of the Son of God that is the death on the cross in Christianity'.[16]

Fujiwara's second orientation is found in his practical contemplations, which follow on from the basic ideas of Yoshimoto Naikan and the

Buddhist *mishirabe* practice from which it derives. The influence of Pauline teachings on the crucifixion and on redemption is also evident. According to Fujiwara, after he met Christ on the road to Damascus Paul returned to Arabia and looked deeply into himself, 'moaning' as he discovered the disruption and discord within his body and soul. Fujiwara has digested the teachings of Paul that followed this crucial moment and in simple poetry has expressed his awareness of his own sins, as revealed through sharp self-criticism in Naikan meditation.[17]

Needless to say, this unity of kenotic Johannine theology and redemptive Pauline theology has been a difficult issue throughout the entirety of Christian history and it would be hard to say that any coherence has been achieved in Fujiwara's writing, which oscillates between these two poles.[18] Since Naikan's strict method does not offer scope for much creative intellectual development, Fujiwara has tended to rely more on the spirituality of Eastern Christianity than on the psychology of Naikan in developing his hybrid thought and practice.[19] In less sophisticated works earlier in his career (such as *Tōzai no hazama de* [*Between East and West*], first published in 1998 with a second printing in 1999, and *Kokoro no uchinaru tabi* [*Inner Journey of the Heart*] from 2002), the confessional quality connected with mourning in Naikan therapy is particularly strong. Fujiwara's explorations of recent years, by contrast, are characterized – according to Satō Migaku – by a 'de-tragedization' torn down from an understanding of the Resurrection as 'mourning work'. In terms of anthropology, attention needs once again be paid to those aspects of Western spirituality that are sensitive to the pain of mourning.[20] Accordingly, in my explorations here I will focus mainly on the works from Fujiwara's early period, including the above-mentioned two books.

### *The sense that the dead are real*

The focus of Catholic Naikan upon the dead comes first from Fujiwara's initial experience of Naikan, which was a meditation on his relationship with his dead father, and second from the diffusion of the method, which occurred in response to demands from middle-aged and elderly nuns. He began to work as a Naikan guide in May 1996 when he received a request from five nuns at the Holy Cross Monastery in Chiba Prefecture, part of a contemplative order called the Congregation of the Benedictines of Jesus Crucified. The nuns decided to engage in Naikan practice following a talk given by Fujiwara about how his father had influenced him.[21] Fujiwara came to regard the area within the folding screens where the Naikan practitioner secludes himself or herself as a kind of 'Purgatory' – a purgatory for the living. I see as a distinctive feature of this theory of a living purgatory the notion that 'purgatory is a purification process that was begun before one was born by the inevitable distress that is given passively in relationships with the most dearly loved deceased'.[22] For Fujiwara, the reality of death is so strong that Naikan meditation is a place where you grasp 'yourself among the coffins or in the graveyard'. One achieves 'a view from the borders of death ... an experience that is like someone who has passed away emerging from the folding screen'.[23] That person somehow lives, and at that moment one's relationship with the dead is preserved through powerfully felt sensations. This is not the 'satori' of Buddhist traditions: the apex of the transformation wrought in Naikan meditation may well be tears. Many of the people who appear in the New Testament shed tears, including Jesus. Drawing on the seventh-century Sinai hermit John Climacus (Ἰωάννης τῆς Κλίμακος) in the high esteem he has for the 'gift of tears', Fujiwara regards tears as 'an important phenomenon in personality transformation'.[24]

A tear-filled 'descent into the netherworld' opens up an immensely deep field of vision, with which one can see 'that tens, hundreds, thousands of people are stretched out behind every single Naikan practitioner'. As each practitioner is 'disturbed' by intense feelings of guilt and by the general weight of their consciousness, they feel an inner reciprocal illumination – as though 'the darkness hidden within is having light shined upon it by another person'.[25]

Fujiwara regards the ability to shepherd a person on a descent into the netherworld as akin to the shamanism of a *miko, yuta, noro,* or *itako* – all Japanese shamanic figures who function as mediums to the world of the dead.[26] He is thinking too of such figures as the Russian *jurodivyj* (юродивый, 'holy idiots') or the biblical prophets.[27] In short, the goal of Catholic Naikan meditation is to engage in a shamanistic exercise in a place where one artificially experiences death. Watched over by a priest as their selves empty out, practitioners seek to achieve an altered state of consciousness of sorts that functions as a 'communion of saints' with their dead fellows. While Yoshimoto secularized Naikan, Fujiwara has 're-religionized' it to an extent: the priest plays a primordial role in bridging the worlds of the dead and the living.

## *Anger*

In both Yoshimoto and Catholic Naikan, expressing anger by projecting such feelings onto others – i.e. 'transference', in psychotherapeutic terms – is regarded as an unhelpful deviation. However, a dissenting view has emerged, based on recent research in psychotherapy. The argument is that this intervention to avoid the external aspects at times is accompanied by an intense psychological invasion; such a condition may be nothing more than that of emotional transference.[28] It is natural for the practitioner to feel antipathy towards the guide, since the expression of negative feelings during the Naikan process go unrecognized by the guide. Given the practitioner's experience of transcending the border between life and death, in order to interact with the dead, it is entirely conceivable that a powerful expression of emotions, deviating from general Naikan principles, might occur. This irrationality is a consequence of conventional poles of good/evil, light/dark, and God/man becoming ambiguous as part of the Naikan experience.

Fujiwara Naikan meditation differs from Yoshimoto Naikan in its use of 'ontological prayer': inhaling is connected with the direction of life itself, exhaling with death – with someone breathing their last. This prayer is practised under the direction of the priest.[29] Every evening, once Catholic Naikan practitioners have completed the day's reflections they gather together in a hall and do these deep breathing exercises, which are reminiscent of yoga but whose purpose and meaning extends far beyond relaxation while also including it.[30] When practitioners return to regular Naikan meditation the next day the distress produced by original sin (self-centredness) – what might be described as an ontological defect – returns like waves ceaselessly breaking on a shoreline. This corresponds to a theme in the psychology of mourning whereby the death of a loved one 'becomes a real issue in that person's mind after the emergency has ended and they have returned to a peaceful life'.[31] In Yoshimoto Naikan, theorizing about psychological phenomena in this way tends to be rejected and Fujiwara's Naikan shares such a rejection.

Anger must not be allowed to run rampant in secret. Ideally, one would develop a refined judgement in regard to anger, which somehow takes mourning into account. In the New Testament we find *orgé* (ὀργή), which is a good sort of anger rooted in a sense of justice and arising when one dwells upon one's hardened heart. There is also *thumos* (θυμός), a 'bad wrath', that has degenerated into pure passion. In situations where the latter arises, by giving meaning to it one can perhaps transform it into the former type. In other words, rather than exhibiting violent emotions toward, say, their mother, a person might instead scrutinize their memories through Naikan and become able to consider the situation in which their mother found herself.[32]

What sort of advice will the Naikan guide be able to provide here? This could be a heavy burden for a guide, who usually lacks relevant training. Most guides are priests but have had scant opportunity to master psychological techniques during or after their seminary days. The spiritual exercises of Ignatius of Loyola, which prepare people for similar situations, might be useful here, in getting guides ready for their work.[33]

## Sharing one's fate with the dead

We have seen already that the sharing of one's fate with the dead, as part of Catholic Naikan practice, begins with the living becoming artificially dead by moving beyond the borders of death. This, however, is not the only way. A further distinctive feature of Catholic Naikan is the possibility of performing a 'proxy' Naikan, done on behalf of others as *daijuku* (suffering for others) or *daizange* (repenting for others). This element in Catholic Naikan is influenced by a text written by the eleventh century Shingon priest Kakuban called the *Mitsugon-in hotsuro sange no mon* (*Religious Confession at Mitsugon Temple*). A Naikan practitioner making contact with a dead parent generates within himself 'the groans of the soul that the parent is shouting out without realizing it'.[34] What results is a further awakening to another person produced by the aforementioned 'good anger'.

According to Fujiwara, this task reaches the point of presenting the essence of the collective Naikan before God by 'looking back over your history of salvation ... and acknowledging the fact that you have done "senseless things"'. Individual faults are not dwelt upon at this point. Instead, there is the invocation of Eastern Orthodoxy's Holy God ("Άγιος Θεός) of the Improperium in ceremonies on Good Friday.[35] This Naikan process – done in a form where the living and the dead are presented as 'sacrifices of thanks'; that is to say, as humans taking on the role of Hosts – is concluded by a Mass that contains a 'cosmic expanse'. The *kenosis* (emptying) of God that became evident in the Descent into Hell overlaps with the *theosis* (divinization) of human beings.[36]

Although this ceremony carries the risk of degeneration into mere formalism, the intention is that the living person develops greater awareness of their own future death – i.e. the ceremony acts as a kind of *memento mori*. However, in terms of theorizing this in Naikan meditation at present, at most it does not go beyond the 'everyday Naikan' that originates in the Yoshimoto method and involves the practitioner finding time in their daily routine to continue to do Naikan.[37] In fact, only a few people actually take part in this ceremony. From having served so often as a Naikan guide, Fujiwara himself has likely felt the presence of the dead through frequently being in places where they 'appear' and from sharing a space where consciousness is altered. In that sense, interactions between the living and the dead motivated by the shared fate of death can easily occur in Naikan meditation; what's more, they are desirable.

A major limitation with Catholic Naikan is that although a lay practitioner can become a guide Naikan retreats are always closed with a Mass, and there is no alternative to the sacramental authority of priests when it comes to this aspect of Catholic Naikan.[38] For this reason Catholic Naikan can do little to change the clergy-centredness of the church – perhaps limiting the scope of what Naikan will be able to achieve within Japanese Catholicism.

### *A vision of being reunited*

Both the living and the dead reunite as 'the dead' when Naikan meditation is practised. Returning to the everyday world once the retreat is over, the living practitioner must somehow manage to hang on to the resonances of the altered state of consciousness they have achieved. Fujiwara has some deeply suggestive comments on this point: 'To do Naikan when you are young is fine', he writes, 'but to engage in introspection about your entire life and to prepare for death when you reach an advanced age may perhaps be the greatest task of your old age'.[39] As psychiatrist Murata Tadayoshi has said:

> One reason why the prayers of the elderly are beautiful is that they are not prayers for favours. Another big reason is that they are the prayers for 'a person who was once an old person', that is to say, they are a dialogue with the dead.[40]

Such innocence looks beautiful in the context of Japanese culture: doing away with rational blinders, which hide the existence of the dead.

The psychiatrist Ōi Gen, who is well versed in geriatric medicine, writes: 'It is a natural process for a person who has relinquished connections with the outside world to try to find connections to the world of their memories'.[41] Engaging in Naikan meditation as part of the ageing process serves as a valuable form of self-enlightenment for acquiring and maintaining a smooth continuity with the past, as the elderly head towards an advanced stage of post-rationality – in a broadly positive sense.

Looking back, one cannot help saying that a spirituality that has achieved inculturation has yet to develop even if we set aside specialized spirituality among elders in the church. However, when Fujiwara's Catholic Naikan meditation has been integrated into the work of curing the souls of the church's elderly commensurate with their lifecycle, the vision of reuniting will pick up on the ideas and sensibilities accumulated in such cultural traditions as Pure Land Buddhism and ancestor worship while showing that mode all the more concretely.

## Remaining issues

As noted earlier, a Catholic Naikan meditation retreat is brought to a close on the final day with a Mass. Mass is a sacrament that celebrates the Passover from death to the Resurrection – highly effective as a form of spiritual care in its own right. The sacrament of Communion, which goes beyond the solace of words, is an experience of being united with the real body and blood of Christ. When it comes to understanding the seven sacraments in theological terms, they were once arranged in a time-oriented way running from Baptism, which marks the person's birth as a believer, to Extreme Unction (or else the Anointing of the Sick), which moves towards death. Since Vatican II, however, this has changed and now the Holy Eucharist is understood as central.[42] The sacrament that Naikan meditation most directly brings to mind is that of Penance and Reconciliation, i.e. confession. Fujiwara places this sacrament on a par with the

Mass.[43] Strangely, however, he says very little about the precise relationship between confession and Naikan meditation.

Certainly, one could argue that because of the close kinship of this sacrament with Naikan meditation the likes of the latter may be seen as unnecessary. Though Naikan meditation is free from the Sacrament of Penance and Reconciliation, the value of this sacrament at the close of a Naikan retreat is clear: a proclamation of forgiveness delivered by a priest, helping to soothe the turmoil created by the necessary invasiveness of Naikan. Naikan meditation can be understood as paving the way for the Sacrament of Penance and Meditation. In any case, one of the issues that remains for Catholic Naikan as it develops is how to position it in relation to Catholic confession.

## Conclusion

Catholic spirituality has been attracting more and more attention in recent years from such people as the literary critic Wakamatsu Eisuke, who was baptized Catholic as a baby and has written lively pieces aimed at the rehabilitation of Catholicism in Japan. His focus has been on exchanges with the dead in the real world, through cultivating the sense that the phenomena of this world are in some sense underpinned by the dead.[44] If intellectual currents such as these from outside the church could be made to resonate sympathetically with existing movements within the church, Fujiwara's Catholic Naikan meditation might begin to make significant headway.

Ever since the triple disasters of 3/11, which shook Japanese society to its core, Japanese people have considerably deepened their relationship with the dead and their practice of mourning. Religious organizations found, through 3/11, a way of contributing to society. And yet the more that traditional religious groups build up their doctrinal systems, the more difficult it will be for new methodological developments to emerge beyond established forms. In that sense, one imagines that Catholic Naikan meditation as developed by Fujiwara Naosato – a priest in a traditional religious group, who has made use of traditional religious spirituality to create an extremely unorthodox form of practice – may attract more and more attention as a form of Catholic spirituality that pays heed to present-day anthropological realities.

This ought to include perspectives not only from others inside Japan but also for exchanges with the outside world – and in fact though small in number since 2006 Fujiwara's Naikan has been finding more and more advocates in Korea. It has also received support from Koreans residents in Japan.[45] If this becomes a full-blown trend, one can imagine some sort of future harmonization and fusion with Korean *Han* theology and further developments leading to a trans-East Asian Christian psychotherapy.[46] Thus, while Fujiwara's Catholic Naikan meditation may currently be small as an operative force, we ought not overlook the possibilities hidden within.

## Notes

1 Translated by Carl Freire. This essay contains material originally published as Terao, 'Naikan to Hiai'.
2 According to Yoshinaga Shin'ichi, a diverse range of individuals – including people interested in psychic research or health management, or who had once been interested in socialism – were active in this area. Mullins' *Christianity Made in Japan* is quite suggestive.
3 For the purposes of this article I have simplified a somewhat complex debate. The concept that corresponds to the soul in the Old Testament is *nephesh* (נפש). This alongside *ruach* (הור), which corresponds to the spirit, refers to the general life principle of humans. However, while *ruach* is used in reference to the relationship between God and man, *nephesh* is used for relationships between one person and another. Based on this, it is evident that *nephesh* is undeniably appropriate as a reference to the soul that underpins one's love for one's neighbours, as an ethical proposition. However, we should take care to note that in the Old Testament this is unconnected to the Greek idea of emphasizing the soul while holding the flesh in contempt, with one separated from the other. The Old Testament hints not at a soul residing in the body. Rather, the soul expresses itself through the body and signifies the entirety of human existence – just as 'flesh' does. The word that corresponds to *nephesh* in the New Testament, meanwhile, is *psuche* (ψυχῆ). In contrast to *pneuma* (πνεῦμα), being the incorporeal essence of humans turned toward God, *psuche* can be thought of as the incorporeal essence of humans turned toward each other and as such has an ethical character. However, such Hebraic vitalism turned into something of a static, rigid doctrinal concept as Christianity Latinized in the early centuries CE.
4 After Vatican II, as the church boosted its social nature in the name of being a more 'open church', words like '*kyūrei*' (salvation of the soul), in its old sense at least, came to be used less frequently. The significance of salvation itself was lost, however, and through contemporary 'spiritual care' it is possible that the term will take on new meaning and strength.
5 Inoue, 'Gendai no reisei o motomete', p. 309.
6 Momose, 'Shingaku to reisei', pp. 248, 253.
7 www.info.sophia.ac.jp/phanthro/, accessed on September 13, 2012.
8 See Etō, 'Health no gogen to sono dōzokugo to no imiteki rensa: Imiteki rensa to iu shiten kara no gogen kenkyū no yūkōsei'.
9 See Uenuma, *Yami o sumika to suru watashi, yami o kakurega to suru Kami*, pp. 25, 174. Using memory as his core concept, Uenuma has focused his attention on the dimension of darkness in the heart, as illuminated in Emmanuel Lévinas and Murakami Haruki in his quest for a 'pre-verbal theology'.
10 Fujiwara, *Kokoro no uchinaru tabi: Naikan no reisei o motomete*, p. 10.
11 Private correspondence between Fujiwara and the author. February 13, 2014.
12 I experienced Naikan for myself under Fujiwara's supervision from August 18–24, 2008, at Himeji Retreat Center of the Hospital Sisters of St. Francis.
13 For further details on Tanaka Teruyoshi's thought, see Terao, 'Tanaka Teruyoshi no ishikiron'.
14 Satō, *Hajimari no Kirisuto-kyō*, p. 63.
15 Others scholars who have worked in this area include Okumura Ichirō, Onodera Isao, and Honda Masaaki, who took part in the Zen–Christianity Roundtable (Zen to Kirisutokyō kondan-kai) and the East–West Religions in Encounter conclaves. Their ideas are definitively based on the 'absolute negation' concept of the Japan's Kyoto School of philosophy, which was pioneered

by Nishida Kitarō (and later Tanabe Hajime). Endō Shūsaku and Inoue Yōji are also important figures in this regard.
16 Fujiwara, *Namu no michi mo āmen no michi mo*, pp. 161–162.
17 Regarding Paul as a Naikan practitioner, see Fujiwara, *Tōzai no hazama de*, pp. 103–105. Fujiwara believes that Paul practised a kind of Naikan during his retreat in Araby. Here are two examples of confessional *tanka* and short poems by Fujiwara, from pp. 28–29 of the same work. 'The immature apprentice monk may cleave the plain and simple heart of a mother with a sharp blade' (Tanjunsoboku na haha no kokoro o/surudoki yaiba de kiru/aonisai no minarai sō ka na). 'At the very end is the sadness of karma, because you come to your senses after you have caused your mother to worry and hacked at maternal affection' (Tokoton wa haha o kurushime/hahagokoro o kitta ato ni/me ga sameru to iu/gō no kanashisa).
18 Fujiwara himself admitted, 'When I reread this pamphlet after having completed it, I sensed that in spite of myself the book's viewpoint is diffuse and for some reason it never settled on one focus'. Fujiwara, *Kokoro no uchinaru tabi*, p. 151.
19 Approaches that strictly retain the methodological principles of the Yoshimoto Naikan method are called *naikan genpō*, while those that incorporate various revisions are referred to as *naikan henpō*. If we glance through the works of influential Naikan practitioners, the bulletin of the Japan Naikan Association, and so forth, we see they call for maintenance of the *naikan genpō* approach almost as a prerequisite. The current situation is such that there are hardly any instances of *naikan henpō* being offered.
20 In that sense, Fujiwara's shift to the East means his failure to hold the pain that arises from consciousness of human sins. Satō also speaks critically of how the anthropologically tragic nature that was clear in the Gospel of Mark was 'rendered harmless' and 'detragedized' by 'the story of the epiphany of the one who was resurrected' in Matthew, Luke, and John. Satō, *Higeki to fukuin*, pp. 158–167.
21 Fujiwara, *Tōzai no hazama de*, p. 1. The congregation was established with the idea of allowing individuals with physical illnesses or disabilities to partake in monastic life the same as able-bodied persons.
22 See Terao, 'Katorikku-teki shigosei no yukue, p. 70.
23 Fujiwara, *Tōzai no hazama de*, p. 77.
24 Ibid., p. 115.
25 Ibid., p. 131, and Fujiwara, *Kokoro no uchinaru tabi*, p. 118.
26 See Shiotsuki, this volume.
27 Fujiwara, *Kokoro no uchinaru tabi*, pp. 88, 133, 135. Minami Jikisai, chief priest attached to the Zen temple Bodai-ji at Osorezan in Aomori Prefecture, speaks frequently about 'powerless sacredness' in his work *Osorezan*.
28 Maeshiro, *Shinri ryōhō to shite no naikan*, p. 162.
29 Fujiwara, *Kokoro no uchinaru tabi*, p. 70.
30 Fujiwara, ibid., p. 148. Fujiwara got his idea from Tamaki's view on Dhamma as found in his book *Nōkan to gedatsu*, and from Suzuki's *Nihon-teki reisei*.
31 Okonogi, *Taishō sōshitsu*, p. 57.
32 This produces an identification in connection with fate as individuals with mutually deep sinful existences. This is a matter of sharing in sadness or weakness, and is likely the feeling that underlies karma in Buddhism.
33 Jesuit spiritual director Thomas Henry Green says, 'The director is someone who engages together with the practitioner in the project of discernment: discerning the emotions of the person receiving direction'. Green, *The Friend of the Bridegroom*, p. 63. He also notes, 'What John [of the Cross] criticized most severely was directors who tried to control the soul of the person receiving direction'. See ibid., p. 90.

34 Fujiwara, *Tōzai no hazama de*, pp. 56–57, 75.
35 Ibid., p. 119.
36 Ibid., pp. 146, 148. In animal sacrifice, which cultural anthropologists view as one of the origins of the Mass, participants bring their sins to mind and then touch the animal so that it will bear their sins for them. The animal is then killed. Naikan offers a similar sort of repentance, with 'Holy God' collectively performing this function.
37 Fujiwara frequently recommended daily Naikan to Naikan practitioners in the pages of *Ibuki* [*Breath*], the quarterly newsletter of the 'Kokoro no ihori' Naikan Meditation Center.
38 Though they are few in number, there are some theologians who advocate that lay believers should have the right to conduct Mass. See, for example, Neyrand, 'Shinto ga misa o sasageru koto no kenkai'. In recent years, there have been instances of lay believers who have gone through Naikan meditation under Fujiwara going on to hold Naikan meditation sessions themselves (for example, Ogura Kazue at Sōsōan in the Nagano Prefecture village of Ōshika). Fujiwara supports making attempts at 'a collaborative form of church', but he does not address any specific examples in his essay 'Shinto no naka ni hataraku seirei', p. 2.
39 Fujiwara, *Tōzai no hazama de*, p. 78.
40 Murata, *Oi no ningengaku*, p. 31.
41 Ōi, *'Chihō rōjin' wa nani o mite iru ka*, p. 127.
42 Matsumoto, *Kami no kuni o mezashite*, p. 95.
43 In the 'Kirisuto-sha no tame no Naikan meisō' [Naikan meditation for Christians] article on the subject of Naikan meditation that appears in each issue of *Ibuki*, the interview done by the guiding priest is clearly described as 'being carried out together with a Mass within the framework of the "sacrament of penance and reconciliation"'.
44 Wakamatsu writes, 'When the dead are close at hand, our souls tremble with sadness. Sadness is a signal that the dead are visiting'. Wakamatsu, *Tamashii ni fureru*, p. 8.
45 Interactions with Korea have been taken up as a topic from time to time in *Ibuki*. For example, Fujiwara reported that in issue 41 (December 2010) the contact with Korea began at the Naikan experience of a Korean pastor working in Osaka, Japan in 2006 and in the same issue he showed us the gist of a lecture delivered at a Catholic social hall in the South Korean city of Incheon. Note was also made in issue 44 (December 2011) of the participation by five Naikan practitioners from Korea and three from Japan's resident Korean community in a training workshop for 'interviewers' (equivalent to guides). Partners within Japan's resident Korean community include clergymen who render service to workers in Osaka's Nishinari district (*Ibuki*, No. 46, July 2012).
46 'Han' is a key concept of feeling in Korean culture. It is a complex feeling deeply connected with sadness at life's contradictions and hope at the possibility of going beyond such suffering. Some Korean theologians, especially those working within Minjung theology, have accepted this concept into their thinking. See, for example, Park's *The Wounded Heart of God*.

## References

Etō Hiroyuki, 'Health no gogen to sono dōzokugo to no imiteki rensa: Imiteki rensa to iu shiten kara no gogen kenkyū no yūkōsei [Etymological analysis on "health" and the linkage of its congeneric words],' *Bulletin of the Nagano College of Nursing*, No. 4 (2002).

Fujiwara Naosato, *Tōzai no hazama de* [*Between the East and the West*] (Tokyo: Katorikku naikan kenkyūkai [Institute for Catholic Naikan Research], 1998).
Fujiwara Naosato, *Kokoro no uchinaru tabi: Naikan no reisei o motomete*, [*Inner Journey of the Heart: Looking for the Spirituality of Naikan*] vol. 1 (Osaka: Katorikku naikan kenkyūkai, 2002).
Fujiwara Naosato, *Namu no michi mo āmen no michi mo: Aru inshūshi to no taiwa* [*Path of Namu and Path of Amen: A Dialogue with a Hermit*] (Osaka: 'Kokoro no ihori' Naikan Meditation Center, 2005).
Fujiwara Naosato, 'Shinto no naka ni hataraku seirei [Holy Spirit Being Actual in Laypersons' Activity],' *Ibuki*, No. 46, Summer 2012.
Green, Thomas H., *The Friend of the Bridegroom: Spiritual Direction and the Encounter with Christ*, trans. into Japanese as *Hanamuko no tomo: Rei-teki dōhan no michi shirube* (trans. Suzuki Ryū and Arimura Kōichi *et al.*) (Tokyo: Musōan, 2005).
Inoue Yōji, 'Gendai no reisei o motomete [In search of the contemporary spirituality]', in Momose Fumiaki and Sakuma Tsutomu (eds), *Kirisuto-kyō no shingaku to reisei: Konnichi dono yō ni shinkō o ikiru ka* [*Theology and Spirituality of Christianity: How Can We Live Our Religious Life In Our Time?*] (New Jersey: Paulist Press, 1999).
Maeshiro Teruaki, *Shinri ryōhō to shite no naikan* [*Naikan as a Psychological Therapy*] (Osaka: Toki shobō, 2005).
Matsumoto Saburō, *Kami no kuni o mezashite: Watashitachi no Dai-ni Bachikan kōkaigi* [*In an Effort to Reach the Kingdom of God: Commentary on the Second Vatican Council as a Great Gift to Us*] (Tokyo: Oriens Institute for Religious Research, 1990).
Minami Jikisai, *Osorezan* [*Mt. Osore*] (Tokyo: Shinchōsha, 2012).
Momose Fumiaki, 'Shingaku to reisei [Theology and spirituality]', in Momose Fumiaki and Sakuma Tsutomu (eds), *Kirisuto-kyō no shingaku to reisei: Konnichi dono yō ni shinkō o ikiru ka* [*Theology and Spirituality of Christianity: How Can We Live Our Religious Life In Our Time?*] (New Jersey: Paulist Press, 1999).
Mullins, Mark R., *Christianity Made in Japan: A Study of Indigenous Movements* (Honolulu: University of Hawaii Press, 1998).
Murata Tadayoshi, *Oi no ningengaku* [*Anthropology of Aging*] (Tokyo: Chūō shuppansha, 1986).
Neyrand, Georges, 'Shinto ga misa o sasageru koto no kenkai [My Opinion on a Tentative Theory that Laypersons Can Conduct a Mass Service]', *Fukuin senkyō* [*Mission of Gospel*], June/July 2003.
Oi Gen, '*Chihō rōjin*' *wa nani o mite iru ka* [*What do the demented Elders See?*] (Tokyo: Shinchōsha, 2008).
Okonogi Keigo, *Taishō sōshitsu* [*Object Loss*] (Tokyo: Chūō kōron sha, 1979).
Satō Migaku, *Higeki to fukuin: Genshi Kirisuto-kyō ni okeru higekiteki na mono* [*Tragedy and Gospel: Something Tragic in Primitive Christianity*] (Tokyo: Shimizu shoin, 2001).
Satō Migaku, *Hajimari no Kirisuto-kyō* [*Christianity in the Beginning*] (Tokyo: Iwanami shoten, 2010).
Sung Park, Andrew, *The Wounded Heart of God: The Asian Concept of Han and the Christian Doctrine of Sin* (Abingdon: Abingdon Press, 1993).
Suzuki, D.T., *Nihon-teki reisei* [*The Japanese Spirituality*] (Tokyo: Iwanami bunko edition, 1972).
Tamaki Kōshirō, *Nōkan to gedatsu: Katachinaki inochi ga tsūtetsu suru* [*Brainstem and Liberation: Formless Life Penetrates the Whole Existence*] (Tokyo: Tetsugaku shobō, 1996).

Terao Kazuyoshi, "Tanaka Teruyoshi no ishikiron" [Tanaka Teruyoshi's Theoretical Imagination on Consciousness], *Ningengaku kiyō* [*Studies in Philosophical Anthropology*], No. 39 (2009).

Terao Kazuyoshi, "Katorikku-teki shigosei no yukue: Seizen rengoku-setsu to naikan meisō," [The Catholic Vision of Afterlife: the Theory of Antemortem Purgatory and Naikan Meditation] in *Shiseikan to chōetsu: Bukkyō to shokagaku no gakusai-teki kenkyū* [*Vision of Life and Death and Transcendence: an Interdisciplinary Research of Buddhism and Scholarships*] (2010-nendo hōkokusho) (Ryūkoku University, 2011).

Terao Kazuyoshi, 'Naikan to Hiai' [Naikan and Grief]', in Takada Shinryo (ed.), *Shūkyō ni okeru shiseikan to chōetsu* [*Transcendence and Views of Life and Death in Religion*] (Kyoto: Hōjōdōshuppan, 2013).

Uenuma Masao, *Yami o sumika to suru watashi, yami o kakurega to suru Kami* [*I Live in Darkness and God Hides in Darkness*] (Tokyo: Inochinokotobasha [Word of Life Press Ministries], 2008).

Wakamatsu Eisuke, *Tamashii ni fureru: Daishinsai to, ikite iru shisha* [*In Touch with the Souls: the Great Earthquake and the Dead who are Alive*] (Tokyo: Transview, 2012).

# 9 Kawai Hayao's transnational identity and Japanese spirit

*Tarutani Shigehiro*[1]

Kawai Hayao was originally a scientifically oriented thinker who had no interest in Buddhism or religion generally. This all changed when he went to the University of California, Los Angeles, to do post-graduate research with the Rorschach expert Bruno Klopfer. Klopfer was unusual in that he was internationally renowned as an expert in Rorschach testing and its statistical analysis, on the one hand, and a student of C.G. Jung (1875–1961) and his analytical psychology, on the other. Klopfer introduced Kawai to the Jungian analyst Marvin Spiegelman. When Spiegelman instructed Kawai to bring him his dreams, Kawai was puzzled as he had been expecting a scientifically oriented clinician. Spiegelman retorted that it would be unscientific to regard dreams as 'unscientific' without having researched the matter. The first dream that Kawai reported to Spiegelman contained a Hungarian coin: 'When I picked up the coin and examined it, I saw that it was embossed with the figure of a hermit sage'. Spiegelman suggested that this could be interpreted as signalling the mutual relationship between Western and Asian thought, and that Kawai might begin to explore this theme through the study of the early Taoist texts of the *Lao-tzu* and the *Chuang-tzu*. For his part, Spiegelman had recently dreamed of 'the Sun rising from the West', which he thought in hindsight presaged Kawai's arrival from Japan. Kawai was to go on to play a major role as a bridge between Japan and the West, and later said that his life was a process of bringing the promise of this initial dream to fruition.[2]

In this chapter, I trace Kawai's intellectual trajectory and examine the rich potential of his distinctive interpretation of transnational identity and Japanese culture. I argue that his clinical work was inseparable from a deepening awareness of his own existence, and that both were influenced heavily by the interplay of Kawai's own thought with that of Carl Jung.

## The birth of Kawai Hayao as a 'spiritual intellectual'

When Kawai returned, in 1965, from his studies in the US and subsequently in Switzerland, the work of Jung was as yet virtually unknown in Japan, although a collection of Jung's works in translation had been published in five volumes (1955–1957). Where he was known in intellectual circles, he was widely regarded with suspicion as having occult tendencies. Even in the West, Jungians have debated amongst themselves as to how they could escape a 'ghetto mentality'[3] and 'amateur expert syndrome'.[4] Today, although Jung has achieved a certain currency in the Japanese popular imagination, he is not regarded highly in academia.

Kawai himself, reflecting on the early period of his time at UCLA and his studies abroad, has written about his encounters with 'true believers' in Jung and the cult-like status surrounding him that has hindered sophisticated, critically informed research.[5]

In view of this general suspicious and marginalized view of Jung, Kawai's success in bringing Jungian psychology into mainstream prominence in Japan is all the more striking. Certainly, he had the advantage of having seen what had happened in the West, and so was able to plot a strategic path for the introduction of Jungian paradigms into Japan. First, before presenting his ideas in specific Jungian terms, he worked to compile a solid foundation of clinical case studies. And rather than use dream analysis, which was Jung's primary clinical method, Kawai initially focused on Sandplay therapy, for which there was a well-established cultural receptivity in Japan.[6]

Once he had established a solid academic foundation for his clinical methods, he gradually and carefully expanded his areas of research and writing into dreams, folk tales, myth, Japanese culture, and so on. Eventually, he became Professor of Clinical Psychology at Kyoto University, the Director-General of the International Research Center for Japanese Studies, a central figure in the establishment of the Japanese Certification Board for Clinical Psychologists, and Japan's Commissioner for Cultural Affairs. Through a large number of public lectures and publications, Kawai became one of the most widely recognized and respected intellectuals in Japan. It would have been impossible to imagine such a career at the outset given his initial strong reaction against Jung and what Kawai perceived to be his occultist tendencies.[7] So how did Kawai come to find his spiritual centre as a Jungian?

Kawai was born in 1928, and his childhood and youth coincided with a period of intense Japanese imperialism, a period of regimentation in which nationalist ideology was inculcated in Japanese people through strict, ritualized education. Kawai, however, seemed to have an innate dislike for over-regimentalization, and is said often to have made jokes and transgressed various rules – a naturally rebellious, trickster figure. Although he could have tried to be a good, patriotic child-citizen, as he grew up through the war years Kawai saw clearly that Japan was going to ruin. He finally seemed to have reached his limit on one occasion when he heard a strident army lecturer irrationally assert that America would lose because invaders always lose. When Kawai confided in his elder brother that he was sure the lecturer was wrong, his brother told him to remain silent about his convictions, even to their parents. On another occasion, Kawai experienced a degree of what he later saw as cognitive dissonance, when the militaristic slogan 'American and English Devils' was displayed alongside a foreign film, in colour, full of references to the human touch. Despite being an excellent student academically, he failed to gain entrance to his first choice of higher school (*kyūsei kōkō*) when he received a C-grade in the required subject of military drills. After the war, Kawai disagreed with the view that Japan had lost because of a lack of material resources; rather, he felt that the US had won on the basis of a superior rationality.[8]

Kawai was an introverted child who excelled in mathematics and Japanese literature.[9] A voracious reader, he loved to recite stories when prompted by busy teachers in need of help in momentarily distracting the class. However, he felt frustrated by his inability to appreciate the aesthetic qualities of the literature he studied, because he remained so preoccupied with the plight of the protagonists. He found himself most attracted to the otherworldly quality of Western folktales, such as those of the Grimm brothers, which he preferred to what he considered the more mundane Japanese tales.[10] He felt ambivalent also about Japanese mythology: he loved the stories of the *kami*, the gods and goddesses, but he was repulsed by the irrationality of the militarists who presented these stories as historical fact.[11] Tensions between fantasy and logic continued throughout Kawai's life.

At Kyoto University, Kawai majored in mathematics, but feeling that somehow he could not fully understand the essence of the subject he decided instead to become a high-school teacher.[12] Desiring to help his students in their personal lives as well as in class, he began to study psychology, but became frustrated with the statistical, scientifically oriented experimental psychology that he encountered, which did not seem to take the lives of individuals into account.[13] It was at this point that he discovered Rorschach testing, a statistically analysable psychological tool that nevertheless took into account the rich diversity of individual human experience.

Travelling to UCLA for further study, Kawai developed friendships with both Americans and students from Japan, and began to notice basic differences in the way he related to them. His sense of individual consciousness was heightened when in the company of his American friends, to the point that he would suddenly find himself exhausted after extended conversations with them. With his Japanese friends, he found that it was as though they related to one another on a pre-cognitive level, as if they were coexisting on a shared plane or field of intuition. He came to recognize that, as much as he enjoyed and attempted to relate to people at the level of individual ego, something remained out of reach, and not primarily for linguistic reasons. These experiences took him out of his comfort zone, and he came to recognize for the first time that there could be radical cultural differences in ways of relating.[14] *The Great Mother* by Erich Neumann provided Kawai with vocabulary to identify these differences. Once, in a dream analysis with Spiegelman, Kawai was at a loss for words when he tried to explain the Japanese concept of *amae*.[15] After struggling for a week to find a way to explain the concept, Kawai felt that it was close to what Neumann called the feeling of dependence on the Jungian archetype of the Great Mother. He came to feel that the pull of the Great Mother tended to be stronger in Japanese society than in the Western cultures he had so far encountered.[16]

Following his work at UCLA, Kawai went to the Jung Institute in Switzerland where he went on to become the first Japanese national to be certified as a Jungian analyst. He underwent a training analysis and a 'control analysis' – two major rites of passage in his career and his life. In both cases, he found his own identity called into question, both personally and more broadly, in a cultural sense. As he took on his own clients, Kawai found life as an analyst to be quite challenging. One moment, he would have five clients; the next, all but one would be gone.

Was it due to his 'otherness' as a Japanese person, and what was the nature of his own inner other, the Jungian 'anima'? He faced moments of great difficulty, such as when one of his clients attempted suicide.[17] Moreover, through the training analysis, Kawai became aware of the collective shadow of the Japanese within him, in relation to Japanese wartime militarism.[18]

Kawai faced a great test too at the oral defence of his thesis. When one of the examiners asked him, 'What are some examples of symbols of the Self?', to which a textbook answer would have been 'mandala' or 'quaternity', instead an expression from East Asian Buddhism came into Kawai's mind: 'Mountain, rivers, grasses, and trees are all manifestations of buddha nature,' he replied. 'Everything, in fact, including this desk!' A heated discussion ensued, and the examiner later said that Kawai lacked basic knowledge of analytical psychology, a reaction which perhaps was to be expected. After some difficulty, Kawai obtained his certification, and when he later thought about how hard he had insisted on his own answer he felt that in the background all the time was the concept of all things being sacred, conveyed to him by the Japanese Buddhist phrase, *shinra banshō*, 'all things in nature'.[19]

Up to that point, many had thought that Kawai was some stereotypical Asian 'Yes'-man, but suddenly he had uttered a 'No' at the establishment – questioning the orthodox foundations of the Jung Institute, according to its then President, Franz Riklin.[20]

Returning to Japan soon thereafter, Kawai found himself engaged in an inner battle with the 'Great Mother', becoming aware through his parapraxes of aggressive feelings towards his own mother.[21] As if by coincidence he found himself consulted by clients with similar symptoms, including a junior high-school boy with a history of absenteeism, who dreamt about being swallowed by a vortex made of raw meat (suggestive of the Great Mother in her devouring form), and a female college student with social phobia, who described an especially strong bond with her mother and who suffered from repeated instances of imaginary earthquakes.[22] As the chapters in this volume on Kosawa and Doi show, maternal themes recur throughout Japanese sociology and psychology, related to fields of intuition, maternal indulgence, anima, collective shadow, and the all-encompassing nature of the Jungian Self.

During the mid-twentieth century, religion and philosophy garnered wide interest among the university-educated in Japan, as seen in major East–West syntheses such as Nishida Kitarō's *The Study of Good*. For Kawai such works were rather abstract and obscure,[23] but later in life he came to appreciate the religious thought of such philosophical thinkers as Izutsu Toshihiko, and his articulations of Sufism and semiotics, as well as Ueda Shizuteru's expositions of Zen Buddhism and philosophy of religion.[24] Kawai himself began to write about Buddhist thought and Japanese philosophy, and he interacted with both men regularly at the Eranos Conferences – in fact, it was Izutsu who introduced Kawai to Eranos.

Kawai went so far as to say that his own philosophical thinking was based on Huayan Buddhism as elucidated by Izutsu.[25] According to Adolf Guggenbühl Craig, Kawai became known as a Jungian with strong Buddhist leanings.[26]

If the Great Mother archetype in Jungian psychology and Buddhist expressions of ultimate reality both point to something beyond the visible, then one could say that Kawai began to open up to a world that he had once thought 'occult' but which he now saw as clarifying something that lay deep within him – something more intimate than he could ever have suspected would be there. This did not mean an abandonment of critical rationality, but rather its more precise application. One can see this in the International Transpersonal Conference held in Japan in 1985, which under Kawai's leadership managed both spiritual depth and scholarly rigour, avoiding extremes of new age occultism or dry scholasticism.[27] The result was genuine enthusiasm for interdisciplinary collaboration among scholars and practitioners representing the best of the fields, such as Jungian analyst James Hillman and terminal care specialist Elizabeth Kübler-Ross. Through Kawai's efforts as a kind of 'spiritual intellectual', educators, clinicians, and the general public were brought into an encounter with the so-called 'Spiritual World'.[28]

## Spirituality in Jung's thought

In order to understand Kawai as a 'spiritual intellectual', one must first briefly examine Carl Jung's place within the spiritual culture of the West. By the late nineteenth century, scientific advances in such fields as evolutionary biology and the idea of the historical Jesus rendered it increasingly difficult for the intellectual class to maintain the faith of earlier generations – including Jung's own father, a Protestant minister. Unlike his father, Jung's mother was highly susceptible to spiritual trances and was influenced by fashionable and quasi-scientific grassroots spiritualist movements, which stood somewhat in contrast to the communal and institutional faith of religious communities since the middle ages. This rootless spiritualism was part of the legacy that Jung inherited. Like Kawai in later years, Jung found himself ultimately dissatisfied with traditional religious culture, with enlightenment rationality, and with modern spiritualism.

Based both on his religious background and a rational approach, Jung dealt with spiritual matters critically but openly. There was an affinity between his approach and that of such contemporaries as Thèodore Flournoy and Pierre Janet. Jung's thesis on *The Psychology and Pathology of So-called Occult Phenomena* (1902) was modelled on Flournoy's study of spiritual mediums and examined the symptomatology of altered states of consciousness in somnambulism with an eye to its compensatory significance as well as the possibility of development into a new personality in the future. After Jung parted ways with his mentor Freud, Flournoy played a kind of paternal guardian role for Jung as the latter developed his thinking.

From Janet, he inherited such notions as *abaissement du niveau mental*, 'lowering the threshold of consciousness', and 'subconscious fixed idea' (1902–1903), the latter Jung renamed 'psychological complex'. Janet himself had an interest in spiritual matters, shown by his historical research on mesmerism, and his work on the transformation of consciousness and the refinement of psychic energy through ritual, myth, and possession. In these areas Janet's later work overlapped with that of Jung.

Jung proceeded with his study of neurosis and psychosis, hypnosis and word association, dreams, and active imagination; in his spiritual interests he researched mesmerism and modern occultism, Gnosticism and inner alchemy, as well as related dimensions of religious culture, all from the standpoint of altered states of consciousness and the transformation of personality.

Freud's influence on Jung lay in other areas, such as interpretation of the unconscious including dream analysis, defence mechanisms, and problems of *ressentiment* or self-deception. This latter problem Jung explored through such notions as the trickster figure and the mercurial character, as expressions of the soul or of the unconscious.

For Jung as well as for Kawai, the awakening to the unexpected turns of the unconscious, and its 'trickster' character, required him to undergo a reappraisal of his whole being, body and soul – a 'confrontation with the unconscious', as Jung described it. Jung had previously sought to approach the religious dimension objectively, from a scientific standpoint or under the rubric of the occult. Through his experience of the unconscious, however, he helped to give birth to a renewed discipline of psychology that found positive significance in a subjective, non-material realm.

In other words, Jung's confrontation with the unconscious made it necessary for him to postulate its objective existence as a psychic reality existing in complementary balance and interaction with the material world of the body, physical matter, society, and nature – rather than being merely a product of repression. What Jung – building on Immanuel Kant – called *esse in anima*, 'existence in the soul', was neither pure materialism nor idealism, but instead involved understanding living reality as an interplay of the material (*esse in re*) and the ideal (*esse in intellectu*): patterns constellate of their own accord in the field of psychic energy, responding to the changing landscape of the material realm.[29] Jung treated the unconscious, or 'soul', phenomenologically, as a field of real experience, without venturing metaphysical speculations about it.

This was a position that ran counter to modern assumptions concerning the fixed separation of subject and object. Jung thought that in order to achieve the state that had existed before the modern separation of subject and object, we must open up our self-consciousness to the 'Other'. In contrast with Freud, he shifted the task of the conscious ego away from preoccupation with the material realm to the continual exploration of how we ought properly to deal with this Other: an ongoing task that requires the ego to become responsive to the ever-changing unconscious, or 'soul', as well as to the shifting contours of social reality. 'Receptivity' here requires not only the application of reason but also affective and intuitive awareness, where multiple significations and ambiguities are often better captured through images than in set concepts. Arguably, the deeper one goes into ambiguity, the more nearly one approaches questions of fundamental existence. From this perspective, life on the surface of consciousness and society is seen as a product of fantasy and imagination working at the depths of the soul.[30]

For Jung, when the focus of existence is shifted from the social and material to the unconscious, then the actual workings of what he called the 'religious factor' – the numinous, the divine – must be accounted for. Regardless of whether a given individual is aware of it or not, this dimension is present and will eventually make itself known through its possession of the entirety of the psyche.

However, a situation where the ego is merely invaded or possessed by impulses arising from the unconscious cannot be regarded as fully 'religious' in character, since to qualify as the latter requires active engagement by, and commitment from, an autonomous individual whose ego consciousness is assuming its proper ethical responsibilities.[31] This view of religion perhaps reflects Jung's background in the family of a Protestant minister, with a modernist view of religion in which each individual takes responsibility for recognizing and attending to the numinous. As Jung notes, '"*Religio*" … means a careful consideration and observation of certain dynamic factors that are conceived of as "powers"',[32] and a 'careful consideration of ever-present unconscious forces, which we neglect at our peril'.[33]

[For Kawai] What it means to be a 'Jungian' was, as Jung had said, to conscientiously and attentively examine the material that is produced out of the unconscious, to determine one's life course taking all of it into account, and to set out on the path of individuation thereby.[34]

'Religion' in this sense had nothing to do with dogma, canonical scripture, denomination, or church.[35] The key lay rather in religious experience, an emphasis that was later inherited by the Transpersonal Psychology movement.

## Undercurrents in Japanese spiritual history

For Kawai the role of the maternal as a psychological force became a major theme following his return to Japan, both in working with clients and in his own life. He articulates this in *The Japanese Psyche: Major Motifs in the Fairy Tales of Japan* (1988),[36] where he points out some of the characteristics of Japanese psychology.

According to Jung's Analytical Psychology, fairy and folk tales carry significant content that emerges from the structures of the collective unconscious. While there are universal themes expressed through these stories, they also contain elements distinctive to the cultures they are found in. Jung differentiated between the universal and culturally delimited dimensions by referring to them as expressions of the 'collective unconscious (archetypes)' and 'collective consciousness', respectively. While collective consciousness is linked to the unconscious, it shows hallmarks of a specific culture. This is especially apparent in myths, fairy tales, religious rituals, and customs. When the collective consciousness takes religious themes and over-secularizes and commodifies them, they tend to become highly ideological and dogmatic. In that sense, they differ from deep expressions of the collective unconscious that remain beyond the reach of immediate commodification.[37]

Collective consciousness is often expressed in the religious ethos of the accepted or dominant traditions of a particular culture, but the conscious aspect is often just the tip of the iceberg of a larger subconscious or unconscious force – this is similar to what Freud conceived of as the super-ego.[38]

Though we are often not conscious of the real significance of the rituals and customs we participate in, since prehistoric times human beings have regulated their desires and ordered their societies – everything from class structure to tribal teachings and marital relations – through ritual and traditional narratives. Such traditions have their own inertia and do not always evolve with the changing circumstances of time and place, though since they are largely a matter of the unconscious the people inhabiting these ritual spaces and narrative topoi often fail to notice that the link between the collective consciousness and the collective unconscious has been lost or broken. This can result in the ossification of culture, with ritual and narrative traditions falling into empty formalism. Yet the forces of the collective unconscious do not disappear, and unless the collective consciousness is reimagined appropriately a crisis can occur at the psychic level that leads to major disturbances and ruptures at the individual and social level.[39]

Christianity has been one of the major dominant forces in the shaping of collective consciousness in the West.[40] Jung sought to excavate and elucidate deep layers of the psyche in Western spiritual history that had been fused with Christian culture, with a view to finding a myth that would genuinely support him. This led him to the study of mythology, the deeper significance of rituals such as the Catholic Mass, and archetypal symbols such as the Trinity. For Kawai it became necessary to unearth the narratives and rituals that underpinned the dominant religion and culture of Japan: Buddhism. He did not precisely adopt Jung's concept of 'collective consciousness' in relation to myths and fairy tales; rather, he understood the function of fairy and folk tales primarily as compensatory for the constraints of a socially acceptable consciousness.[41] Eventually, he discovered a subterranean stream of cultural traditions fused with Buddhism, which the Japanese thinker and friend of Kawai, Tsurumi Shunsuke, has termed *kakure bukkyō*: hidden, or latent, Buddhism.[42]

Where Kawai was drawn to Western fairy and folk tales for the richness of their happy endings, of romance and salvation, he found Japanese tales lacking in many of these same areas. He was disappointed by their blandness, their lack of excitement. Stories often contained unhappy or incomplete romance, with the male character breaking a taboo and causing a female character to turn into an animal and depart, out of resentment. There seemed to be no moral to the story, no ethical consequence for the breaking of the taboo, and the lingering tone at the end would be one of ephemeral beauty or the pathos of things.

The well-known story of Urashima Tarō is emblematic of some of these tendencies. Although Urashima enters the undersea Dragon Palace, there is no battle with the dragon. And even though he lives with the princess of the Dragon Palace for many years, they never marry. When he returns to the surface out of longing for his previous life, he breaks a taboo against opening a particular jewel box, and is instantly turned into an old man. In this and many other stories, the male protagonist fails to take charge, to show autonomy. There are Japanese stories that do result in marriage or romantic consummation, but in the majority of such narratives, the protagonist is female. In those cases where the protagonist is male, the truly proactive character tends to be female. In the rare cases where there is an active male protagonist in a narrative that leads to successful romance, the male tends to be subservient to a mother or maternal force, so that he never really comes into his own and ends up a kind of impish trickster figure.

This stands in contrast to the hero narrative of Western myth and folk tales, which correlates with the dominant male divinity that provides the sacred canopy under which the hero's story unfolds.

In the Japanese narratives, the power of female characters and their stories of successful romance are not those of heroic conquest but rather perseverance and endurance supported by a sense of absolute nothingness. According to Kawai, Japanese narratives revolve not around a dominant male hero but a spacious or hollow centre that has a balancing and harmonizing function, allowing various characters or elements to enter the stage provisionally and temporarily.

Thus, Kawai brings out a contrast between the dominant centre of Western narratives, with the male God in Heaven and the human hero below, and Japanese stories, with a hollow centre and receptive rather than proactive characters. One should keep in mind that this image of feminine receptivity that Kawai associates with Japanese psychology is not gender-specific in a social sense. That is, both men and women in Japan tend to be more receptive than proactive. This receptivity, however, is not passivity. The hollow centre is not merely an empty nothingness; rather, it is more like an active nothingness, in the sense of receptive sensitivity. According to Kawai, it is not that 'nothing happens' but rather that '*the* nothing *happens*'. The entirety of the folk or fairy tale narrative gives expression to this nothing that is happening.[43]

Kawai considered the traditional Japanese self-image to be a feminine one supported by absolute nothingness, which 'tries to accept whatever comes or happens, and aims at completeness'[44] – something akin to the inclusiveness of nature. Thus, for example, unusual natural phenomena are not given exceptional status as 'magic' or 'witchcraft' in Japanese stories, but are accepted simply because everything that occurs is part of nature.[45] Such inclusiveness can be morally superior *or* inferior to masculine exclusiveness: there are times when the exclusion of evil may be ethically necessary, and when inclusiveness leads to corruption. The key is simply to recognize diverse psychological modalities: feminine inclusiveness and masculine exclusiveness. For example, the only socially acceptable image of the 'mother' in Japanese society is that of absolute good. The negative side of the maternal is found instead in stories such as 'The old woman of the mountain' (*Yamauba*) or those that feature cruel stepmothers. These are cases of inclusiveness where the maternal threatens to devour the male protagonist. There are also stories of close bonds between siblings where the older sister becomes a kind of surrogate mother and the younger brother takes a passive role.

In *The Japanese Psyche: Major Motifs in the Fairy Tales of Japan* (1988), Kawai introduces the story 'The home of the bush warbler' (*Uguisu no sato*). The protagonist is a woodsman who falls in love with a beautiful woman. But he breaks a taboo, and she turns into a bush warbler and leaves him out of resentment. He stands by helplessly and watches as the bush warbler takes flight. 'Looking in the direction of the bird as it disappeared, he picked up his axe, yawned, and relaxed. When he regained his senses, he found himself standing in the middle of the meadow without finding even a trace of the splendid mansion he had seen before.'[46] This may appear to be a story of female exclusiveness, but what we see here more than anything is the failure of engagement, both literal and figurative, by the male protagonist. It is as if the female character departs so as to return to nature, or the collective unconscious, as suggested by the warbler. What is striking is that the failure to achieve any male–female union is so widespread in this type of narrative, with the return to nature also quite common.

Kawai considers another folk tale – *Sumiyaki-Chojya* (The charcoal maker millionaire) – in which the female protagonist shows her true colours. In this tale, rather than escaping back to nature or into the unconscious, this disclosure of her true nature frees up her intuition to enable her to see into men's true natures. After enduring trials that take her through various twists and turns, she emerges stronger, and as a woman of will is able to achieve a happy marriage. Although the female–male union is achieved, it is notable here that the power of the will is expressed through the female character.

In the context of these Japanese stories, the feminine consciousness does not develop according to a linear progression, as Erich Neumann suggests often happens in Western narratives, but images of the feminine undergo a series of overlapping, ambiguous transformations in which their multivalent, multivocal, synchronic resonances often outweigh their diachronic development. Contradictory or polar traits or characteristics are often embraced simultaneously or in close succession, such as that of old age and youth, *senex* and *puer* consciousness. Due to its polysemy, the maternal principle that Kawai has illuminated does not simply stand in clear contradistinction to the paternal principle but rather embraces it, at times allowing for its development, at other times appearing to bind or devour it, but seemingly never quite letting it out of its grasp.

## Inheritance from Jung

Kawai often said that during his time abroad he learned the three 'C's: complex, constellation, and commitment. Of these, he made 'constellation' the topic of his farewell retirement lecture at Kyoto University in 1992.[47] In this lecture, he clarified his own views on the subject and related them to those of Jung. Here I would like to examine some ramifications of his views, drawing on a number of his other published works and placing them in the context of his spirituality.

While developing his word association test (1905–1906), Jung had often used the word 'constellation', closely related to his definition of 'complex'. Jung had noticed that some stimulus words produced lags in response time, or an inability to respond, a misunderstanding of the word itself, or strange or unusual responses. Taken together, these noteworthy difficulties resembled the way that stars seem to form patterns, or 'constellations'. Jung used the word 'complex' to refer to a similar, usually undesirable situation whereby a composite body of ideas charged with strong emotions coalesce due to some aspect of an individual's personal history. Jung wrote initially of 'a complex that had constellated', but from around 1940 he began to write more about the 'constellation of an archetype'.

In one piece of writing, Jung referred to 'irrational, affective reactions and impulses, emanating from the unconscious', saying:

> The more clearly the archetype is constellated [i.e. the more clearly an archetype comes through in a particular pattern of associations], the more powerful will be its fascination, and resultant religious statements will formulate it accordingly as 'daemonic' or 'divine'. Such statements indicate possession by an archetype.[48]

A progression from this was Jung's development of his theory of synchronicity, in the 1950s. This involved detecting significance in simultaneously occurring phenomena that were not linked by linear causality – instead what Jung called 'an acausal connecting principle' was at work. When an archetype is constellated within the psyche of an individual, a correlative constellation may occur in the external world, as if to echo the psychic significance of the archetype. To attribute such correspondence to a linear causal link between these inner and outer realms runs the risk of falling prey to the delusion of omnipotence of thought.

Instead, synchronicity as an acausal connecting principle leads us to ponder the significance of inner and outer events more holistically, in a way that calls into question the assumed existence of an isolated, willful individual acting alone.

Discussing these ideas of Jung's in his farewell lecture, Kawai pointed out the importance of a therapist's personality and reflexivity in accurately reading constellations. This has the added benefit of enabling a closer relationship between therapist and client.[49] In other words, the third 'C', commitment, is required. This is no ordinary commitment. If faced with a client who expresses a desire to commit suicide, the therapist must commit fully to the situation: seeking neither to dissuade the client, nor to approve or assist, but rather entering fully into the client's particular field of constellation without prejudice and without hesitation based on any expected outcome. Commitment in this sense is 'to commit one's whole being', though without undue interference at the level of waking or ordinary ego consciousness.[50]

This open attitude on the part of the therapist, said Kawai, may also facilitate the same openness in a client, which then allows the archetypal constellation to unfold, to be cognized, and to be interpreted. This attitude of nonjudgmental openness is similar to what Freud called 'evenly suspended attention': a receptive attitude that should not be mistaken for mere passivity, since the therapist must guard against falling into an ego-defensive attitude and must be attentive to the undercurrents of emotion so as to facilitate the broadening of the client's field of vision, in which the right grasp of a constellation through subjective and objective perceptions is made possible.[51]

For Kawai, both the therapist's 'evenly suspended attention' and the client's state of 'free association' represent altered states of consciousness. Unlike hypnosis, the link with waking consciousness is maintained; therapist and client work together in opening themselves to that which had previously been 'other' to conscious awareness. Both should be open and sensitive not only to the body and to desire but also to the contours of the social, cultural, and natural landscape. Time and space are made specific to each particular therapeutic setting: the analyst's office or counselling room as well as the length and schedule of the therapeutic sessions are designed to open both therapist and client to the therapeutic moment. Freed from the constraints of ordinary everyday life, they are initiated into non-ordinary forms of consciousness. As Jung puts it, they are brought into 'the *vas Hermeticum* of alchemy, [which is] hermetically sealed (i.e. sealed with the sign of Hermes).'[52] It is a sacred space, a sanctum, *temenos*.

This is what Jung understood to be the truly religious attitude, one based on what, as we have seen, he called *esse in anima*. There are varying degrees of depth to this attitude, from spontaneous experiences occurring in lay people to the mature therapist, shaman, or awakened religious master. Regardless of difference in depth, the same definition, of 'spirituality', applies: an opening to a deeper level of consciousness and the widening of the horizon of awareness and self-awakening. The significance of spirituality does not depend on the depth of realization but rather on our flexibility in adapting to the diversity of human experience, ensuring that the singular significance of each individual is not lost in a fixed grid of dogma, morals, and values. This is how I interpret Jung's and Kawai's views on 'spirituality'.

Kawai also discussed art and Sandplay therapy as sources of insight about archetypal constellations. Showing slides of Jung's mandalas and his own case studies of Sandplay therapy, Kawai explained:

> These examples show how an entire world is expressed in one constellation. ... I think there is a story waiting to get out from each person, each of you. ... When you try to convey to others a constellated moment of synchronicity, then it has to unfold diachronically, as a story.[53]

One can see here that Kawai, like Jung, placed great emphasis on image and fantasy as the loci where the separation of subject and object are transcended.

## Hidden Buddhism and the establishment of the individual

One of Kawai's major contributions was to bring to light the situation of the collective consciousness in Japan through his research into folk and fairy tales. However, the complex and fragmented nature of modern life has made it impossible even for the fully articulated collective consciousness to embrace everything. This fragmentation of culture and collective consciousness has been a topic of intense debate since at least the nineteenth century, and various responses have been proposed from the political through to the psychological and religious.[54] Both Jung and Kawai sought the key in 'spirituality': Jung turned to the study of 'heterodox' spiritual lineages, from Gnosticism to alchemy, while Kawai turned to alternative narratives of Japanese Buddhist history and focused on the Buddhist high priest Myōe (1173–1232), whom Kawai thought underappreciated compared with his contemporaries. Kawai wrote a series of articles on Myōe and ultimately devoted an entire monograph to him – *The Buddhist Priest Myōe: A Life of Dreams* – which focused on the Buddhist monk's dreams.[55]

According to Jung, individual dreams and visions often arise spontaneously from the collective unconscious as compensatory for or corrective of imbalances in the general cultural situation in which that individual finds himself or herself.[56] In this sense, individual dreams and visions differ from myths and folk tales, since the latter tend more to express the collective consciousness as well as carrying content reflective of the collective unconscious. Kawai took an interest in Myōe because he left behind a detailed journal of his dreams and visions that reflected his spiritual development; a record that is singular in Japanese religious history. The key here is that Myōe's legacy is not primarily one of Buddhist philosophical precision (although he had that also) but rather a dream journal that Kawai believed vividly expressed the workings of the collective unconscious.[57]

By the time of Myōe, Buddhism had been in Japan for over six centuries and had reached a certain level of maturity, with high-level debates concerning canonical scriptures and textual passages. At the grass roots, Buddhist notions had taken hold, including those relating to karma (both individual and collective), and there was a widespread sentiment that *mappō*, the final age of the dharma, had arrived, such was the collective decadence and corruption of the Buddhist priesthood. In reaction, there arose a movement to revive the practice of Buddhist precepts that had fallen into disuse. These included the eight primary precepts: prohibitions against murder, theft, sex, lying, imbibing alcohol, cavorting, wearing makeup, and eating more than one meal after noon. Yet, many of the monks continued their dissolute ways. There was a great deal of elitism within the aristocratic priesthood, and wealthy temples not infrequently armed their monks for the invasion of rival temples.[58] Monks who had sincere religious aspirations left these worldly temples, and a number of them attempted to initiate reform movements.

These included the Pure Land leaders Hōnen and Shinran, the Zen master Dōgen, and the Lotus advocate Nichren. In contrast to these figures, who became the founders of the major sects of Buddhism in present-day Japan, the likes of Myōe and Jōkei attempted to revive the older established sects through the reinstatement of monastic precepts.

One of the ideological bases of decadent, aristocratic Buddhism was the concept of *hongaku*, or 'original enlightenment', which held that all beings are originally enlightened by virtue of their buddha-nature. Since all beings are enlightened by their very nature, all natural actions may also be regarded as enlightened, including the imbibing of alcohol and engagement in sexual activity. Furthermore, 'all beings' was held to include mountains, rivers, trees, and grasses – a naturalistic tendency within Japanese religion that runs throughout Japanese history, despite periodic efforts to resist it. This 'Hidden Buddhism', with its emphasis on original enlightenment, came to the fore during Myōe's time, and the naturalistic affirmation of this world influenced not only developments within Buddhist temples but far beyond into the realms of art, literature, and entertainment.[59] For all their rejection of original enlightenment, such figures as Myōe nevertheless drew upon the rich artistic culture that was inspired by it, a feature of which was the inextricable interweaving of transcendence and immanence. This undercurrent within Japanese Buddhism tended to affirm things as they were without need for disciplined practice, offering an inclusive and permissive maternal dimension that Kawai grappled with and for which he found Myōe a compelling case study.

Myōe was a strong-willed and highly disciplined monk, the type of male figure that is distinctly absent from Japanese folk tales. Rather than affirm things 'as they are' (*arugamama*),[60] he sought through rigorous religious practice to implement things 'as they should be' (*arubekiyōwa*). He rejected the status quo in Japan and even sought to make a pilgrimage to India as the authentic land of Buddhism. There are numerous episodes indicating his rejection of this world of natural desire in favour of the other world of religious transcendence, such as his call for the revival of the precepts, his attempt to leave for India, the amputation of his ear, and his intense asceticism. At the same time, he was not merely an ascetic who cut himself off from the world of desires. His founding of a convent as a refuge for widows of deceased soldiers, his compassion for lay people, his dreams and visions rich with affection and even tantric themes of sexuality all show that he remained connected to his emotions and his body. In Jungian terms, his *anima*, or feminine consciousness, connected him with the collective unconscious, but also with the world around him and the collective consciousness.

Kawai's research on Myōe constituted a case study of a kind of individuation process, wherein the dream journal, biographical texts, and other materials were used to show how the Buddhist priest evolved his religious praxis as a way to open to and integrate contents arising from the collective unconscious, and how he dealt with various mental and physical afflictions as well as unexpected events, both psychic and external.[61] From the available biographical records, it is apparent that Myōe had a strong aversion to the defilements of this world, of *samsara*, and a desire to withdraw as a hermit, but by being open to the collective unconscious he also had to attend to the suffering of the collective consciousness – even while this exposed him to potential transgression, including contact with women, physical ailments and conditions, animals and the natural environment.

And it was precisely via these sorts of contacts that Myōe was in fact able to deepen his religious awakening, embraced in what the Mahayana Buddhist tradition describes as the light of boundless compassion, emptiness/oneness, in which all beings and things are seen to interpenetrate one another. It is this realization of oneness that characterized Myōe's spirituality.

Of course, Myōe was also a finite, limited human being, and there were contents of the collective unconscious that he failed to recognize or to integrate with his conscious awareness. Kawai hints at some of these areas, including Myōe's disagreements with his contemporary, the Pure Land Buddhist priest Hōnen. Hōnen was one of the most respected monks of his day, who took a radical turn at the age of forty-three when he came to think that all beings are so burdened with karmic evil – laity and priesthood alike – that they should abandon all religious practices except for the single-minded repetition of the Name of Amida Buddha, the buddha of infinite light: 'Namu Amida Butsu' ('I entrust myself and bow to the awakening of infinite light').

After Hōnen's death in 1212, Myōe composed a highly charged, polemical critique, the *Zaijarin* (Breaking the circle of heresy), in which he sharply criticized Hōnen's main work, *Senjaku hongan nembutsu shū* (Collected sayings on the selected original vow of the name), in which he had advocated the practice of the Name. Myōe was particularly incensed by Hōnen's exclusion of other practices – and by implication other Buddhist sects – and with his sweeping criticism of the contemporary monkhood as 'bandits and robbers'. Myōe called Hōnen 'a limb of the devil' and condemned him for making universal evil the basis for seeing everyone on the same level, regardless of their efforts as priests or as laypeople.

Yet, in the very midst of making these criticisms, Myōe saw a dream in which Hōnen appeared to him as a holy man. Thus, Myōe's conscious view of Hōnen was contradicted by his unconscious. Although Kawai does not state this explicitly in his work on Myōe, he seems to suggest that Myōe had an imbalanced view of Hōnen at the conscious level and so the unconscious provided a compensatory vision.[62] Certainly, viewed against the historical background, Myōe's criticism was excessively severe. For, even in his lifetime, Hōnen's sect suffered from unprecedented pressure from the establishment. Having passed away in this political situation, he could no longer respond himself to Myōe's criticism against his thought. And though it was clear that Hōnen's denial of religious service as a means of salvation was an antisocial, dangerous element,[63] in terms of the Buddhist morality that thereby spread among the common people, Hōnen was a highly disciplined monk and accomplished practitioner who had tapped into the deepest levels of the mind through his constant practice of the Name.[64] Through his experience of an altered state of consciousness, Hōnen perceived 'the structure of invisible power', and preached salvation brought equally to all people.

As an expression of compensation for the contemporary collective consciousness, Hōnen's teachings fulfilled the needs of the times by saving those excluded from the community.

For Myōe's part, his call to return to practices 'as they should be' (*arubekiyōwa*) was a negation of the status quo to an extent, but his overlooking of the oppression of the peasants by the aristocracy, including by the priesthood, amounted to a kind of complicity in reinforcing that status quo. The 'Hidden Buddhism' of medieval Japan, which contained a more authentic or profound affirmation of the oneness of all beings, nature, and the cosmos, remained partially hidden for Myōe, who could not connect with the masses at their own level; Hōnen remained limited in another way, through his exclusion of the wide range of practices developed by the Buddhist priesthood.

## Hidden Buddhism and exclusivism

Jung was deeply concerned with the psychic as well as societal fallout of the dominance of discursive reason in a Western spiritual climate underpinned by dichotomous – 'either-or' – thinking. In particular, he focused on problems of exclusion: of women, the body, and the dark or shadow side ('evil'). In the case of Japan, however, with its powerful, inclusive, maternal forces, it was more difficult to discern the hidden exclusivism operating within its psychology. Kawai thought that the ambiguity of the maternal made it difficult to distinguish what Japanese society traditionally deemed acceptable or proper.[65]

In Kawai's view Japanese morality has not been based on the clear distinction between good and evil in the way that Western morality has. Although Japanese society is patriarchal, its psychology, in particular with respect to its unconscious, is strongly maternal.[66] Social patriarchy is just an articulation of differentiation within a greater undifferentiated totality, symbolized by the (circular) uroboros of religious mythology around the world. It was the uroboric father – patriarchy arising out of the maternal – that Kawai rejected when he rebelled against Japan's militarism in the early twentieth century, even before the Pacific War.[67] And he was disturbed to discover, during a training analysis at the Jung Institute, that this uroboric father lurked in the depths of his own psyche, as part of the unsettled collective shadow.

Kawai later explored this problem through his interpretation of the folk tale of Katako, the 'half-child'.[68] A Japanese man once had the thought that he liked sweet-bean rice cakes so much that he would be willing to trade his wife for one, whereupon a devil (*oni*) came to him, let him eat to his heart's content, and kidnapped his wife. Ten years later, he finally found her on the Island of the Oni. By then, his wife had had a child by the devil, a 'half-child'. Thanks to the child's knowledge and cleverness, the man, his wife, and the child were able to escape. Once back home in Japan, however, the 'half-child' was rejected by everyone due to his mixed heritage, and he ended up committing suicide. Before his death, the half-child had left instructions that, should his father the devil come in search of him, those left behind were to cut the devil-portion of the half-child's flesh into pieces, put these on skewers, and leave them by the door. When the devil came to attack them they had already done this, according to the half-child's instructions, and the devil was turned away. He left, muttering: 'Japanese women are terrible'.

Key features of this story include the unreliability of the Japanese man, the son (half-child) devoted to his mother, and the primacy of the mother–son bond. Kawai states: 'The maternal within the Japanese ... does not tolerate the 'half-child' and instead valorizes homogeneity. This is symbolized by the parents who silently look on as their half-child commits suicide.'[69] The devil symbolizes the 'strong male' that is lacking in Japanese culture, and the half-child the possibility of forming a bridge between the two. In Grimm's fairy tales the devilish character is often killed but then reborn, freed from the evil spell that has been cast. In contrast, in Japan where nature (mother earth) is at the fore, the half-child must live on as he is. Kawai urges the necessity of taking time to recreate a half-child fantasy in ourselves, involving a completely new image of a father, which neither excludes evil in a Western manner nor refrains from facing the world in a Japanese manner.[70]

## Conclusion

In one sense, Japan may be said to be a culture of wholeness or completeness, but as Jung says, without the principle of perfection (the inclusion of the strong male or paternal), there can be no true wholeness.[71] One might suggest, on this basis, that Japan cannot merely pursue 'Westernization' to find its place in global society. If that were possible, then thinkers like Jung and Kawai would not have had to undertake the enormous task of elucidating the social unconscious in order to achieve informed cross-cultural integration. Jung regarded it as a self-deception for Western people to leap at and imitate what he called Eastern spirituality, setting aside their traditions and collective consciousness, because a mere negation of these traditions risked dragging out their own collective shadow. What he thought had to be done was to endeavour to understand it as far as possible with the Western mind.[72] And for Kawai, Westernization of the Japanese was out of question. Just as the structure of a language imposes a limiting framework on one's way of thinking, so one cannot simply deny the collective consciousness of the place and the time in which one was brought up: instead, in order to develop a spirituality open to both immanence and transcendence, one must relive that collective consciousness with renewed awareness, in the depths of one's own consciousness.

Kawai was prescient in understanding that for Japanese, there is ultimately no way to feel at home in global society without somehow rescuing the half-child. This was not just a theory but something that came out of his own life and extended not only to the Japanese but to other peoples as well. Having studied abroad at the most crucial juncture in his life, he became, in his own words, 'half Western, half Japanese' – a half-child himself, with an unusually keen sense of the collective consciousness of both cultures in which he had experience of living. The task of rescuing the half-child was an urgent one for Kawai himself and, as he increasingly found, for members of his audiences – including in the US. He began to realize that the problem of feeling ostracized from the communal was a universal one, and not easily resolved.[73]

Indeed, Kawai himself never fully resolved the problem, and his son Toshio, who succeeded him at Kyoto University, has continued to grapple with it. Speaking of his father, he described a scene at the Eranos Conference where the elder Kawai gave a speech. When he addressed the problem of the half-child, and similar characters such as Hiruko, the Leech Child, he became filled with emotion and tears rolled down his cheeks.[74] The half-child must have been an acute problem, central to his existence. However, Kawai, always cautious and measured with regard to publicizing problems of the unconscious, did not feel ready to put his thoughts on this into writing. Perhaps he had further ideas of which we shall never know.[75] But as this problem of ostracism becomes ever more urgent, we begin to see that Kawai has left invaluable clues as to how we might open new paths for inquiry and self-discovery.

## Notes

1 Translated by Mark Unno.
2 Kawai, *Mirai e no Kioku ge*, p. 17, pp. 36ff.; Kawai, *Buddhism and the Art of Psychotherapy*, p. 17.
3 Casement, 'Introduction', in Ann Casement (ed.), *Post-Jungians Today*, p. 2.
4 Samuels, 'Will the post-Jungians survive?', in Casement, ibid., p. 29.
5 Kawai, *Mirai e no Kioku ge*, pp. 64, 95.

6 Kawai, *Shinsōishiki e no Michi*, pp. 111ff. Kawai favoured the means of self-expression afforded by Sandplay over the requirement in dream analysis for patients to verbally articulate themselves at length – something he noted was relatively unfamiliar in the Japanese context. Classic forms of self-expression in Japanese culture include Buddhist art (such as mandala), haiku poetry which describes both nature and sentiment, and miniature gardens and bonsai.
7 Kawai, *Mirai e no Kioku ge*, p. 23
8 Kawai Hayao, *Mirai e no Kioku jyō*, p. 29, pp. 41ff., pp. 73ff., p. 85; Kawai, *Buddhism and the Art of Psychotherapy*, p. 15.
9 Ibid., pp. 24ff.
10 Kawai, *Shinsōishiki e no Michi*, p. 11; *Mirai eno Kioku jyō*, pp. 88ff.
11 Kawai, *Mirai e no Kioku jyō*, pp. 50ff.
12 Ibid., pp. 89ff.
13 Ibid., pp. 154ff.
14 Kawai, *Mirai e no Kioku ge*, pp. 35ff.
15 See Ando, this volume.
16 Kawai, *Shinsōishiki e no Michi*, pp. 73ff.
17 Kawai, *Mirai eno Kioku ge*, pp. 105ff.
18 Kawai, *Shinsōishiki e no Michi*, pp. 89ff.
19 Kawai, *Mirai e no Kioku ge*, pp. 162ff.; *Buddhism and the Art of Psychotherapy*, pp. 22ff.
20 Kawai, *Mirai e no Kioku ge*, pp. 162ff.; *Buddhism and the Art of Psychotherapy*, pp. 22ff.
21 Kawai, *Monogatari to Ningen no Kagaku*, pp. 59ff.
22 Kawai, *Yung Shinrigaku Nyūmon*, pp. 89ff.; Kawai, *Buddhism and the Art of Psychotherapy*, pp. 23ff.
23 Kawai, *Mirai e no Kioku jyou*, p. 83, p. 117.
24 Kawai, *Shinsoisiki e no Miti*, p. 35, p. 76, p. 167, pp. 181ff.; Wakamatsu, *Izutsu Toshihiko*, pp. 389ff.; Otsuka, *Kawai Hayao: Monogatari wo Ikiru*, p. 144.
25 Otsuka, *Kawai Hayao: Shinri ryōhōka no tanjyō*, p. 338.
26 Ujihara, *Yungu wo yomu*, p. 2.
27 Kawai, *Shūkyō to Kagaku no Setten*, p. 10.
28 The term 'spiritual intellectuals' was coined by Shimazono Susumu to refer to cholars and intellectuals who played a major role in mediating between the Spiritual World movement and the academic world. Shimazono regarded Kawai Hayao as one of them. See Shimazono, *From Salvation to Spirituality*, pp. 277ff. On the 'Spiritual World', see Harding (Introduction), this volume.
29 Jung, *Spirit and Life*, CWVIII, §624; *Psychology and Religion*, CWXI §11.
30 Jung, *Psychological Types*, CWVI §77f; *Psychological Commentary on The Tibetan Book of the Dead*, CWXI §766, 769; *Memories, Dreams, Reflections*, p. 31.
31 Jung, *Psychology and Religion*, CWXI, §142.
32 Ibid, §8.
33 *The Psychology of the Transference*, CWXVI, §395.
34 Kawai, *Buddhism and the Art of Psychotherapy*, p. 33.
35 Jung, *Psychology and Religion*, CWXI, §9ff.
36 Kawai, *The Japanese Psyche*.
37 Jung, *Archetypes of the Collective Unconscious*, CWIX/i, §6.
38 Jung, *Archetypes of the Collective Unconscious*, CWIX/i, §2n.
39 Jung, *Mysterium Coniunctionis*, CWXIV, §602, §743.
40 Jung, *Psychology and Alchemy*, CWXII, §91ff.
41 Cf. Kawai, *The Japanese Psyche*, p. 26, p. 181.
42 Tsurumi has said that by continuing to read Kawai's works after his death, he has become aware of himself as part of the unseen Buddhist tradition latent in Japanese culture. Tsurumi, *Kakure Bukkyō*, pp. 175ff.

43 Kawai, *The Japanese Psyche*, p. 20ff, p. 167, p. 177.
44 Ibid, p. 187. Jung referred to the contrast between the paternal principle and the maternal one as perfection (*Vollkommenheit*) versus completeness (*Vollsändigkeit*).
45 Ibid., pp. 134ff.
46 Ibid., p. 195.
47 Kawai, 'Constellation', in *Monogatari to Ningen no Kagaku*, pp. 46–82.
48 Jung, *A Psychological Approach to the Dogma of the Trinity*, CWXI, §223. The treatise is based on his lecture at the Eranos Conference entitled *Zur Psychologie der Trinitätsidee* (1940).
49 It is said that 'deep' transference often takes place on such occasions. However, it should not be confused with the 'shallow and strong' transference that causes a client to act out. Kawai, *Shinriryōhō Nyumon*, pp. 161–164.
50 Ibid, p. 138.
51 Kawai, *Yung Shinrigaku Nyūmon*, pp. 257, 12, 16.
52 Jung, *The Spirit Mercurius*, CWXIII, §245.
53 Kawai, *Monogatari to Ningen no Kagaku*, p. 79f
54 See Harding (Introduction), this volume.
55 Kawai, *The Buddhist Priest Myōe*.
56 Jung, *Archetypes of the Collective Unconscious*, CW IX/i, §6.
57 Kawai, *The Buddhist Priest Myōe*, pp. 47ff.
58 Taira, *Rekishi no nakani miru Shinran*, pp. 41ff.; Machida, *Hōnen*, pp. 24ff., 28.
59 Sueki, *Hongaku Shisō*, pp. 188ff.
60 See Kondo and Kitanishi, this volume, on Buddhist influences in Morita Therapy.
61 Kawai, *The Buddhist Priest Myōe*, pp. 88ff., 91ff., 143ff.
62 Ibid., p. 132.
63 Machida, *Hōnen*, p. 34
64 Ibid, pp. 63ff., 21ff., 137ff.
65 Kawai, *The Japanese Psyche*, p. 167.
66 Ibid., p. 17.
67 Ibid., pp. 55, 127.
68 Kawai, *Katagawa ningen no Higeki*; *Japanese Mythology*.
69 Kawai, *Sei to Shi no Setten*, p. 255.
70 Ibid., pp. 265, 267ff.
71 See Jung, *Answer to Job*, CWXI, §620, 627.
72 Jung, *Psychological Commentary on The Tibetan Book of the Great Liberation*, CW XI, §802; *The Psychology of Eastern Meditation*, CW XI, §933, 939. After his criticism of the Western imitation of yoga, Jung states: 'In the course of the centuries the West will produce its own yoga, and it will be on the basis laid down by Christianity' (*Yoga and the West*, CW XI, §876).
73 Kawai, *Josetu; Kokusaika no Jidai to Nihonjin no Kokoro*, ix.
74 Izanagi and Izanami, conjugal god and goddess, brought forth the Japanese islands and various gods and goddesses, including Amaterasu. However, when they gave birth to Hiruku and found her unable to use her leg, they banished her from the pantheon, from which she went with the wind or adrift on the waves.
75 Kawai, *Kawai Hayao to Nihon-shinwa*, pp. 254ff.

## References

Casement, Ann (ed.), *Post-Jungians Today: Key Papers in Contemporary Analytical Psychology* (London: Routledge, 1998).
Jung, C.G., *Answer to Job, CWXI* (Princeton: Princeton University Press, 1969).
Jung, C.G., *Archetypes of the Collective Unconscious, CWIX/I* (Princeton: Princeton University Press, 1969).
Jung, C.G., *Memories, Dreams, Reflections,* recorded and edited by Aniela Jafe. trans. by Richard and Clara Winston (New York: Vintage Books, 1965).
Jung, C.G., *Mysterium Coniunctionis, CWXIV* (Princeton: Princeton University Press, 1970).
Jung, C.G., *A Psychological Approach to the Dogma of the Trinity, CWXI* (Princeton: Princeton University Press, 1969).
Jung, C.G., *Psychological Commentary on the Tibetan Book of the Dead, CWXI* (Princeton: Princeton University Press, 1969).
Jung, C.G., *Psychological Commentary on the Tibetan Book of the Great Liberation, CWXI* (Princeton: Princeton University Press, 1969).
Jung, C.G., *Psychological Types, CWVI* (Princeton: Princeton University Press, Bollingen Paperbacks, 1976).
Jung, C.G., *Psychology and Alchemy, CWXII* (Princeton: Princeton University Press, Bollingen Paperbacks, 1968).
Jung, C.G., *Psychology and Religion, CWXI* (Princeton: Princeton University Press, 1969).
Jung, C.G., *The Psychology of Eastern Meditation, CWXI* (Princeton: Princeton University Press, 1969).
Jung, C.G., *The Psychology of the Transference, CWXVI* (Princeton: Princeton University Press, Bollingen Paperbacks, 1980).
Jung, C.G., *Spirit and Life, CWVIII* (Princeton: Princeton University Press, 1969).
Jung, C.G., *The Spirit Mercurius, CWXIII* (Princeton: Princeton University Press, 1970).
Jung, C.G., *Yoga and the West, CW XI* (Princeton: Princeton University Press, 1969).
Kawai Hayao, *Yung Shinrigaku Nyūmon [Introduction to Jungian Psychology]* (Tokyo: Baifūkan, 1967).
Kawai Hayao, 'Japanese mythology: Balancing the Gods', in *Dreams, Myths and Fairy Tales in Japan* (Einsiedeln: Daimon Verlag, 1995).
Kawai Hayao, *Shūkyō to Kagaku no Setten [The Points of Contact between Religion and Science]* (Tokyo: Iwanami Shoten, 1986).
Kawai Hayao, *The Japanese Psyche: Major Motifs in the Fairy Tales of Japan* (Dallas: Spring Publications, 1988).
Kawai Hayao, 'Katagawa ningen no Higeki [Tragedy of unilateral figures]', in *Sei to Shi no Setten [A Point of Contact between Life and Death]* (Tokyo: Iwanami Shoten, 1989).
Kawai, *Sei to Shi no Setten [A Point of Contact between Life and Death]* (Tokyo: Iwanami Shoten, 1989).
Kawai Hayao, *The Buddhist Priest Myōe: A Life of Dreams* (trans. by Mark Unno) (Venice, Calif: Lapis Press, 1991).
Kawai Hayao, *Monogatari to Ningen no Kagaku [Tales and The Science of Human Being]* (Tokyo: Iwanami Shoten, 1993).
Kawai Hayao, 'Josetu; Kokusaika no Jidai to Nihonjin no Kokoro [Introduction;

international era and Japanese psyche]', in *Kawai Hayao Chosakushū 8: Nihonjin no Kokoro [Collected Works of Kawai Hayao Vol. 8: Japanese Psyche]* (Tokyo: Iwanami Shoten, 1994).

Kawai Hayao, *Mirai e no Kioku jyō [Memory for the Future Vol. 1]* (Tokyo: Iwanami Shoten, 2001).

Kawai Hayao, *Mirai e no Kioku ge [Memory for the Future Vol. 2]* (Tokyo: Iwanami Shoten, 2001).

Kawai Hayao, *Shinsōishiki e no Michi [The Path to Depth Consciousness]* (Tokyo: Iwanami Shoten, 2004).

Kawai Hayao, *Buddhism and the Art of Psychotherapy* (Texas: Texas A&M University Press, 2008).

Kawai Hayao, *Shinriryōhō Nyumon [Introduction to Psychotherapy]* (Tokyo: Iwanami Shoten, 2010).

Kawai Toshio, 'Kawai Hayao to Nihon-shinwa [Kawai Hayao and Japanese Mythology]', in *Nihon-shinwa to Kokoro no Kōzō [Japanese Mythology and the Structure of Psyche]* (Tokyo: Iwanami Shoten, 2009).

Machida Soho, *Hōnen: Seikimatu no Kakumeisya [Hōnen: A Revolutionalist at the End of a Century]* (Kyoto: Hozokan, 1997).

Otsuka Nobukazu, *Kawai Hayao: Shinri ryōhōka no tanjyō [Kawai Hayao: The Birth of a Psychotherapist]* (Tokyo: Transview, 2009).

Otsuka Nobukazu, *Kawai Hayao: Monogatari wo Ikiru [Kawai Hayao: Live his Tale]* (Tokyo: Transview, 2010).

Samuels, Andrew, 'Will the post-Jungians survive?', in Ann Casement (ed.), *Post-Jungians Today: Key Papers in Contemporary Analytical Psychology* (London; New York: Routledge, 1998).

Shimazono Susumu, *From Salvation to Spirituality: Popular Religious Movements in Japan* (Melbourne: Trans Pacific Press, 2004).

Sueki Fumihiko, 'Hongaku Shisō [Doctrine of original enlightenment]', in *Nihon Bukkyōshi [A History of Japanese Buddhism]* (Tokyo: Shinchosha, Shincho-bunko Library, 1996).

Taira Masayuki, *Rekishi no nakani miru Shinran [Shinran in History]* (Kyoto: Hozokan, 2011).

Tsurumi Shunsuke, *Kakure Bukkyō* (Tokyo: Daiamondosha, 2010).

Ujihara Hiroshi, *Yungu wo yomu [Reading Jung]* (Kyoto: Minerva Shobō, 1999).

Wakamatsu Eisuke, *Izutsu Toshihiko: Eichi no Tetsugaku [Izutsu Toshihiko: Philosophy of Wisdom]* (Tokyo: Keiōdaigaku Shuppankai, 2011).

# 10 The contemporary view of reincarnation in Japan
## Narratives of the reincarnating self[1]

*Horie Norichika*

This paper discusses the contemporary view of reincarnation in Japan, focusing on how it differs from traditional Japanese conceptions of reincarnation. By examining examples of past-life therapy (PLT), also known as regression therapy, it aims to illustrate the transition that has taken place in recent years from a religious to a spiritual view of life and death. This concept of reincarnation holds a significant place in the contemporary culture of spirituality in Japan,[2] operating as a fundamental basis for understandings of life and death.

Various definitions of 'spirituality' can be classified into two types: the analyst's and the practitioner's. The analyst's definition would be as follows: *Spirituality refers to both belief in what cannot usually be perceived but can be felt internally, and practices to feel it with the whole mind and body, accompanied more or less by attitudes of individualism or privatism, anti-authoritarianism, and selective assimilation of religious cultural resources.*[3] Practitioners, for their part, understand spirituality as being spirit in a literal sense; it refers to the fact that human beings are originally 'spirit' and the realization of it. This definition was shared by the leading lights of Japanese popular spirituality in the 2000s, and is what authors such as Ehara Hiroyuki would mean by the term *supirichuaru* ('spiritual').[4] Around the same time, psychologists and medical and nursing practitioners started talking about *supirituariti* – a phonetic import of the English word 'spirituality', rendered in *katakana* script – to describe a stance in which one pursues life's ultimate meaning, incorporating the notion of an afterlife. This was in order to circumvent the negative connotations and imagery that sometimes attach to the word *reisei* (spirituality) or particularly *rei* (spirit): associations with evil spirits, for example, or spectres of some sort. Authors of books on popular spirituality such as Ehara brought a breath of fresh air into the word *supirichuaru* (spiritual) by intentionally using the term to discuss the *rei* (spirits) of the dead, *shugorei* (guardian spirits), and one's previous lives.[5] This popular concept of 'spirituality', which suggests an awareness of oneself as spirit, can be related to the Christian concept of the 'Holy Spirit', to the Japanese traditional animistic notion of 'spirits', and various types of belief in spirits in other parts of the world. Practitioners believe 'spirituality', in this sense, to be at the core of what we call religion, when stripped of its superficial artefacts.

The concept of reincarnation in the culture of spirituality is characterized by a strong emphasis on awareness of oneself as a spirit; the 'Self' as a consistent entity outside of any spatial or temporal confinement. The so-called 'spiritual boom' in contemporary Japan[6] offers various examples of the concept of past lives, which are a principal focus here. People who are interested in spiritual issues sometimes consult a spiritual medium who tells them about their past lives, or a therapist who uses PLT to help clients recall memories of their past lives by putting them in a hypnotic state.

The view of reincarnation in Japan is often thought to be based on traditional Buddhist teachings.[7] However, ancestor worship in Funeral Buddhism, as widely practised in Japan, is theoretically incompatible with the original concept of reincarnation. The first part of this paper discusses how the contemporary individualistic and growth-oriented view of reincarnation in Japan has diverged from traditional views of reincarnation, that is, from the original aims of Buddhist practice to be liberated from an endless cycle of suffering, and from the Japanese folk view of reincarnation based on *ie* (house/kinship) as the fundamental unit of identity. The second part of the paper illustrates these trends with findings from recent research.

## Is reincarnation the traditional Japanese view on life and death? Buddhist and folk views of reincarnation

In the Buddhist view of reincarnation, it is believed that karma determines one's mode of existence within the six realms: Hell, hungry ghosts, animals, jealous gods, humans, and Heaven). The aim of Buddhist practice is ultimately to liberate itself from the eternal suffering of death and rebirth.[8] This view of reincarnation is theoretically inconsistent with traditional ancestor worship in Japan: if spirits are reborn, it makes no sense to worship a 'dead spirit' or an ancestor's spirit.[9] There is no meaning in worshipping one's great-grandfather if he has been reborn.

There are a few ways to solve this problem. One is to use the two different belief systems for different purposes, and disregard the contradictions. Another is to believe that a dead person is not reborn immediately, and so the mourning of close relatives remembered by the living (memorialism) is permissible.[10] However, this kind of memorialism diverges from true worship of ancestors in the family lineage, who are remembered in an abstract sense of 'ancestors' rather than as particular individuals. Also, some believe that a dead person goes to the Pure Land straight after death, or attains Buddhahood around forty-nine days after a series of memorial services. In this case the idea of six possible realms of reincarnation applies only to people who do not enter the Pure Land or attain Buddhahood. On the surface of it, this belief seems consistent with traditional

Buddhist doctrine. However, this kind of shortening of the term of reincarnation is tantamount to actual rejection of the doctrine itself.

The belief most theoretically consistent with the practice of ancestor worship is what we call here the folk concept of reincarnation. Lafcadio Hearn wrote in 1896 that the Western concept of an individual 'ghost' dwelling inside the body does not exist in Japan.[11] According to Hearn, the Western notion of 'self' is understood in Buddhism to be but a temporary illusion created by karma; that is, a collection of countless actions and thoughts in preexistence.[12] Similarly, in Shintō the Western 'self' is considered to be just an aggregation of dead spirits (ancestors/deities). Hearn claimed that these concepts of 'self', made up of past lives or ancestors, were commonly believed by everyone in Japan, from young educated students through to illiterate peasants.[13] The Japanese view of life and death that Hearn observed in his day, therefore, was a type of reincarnation from plural past lives and an aggregate of ancestral spirits. There he might find no contradiction between reincarnation and ancestor worship.

Yanagita Kunio, Japan's first modern folklorist, later argued that the concept of six-realm reincarnation did not exist in Japan, as it was widely believed that once dead spirits were purified they became merged into 'the body of the great spirits' called '*Kami*' (deity), in which one's individuality was lost. That is why one could never be reborn with one's previous individuality.[14] On the other hand, he referred to some evidence of belief in reincarnation – including the burial of a dead infant under the floor, in order to hasten rebirth back into the family.[15] According to Yanagita, 'a number of instances of people declaring that a certain child is such a one reborn [the rebirth of a dead member of the family]' suggests that 'one would surely be reborn to the same kin group and to the same bloodline'.[16] This view of reincarnation, based on the spirit's fusion with a group of ancestors of *ie* (clan or extended family) or *ujigami* (ancestral deity or tutelary deity) before being reborn, seems to render reincarnation and ancestor worship somewhat compatible.

The concept of reincarnation via the exclusive local community, to which the *ie* belongs, implies the existence of a similar spiritual group of ancestral spirits of the community, which is worshipped until the spirits are reincarnated from it. *Katsugorō's Report on Reincarnation* compiled by the great eighteenth- and early nineteenth-century scholar Hirata Atsutane, from which Yanagita quoted, tells the story of a boy who remembers having lived a previous life in a nearby village. The story ends with the two families – that of his past life, and that of his present – embarking upon a new relationship as relatives.[17] This suggests that their belief in reincarnation was not always restricted to their kinship group but could extend to unrelated families living in relative proximity and in a similar time period. Hirata's interpretation was that the tutelary deities of the present life and of the previous life had had a consultation about the destination of the boy's spirit – since it was believed to be normal that a single tutelary deity alone decided reincarnation inside a single village community.[18] It is recorded that this boy hated Buddhism, deeming the idea of paradise as falsehood.[19] Hirata himself also relativized the Buddhist view of reincarnation as additional decoration of common concepts, such as Heaven and Hell, a cycle of life, and cause and effect, which exist in all countries.[20]

Naturally, no single view can do justice to Japanese ideas about the afterlife, which have taken various forms across history. We cannot say that the tales of reincarnation originating in India were uniformly accepted and believed in Japan. One has also to question to what extent elite notions of reincarnation were shared amongst the rest of the population.[21] Practices of ancestor worship and Japanese formulations of instant rebirth in the Pure Land or instant Buddhahood after death, all of which make ineffective the original doctrine of Buddhist reincarnation, are not permanent in Japanese history because they have been dependent upon the *ie* system and the *terauke* (temple certification) systems since the early modern period. In spite of the efforts of Yanagita and other folklorists, it cannot be shown that the folk view of reincarnation described above has been permanent throughout Japanese history and has permeated all levels of society. To be closer to the reality of Japanese religious history, it is better to presume that there have been different views of the afterlife, and to understand that the extent to which emphasis has been placed on one or another has depended upon time, region, and social class.

## Three characteristics of the contemporary view of reincarnation

The contemporary view of reincarnation in Japan is not merely a continuation of these traditional views. Instead, three points stand out. First, there is now a belief in reincarnation from long-ago and far-away contexts: what we might call 'transcultural reincarnation' – a past life as a medieval European knight, for instance. This, of course, is a theoretical contradiction with ancestor worship. Second, there exists a tendency of explaining and giving positive meaning to reincarnation in the form of one's 'personal growth through reincarnation' or one's fulfilment of a life mission through rebirth. Third, clients of 'spirit viewing' or other forms of hypnotic regression place great value upon their own convictions and experiences. Let us call this an 'emphasis on experiential reality' rather than objective reality.

The first of these themes, transcultural reincarnation, mirrors the decline in modern Japan of ancestor worship. Factors such as the rise of the urban nuclear family, steep depopulation in rural areas, a decline of consciousness of *ie*, an increasing divorce rate, and an increasing number of unmarried persons, have all contributed to a trend towards memorialism, natural burial and individual memorial services, which have started to reflect the dwindling impact of ancestor worship based on *ie*.[22] In this context, the folk view of reincarnation, which used to bridge the gap between ancestor worship and reincarnation, is becoming obsolete and the notion of reincarnation from a distant past or place less contradictory.

This connects to the second feature of the contemporary view of reincarnation: personal growth through reincarnation. By today's standards of individualism it is acceptable to provide a genealogical narrative of the reincarnating soul, not of the *ie*, to an individual who no longer feels attached to his or her *ie*. One is thought to develop one's spirituality through reincarnation, not the status of the *ie*. Spirituality here refers to the extent of one's awareness of the self as a reincarnating spirit and one's capability to act with this awareness. By examining one's past life one can have a clearer understanding of the present ego, liberate oneself from the state of one's karma, and awaken to one's own mission. These all lead to self-actualization; that is, the accomplishment of the original plan made by oneself before birth. This positive outlook on reincarnation is of course antithetical to Buddhism's negative view of it as a source of suffering. 'Funeral Buddhism', based on the concept of instant Buddhahood after death without the need for ascetic practices, may seem optimistic. However, it leaves behind the fear of becoming an unpurified spirit, destined to endure reincarnation into one of the six realms. The concept of reincarnation itself remains inherently negative. By contrast, personal growth through reincarnation is undoubtedly a positive take on the concept.

This is linked to the third characteristic: an emphasis on the experiential reality of reincarnation. In the Heian period, people may have taken some interest in their *chigiri* (a promise between a man and a woman from their past lives), but this remained speculation.[23] However, nowadays there are '*Nōryokusha*' (a person with abilities)[24] who give accounts of clients' previous lives. It is believed that even clients without 'abilities' can recollect past life memories under hypnosis. Such memories being of course incapable of substantiation, it is unclear the extent to which clients take these visions literally. They are apparently accepted, however, with personal conviction.[25]

## The past life boom of the 1980s

It is difficult to say precisely when the contemporary view of reincarnation with the three characteristics mentioned above emerged amongst the masses in Japan, but its pioneers have been the so-called 'new religions' that have a belief in the spiritual world (*reikai*). Religious organizations such as the God Light Association (GLA), from the 1970s onwards, started experimenting with speaking in tongues and with the idea of transcultural reincarnation.[26] Takahashi Shinji, the founder and leader of GLA, was believed to be the reincarnation of the Buddha, and after his death it was believed for some time that his daughter Takahashi Keiko was Archangel

Michael.[27] The organization has a doctrine of a main body (*hontai*) and its doubles (*bunshin*), which is similar to the spiritualist's theory of 'group soul'. They also share with spiritualists the concepts of guardian spirit and guide spirit.[28] Holding reincarnation as a basic doctrine, they claim that it is the harmonious life of the offspring, rather than the performance of formalistic ritual or worship, that will guide the stray ancestors. This is the real point of memorial services for ancestors, they say. Takahashi often attacks Funeral Buddhism and encourages his adherents to maintain the harmony of their own mind by reflecting on it every day. This teaching is actually a denial of ordinary ancestor worship, ranking the ancestors lower than the guardians, the guides, and the members of the group who have awoken to their reincarnation.[29] Hirai Kazumasa, the author of the novel *Genma Taisen*, was strongly influenced by GLA. The novel includes characters who are related to each other from their previous lives and who possess supernatural powers, which are used to fight against evil forces.[30] The novel was made into an *anime* in 1983 by the film director Kadokawa Haruki, who also made *Satomihakkenden*, a movie about reincarnated light warriors waging a battle against dark forces.

In the mid-1980s there was a noticeable surge of people looking for others who might share the same memories, suggesting a past-life connection. They searched for one another in the readers' section ('contact plaza') of magazines such as *Mū*. The average age of someone looking for someone else to share their past life in *Mū* was 16.7 years in 1985 and 17.3 years in 1986, of which 81 per cent were female and 19 per cent male. As a social phenomenon it peaked in 1985/6, before it suddenly disappeared in 1988. According to Asaba (1989) this was due to editors' shying away from such letters.[31]

Here is an example of a post on contact plaza:

> If you believe in reincarnation, believe that you have lived on the Continent Mu, and remember the names Rimuru and Anja, please contact me.[32]

This may or may not have been a genuine request: it may have been a prank of some sort. *Mū* never focused specifically on the concept of reincarnation, with the exception of the August 1986 special issue. Perhaps the editors could not ignore readers' growing interest in reincarnation. However, the publisher might become reluctant to adopt their letters looking for friends from past lives for fear that young readers were starting to indulge in an extreme fantasy. Soon after they stopped printing such letters, a manga called *Protect my Planet*[33] emerged, parodying *Mū* by featuring a character who recalls his past life as an alien.

In March 1989, it came to media attention that a sixth grader, an avid reader of occult magazines, had committed suicide leaving a note that read: 'the spirit is calling me'. In August of the same year, some girls from

Tokushima prefecture took a large quantity of antipyretics in an effort to see their past lives as princesses.[34] Usually the media is blamed for influencing young children when this kind of incident happens. However, right from the beginning, *Mū* had been reluctant to deal with the concept of reincarnation, and *Protect my Planet* was no more than a parody of the readers' letters in *Mū*. The media can hardly, then, be considered to be behind the 'past-life boom' of these years. Instead, the impact of the novel *Genma Taisen*, which preceded the boom, cannot be ignored. And yet how did a simple piece of fiction become so influential amongst young readers? Was it just this single novel? How about *Out on a Limb*,[35] the actress Shirley MacLaine's account of her belief in reincarnation? Was it solely down to this book that the concept of reincarnation received widespread acceptance in the US? It seems that the concept of reincarnation is deeply rooted in Japan's and America's counter-culture, and publications such as these had the power to act as triggers for the popularization of the concept.

The so-called 'New New Religion' emerged around 1990, right after the past life boom, including *Aum Shinrikyō* and *Kōfuku no Kagaku* (Happy Science). Reincarnation was their foundation, and they emphasized spiritual growth or evolution and an imminent Armageddon. This latter idea lost power after the Aum sarin gas attack on the Tokyo subway in 1995[36] and when the world survived Nostradamus' prediction of catastrophe (an interpretation popular among Japanese people) for the year 1999. From 2000 onwards Ehara Hiroyuki helped to lead a spiritual boom, focusing on reincarnation, but there is no grandiose narrative in this boom that a group of light warriors are reborn with a common mission to fight the final battle between good and evil; that they become aware of their mission and reassemble to be in solidarity. Iida Fumihiko, who along with Ehara strongly influenced Japanese views of reincarnation around this time, argued that by accepting reincarnation one is able to attain 'vivacity' and the meaning of life because it contributes to a search for an 'authentic self'.[37] In this way, a metanarrative of apocalypse turned into a narrative of growth or evolution of a reincarnating 'Self' that transcends the present ego.

According to the database of the National Diet Library, published titles including the word 'reincarnation' have been increasing year on year since the late 1980s. Where past life therapy is concerned, American past-life therapist Brian Weiss' works were available in Japanese from the early 1990s, but only after 2004 did the number of titles including the words 'past life therapy' rapidly start to increase.[38]

## Reincarnation after the spiritual boom

A shift in public interest, away from the crisis of the world in the near future and towards past lives, became increasingly noticeable in the mid-2000s, as the spiritual boom grew. There seem to be three ways in which people pursue this interest.

1   *Past life divination*. A Japanese internet search for 'past life' yields 'past life divination' websites at the top of the list. However, the 'past life' offered there is automatically generated based on one's birth date, blood type, psychological tests, etc. According to GoisuNet's 'Past Life Check', the author of this paper was, in a past life, 'a shamanic priestess who ruled the world in ancient times'. According to 'Time travel: Past life, present life and next life', he was a (female) 'dancer' and will, in the next life, be 'one that saves the world'.[39]

    It seems unlikely that these kinds of judgements are taken literally by users. It is not an inquiry into past lives based on any particular view of reincarnation: rather, a type of divination using characters such as king, soldier, peasant and priestess that symbolize particular fates. However, this does not mean that such phenomena are unimportant in understanding the contemporary view of reincarnation in Japan. On the contrary, it illustrates the fact that people don't believe in past lives literally but enjoy using the idea as a way of deepening self-understanding. It shows an expanded sensibility, which includes the pleasure of imagining oneself as a past life character and a feeling of the plurality of the self.

2   The second way of pursuing one's past life is via a reading from a '*Nō ryokusha*', including spiritual counsellors. The most well known of these is Ehara Hiroyuki and his '*reishi*' (spiritual or psychic clairvoyance) in a television programme called 'The Spring of Aura', which aired between 2005 and 2009. Below is a conversation between Ehara and the actress Katō Koyuki, or 'Koyuki' [best known in the West for her role in the film *The Last Samurai*].

EHARA: 'You were a spiritual medium in a past life; engaged in what is called 'healing' in today's terms. *This may be why* you once wanted to become a nurse. The reason you were employed or incarcerated in the castle was because of your special ability'.
KOYUKI: 'Ah'. [Tilts her head to the side and laughs]
EHARA: 'You were constrained in that condition. *That's why* you now hate working only for a particular group of people. You had a strong desire to heal the less fortunate, but you were kept inside the castle because of that special ability. I think this was in Europe. This might seem far-fetched, but I think it was in France. *That's why* you partook in Paris Fashion Week'.
KOKUBUN TAICHI (MC): 'You said something like 'Ah' when the word incarceration came up. Does it ring a bell?'
KOYUKI: '*I've often been told something similar* by my sister, who is said to have such [psychic] abilities'.

MIWA [PANEL GUEST]: 'How so?'

KOYUKI: 'When I was really young, my sister kept on telling me that I, or my ancestor, had been in Europe, and had been kept inside a castle ... and *that's why* now I am afraid of this and that. I used to think, what is she talking about?'[40]

This conversation focuses on the correspondences between present and past lives. Koyuki was a healer in a past life, and also wanted to become a nurse in her present life. However, she was incarcerated in the past life, and instead of becoming a nurse she became a model/actress in the present life. She has a connection with France in both her past and present lives. She had already been told about her past life by her sister. Based on these correspondences, Koyuki seems to be very much convinced of her past life story told by Ehara and her sister. (No one can tell whether she genuinely believes in it or merely behaves as though she does; or, if she believes, to what extent she is sure.)[41]

By its very nature, *reishi* (spiritual or psychic clairvoyance) is not verifiable in empirical terms. Instead the client develops confidence in the result by using it to understand coherently his or her present situation. The programme makers warn that the results of spiritual seeing are not to be taken as literal truth. At the end of the programme, the caption reads: 'concepts such as "past life" and "guardian spirit" have not been proven by contemporary science. They should be treated as assistance in living a good life'. This is designed to guard against accusations or complaints being made[42] that the programme is imposing a particular spiritual view upon its audience. It also shows that a criterion of acceptance of one's past life narrative is practicality rather than scientific verifiability.

A recipient of a past life reading constructs a narrative of a reincarnating 'Self' that transcends time, space, and *ie*, based on correspondence between an unverifiable vision of past 'me' and a present *I* or ego that is taken for granted. For this narrative to be accepted it must correspond with the present ego, help one understand one's life coherently, and provide practical guidance for future life.[43] One might say that the main criterion for its acceptance is whether the narrated content of a past life functions as a part of the reincarnating Self, which is a frame of reference to understand the present ego. In spiritual reading, narrative reality brings an effect that is similar to experiential reality, one of the contemporary features of reincarnation.

Transcultural reincarnation, another feature, is also a significant element in Ehara's work. As the example above shows, Ehara's past life stories often take place in Europe (as frequently as they do Japan).

Personal growth through reincarnation, the third feature, is less noticeable on television. In the above example Ehara might want to point out indirectly Koyuki's strong ego and encourage her to accept the career path she has taken – but with no explicit urge to attain greater 'growth'. Ehara's writings, on the other hand, underscore the importance of realizing oneself as a 'subject of responsibility' on the journey of the 'soul's evolution and improvement through reincarnation'. The major problems and sufferings in this life are planned before birth, and one is responsible for them. Even karma is taken positively as some kind of grace that might suggest the soul's disposition and provide a chance to improve past misdeeds.[44]

## Testimonies of past life therapy

The third method of inquiring into past lives is to envision and experience that past life for oneself, in an altered state of consciousness. This envisioning gives one a sense that one has 'recalled' that past life, thus creating a strong experiential reality.

Past Life Therapy (PLT) is a type of hypnotherapy devised by a psychiatrist, Brian Weiss. The technique involves the client regressing, under hypnosis, back beyond birth.[45] It is said that in recollecting a past life the client is healed by deepening his or her self-understanding and awareness of current problems and finding the key to a solution of them. Most past life therapists, however, lack credible qualifications, such as that of certified clinical psychologist,[46] and they just have a kind of certificate issued by seminar companies that is accepted only amongst those who are interested in spirituality.

There are two principal advantages of examining PLT cases. First, we are dealing with ordinary people's views of reincarnation, rather than those of celebrities on television. Second, thanks to the advertising efforts of therapists there are ample cases publically available for study. The down side, of course, is that there are no cases showing unsuccessful treatment. It is difficult, then, to know the reality behind PLT but relatively straightforward to grasp the ideal for practitioners. The case examples used here are drawn from online websites run by practitioners of PLT.

I collected my examples as follows. I used homepages featured in 'The list of past life therapists (Eastern Japan)' and 'The list of past life therapists (Western Japan)'.[47] These pages contain lists of therapist websites. Data was collected from pages describing clients' experiences where such a link appeared at the top page of a website. I chose the first example that was comprehensible and which included the age and sex of the client. Only one example was collected from each PLT website, in order to avoid bias. Data collection began in Hokkaido, moving southward, and stopping at Okayama when twenty suitable examples had been collected. The websites were accessed on 11th September 2008.

In all, these target sites contained 128 cases, including the twenty samples, and revealed the age and sex of the client. The average age was 34.8 years, which places many of these individuals in middle school during the past life boom of the 1980s.[48] There were twenty-four male cases (19%) and 104 women (81%). The typical client, then, was a thirty-five-year-old woman.

## Characteristics of the testimonies

The collected data for the twenty chosen case studies is summarized in Table 10.1, 'PLT analysis', under the following headings: present problem, character in the past life, events in the past life, and awareness and findings. The average age of the case study clients was thirty-seven, and all except two were female.[49] To understand some of the general patterns that emerged, let us begin with one illustrative case. Case 6 is an experience of a forty-year-old woman. Under hypnosis she claims to have seen her past life as a man in ancient Greece:

> I was worried about my family and myself, and my relationships with people around me. Now, though, *I am able to understand once again that my children are the most important thing*. That strange feeling came upon me when I was talking [about the past life under hypnosis] ... I couldn't stop crying when I thought of my children. *This must be from my past life memory* (perhaps hidden inside me).
>
> Truth be told, I was not confident about this therapy, and I used to think that it would be simply my creation, but I was taken aback by these unexpected developments. Distanced from myself, I was able to remember my name *as a Greek man*. I could even *remember the texture of my hair*. That *real feeling of sadness* when I lost my child ... still makes me cry.
>
> My unexpectedly peaceful death, and the thoughts and messages coming from someone who is both myself and yet someone else *taught me what is necessary for me now*, and, thanks to him, I realised I must accept that.
>
> This extraordinary experience *broadened my horizons a little*, which had been narrow up until that point. I would like to keep in mind the messages given via this therapy and put them into practice *to move in a positive direction both for those around me and myself*.[50]

This case encompasses all the major characteristics of the contemporary view of reincarnation. First, it is set in ancient Greece: 'unexpected', and presupposing transcultural reincarnation. Second, the concept of personal growth through reincarnation is evident: the client understands the importance of her children once again, broadens her horizons, and becomes determined to 'move in a positive direction'. This narrative suggests the decision she made before birth that she ought to cherish her child in this life because she lost her child in the previous life. Past life therapy is understood to be a reminder. Through this act of recollection, the 'me' in the past life (the man in ancient Greece) and the 'I' in the present life (a Japanese woman) are reconnected, thus forming a narrative of the reincarnating Self which reconstructs the present ego and allows it a broader field of vision. Third, rather than being a mere speculative inference, this reconstruction involves experiential reality. She felt 'the texture

Table 10.1 Analysis of experiences of past life therapy

| Case | Age | Gender | Present problem | Character in the past life | Events in the past life | Awareness and findings | Notes |
|---|---|---|---|---|---|---|---|
| 1 | 20s | Female | Low self-esteem. | A noblewoman in Europe. | An attractive past life. | She became aware of the power sleeping inside. | |
| 2 | 50s | Female | Divorced ten years ago, single, anxious. | A knight in medieval Europe. | Killed in a war before marriage. | Value of peace and love. | War should never happen again. |
| 3 | 27 | Female | Hatred toward her mother-in-law. | 1600s in England. | A competition for her present husband with her mother-in-law. | A message from herself in the past life that she should be gentle to her mother-in-law because she is lonely. | |
| 4 | 52 | Female | Living separately from her husband. Her only son aged thirty is sick and withdrawn. Living in her old mother's house. No hope in the future. | A pre-modern Japanese peasant's daughter. | Cheerful character. She became an adopted daughter in the house where she was employed. A happy marriage and life. | Life will be opened if you do not worry about it. | She wanted to experience the happiest past life to improve her dark moods. |

*continued*

Table 10.1 Continued

| Case | Age | Gender | Present problem | Character in the past life | Events in the past life | Awareness and findings | Notes |
|---|---|---|---|---|---|---|---|
| 5 | 35 | Female | Her unreliable husband, a bad relationship with her mother-in-law, and her work makes her uneasy and irritated. | A seaman in c.16th century Norway. | He (she) fought egoistically to survive alone and felt regretful. | It does not matter what the past life was but what one can learn from it. | Later she realized her husband's Kannon-like love when she depended upon alcohol as a student and felt ashamed that she said he is unreliable. |
| 6 | 40s | Female | Problems in family relationships and human relationships. | A man in [ancient] Greece. | She lost his (her) child and felt sad. | She realized that children are the most precious thing in her life. | She could not stop crying during therapy and got a real feeling that it must be her past life. |
| 7 | 41 | Female | Unexplained | A man in the Edo period (1603–1868). | He (she) got married with a tender woman but led a life of pleasure, and the wife ran away from home. He regretted that when he died. | She realized that she must take better care of her husband. | |

| 8 | Late 20s | Female | She always falls in love with men who have some kind of addiction. | A noble woman in Europe. | Her lover, a knight, was killed in front of her, and she was stolen away. | The robber is a friend of hers from her high-school days with whom she had been secretly in love. Later she encountered a man and became convinced that he was the knight who had been killed. She went together with him without depending on him. | A vivid experience. |
| 9 | 29 | Female | Misanthropy. Tendency to put herself in the shade in human relationships. | A poor boy in Turkey in ancient Roman days. | All family members were killed before his (her) eyes. Misanthropy, wariness, living in the shade. | She realized the cause of the present character. The therapist freed her from the fear [by suggestion?]. | She knows that she cannot prove that it was a past life, but admits that she was healed. |
| 10 | 30s | Female | Depression. Anxiety about returning to society. | In France. | Experience of a success. | A will to go to France, and a will to return to society. | She wanted to experience a success story in the past life to get better in this life. |

*continued*

Table 10.1 Continued

| Case | Age | Gender | Present problem | Character in the past life | Events in the past life | Awareness and findings | Notes |
|---|---|---|---|---|---|---|---|
| 11 | 32 | Female | Much stress caused by taking care of her mother, difficulty in controlling her feelings, an outburst of anger toward her child, right eyelid twitches. | A man in his 40s. | He (she) took care of his parents rather than himself and got sick. He moved away from his family and died alone [an infectious disease]. | She came to give more priority to her own time, which alleviated her problem. | |
| 12 | 30s | Female | Unexplained | An owner of a stock farm in an English speaking country. | Father abandoned the family, and she did not get married and ran the stock farm with her mother. | She realized a cause of her present distrust of men. Her interpretation was that loneliness made her choose a big workplace and a big family. | Life is what you choose. It is meaningful, and you must be thankful. |
| 13 | 50s | Female | Unexplained | An Olympian in ancient Greece. | He (she) became arrogant, incurred displeasure, and got his leg crushed. | Positive attitude toward life. Do not waste time. | |

| 14 | 30s | Female | Negative attitude toward love. She wants to meet her soul mate. | A princess or daughter of a grand landowner in Japan's Heian period (794–1185). | She betrayed her lover, causing his death, by breaking a promise to run away with him. | It was because she wanted to meet him again that she had avoided loving anyone else. Later she met him (she could recognize him by his eyes). After three months he proposed to her. |
| 15 | 20s | Female | Sense of inferiority towards her lover. Strained relationship with him. | Unexplained | A family problem. | A family problem in the past life caused the problems in her present relationship with her lover. |
| 16 | 20s | Male | A famous psychic told him that he was an Indian in his past life. | A man in India. | He was shy and lonely and did not work. He lost his house and died by himself. | Value of surrounding people. Happiness of his present life. |
| 17 | 50s | Female | Unexplained. Anger at something unknown. | A monk in Tibet. | Religious practice. | Sudden interest in books on religious philosophy. |

*continued*

Table 10.1 Continued

| Case | Age | Gender | Present problem | Character in the past life | Events in the past life | Awareness and findings | Notes |
|------|-----|--------|-----------------|----------------------------|-------------------------|------------------------|-------|
| 18 | 30s | Female | Unexplained | A girl in Poland. | Her mother did not love her. She was buried in the snow by her father and died. | She realized the value of her present family. | |
| 19 | 30s | Female | Divorce of her parents. Anxiety about not being loved. Loneliness. | A woman who lived near the coast somewhere in Southeast Asia. | A ruthless mother. The father did not stand up for her. A black sheep in the family. She got married but died and left her young child. | Such sadness that the therapist broke the hypnosis. She went beyond it towards the light in the second hypnosis. Then she realized that the past life has no influence on the present life. Refreshed. Self-affirmation. She realized the cause of feeling persecuted by her parents and the cause of special feelings toward her nephew (her son in the past life). | Exhausted but refreshed. Increased self-affirmation. Tears when she held her nephew. |
| 20 | 30s | Male | Unexplained | A man in Mongolia. | His wife's death. Marriage of her daughter. | Relieved to know that he had no regret in the past life. Link to the present life is not explained. | |

of the hair' and a 'real feeling of sadness' at losing a child. She seems confident that these feelings must be from memories of a past life.

## Evaluation of case studies

Eleven of the twenty cases are set in Europe, three in Japan, four in the rest of Asia, and two unknown. So 83 per cent of clients were non-Japanese in their past life – an overwhelming majority for transcultural reincarnation. The four cases set in Asia were found only on websites in Kanagawa Prefecture and westward, whereas cases set in Europe were prominent in Tokyo and northward. Melton's study of E. Casey's spiritual reading showed that most past life situations read by him were limited by the historical knowledge of American people at the time.[51] The twenty cases featured here frequently involved Europe and rarely Africa or South America, possibly because most Japanese people are familiar with European culture from a young age through stories for children. Since PLT directs clients to their past life through regression, it is conceivable that childhood memories of the stories might have a significant effect on the past life they recall. The frequency of Asian past life settings amongst people living in West Japan might have something to do with their proximity to these Asian countries.[52]

Looking at the column *present problem*, seven of the twenty cases involved family problems, five of which concerned the client's personality; three cases were about relationship problems, with a further six unknown. There is a common belief in Japan that women become interested in spirituality because their life is unstable – employment or marriage problems; anxiety about the future, etc. However, in these cases most problems seem to originate within family relationships.

The ways clients relate themselves with *events in the past life* include two main reactions: resemblance and contrast. There were ten cases in which they regard current problems as being rooted in the past life (case 3, 6, 8, 9, 11, 12, 14, 15, 17, 19). In nine cases the clients learned to appreciate their present situation in comparison with a terrible past life (2, 5, 6, 7, 11, 13, 16, 18, 19). Case Six, dealt with above, contains both features: the client lost her child in the past life, and that is why she wishes to be close to her children now and why she realizes that she must appreciate her current situation. In contrast to this kind of negative case scenario, there are only four cases in which clients were encouraged by success in a past life (1, 4, 10, 20). Past life visions cannot, therefore, necessarily be understood purely as a projection of current desires. On the contrary past lives are often unfortunate and turbulent – albeit one might interpret this as a desire to become thankful for the present situation.

Under the heading '*awareness and findings*', we find only one case where the present life was understood as something that the client had chosen (case 12), but in four cases the conclusion was that present predicaments were due to the events of the past life (9, 12, 15, 19). A dominant idea in contemporary views of reincarnation expressed by spiritualists such as Ehara is that one determines one's present life before birth. Somewhat in opposition to this view, the cases presented here emphasize past life deeds determining the present situation. Both approaches seem valid if it is understood that the clients willingly face challenges left unsolved in previous lives, but the significant element here is the contrast between predominantly male writers on reincarnation, who argue for self-determination, and mainly female clients who are facing actual problems that they cannot solve by themselves.

However, even where the present life is held to be determined by the past life, rather than adopt a Buddhist approach of simple acceptance some clients tend to show a more proactive attitude by living positively to cherish the time given to them (4, 5, 10, 11, 13). There are two ways of sweeping away the traditional negative view of reincarnation. One is to strengthen a sense of self-assertion by breaking the relationship of co-dependency that has continued since a past life. The other way, which is adopted by more clients, nine cases, is to appreciate the wonder of love and bonds that transcend reincarnation, especially within families, and to realize the value of one's peaceful family in the present life (2, 3, 5, 6, 7, 14, 16, 18, 19).

Clients expect to sense some sort of reincarnating Bond corresponding with the reincarnating Self. The particular narrated 'Bond' in the past life may be a cause of problems in a present relationship, but this reincarnating Bond between family members that stretches across particular incarnations is retold as something wonderful.[53] It is by appreciating the wonder of such Bonds and deepening affection actively, not passively grieving over his or her unhappiness, that the client is able to find solutions to current problems.[54]

There is a tension between the reincarnating Self and the reincarnating Bond. Some clients prioritize the former, rejecting past life bonds in order to attain personal growth. By contrast the second strategy, cherishing the reincarnating Bond, involves the client seeing the improvement of the Bond as key for themselves and others to grow together through reincarnation. They feel that 'it is I that improve it because only I realized it via a past life therapy'. In either narrative, the Self is an active subject that progresses the reincarnation, not a passive sufferer of it.

One wonders whether the 'memorialism' mentioned above, practised in regard to close relatives, plays an influential role here: the concept of a 'Bond' between close relatives, which allows for communal reincarnation, bridges the gap between memorialistic ancestor worship and the more individualistic contemporary view of reincarnation.

However, the range of memorialism does not necessarily overlap neatly with the range of the Bonds continuing across incarnations. It is believed that such Bonds extend only to people who have been chosen or 'authorised' by the client. So not all the family members are included within the Bond, but rather perhaps an intimate friend, a boyfriend/girlfriend, or an important acquaintance may come into it. And if the client has chosen his or her present family before birth in order to develop the self, the naturalness of the family *unit* collapses. Memorialism, as a modernized version of ancestor worship, breaks down at this point and becomes subservient to the narrative of a reincarnating Self.

There are many personal testimonies that suggest the past life being accepted only as an experiential reality rather than an historical fact. As the client in Case 9 puts it: 'I think it would be hard to prove that it is my past life, but I remember the image vividly and it is true that my heart (*kokoro*) was healed'. The basis for believing in a past life is clearly very intuitive and sensory: extreme emotions, refreshment (catharsis), and a sense of being healed. Clients who accept the narrative of a past life are often agnostic and have a pragmatic attitude towards meaningful psychological/emotional change.

## The 'individual–universal' and 'private life' principles: metaphysics versus utility

One might suggest that 'transcultural reincarnation' and 'personal growth through reincarnation', seen in these case studies, are related to modern individualism. However, there is a trend in these cases towards explaining present problems in terms of a past life: the idea of self-responsibility for the present problems from the viewpoint of reincarnation is replaced by the idea that a past life is the cause of the current situation. One escapes responsibility for such problems.[55] The idea that the present ego can solve these problems does not directly correlate with individualism. Not only the Self but also the Bond with others is developing through reincarnation, and the client is the one who can realize this and should sustain the growth of the Bond. It is not a simple individualism because one romanticizes one's relationship with others. Thus the reincarnating Self has an ambiguous nature, a 'sufferer' of fate and at the same time an agent of the Bond.

Ehara Hiroyuki's spiritualism teaches his readers to move on from the small self to the big Self and to realize spiritual connections with other people.[56] Once one assumes reincarnation, one is able to deconstruct one's present ego by portraying it as multiplex, attempting to relate it to past lives and to group souls (guardian spirits and guide spirits), integrating it into a Self with greater temporal dimensions than the present. This is not merely salvation for an ego that is a victim of fate, but also a realization of one's own spirituality through relationships with other spiritual beings – reincarnating others. To the extent that this becomes an awareness of the fluid and multiple nature of the self as a spirit, it might be similar to the Buddhist realization of 'no-self'. As we have already seen, the goal of spiritual evolution in spiritualism is to achieve unity with the 'Great Spirit' – an impersonal God – and to erase one's individuality.[57] This is comparable to Buddhist *moksha* (liberation) from reincarnation, or a fusion with ancestral spirits in the Japanese folk view of reincarnation.

However, union with the Great Spirit cannot be set as a practical goal, and so Ehara does not specifically refer to it on television for the general public. However, he does in his books. As a result, there are Buddhists who argue that spiritualism is fundamentally different from the idea of 'no-self' and is tantamount to worship of the individual.[58] The clients in the selected examples showed a great deal of interest in the Bond with other reincarnating beings, but none of them expressed their desire to unite with the Great Spirit in the afterlife. Even if they realize the importance of Bonds with others, this tends to be limited to close personal relationships.

To put it in simple terms, there is a dichotomy between an 'individual–universal' principle on the one hand and a private life principle on the other. On a theoretical level, the contemporary view of reincarnation links up individual reincarnation with the spiritual evolution of the universe itself – connecting individualism with universalism. However, at the practical level various spiritual resources such as the Great Spirit, guardians, and group soul, which have originally cosmological implications, are mobilized towards the betterment of an individual's private life, but none of the clients expect it to contribute to universal evolution.

This connection between the individual and the universal was widely accepted in the 1980s in fantasy genres within Japanese culture. A brotherhood of 'warriors' from a past life was imagined, and it was actually believed within 'New New Religions' that a future apocalyptic war would give them a chance of spiritual evolution. Bearers of such beliefs are of a similar generation to the typical clients for PLT: interest in grand universal themes has faded away in the course of ordinary lives. More occultist clusters of people in present-day Japan still believe in the 'Ascension' of the planet Earth, the simultaneous catastrophe on unharmonious parts of the Earth and the spiritual evolution of awakened people.[59] Yet this is rarely a feature of PLT. PLT aims at moral growth of the Self and evolution or deepening of the Bond with partners or other family members, but it goes no further and its actual effect is not too different from that of secular therapy.

This kind of private life principle, or simply privatism, leads to an emphasis on an experiential reality that has epistemological value. Authors writing about reincarnation believe it to be literally true, and treat PLT as a means to connect with and experience this truth. However, such claims' basis in immediate experience weakens their objectivity. For recipients of PLT, the prioritization of experiential reality as the measurement of truth gives rise instead to an agnostic pragmatism. One might criticise that recipients show a certain credulity in believing in a mere hypnotic illusion, but in fact they are aware that it is nonsense to try to demonstrate the literal truth of the vision. As the cases show, they are modest enough to admit that their conviction is only a personal one, based on experiential reality. In a way, their attitude might be akin to the pragmatic theory of truth whereas the critics presuppose naïve positivism.[60]

## Ancestor worship, memorial devices, and reincarnation from the point of view of gender

For female PLT clients, family is ambiguous. Family is the source of many problems, but at the same time such problems are resolved by re-evaluating the Bond with family. Clients' self-images are also ambiguous. There is the self who is bound by a past life 'bond', and there is the self who realizes a Bond across incarnations and tries to improve it as a responsible subject. A female client might try to escape stressful family situations as an independent individual, but at the same time she is willing (or obliged) to act as a mediator within her family and to maintain its emotional unity.

Let us sketch some of the historical developments from ancestor worship through to the contemporary view of reincarnation from the hypothetical perspective that the female gender role is the basis for the role of mediator where a reincarnating Bond lost from sight is a source of present problems.[61]

1   The traditional *ie* system was patriarchal, preserved down generations through the worship of ancestors within the framework of Funeral Buddhism. As Yanagita has argued, the duty of the head of the family was to conduct services properly for their 'ancestor' as a non-individual deity. By doing so he is expected to become the 'ancestor', posthumously (patriarchal agency by familial priesthood).

2   In modern families (which started in the Taishō period (1912–1926) and became dominant around the 1970s when the number of house-wives peaked in Japan), males' social activities often separated them from local communities, so females were expected to take on the role of emotional mediator within the family. Ancestor worship did not decline immediately, but – as we saw above – was transformed into memorialism, which left behind the problem of the purification of the souls of the old family that date from before the time that the living can remember. If there is a problem within the family, a concern arises about the possibility of an unpurified soul that has diverged from the path of becoming an ancestral spirit and instead is suffering, feeling resentful, and even cursing its family. Holding a memorial service for such souls is believed to keep the family bond intact, thus reconciling conflicts. This act of saving terrible souls and helping

them become one with the ancestral spirit, in order to protect the present family and its spiritual health, involves a high degree of female participation, which represents strong and merciful 'maternity'. Women feel that they cannot leave ancestor worship to men any more because they are not seriously committed with family rituals, and in some cases they engage the help of psychics or new religions to revive the effect of ancestor worship. This gives women a pride in their status in the family (matriarchal agency through the practice of memorial services).[62]

3   With decreasing marriage rates and increasing divorce rates, trends towards simplification and liberalization in funeral services, and declines in the number of *danka* (Buddhist parish members) and people engaging in ancestor worship, women can no longer develop and assert themselves through holding memorial services. As their role in family ritual has eroded, they do not have to take on the symbolic 'maternity' of *ie* any more. Nevertheless they experience guilt as their relative detachment from family members becomes clear. This leads them to have a sense of a mission to rebuild the family. At this stage, clients of PLT do not resort to the collective rituals of religion but rely on non-religious spiritual resources like PLT. Involvement in a private session of PLT can encourage them to search personally for a narrative of the reincarnating Self. However, in the course of the session they become aware of their reincarnating Bond and make up their minds to improve the reincarnating Bond, with a sense of privilege that 'it is only *I* who can do it'. This process does not involve other people and remains instead a personal awakening. As we saw above, 'family' in such contexts are the client's close relatives or partners who are chosen by her as having a significant relationship with her reincarnating Self. If lifestyle trends towards single living continue, the range of relationships to which women refer in PLT may well continue to shrink. This will be possible because the most important thing is the Bond discovered by the Self, independent of blood relations (Self-agency through furthering the growth of the reincarnating Bond).

From the perspective of gender, female clients are in a double bind: on the one hand family becomes the source of the problems that they want to transcend; but on the other hand they cannot identify themselves with the universal as a potential resource for autonomy. The 'universal' here is human spiritual evolution, with which male reincarnation authors identify themselves. Ideally, an individual soul plans his or her life before birth and can live this life responsibly when becoming aware of the plan. This leads to universal spiritual evolution, coming closer to the Great Spirit. In contrast, none of the female clients studied here refer to such planning or universal evolution since they are unable to see their lives as something that they have planned. That is the reason why a private life principle is preferred over an individual–universal one. They deepen their awareness of the reincarnating Self and the Bond and of their spirituality in a lonely private session separated from both the universal and from given family conditions. This lonely awareness then turns into a sense of privilege that 'only *I* am aware of spirituality, aware of "my being spiritual"'. Behind this lies a sense of mission to burden oneself with the Bond even if others do not appreciate it. Such a sense of burden, isolation, and privilege may be heightened by a male partner's lack of interest in spirituality, and it can also be said that the partner's disinterest conversely heightens a woman's convoluted devotion to spirituality. This becomes a vicious circle.

## Conclusion: from the darkness of *rei* (spirit) to the brightness of spirituality

What impact are these contemporary views of reincarnation having upon the Japanese religious context? More than anything, spirituality in the sense of being a spirit, as a reincarnating entity, is transforming the negative and dark images formerly attached to the word *rei* (spirit).

First, Self as spirit is thought to be purified in the bright middle world – what Weiss calls the 'in-between state'[63] – existing between past and present lives. Here one plans how one will accomplish the tasks of the past life in the present life and takes a new birth spontaneously. The word 'karma', in the context of this view, means only something like 'tendency' and has no binding power. Such presuppositions underlie clients' lightness and positivity even after they know their dark past in a previous life.

Second, the realization of the spirituality of the Self and others that share the Bond has no connection with other spiritual beings, '*rei*', and the misfortune caused by them. They used to be thought of as unpurified spirits that had strayed off the course leading towards uniting with the ancestral spirit. However, with the general decline of ancestor worship, people have become less scared of unpurified spirits. Ehara indeed admits the existence of unpurified *rei* and its possession of the living but also writes that such a phenomenon is attracted by one's low wavelength (*hachō*) of mind,[64] and that it is more important to lighten oneself and to heighten one's vibration than to worry about the *rei*.[65]

Thus spirituality as an internal realization of the Self as a reincarnating spiritual being has added to the word '*supirichuaru*' ('the spiritual' often used as a noun in Japanese context) fresh connotations of lightness, positivity and agency. It has pushed into the background the connotation of '*rei*' as an external transcendent being outside the self. And yet there remains a negativity and a sense of burden, relating to the Self, in the cases we have discussed. It is as if the client, as the only one who understands the spiritual dimension around the family, is a kind of *rei* for the rest of the family. Is it an ongoing process towards greater subjectivity and light? Does it perhaps reveal a hierarchy and a dislocation between the male authors who lead the culture of spirituality and the female readers who follow them? Is it a gender strategy that privileges the isolated awareness of burden and mission? We wait to see how this area of Japan's spiritual culture develops, especially in relation to changes in family and gender status.

## Notes

1 Translated by Inoue Yoshinobu, Christopher Harding, and Horie Norichika. This article is a modified version of Horie, 'Gendai no Rinne-tenshō-kan: Rinne suru Watashi no Monogatari'.
2 Shimazono Susumu coined the term '*Shin-Reisei Bunka*' (New Spirituality Culture) and '*Shin-Reisei Undō*' (New Spirituality Movement) to refer to the whole realm of New Age in Anglophone countries. 'Seishin Sekai' (Spiritual World) broadly corresponds to New Age in Japan (Shimazono, *Supirichuariti no kōryū*: 53). The term 'New' implies people's expectation of the coming of an alternative to religion (50). 'Spirituality' here implies something to be searched for principally by individuals, not via religion.
3 See Horie,'Nihon no Supirichuariti Gensetsu no Jōkyō': 36 and note 1; 'Narrow new age and broad spirituality': 111–112.
4 Ehara holds 'the Principle of Soul' that 'humans are spiritual beings', as the first of the Eight Principles of Spiritualism (Ehara, *Supirichuaru na Jinsei ni Mezameru tameni*: 85).
5 Horie,'Nihon no Supirichuariti Gensetsu no Jōkyō': 47).
6 'Spiritual boom' refers to the rise of Ehara's popularity and related phenomena around 2007 such as frequent use of the word 'spiritual', and growing interest in auras, guardian spirits, and past lives.
7 According to a survey, 29.8 per cent of Japanese people believe in reincarnation while 23.8 per cent believe in an 'other world', and 9.9 per cent believe that the deads' souls reside in the cemetery. To sum up, 63.5 per cent believe in an afterlife in general. The same survey shows that 20.6 per cent are interested in 'supirichuaru' (spiritual) in the sense of a trend towards obtaining peace of mind by connecting oneself to invisible spiritual beings or phenomena such as past lives, guardian spirits, and auras. See Yomiuri Shinbun, 'Nenkan Renzoku Chosa'.
8 Taishō Daigaku Sōgō Bukkyō Kenkyūjo (ed.), *Rinne no Sekai*.
9 Ōsumi, 'Sōron: Inga to Rinne wo Meguru Nihon-jin no Shūkyō-ishiki': 48–49.
10 Smith, *Ancestor Worship in Contemporary Japan*: 223.
11 Hearn, *Kokoro: Hints and Echoes of Japanese Inner Life*: 225–226.
12 Hearn, *Kokoro: Hints and Echoes of Japanese Inner Life*: 239–240.
13 Hearn (1896: 232–235).
14 Yanagita, *About Our Ancestors*: 171.
15 Yanagita, *About Our Ancestors*: 173.
16 Yanagita, *About Our Ancestors*: 174.
17 Hirata, 'Katsugorō Saisei Kibun': 374.
18 Hirata, 'Katsugorō Saisei Kibun': 383–384.
19 Hirata, 'Katsugorō Saisei Kibun': 376–377.
20 Hirata, 'Katsugorō Saisei Kibun': 394.
21 Ōsumi, 'Sōron: Inga to Rinne wo Meguru Nihon-jin no Shūkyō-ishiki': 53.
22 Inoue, *Haka to Kazoku no Hen'yō*.
23 For example, at the beginning of the 'Tale of Genji', there is speculation that it

is due to a deep *chigiri* between the Emperor and Kiritsubo no Kōi that such a beautiful prince as Hikaru Genji was born (Murasaki, 'Genji Monogatari': paragraph 2, Chapter 1: Kiritsubo).
24 Some people who are interested in New Age spirituality in Japan recently prefer the word '*nōryokusha*', which means only 'a person with ability', to '*reinō ryokusha*', which has been used for spiritual mediums or psychics. This suggests that they do not like the word '*rei*' (spirit or ghost), as well as an emerging notion that it is via one's natural abilities that one can be aware of a past life.
25 The term 'experiential reality' can be replaced by other terms such as 'psychic reality' or 'narrative reality', as the theoretical viewpoint changes. An experiential realization of a past life would be accepted as evidence in the psychic world. However, from the viewpoint of analysts, such an experience is accepted only when a narrative of it successfully describes or constructs the self. According to Paul Ricœur, even a fiction can 'redescribe' reality in the same way as scientific models or theories in the field of astrophysics construct reality without immediate data (what philosophers of science call 'redescription'). In this way, a narrative of the self constructs a narrative identity (Ricœur, *Time and Narrative*): it is not that one constructs one's narrative but rather that the narrative constructs the self. Here, a narrative of past lives and the greater narrative of a reincarnating Self redescribe the 'reality' of reincarnation when it is successfully narrated – even if it is not verified.
26 Takahashi, *Kokoro no Hakken*: 310.
27 Numata, 'Gendai Shin-Shūkyō ni okeru Karisuma no Sei to Shi': 24–26, 27–28.
28 Numata, 'Gendai Shin-Shūkyō ni okeru Karisuma no Sei to Shi': 17–18.
29 Takahashi, *Kokoro no Hakken*: 181. Kumata pointed out that GLA and its factions share 'a selective view of reincarnation', wherein one selects one's condition of life and leads a life of training or practice (Kumata, 'Rinne-Tenshō': 36.
30 Hirai, *Genma Taisen*.
31 Asaba wrote 'you can find four or five strange letters from readers in each monthly issue' (Asaba, 'Okaruto Zasshi wo Kyōfu ni Furuwaseta Nazo no Tōkō Shōjo tachi!': 12), but this statement was exaggerated. According to my research, ten letters in 1985 and eleven letters in 1986 were found in which people were looking for friends in past lives.
32 *Mū*, January 1985.
33 Hiwatari, *Boku no Chikyū wo Mamotte*.
34 *Asahi Shimbun*: 12.
35 MacLaine, *Out on a Limb*.
36 See Harding (Introduction), this volume.
37 Iida, *Ikigai no Sōzō*: 266–271.
38 Nine of seventeen titles including 'past life therapy' were published after 2004. Before then four of eight are the translated books written by Weiss (accessed on 14 June 2010).
39 http://goisu.net/cgi-bin/psychology/psychology.cgi?menu=c036, www.jikan-hikou.jp/.
40 Broadcast on 20 October 2007, emphasis added.
41 One might make the criticism that responses of guests on a variety show are not credible, but this article is not concerned with the truthfulness or otherwise of such responses. The aim here is to abstract the patterns of how stories about past lives are received and passed on. Even where people are performing on a talk show according to a script, we are able to analyse what is natural for them as a scene of agreeing upon the stories.
42 'A Request' of Zenkoku Reikan Shōhō Taisaku Bengoshi Renrakukai [National Association of Lawyers Against Spiritual-Pressure Sales Method] to NHK

[a government-run broadcasting station] and NAB [an association of commercial broadcasting stations] on 21 February 2007, www1k.mesh.ne.jp/reikan/shiryou/siryo4.htm.
43 In this article, lower-case 'self' with quotation marks, ego or *I* without quotation marks, and capitalized Self, are strictly used to distinguish the narrated self in the past life, the present self, and the constructed self beyond reincarnations.
44 Ehara, *Akui Zen'i*: 26–27).
45 Weiss, *Many Lives, Many Masters*.
46 Cf. The website of the Foundation of the Japanese Certification Board for Clinical Psychologists, www.fjcbcp.or.jp/, accessed on 9 March 2014.
47 www.geocities.jp/hypno_pastlife/e-jp.html; www.geocities.jp/hypno_pastlife/w-jp.html.
48 Round numbers, for example '30s', are calculated here as thirty-five. The exception is 'teenager', which is calculated here as eighteen on the basis of content on the site and on the basis that clients pay as much as 15,000 to 30,000 yen.
49 All data was collected by the means written above, with no intervention or selection by the author.
50 Emphasis added. http://therapyroomaube.jp/taikendan.html.
51 Melton, 'Edgar Cayce and reincarnation'.
52 This is not an assertion that 'past lives' are invented by clients. Believers would probably explain an association of a past life with memory of a client's childhood as below: the client sees the particular past life that has the greatest resonance, of all past lives, with his or her present existence. Of course, verification is not the purpose of this article. The main purpose here is to find out how patterns of narrative produce reality, based on the narrative point of view that the self is constructed by narrative (Asano, *Jiko eno Monogatariteki Sekkin*: 5–7).
53 Hereafter, lower-case 'bond', with quotation marks, and capitalized Self are used to distinguish the narrated 'bond' in a particular past life from the imagined Bond transcending incarnations.
54 The word 'soulmate' is often used to refer to a partner with whom one has formed a bond since past lives. According to Weiss, one is connected with one's soulmate by love forever and necessarily meets him or her every time one is reborn (Weiss, *Only Love Is Real*). In his examples, soulmates are very often boyfriends or girlfriends. In our cases, the clients of cases three and fourteen regard their boyfriends as 'soulmates' who were loving partners in their past lives, too. However, Iida (*Sourumeito*) and Ehara (*Ningen no Kizuna*) claim that every person in connection is a 'soulmate' in a broad sense.
55 In *Serapii Bunka no Shakaigaku*, Koike contrasted the principle of self-responsibility in large-group awareness training and self-help manuals with a tendency towards escape from responsibility in the theory of adult children of dysfunctional families. In *Supirichuariti no kōryū*, Shimazono applied this typology to spirituality and called the latter type 'spirituality of liberation'.
56 Ehara, *Ningen no Kizuna*: 30). He does not give clear definitions of concepts, but his idea appears to be as follows: the big Self loves other selves like itself rationally, recognizing spiritual connections with others; the small self (or ego) gives priority to self-fulfilment over others' needs, searching for physical satisfaction (cf. Ehara, *Akui Zen'i*: 82–89).
57 Ehara, *Supirichuaru na Jinsei ni Mezameru tameni*: 142.
58 Gen'yū, 'Kosei wo Kyōyō Sareru Gendaijin wo Hikikomu "Mitsu"'.
59 Asakawa, *2012-nen Asenshon Saigo no Shinjitsu*.
60 In 'Zense Ryōhō no Rinshō Shinrigaku teki Kenshō', Ishikawa points out as a clinical psychologist that PLT has developed out of existing psychotherapy systems and is in danger of getting out of control. At the same time, he

recognizes its efficiency when a skillful psychotherapist practises it as an imaginative therapy that treats past lives phenomenologically.
61 In 'Pāsto Raifu Serapii Mūbumento wo Dō Yomu ka', Shimada commented on Weiss's PLT right after it was introduced to Japan. He predicted that it would be just a transitory fashion if it were not taken into traditional spiritual culture in Japan. In fact, it did not become popular at all in 1990s. As the present article shows, it became popular around 2004, but the reason for its rise is that traditional ancestor worship has been weakening, contrary to Shimada's argument.
62 See part four of Kōmoto, *Gendai Nihon niokeru Senzo Saishi*, though it dealt with only Reiyūkai and its factions.
63 Weiss, *Many Lives, Many Masters*: 46.
64 'Wavelength' is an important concept not only in Ehara's thought but also in GLA and *Kōfuku no Kagaku* (Happy Science). The higher the wavelength your mind has, the higher the spirit you can communicate with, and the better things you can attract. In Anglophone New Age, 'vibration' is used more often in this context. cf. Hicks and Hicks, *The Law of Attraction*.
65 Ehara, *Supirichuaru na Jinsei ni Mezameru tameni*: 109, 113–114.

## References

Asaba, Michiaki. 1989. 'Okaruto Zasshi wo Kyōfu ni Furuwaseta Nazo no Tōkō Shōjo tachi! [Strange girl readers threatened an occult magazine!]', *Bessatsu Takarajima 92: Uwasa no Hon [Takarajima, extra issue 92: a book of rumor]* (Tokyo: JICC Shuppankyoku).

*Asahi Shimbun, Evening ed.*, 17 August 1989.

Asakawa, Yoshitomi. 2009. *2012-nen Asenshon Saigo no Shinjitsu: Maya Yogen no Himitsu to Kurarion Seijin no Keiji… Tamashii no Go-jigen Jōshō ga Ima Hajimaru! [The final truth of the Ascension in 2012: secrets of Mayan prophecy and a revelation from the planet Clarion … telling that the soul's rise to the fifth dimension starts now!]* (Gakushū Kenkyūsha).

Asano, Tomohiko. 2001. *Jiko eno Monogatariteki Sekkin: Kazoku Ryōhō kara Shakaigaku e [Narrative approaches to the self: from family therapy to sociology]* (Tokyo: Keisō Shobō).

Ehara, Hiroyuki. 2003. *Supirichuaru na Jinsei ni Mezameru tameni: Kokoro ni 'Jinsei no Chizu' wo Motsu [To awake to a spiritual life: to have a 'map of life' inside your mind]* (Tokyo: Shinchōsha).

Ehara, Hiroyuki. 2007. *Ningen no Kizuna: Sourumeito wo Sagashite [Human bond: in search of soulmate]* (Tokyo: Shōgakkan).

Ehara, Hiroyuki. 2008. *Akui Zen'i: Tamashii no Sugao [Ill will and good will: The soul as it is]* (Tokyo: Shōgakkan).

Gen'yū, Sōkyū. 2006. 'Kosei wo Kyōyō Sareru Gendaijin wo Hikikomu "Mitsu" ["Honey" that attracts and forces people today to search around individuality]', *Chūō Kōron*, 121(12), 153–159.

Hearn, Lafcadio. 1896. *Kokoro: Hints and Echoes of Japanese Inner Life* (Tokyo: Tuttle Shokai, 2002).

Hicks, Esther and Hicks, Jerry. 2006. *The law of attraction: The basics of the teaching of Abraham* (Carlsbad, CA: Hay House).

Hirai, Kazumasa. 1979–83. *Genma Taisen [Genma wars]*, Vol. 1–20 (Tokyo: Kadokawa Shoten).

Hirata, Atsutane. 1829. 'Katsugorō Saisei Kibun' [A record of tidings of Katugorō's rebirth]', *Senkyō Ibun and Katsugorō Saisei Kibun [Strange tidings from the realm of immortals and a record of tidings of Katugorō's rebirth]* (Tokyo: Iwanami Shoten, 2000).

Hiwatari, Saki. 1987–1994. *Boku no Chikyū wo Mamotte [Protect my planet]*, Vol. 1–12 (Tokyo: Hakusen-sha, 1998).

Horie Norichika. 2007. 'Nihon no Supirichuariti Gensetsu no Jōkyō' [The situation regarding discourses on spirituality in Japan]', in Nihon Toransupāsonaru Shinrigaku Seishin'igakukai [Japanese Association for Transpersonal Psychology/Psychiatry] (ed.), *Supirichuariti no Shinrigaku [Psychology of Spirituality]* (Osaka: Seseragi Shuppan), pp. 33–54.

Horie Norichika. 2010. 'Gendai no Rinne-tenshō-kan: Rinne suru Watashi no Monogatari', in Tsuruoka Yoshio and Fukasawa Hidetaka (eds), *Supirichuariti no Shūkyōshi (Jōkan)* (Tokyo: Liton).

Horie Norichika. 2013. ' "Narrow new age and broad spirituality": A comprehensive schema and a comparative analysis', Steven J. Sutcliffe and Ingvild Saelid Gilhus (eds), *New age spirituality: Rethinking religion* (Durham: Acumen, November 2013), pp. 99–116.

Iida, Fumihiko. 1996. *Ikigai no Sōzō: "Umarekawari no Kagaku" ga Jinsei wo Kaeru [Creation of vivacity: "a science of reincarnation" will change your life]*, (Kyoto: PHP Kenkyūjo, 2007).

Iida, Fumihiko. 2005. *Sourumeito: 'Unmei no Hito' nitsuiteno Nanatsu no Kōsatsu [Soulmate: seven considerations on 'the one for you']* (Kyoto: PHP Kenkyūjo).

Inoue, Haruyo. 2003. *Haka to Kazoku no Hen'yō [Transformation of grave and family]* (Tokyo: Iwanami Shoten).

Ishikawa, Yūichi. 2004. ' "Zense Ryōhō no Rinshō Shinrigaku teki Kenshō": Sono Mondaiten to Kanōsei [An Inquiry into "past life therapy" from a standpoint of clinical psychology: its problems and possibilities]', *Toransu Pāsonaru Shinrigaku/Seishin Igaku* 5 (1), 66–76.

Koike, Yasushi. 2007. *Serapii Bunka no Shakaigaku [Sociology of therapeutic culture]* (Tokyo: Keisō Shobō).

Kōmoto, Mitsugu. 2001. *Gendai Nihon niokeru Senzo Saishi [Ancestor worship in contemporary Japan]* (Tokyo: Ochanomizu Shobō).

Kumata, Kazuo. 1996. 'Rinne-Tenshō [Reincarnation-rebirth]', Nihon Bukkyō Kenkyū-kai (ed.), *Nihon no Bukkyō [Japanese Buddhism]*, No. 6 (Kyoto: Hōzōkan).

MacLaine, Shirley. 1983. *Out on a limb* (N.Y.: Bantam Books, 1984).

Melton, J. Gordon. 1994. 'Edgar Cayce and reincarnation: Past life readings as religious symbology', *Syzygy: Journal of Alternative Religion and Culture* 3 (1–2).

*Mū*, January 1985 (Tokyo: Gakushū Kenkyūsha).

Murasaki Shikibu. *Genji Monogatari [The tale of Genji]* in *Genji Monogatari no Sekai: Saihenshūban [World of the Genji Monogatari: re-edition]*, www.genji-monogatari.net/, updated on 20 August 2006.

Numata, Ken'ya. 1986. 'Gendai Shin-Shūkyō ni okeru Karisuma no Sei to Shi: Takahashi Shinji to GLA no Kenkyū [Life and death of a charismatic leader of a New Religion in contemporary age: a study of Takahashi Shinji and GLA]', *Momoyama Gakuin Daigaku Shakai-gaku Ronshū*, 20(1), 1–33.

Ōsumi, Kazuo. 1986. 'Sōron: Inga to Rinne wo Meguru Nihon-jin no Shūkyō-ishiki' [General introduction: Japanese religious consciousness about cause–effect and reincarnation]', Ōsumi (ed.), *Inga to Rinne: Kōdō-kihan to Takai-kan no Genri*

*[Cause–effect and reincarnation: principles of the norms of action and the views of the other world]* (Tokyo: Shunjūsha).

Ricœur, Paul. 1983–1985. (translated by Kathleen McLaughlin and David Pellauer) *Time and narrative*, vol. 1–3 (Chicago: University of Chicago Press, 1990).

Shimada, Hiromi. 1992. 'Pāsto Raifu Serapii Mūbumento wo Dō Yomu ka [How to understand past life therapy movement]', Takarajima Henshūbu (ed.), *Kakoze Kaiki* (Tokyo: JICC Shuppankyoku).

Shimazono, Susumu. 2007. *Supirichuariti no kōryū: Shin-reisei bunka to sono shūhen [The rise of spirituality: New spirituality culture and its surroundings]*, (Tokyo: Iwanami Shoten).

Smith, Robert. 1974. *Ancestor worship in contemporary Japan* (Stanford University Press).

Taishō Daigaku Sōgō Bukkyō Kenkyūjo Rinne Shisō Kenkyūkai (ed.). 2001. *Rinne no Sekai [The worldview of reincarnation]* (Tokyo: Seishi Shuppan).

Takahashi, Shinji. 1973. *Kokoro no Hakken: Genshō-hen [Discovery of mind: its phenomena]* (Tokyo: Sanpō Shuppan).

Weiss, Brian L. 1988. *Many lives, many masters* (N.Y.: Simon & Schuster).

Weiss, Brian L. 1996. *Only love is real: A story of soulmates reunited* (N.Y.: Warner Books).

Yanagita, Kunio. 1946. (translated by Fanny Hagin Mayer and Ishiwara Yasuyo) *About our ancestors: The Japanese family system* (New York: Greenwood Press, 1988).

Yomiuri Shinbun. 'Nenkan Renzoku Chosa: Nihonjin (6) Shukyokan [Annual survey: Japanese (6) views on religion]'. *Yomiuri Shinbun* (29 May 2008).

# 11 A society accepting of spirit possession
Mental health and shamanism in Okinawa

*Shiotsuki Ryoko*[1]

Late modernity has for the most part considered insanity to amount to irrational behaviour, and insane people have been segregated, confined or ostracized.[2] Spirit possession has been regarded as a form of insanity; a disease requiring segregation and treatment via modern western medicine. This was true of mainland Japan during its process of rapid modernization beginning in the Meiji era (from 1868). And yet in Okinawa some forms of possession phenomena have been regarded as sacred – 'blessed insanity' – and not as a disease. 'Spirit possession' here refers to a combination of unusual physical and mental states, through which a potential shaman passes in the process of becoming a shaman.

In Okinawa shamans are known by a number of terms, including *yuta* (principally on the main island of Okinawa and Amami), *kankakarya* ('person possessed by the divine'; used mostly in the Miyako district), and *munushiri* ('knowledgeable persons'; used widely in Okinawa). In this chapter, the term *yuta* will be used to refer to shamans in Okinawa, based on field research findings on Okinawa's main island and in recognition of the fact that the term has now come to be widely used on Miyako island and the Yaeyama islands as well.

Many *yuta*, being folk- rather than official shamans, are female. Prior to the annexation by the Meiji government of what became known as 'Okinawa prefecture', these islands to the south of mainland Japan were known as the Ryukyu Kingdom. An organization within the Kingdom called *Kikoeno ōkimi*: priestesses of royal blood, devoted to the gods. Below these were regional networks of *noro* ('ceremonial women') who oversaw the work of the *kaminchu* ('gods' people') who conducted village religious rituals. In Okinawa, the long-held *onari gami* belief that sisters spiritually protect their brothers was widely held. People believed that females had strong spiritual power and accordingly females were positioned higher than males in religious contexts.

*Kaminchu*, as priestesses, were accorded respect. But after the Ryukyu Kingdom ceased to exist, few successors were trained and these priestesses are now in danger of disappearing. On the other hand, *yuta* have continued to be active despite occasional suppression by the authorities, and the number of *yuta* is actually increasing today. Socially, however, they have come to be disrespected as a result of official prohibition; looked down upon as similar to prostitutes. People commonly say that 'men pay for prostitutes and women pay for *yuta*'. *Yuta*, unlike *kaminchu*, engage in activities relating to death, such as channeling and acting as a mouthpiece for the spirits of the deceased; conducting burial rituals; and summoning the spirits of gods and ancestors to deliver their messages, predict someone's future or treat disease. *Yuta* have also come to play the role of counsellors, performing an essential function in people's lives.

Whereas *kaminchu* do not always undergo a state of being possessed by supernatural beings, most *yuta* put themselves into such a state when becoming shamans and when conveying oracles. People generally do not see such phenomena as negative, and in need of elimination, and in this sense Okinawa can be seen as a society that accepts spiritual possession. Why is it that people in Okinawa have not denied, excluded or segregated experiences of spiritual possession in the modern age as in mainland Japanese and most western societies?

In Okinawa, becoming insane is called *furiyun*, and an insane person is called *fura* or *furimun*, literally meaning to be touched by something. A person in such a state is known as a *tāringua* or *tārimun*, meaning that something has got into that person. These terms imply losing one's senses and often have negative connotations – of foolishness or delinquency. At the same time, however, this possession is regarded as a 'possession by divinity'; such people are regarded as *kamiburi* (touched by god) or *kamidāri* (god has entered into one) – similar to the sacred phenomenon that occurs when a person is spiritually possessed on their way to becoming a *yuta*.

The charismatic and uncontrollable nature of 'sacred insanity' has often been regarded as a threat by authorities in Okinawa, and from time to time they have sought to suppress it. In particular, *yuta*, whose ability to become possessed is more important to their legitimacy than their genealogy, have faced severe suppression from the seventeenth century down to the present day – by local rulers and, in the modern era, by police and the press. One way for *yuta* to handle this problem has been to employ a 'bricolage' tactic: creating their worldview by flexibly combining whatever elements were available around themselves – established religions, folk beliefs, and scientific terminology. They have also been able to obtain support from clients. The cultural anthropologist I. M. Lewis attaches a high value to the state of a voluntarily possessed shaman. He points out the syncretic, active, and flexible nature of shamanism by saying that shamans mitigate the shocks of suppression and change them in their own favour by responding as if they had been earnestly looking forward to the unavoidable. He says:

> old religious forms stretch out their arms to embrace and come to terms with new experience ... bowing to the inevitable (i.e. innovation

or change), and accepting it, as it were, with open arms, they soften its impact, making it seem that they passionately desire what they cannot avoid.[3]

Tactics such as this worked well, and still now demand for *yuta* is unceasing in Okinawa. Common phrases include 'asking for help, half from a doctor, half from a *yuta*' and 'a prayer on one hand, a doctor on the other'.

In this way, clients may visit both *yuta* and medical doctors trained in modern western medicine, depending upon their symptoms and conditions, to seek healing and salvation. Modern medicine and traditional practices coexist.

There are few regions in which modern medical doctors and shamans coexist as they do in Okinawa. To trace the changes in people's views on shamanism and associated insanity or spirit possession, it is important to pay attention to the pattern of the spread of modern western medicine, and in particular the introduction of psychiatric care. The history of the spread of psychiatric care has influenced profoundly people's views on shamanism, insanity and spirit possession. This chapter will argue that the view commonly found elsewhere, that insanity should be isolated, confined and ostracized, is not a major feature of the history of insanity in Okinawa.

## Phases of spirit possession in Okinawa

As mentioned already, some aspects of insanity and spirit possession have been regarded as sacred in Okinawa. Alongside the unusual physical and mental states through which a *yuta*-to-be passes in the process of becoming a shaman, there is the practice of *tamahati* on Yonaguni Island: housewives or women conducting rituals put on sacred talismans (necklaces, spears, abacuses), which have been passed down generation to generation in their families, and call up the spirits of these objects in order that they can become possessed by them and perform ritual dances.[4]

Despite this, from the period of the Ryukyu Kingdom up to the end of the Second World War, *yuta*, as practitioners of spirit possession, were suppressed, and *noro* and other types of *kaminchu* were subject to control by the authorities. Even after the Second World War, criticism of the premodern nature of *yuta* was frequently taken up in newspapers, in connection with the '*tōtōme* (spirit tablets) problem'. Traditionally in Okinawa, the first son or another male relative had inherited the family spirit tablets along with the rest of the family property. These were palm-size objects made from wood, whose colour would be altered from white to red following a memorial service held to mark the forty-ninth day after death (a custom developed partly under the influence of Buddhism). Where a family possessed more than one tablet, these were placed in cases, arranged from right to left in descending order of the age of the tablet, and with men's tablets facing up and women's tablets facing down. After the Second World War, this practice of passing on spirit tablets was discouraged under new gender-equality laws. *Yuta* told many of their clients who observed the law that the cause of their troubles was that they had not followed the traditional way of passing down the family spirit tablets. Hence, they came to be criticized as going against the current law – an example of suppression by the media. Nevertheless, belief in *yuta* is still strong, and the number of people becoming *yuta* is increasing. The need of authorities to maintain the social order via promoting consistent standards of behaviour of individuals and ordinary states of consciousness means that the taking of an affirmative view of spirit possession is a potential threat. This threat is heightened because, unlike the *kaminchu* who were authorized and controlled by the Ryukyu Kingdom Office and later the Meiji government, *yuta* operate on an individual basis and do not rely upon genealogy or licencing for their legitimacy with the general public.[5]

*Yuta* have been seen as liars or deceivers by some Okinawans, and have been discriminated against and placed in the lowest stratum of the society for a long time, particularly on the main island of Okinawa. This view seems to have taken root when 'modern' policies were initiated by the Shimazu clan, which invaded Okinawa in 1609. Under the 'Haneji Shioki' (judicial rules) issued by Shō Jyōken (aka Haneji Chōshū), a politician and scholar in the seventeenth century, shamans were regulated for the first time in the history of Okinawa because it was thought that they would impede the new political reforms.[6] Later, Sai On, a famous politician of the eighteenth century, carried on Shō Jyōken's policy and subjected the *yuta* to strict control.[7]

In the Meiji era, feudal domains (*han*) were abolished, and a centralized prefecture system was instituted by the government in 1871. The Ryukyu Kingdom ceased to exist, but the policies of the Kingdom were succeeded by the Meiji government, and the control and suppression of *yuta* was reinforced. Influenced by the stance of the Meiji government, one local newspaper appealed for stronger control over the *yuta* from the time of its foundation in the 1870s onwards.[8] The cultural assimilation of Okinawa into mainland Japan further weakened the *yuta*, exacerbated by patriotic Japanese feeling stoked during wars against China (1894–1895) and Russia (1904–1905). *Yuta* practices were considered to be an impeding factor in the modernization of Japan, and *yuta* were accused of being anti-nationalists who circulated false or groundless rumours.

*Yuta* tend to embrace ancestors and the gods they believe in and follow what they say, living according to the concepts of 'the other world' rather than the values and systems of 'this world' – on which political rulers insist and which ordinary people understand as common sense. As such they may inadvertently confuse and damage the existing social system and order. Fear of this has caused rulers, across history, to suppress and control *yuta*, while ordinary people, in their suffering, have often earnestly supported them.[9]

The suppression of *yuta* prior to the Second World War might have influenced the thinking of people to some extent, causing them to consider *yuta* to be anti-social and bad. Even so, it has not inculcated an idea that *yuta* spirit possession is a disease to be avoided. And since suppression and regulation of *yuta* have come to an end since the 1990s, evaluation of them is rising in some parts of society. We can attribute this also to a recent change in the understanding of insanity in psychiatry: the advocacy of 'the usefulness of spiritual possession (insanity)'.[10] In some areas of contemporary psychiatry, spirit possession and insanity are starting to be considered a positive human activity. This kind of affirmative view on spirit possession is increasingly reflected in literature, films, manga, animation, and other fields.[11]

### The definition of *kamidāri* in psychiatry

Where clients visit both trained medical doctors and *yuta*, sometimes yuta have recommended their clients to go to hospital, depending on their conditions, while doctors sometimes suggest that their clients visit *yuta* – not least because modern western medicine is not always good at dealing with mental illness. So what view does psychiatry take when it comes to the *kamidāri* (or *kamiburi*) phenomenon?

In psychiatry, *kamidāri* is seen as 'an abnormal mental situation connected with gods-related rituals',[12] or in terms of 'mental and physical abnormalities accompanied by hallucinations or noctambulation, understood [by patients and by society more widely] to be related to supernatural entities including gods and ancestors'.[13] Symptoms include autonomic nervous disorders, behavioural abnormalities and Ganser Syndrome (twilight state), personality transformations (spirit possession), breakdown, anorexia, numbness, dizziness, loitering, sleeplessness, visual hallucinations, auditory hallucinations and delusions.[14] Causes are regarded as being unknown, but it has been said that affected people may recover sooner or later.[15] These conditions are treated as a 'culture-bound syndrome' specific to Okinawa and thus not to be classified under the so-called International Classification of Diseases. As they are transient phenomena and persons suffering these conditions have good communication capabilities, some argue that they are different from ambulatory schizophrenics, and diagnose them instead in terms of neurosis, psychosomatic response, prayer-related mental disorder, or *kamidāri* syndrome. Medicines and other modern medical treatments are rarely effective,[16] and when patients do not recover in hospital, doctors finally resort to consulting senior *yuta*. According to conventional modern western medicine, then, these conditions relate to a treatable 'disorder' and possibly a form of 'insanity'.

In fact, two kinds of attitudes to insanity coexist in Okinawa: whether 'to exclude *kamidāri* as insanity or accept it as a usual practice in daily life'.[17] However, as mentioned in the previous section, the evaluation of *kamidāri* is changing in the psychiatric community. Some find a positive aspect, in terms of patients' mental stability and improved relations with their families,[18] and *kamidāri* is no longer denied or excluded to the extent that it was in the past.

## People with *kamidāri* symptoms visiting psychiatrists

In order to examine the relationships between modern western medicine and spirit possession in Okinawa, two clients who presented *kamidāri* symptoms were chosen at random from among the patients of psychiatrist A, and their experiences are outlined in what follows. One is a middle-aged woman (Interviewee 1) who is working as a *yuta*. The other is a young man (Interviewee 2), a candidate to become a *yuta*.[19] This overview begins with a general introduction to both individuals, before discussing their *kamidā ri* experiences.

### *Interviewee 1:*

First visit in 1984. Woman, aged 55, *yuta*, divorced, living alone

*First interview*

Major complaints: heaviness of the head, sense of constriction of the chest, general malaise, sense of exhaustion, unpleasant sensation in the pharyngeal area, and temperature over 37°C. Doctors examined her suspecting infections, tuberculosis, schizoid disorder, hypertension and neural disorder, or bronchial pneumonia. But no such problems were found. Being unable to control her symptoms herself, she was hospitalized. After leaving the hospital, she visited sanctuaries and mountains all around the island for *uganmāi* (making a wish to the gods), but after getting wet in the rain her cold has worsened and she has become a little feverish.

She has been practising as a *yuta* for the past four years, or more precisely, this is the third year since she began working on a full-time basis. Sometimes she is unable to control her mental condition and is hospitalized. She sometimes sees three clients a day. She charges a fee of around 3,000 yen per consultation [the fee in 2014 ranges from 3,000 yen to 5,000 yen per consultation]. She visits colleague *yuta* to ask their help. She can help others but not herself, so she has to ask her colleagues for their suggestions – as it is said, 'we can see Kerama island but not our own eyelashes'. Since she has to pay them, she ends up earning little.

She married a Filipino-American serviceman who died in the war in Vietnam. A daughter was born (28 years old at the time of interview). Later, she remarried a man from Okinawa and had a son and a daughter. The son died from leukemia when he was a senior high school student.

As her husband became violent when he was drunk, she divorced him. He took the daughter with him. She underwent a *kamidāri* experience nine years ago, and stayed in H hospital for six months. She also visited other hospitals seeking a diagnosis, but all the doctors she saw said that they found nothing wrong with her.

*Second interview*

She is in hospital. She is worried about her house because the doors and windows are all closed. She is sorry for her god, who is enshrined in a home shrine. She wants to be close to her god. Her temperature was normal in the morning, but she became feverish in the afternoon. She wants to go home. While she has been away, telephone calls have been received and clients have visited her a number of times to ask her for help. As many as five clients have visited her in the hospital. She is not so sure, but people have often said that what she said to them has come true. The other day, she guessed that a client's grandfather who had died had hidden money in the bottom of a chest drawer. The family found it there, and was thankful to her.

*Third interview in the hospital*

She had a high fever of forty degrees two days ago. One night before she was going to leave the hospital, her temperature was still as high as 39 or 40°C. While she felt it unsafe to leave the hospital, she also felt a responsibility to perform her duties for her god, and was worried about other things as well.

*Fourth interview at an outpatient room*

Low fever continues at 37.8°C. She felt nauseous, and visited C hospital where she was given medicine.

**Interviewee 2:**

> First visit in 1985. Male, aged 14, a second year student in junior high school. He seems to be in the process of becoming a shaman.

From January last year, he began to be absent from school, not attending school for the first and second terms after he became a second year student, and managing only occasionally to attend school in the third term. Instead he spent time visiting sanctuaries to make wishes, and psychics to ask for omens, messages or divination. According to his mother, the family spent a few million yen, and borrowed more money besides, spending five or six million yen in total on fortune telling and divination by *yuta* and spiritualists. He is the first of three children. His father, fifty-seven, is from the northern part of the island, and his mother, fifty-two, from the central part of the island.

He developed a fever when he was a first-year student in junior high school. Then he got diarrhoea, syncope after melena, and collapsed three times. He was taken to the prefectural hospital by ambulance. He visited various medical facilities for examination, but no problems were found. In the process of visiting these facilities, it was once suggested that he be transported to C hospital, which had a psychiatric department, but due to time constraints in the end he was not hospitalized. Currently, he attends a Ryukyu Dance school, having been advised by the Goddess Kannon (Deity of Mercy) to do so [under the influence of Buddhism, some Okinawans believe in Kannon, although they have no great depth of knowledge about her].

## *Kamidāri* experience

### *Interviewee 1:*

It was when she was a 5th-grade pupil that she began to hear the voice of a god. It was triggered by the death of her father. During *umachī* (gathering of relatives to worship a god) nine years ago, she had a skull-splitting headache like cerebral meningitis. She ran a high fever, followed by auditory and visual hallucinations. She was in a state of *kamidāri* and continued to stay in bed for two years. Because of her suffering, she tried to commit suicide a number of times, attempting on one occasion to tie herself down with an electric cord, and on another to drown herself. She desperately wanted to die to be freed from her sufferings. But her god stopped her. People around her said that she was lazy and unwilling to do anything. But it was not laziness; rather her physical condition was so bad that she was unable to do anything. She visited a number of hospitals in the region, but the diagnoses were 'nothing abnormal', or 'cause unknown'. When she felt pains in the head and had dim sight she went to an eye doctor, and was told that she might lose her sight.

### *Interviewee 2:*

When he became a first-year junior high school student, he dreamed a great deal – often on themes of *kami* (gods) – and frequently fell over. He underwent a personal transformation, becoming possessed by a supernatural being. He engaged in automatic writing and sometimes became violent. After an attack he would be exhausted, and would sleep well. A paternal uncle living on an island in the northern part of the Okinawa island also had spiritual power, and often dreamed. He helped his nephew in judging whether a dream was positive or negative and assisted him in many other ways besides. He helped the boy to summon the spirit of Kannon, and conducted a ritual. When he was possessed by the spirit and spoke as its mouthpiece, he did not later remember what he said nor in what manner. He heard about it only from his mother, afterwards. Figures of high ranking women from the Ryukyu Kingdom appeared in his dreams and daydreams, and he kept drawings of them.

The above cases suggest that people suffering *kamidāri* consult psychiatrists and visit other hospital departments. According to psychiatrist A, both Interviewees 1 and 2 were generally calm and settled, with sufficient communication ability and empathy. He did not find any signs of hysterical personality, schizophrenic disorder or other personal characteristics that could be categorized as psychiatric disease. In parallel to seeing modern medical professionals, both interviewees visited *yuta* or *yabū* (a type of folk practitioner). Interviewee 1 was a professional *yuta* at the time of the interview series. In general, a person who has overcome *kamidāri* and become able to control spirit possession is recognized as having become a shaman (fully qualified *yuta*). But the *kamidāri* condition reoccurs, and at such times they visit both folk medical care workers and doctors trained in modern western medicine. They occasionally engage in *kamigoto* (spiritual rituals) at the same time as taking antipsychotic drugs.

## Psychiatric treatment in Okinawa: history and the law

In contemporary medicine, the utility of spirit possession (insanity) has begun to be advocated. Many cases of *kamidāri* symptoms like those outlined above are not diagnosed immediately as schizophrenic disorder or another psychiatric disease. Whereas in mainland Japan, modern western medicine has been applied since the early modern period, and the confinement of the insane practised in the name of treatment, in Okinawa these forms of modern medicine were not widely introduced before the end of WWII and instead some forms of insanity seemed to be accepted. Takehiko Yoshikawa says that 'in prewar Okinawa, psychiatric care in its modern sense was absent.... Okinawa has a long history of having accepted people with mental disabilities, which can be considered as the way mental care should be'.[20] Okinawa's legal system differed from that of mainland Japan from the late Meiji period up until the reversion of the islands' administration from the United States back to Japan in 1972. This psychiatric history, specific to Okinawa, seems to be a major contributing factor in the tendency for people not to consider spirit possession as something to be excluded, segregated or treated.

The process of establishing psychiatric hospitals in Okinawa is closely associated with the spread of psychiatric concepts in the general population. There were no psychiatric hospitals in Okinawa in the prewar period (neither public nor private), and it was only after the Second World War that psychiatry spread. In mainland Japan, a private hospital for insanity was founded in Kyoto in 1875, which was followed by a private hospital for mental disorders in Tokyo in 1878. At the same time, the confinement of patients by the Metropolitan Police Department was authorized. In 1919, a Law on Psychiatric Hospitals was enacted, under which applications for the establishment of psychiatric hospitals had to be submitted to prefectural governments. But only private hospitals were established as compulsory quarantine facilities. In Okinawa, mentally troubled people were controlled by the police if they were registered. Otherwise, families were entrusted to take care of them.[21]

The beginning of psychiatry in Okinawa is considered to be 1945, when the first department of psychiatry was opened in a US military-government hospital.[22] In 1946, the first psychiatric clinic in Okinawa was opened in Ginoza Hospital. When the Mental Hygiene Law was promulgated in Japan in 1950 to endorse the responsibility of the government in the provision of psychiatric care, in Okinawa, Ryukyu Governmental Psychiatric Hospital (later renamed National Ryukyu Psychiatric Hospital) was established next to a tuberculosis sanatorium in the town of Kin. In 1951, Shima Clinic, a private clinic, was opened, followed by other private psychiatric hospitals just as on the mainland. After the reversion of Okinawa to Japanese control a number of psychiatric hospitals were established.[23]

With the establishment of these hospitals in the postwar years, the question began to be posed of whether *kamidāri* and other types of spirit possession ought to be considered forms of 'disease' to be treated. Some psychiatrists, however, have advocated the usefulness of spirit possession (insanity).

Differences in Okinawa's legal system have also been a contributing factor in the acceptance and affirmation of *kamidāri* and other phenomena of spirit possession in Okinawa. The Meiji government enacted the Law on the Care and Custody of Psychopaths in 1900 to entrust the care and custody of members with mental disorders to families. This was applied to Okinawa when it formally became a part of Japan.[24] The law obliged families to designate the responsible person to give care and custody to member/s with mental disorders and to register them with the police. It also legally allowed families to keep them under court-ordered confinement in their homes. This Law on Care and Custody was abolished in 1950 and replaced with the Mental Hygiene Law on the mainland, but it continued to apply in Okinawa under the US civil administration until 1960 when the Ryukyu Mental Hygiene Law was enacted. Compared with the earlier Mental Hygiene Law this law focused on medical issues more than it did public order ones. It also featured social security provisions, guaranteeing the payment of medical expenses from public funds – although its relatively progressive nature was limited by Ryukyu government budgetary constraints, which led to people having to pay the cost of hospitalization themselves. As a result, home confinement continued even after the enactment of the law.

On top of this, the Ryukyu government and US Civilian Administration prioritized the prevention and treatment of infectious diseases such as tuberculosis, malaria and filarial infections which might have affected US servicemen, with mental health policies not a major concern and little funding made available for psychiatric treatments.

So concerned about the situation in Okinawa was the government in mainland Japan that a programme began in 1964 of dispatching medical doctors to Okinawa, psychiatrists amongst them. The Ryukyu government conducted its own fact-finding investigation of mental hygiene in 1966, finding that the number of people with mental disorders was nearly twice that of the mainland. Demands now began to emerge for the improvement of psychiatric facilities.

The pattern of mental health nursing has also differed in Okinawa. When the 1950 Mental Health Law was enacted on the mainland, public health centres opened in Okinawa and maintained oversight of people with mental health problems, succeeding the power of the police authority to keep them in custody. Later, specialized psychiatric services were included in the work of the public health centres, and affiliated public hygiene nurses began to visit mentally disturbed people and their families at their homes, to offer informal counselling. Through their visits, they surveyed the use of home custody and sometimes, recommended hospital treatment. These nurses played an essential role in the spread of psychiatric awareness and care in Okinawa. This did not, however, lead to *kamidāri* and other phenomena of spirit possession coming to be seen as a 'disease' to be treated, such was the wide persistence in the population of belief in shamanism. This system of public hygiene nurses in Okinawa was terminated after the reversion of the islands to Japanese administration and the enactment of the Community Health Act in 1947 – applied in Okinawa only in 1994.

For historians of Japanese psychiatry the relatively lengthy period of the home custody system in Okinawa from 1900–1960 is 'the period left unattended'. Since giving care to mentally troubled persons was entrusted to families, except for severe cases that were registered with the police authority, mentally ill people lived an ordinary social life in their communities.[25] The period up until the reversion of Okinawa to Japanese control is considered by the psychiatric community as the 'predawn' of psychiatry in Okinawa, and the years since 1972 the 'enhancement' period.[26] Since the 1990s, following the establishment of psychiatric hospitals and the improvement of psychiatric services, positive views of *kamidāri* and other phenomena of spirit possession began to be expressed in the medical community. This was around the time that the importance of 'normalization' was being recognized, and people with mental illness were encouraged to live with other people so that they could benefit from social interaction within communities.

## Conclusion

The most important reason why cases of spirit possession such as *kamidāri* tend not to have been written off as 'disease' in Okinawa is that the non-existence of psychiatric hospitals in prewar Okinawa meant that those who experienced such spirit possession were not isolated or hospitalized. Japan's Psychiatric Hospital Law of 1919, which aimed at the establishment of psychiatric hospitals in all prefectures (although, for the most part only private hospitals were established, which were eventually used as compulsory segregation facilities), had no influence in Okinawa. The first fully fledged psychiatric hospital in Okinawa was not opened until after Okinawa reverted to Japanese control in 1972. By the late 1990s, Japan's psychiatric community had begun to question the treatment of *kamidāri* and other types of possession and their categorization of them as 'disease'. Some psychiatrists were instead beginning to advocate the 'usefulness of possession (insanity)'.

Second, the difference in the legal histories of mainland Japan and Okinawa prevented the exclusion of the 'insane' from society in most cases. The mentally ill tended to remain with their families, as per the provisions of the 1900 Law on the Care and Custody of Psychopaths – all the way up to the time of the Ryukyu Mental Hygiene Act in 1960. Although the Ryukyu Mental Hygiene Act echoed the provisions of the mainland's Mental Hygiene Act, with the government made responsible for accommodating mentally disturbed people in hospitals, this law was not effectively enforced in Okinawa under the US civil administration. This meant that except for severe cases, mentally disturbed people lived a normal social life amongst the people of their communities.

In spite of frequent suppression by political authorities down the centuries, some aspects of spirit possession phenomena such as *tāri*, *furi*, and *kakai* have successfully maintained their image as 'sacred insanity'. In recent years, a mutual aid association – what one might call a 'psychic power development school' – has been founded, inviting children who are touched by the *kamidāri* phenomenon. There, their capacities are positively evaluated and interpreted, and what is held to be their psychic power is further developed.[27] The combination of this folk societal background and Okinawa's unique psychiatric history help to explain why spirit possession in Okinawa has been insulated from the standard critiques of western modernity. It remains possible for people in Okinawa to consider seeking medical help 'half from doctors and half from yuta', and their society remains one that is unusually accepting of spirit possession.

## Notes

1 Translated by Hayashi Chine. This essay includes material from an earlier work by the author: 'Hyōi wo Kōteisuru Shakai – Okinawa no Seishin Iryōshi to Shamanism (A Society that Accepts Spirit Possession: Psychiatric History in

Okinawa, and Shamanism', in *Hyoi no Kindai to Politics (Modern Age of Spirit Possession and Politics)* (Seikyusha, 2007), pp. 197–224.
2  Michel Foucault, *Histoire de la folie à l'âge classique.*
3  On 'tactics' as wisdom of the weak see de Certeau, *The Practice of Everyday Life* (tr. Yamada Toyoko), pp. 25–27. On bricolage tactics see Oda, 'Minshū Bunka to Teiko toshiteno Bricolage', p. 201. On concrete bricolage tactics, see Shiotsuki, 'Seinaru Kyoki' pp. 43–62. I.M. Lewis, *Ecstatic Religion*, p. 89 and p. 183.
4  On *tamahati* in Yonaguni Island, see Ikema, *Yonaguni no Rekishi*, and Yonaguni Town History Compiling Committee Office (ed.), *Cho-shi Bekkan.*
5  After the invasion by the Satsuma clan, both *yuta* and *kaminchu* were outlawed under the clan's prohibition law. But *noro* and other *kaminchu* were under the protection of the Ryukyu government in spite of the prohibition policy by the Satsuma clan, and in the early Showa period (1930s) after the abolition of feudal domains (*han*) and the institution of a centralized prefecture system, they were authorized as shrine children by the government under its policy to integrate shrines into a state Shinto system. As a result, they followed a different history from *yuta* who had no protection.
6  Okinawa Historical Document Compilation Office, *Shuri ōfu Shioki.*
7  Ibid.
8  The first newspaper in Okinawa was *Ryukyu Shimpo*. It was established by former descendants of Okinawa's warrior class and court nobles around Shuri. (Ōta, *Shimpan Okinawa no Minshū Ishiki*, p. 92.
9  The rulers of those days also feared *juri* (prostitutes) as people who might undermine the social system and social order. Specifically, unlicenced prostitutes were suppressed because they were outside of government control. For further details see Shiotsuki and Shibuya, *Fujyo to Yujyo no tosei-shi*, pp. 133–145.
10  Takahata, Shichida and Uchigata (eds), *Hyōi to Seishin-byō*, pp. 320–332.
11  Shiotsuki, 'Hyōshō toshiteno Shamonism', pp. 1–20.
12  Shimabukuro, 'Comment on Tokuyama Tomohiro', p. 80.
13  Takaishi, 'Utaki Shinko to Seishinka Iryō no Setten – sono 1', p. 78.
14  Naka Koichi, Toguchi Seijun, Takaishi Toshihiro, Ishizu Hiroshi, and Sasaki Yuji, 'Yuta (shaman) and community mental health on Okinawa', p. 268.
15  Ibid., p. 268.
16  Ibid., p. 268.
17  Takaesu, 'Minzoku Seishin Igaku', p. 400.
18  Yoshinaga and Sakaki, 'Bunka Ketsugo Shōkōgun no Konnichiteki Ronten to sono Tembō, p. 160.
19  Shiotsuki and Naka, '"Kōteiteki Kyōki" toshiteno Kamidāri Syndrome', pp. 109–123.
20  Yoshikawa, 'Okinawa ni okeru Seishin Eisei no Ayumi', p. 134.
21  Takaishi, 'Okinawa no Seishin Iryō', pp. 220–224.
22  Ogura, 'Okinawa ni okeru Rekishi/Bunka to Seishin Igaku Iryō', pp. 115–126.
23  According to Shima Shigeo, the increase in number of psychiatric hospitals and beds in Okinawa after its reversion to Japanese administration was so rapid that it gained in a short period of time what it had taken the mainland the preceding 30 years to achieve. Shima, *Seishin Iryō no Hitotsu no Kokoromi*, pp. 192–193.
24  Yoshikawa Takehiko says 'The Law on the Care and Custody of Psychopaths enacted in 1990 might have brought in Okinawa an idea that *furimunu* (people touched by something) were targets to be kept under custody, or forced to do so'. He also says, 'mainland Japanese might have inculcated the idea of discriminating against *furimunu* to Okinawa communities'. (Yoshikawa, 'Okinawa ni okeru Seishin Eisei no Ayumi', pp. 134–135.

25 According to Yoshikawa, a person who was out of his mind in the middle of the Meiji period was often not put into home custody. He would spend days at home, go out and loiter around when he was feeling better – and when he was feeling much better he might invite children around and tell them stories. Yoshikawa, 'Okinawa ni okeru Seishin Eisei no Ayumi', p. 134.

26 *Okinawa ni miru "no no counselor" – Gendai Iryō to Minzoku Iryō (Counselor in the Field in Okinawa – Contemporary Medicine and Folk Medicine)*, video program. Nakamura Eitoku and Ohashi Hideshi (supervising editors), Ogawa, Sumiko (responsible editor), Video Pack Nippon (production collaborator), Japan International Cooperation Agency (JICA) Okinawa International Center (planning and production) (2003).

27 Shiotsuki, 'Shakai Byōri to Okinawa Shamanism', pp. 87–95.

## References

de Certeau, Michel. *The Practice of Everyday Life*, Japanese translation by Yamada, Toyoko (Poligolos Collection) (Tokyo: Kokubunsha, 1987).

Foucault, Michel. *Histoire de la folie à l'âge classique,* Japanese translation by Tamura Toshi (Tokyo: Shinchosha, 1975).

Eizo, Ikema. *Yonaguni no Rekishi (History of Yonaguni)*, printed as manuscript, 2003 (1959).

Lewis, I. M. *Ecstatic Religion: A Study of Shamanism and Spirit Possession* (London & New York: Routledge, 2002).

Naka Koichi, Toguchi Seijun, Takaishi Toshihiro, Ishizu Hiroshi, and Sasaki Yuji. 'Yuta (shaman) and community mental health on Okinawa', *The International Journal of Social Psychiatry* Vol. 31(4), Winter 1985, pp. 267–274.

Oda Makoto. 'Minshū Bunka to Teikō toshiteno Bricolage – Benandanti to Okinawa no yuta heno manazashi (Bricolage of Folk Cultures and Resistance – Views on Benandanti and *Yuta* in Okinawa)', in Tanaka Masakazu (ed.), *Bōryoku no Bunka Jinruigaku (Cultural Anthropology of Violence)*, report of a joint study by Institute for Research in Humanities, Kyoto University (Kyoto University Press, 1998).

Ogura Chikara. 'Okinawa ni okeru Rekishi/Bunka to Seishin Igaku/Iryō (History and culture in Okinawa and psychiatry and its care', in Research Center of Community-Based Medicine and Primary Care, Hospital, University of Ryukyu (ed.). *Okinawa no Rekishi to Iryōshi (History of Okinawa, and its Medical History)* (Fukuoka: Kyushu University Press, 1998).

Okinawa Historical Document Compilation Office. *Shuri ōfu Shioki (Ryukyu Kingdom government Criminal Rules)*, (Okinawa Prefecture Historic Document – Premodern times 1) (Okinawa Board of Education, 1981).

*Okinawa ni miru 'no no counselor' – Gendai Iryō to Minzoku Iryō (Counselor in the Field in Okinawa – Contemporary Medicine and Folk Medicine)*, video program. Nakamura Eitoku and Ohashi Hideshi (supervising editors), Ogawa Sumiko (responsible editor), Video Pack Nippon (production collaborator), Japan International Cooperation Agency (JICA) Okinawa International Center (planning and production) (2003).

Ōta Masahide. *Shimpan Okinawa no Minshū Ishiki (New Edition, Okinawans' Consciousness)* (Tokyo: Shinsensha, 1995).

Shima Shigeo. *Seishin Iryō no Hitotsu no Kokoromi (A Trial in Psychiatry)* (Tokyo: Hihyosha, 1982).

Shimabukuro Yasuyuki. 'Comment on Tokuyama Tomohiro, Kamidāri wo teishita Shōrei (Cases of being haunted by spirits)', in Takaishi Toshihiro (ed.), *Research Papers of Motobu Memorial Hospital* (1993).

Shiotsuki Ryoko and Shibuya Mime *Fujyo to Yujyo no tosei-shi –Meiji-ki kara Showa Shoki made no Okinawa Kindaika Seisaku wo megutte (A History of controls over shamans (yuta) and prostitutes (juri) – Policy of Okinawa's Modernization from the Meiji to the Early Showa periods)* (Japan Women's University Annals – Faculty of Integrated Arts and Sciences, No. 10 (2000).

Shiotsuki Ryoko. 'Seinaru Kyoki – Okinawa Shamanism ni okeru Hyōi Genshō (Sacred insanity – spirit possession phenomena in shamanism in Okinawa), in Tachikawa Musashi (ed.), *Iyashi to Sukui – Ajia no Shukyō-teki Dentō ni Manabu (Healing and Salvation – Learning from Religious Traditions in Asia)* (Tokyo: Tamagawa University Press, 2001).

Shiotsuki Ryoko. 'Hyōshō toshiteno Shamanism – Okinawa no Eiga to Bungaku ni miru Identity Politics (Shamanism as representation – Identity politics observed in movies and literature in Okinawa)', in *Tetsugaku* No. 107 (Mita Tetsugakukai, 2002).

Shiotsuki Ryoko. 'Shakai Byōri to Okinawa Shamanism – Futōkō Jidō Seito to sono Oya no tame no Sogofujo Kyodotai no Jirei kara (Social pathology and Okinawa Shamanism – Case studies of the mutual help association of elementary and junior high school children not attending school and their parents)', in Nihonbashi Gakkan University Annals, No. 4 (2005).

Shiotsuki Ryoko. 'Hyōi wo Kōteisuru Shakai – Okinawa no Seishin Iryōshi to Shamanism (A society that accepts spirit possession: Psychiatric history in Okinawa, and shamanism', in *Hyoi no Kindai to Politics (Modern Age of Spirit Possession and Politics)* (Tokyo: Seikyusha, 2007), pp. 197–224.

Shiotsuki Ryoko and Naka Koichi. 'Kōteiteki Kyōki toshiteno Kamidāri Syndrome – Shinri Rinshōka wo otozureta client no case bunseki (Kamidāri Syndrome – Analyses of Clients visiting Clinical Psychologists)', *Nihonbashi Gakkan University Annals Vol. 1* (Tokyo: Nihonbashi Gakkan University, 2002).

Takaesu Yoshihide. 'Minzoku Seishin Igaku (Folk psychiatry)', in Takahata Naohiko & Mita Toshio (eds), *Tabunka-kan Seishin Igaku (Multi-cultural Psychiatry)* (Rinshō Seishin Igaku Koza (Clinical Psychiatry Lecture Series) vol. 23 (Tokyo: Nakayama Shoten, 1998).

Takahata Naohiko, Shichida Hirofumi and Uchigata Ichiro (eds), *Hyōi to Seishinbyō – Seishinbyōrigaku-teki / Bunka seishin-igakuteki kento (Spirit Possession and Mental Disease – Psychopathological and Cultural Psychiatric Consideration)* (Sapporo: Hokkaido University Press, 1994).

Takaishi Toshihiro. 'Utaki Shinko to Seishinka Iryō no Setten – sono 1 (Interface between belief in spiritual sanctuaries and Psychiatry No. 1)', in *Psychiatry in Okinawa*, No. 4, (Psychiatry Compilation Office in Okinawa, 1978).

Takaishi Toshihiro. 'Okinawa no Seishin Iryō (Psychiatry in Okinawa' in *Lectures at the 10th Anniversary of Motobu Memorial Hospital* (Motobu: 1994).

Yonaguni Town History Compiling Committee Office (ed.), *Cho-shi Bekkan (Town History Annex I), photo album, Yonaguni – Chinmoku no Dotō, Do-nanno Hyakunen (Yonaguni – Fierce Surge of Silence – What will happen in 100 years?)* (Yonaguni Township, 1999).

Yoshikawa Takehiko. 'Okinawa ni okeru Seishin Eisei no Ayumi (History of mental hygiene in Okinawa)', in *20th Anniversary Report of the Okinawa Prefectural*

*Mental Hygiene Association* (Okinawa Prefectural Mental Hygiene Association, 1979).

Yoshinaga Mari and Sakaki Yuji. 'Bunka Ketsugo Shōkōgun no Konnichiteki Ronten to sono Tembō (Contemporary issues of culture-bound syndrome and its future perspective)', in Takahata Naohiko and Mita Toshio (eds), *Tabunkakan Seishin Igaku (Multi-cultural Psychiatry)*, Rinshō Seishin Igaku Koza (Clinical Psychiatry Lecture Series) vol. 23 (Tokyo: Nakayama Shoten, 1998).

# 12 Chaplaincy work in disaster areas
## Potential and challenges

*Taniyama Yōzō*[1]

I am a Buddhist monk belonging to the Ōtani branch of Jōdo Shinshū. My fulltime work as a chaplain began in 2000 on the Vihāra ward of Nagaoka-nishi Hospital.[2] 'Vihāra monk' refers to a Buddhist chaplain. As the hospice movement grew in Japan towards the end of the 1980s, Tamiya Masashi promoted the use of the Sanskrit word Vihāra, meaning 'dwelling' or 'refuge', as an alternative to the word hospice, with its Christian undertones. The Vihāra ward was founded in 1992 by Tamiya's older brother, who was the director of the hospital at the time, making it the first hospital ward in the country to offer Buddhist end-of-life care. Buddhist monks in Japan traditionally played an important role in nursing the dying, but this tradition has been lost over time: Tamiya's movement aimed at something of a revival.

There is a Buddhist chapel situated on the ward, where sutra recitation takes place twice a day, morning and evening. About one-third of the patients gather at the chapel, while the rest can participate in sutra recitation via television screens in their rooms. After the daily morning announcement, Vihāra monks visit each and every room to meet with the patients face to face. The monks take an active part in Buddhist ceremonies, ward events, conferences, and meetings. They are expected to be present at pre-admission discussions and at the time of admission, and to accompany the doctor when he or she explains a patient's condition to their family. They escort patients when they want to go outside, and they show visitors around the ward. When a patient dies, monks gather at the chapel to recite a farewell sutra, both for the deceased and for the benefit of the bereaved family and the medical staff.

After three years of work as a Vihāra monk, I began working at a university in Osaka while continuing to volunteer as a chaplain at various public hospitals in the area. My activity extended beyond end-of-life care, providing care for general patients, family members, and hospital staff. I also took part in devising a staff training programme at Share-house Nakai: a new type of end-of-life care home where less fortunate people, such as the abandoned elderly, are able to stay during their last years. They live with the support of home care services, and Buddhist and Shintō chaplains.

With the help of a Christian pastor, I also started a chaplaincy training programme at Sakai Municipal Hospital, based on American clinical pastoral education. Each unit of training lasted only fifty hours but this allowed more than 100 people to go through the training programme. Around 10 per cent of them went on to become fulltime chaplains.

I was living in Osaka at the time of Great East Japan earthquake (11 March 2011), preparing to leave my work at the Osaka Campus of Sophia University's Grief Care Institute in order to study at Ōtani University. On hearing about the disaster, I found myself returning to Sendai, where I had spent my university years. There I co-operated with Buddhist monks, Christian clerics, Shintō priests and medical practitioners in providing grief care and funeral/memorial ceremonies for disaster victims. The early activities of our 'Counselling Room for the Heart' [*kokoro no sō danshitsu*] revealed the need for an organized training programme for chaplains – a need to which the United Church of Christ in Japan, the World Conference of Religions for Peace (Japan Committee), and various other clerics from Japan and abroad responded by supporting the establishment of a Department of Practical Religious Studies at Tohoku University. In April 2012, I was appointed an associate professor at this new institution.

## Japanese chaplains

The word 'chaplain' is used broadly here, encompassing roles such as pastoral care worker, Vihāra monk, and spiritual care worker. Outside Japan, chaplains work in schools, hospitals, welfare institutions, prisons, police departments, fire departments, and armed forces. But because of Japan's strict post-war secularization policies, Japanese chaplains are unable to obtain the necessary funding from public institutions. There are volunteer prison chaplains for prisoners but not for prison officials, for example. There are also chaplains in hospitals, welfare institutions, and schools affiliated with Christianity (and with some new religions), though this is relatively rare. On the whole, the concept of 'chaplain' has not yet penetrated far into Japanese society: few Buddhists in Japan know the term 'Vihāra', and there is an acute shortage of chaplains overall. Moreover, in recent years there has been a trend towards resisting the involvement of Buddhist monks in medical care. When monks visit hospitals, it is not uncommon for them to be asked to either take off their religious dress or leave. This is because Japanese people often associate Buddhist monks with death, creating a conflict with medical aspirations to save lives.

For these sorts of reasons, chaplaincy work during natural disasters has not garnered much public attention until recently. And although many religious organizations took part in volunteer activities in the aftermath of the Great Hanshin (Kobe) earthquake in 1995, they faced criticism for failing to provide adequate spiritual support.

A translation of *Psychological First Aid: Field Operations Guide* was widely circulated amongst volunteers after the Great East Japan earthquake in 2011. This booklet includes a section entitled 'Attend to grief and spiritual issues',[3] which lays out the importance of teamwork between various experts in providing religious care. Regrettably, co-operation between medical professionals and clerics during field operations in the recent disaster was far from satisfactory.[4] The case studies of religious care that follow here are intended to demonstrate both the potential and the challenges of chaplaincy work during disasters.

## Spiritual care and religious care

Quoting from the 'Introduction' to *Disaster Spiritual Care*:[5] 'spiritual care in the context of a disaster responds to the poignant need for spiritual meaning and comfort by providing accompaniment and prayer, both individual and communal.'[6] It encourages us, in the midst of the chaos of a crisis, to stand with others, pray with them, accompany them at the hardest times (such as confirmation of the death of loved ones), and provide a sacred space where the person can sit quietly with his or her God and experience some form of comfort. 'Religious care in a disaster', the booklet continues, 'is particularly focused on facilitating the ability of people to practice their own particular faith without fear of intimidation or proselytizing'.[7] There is a need to provide access to religious worship; access to sacred scripture and texts (in a way that others will not consider to be proselytizing); access to food that meets the person's religious needs; a multi-faith space that can be used for meditation and prayer; and appropriate and timely religious care for the dead.

*Disaster Spiritual Care* is full of valuable suggestions, and I agree that neither spiritual nor religious care ought to be missionary work in disguise. But bearing in mind general public attitudes towards, and relative lack of awareness about, religion, it is not always easy to establish a clear differentiation between 'prayer', 'worship' and 'sacred space'. Ideally, 'prayer' and 'sacred space' in the context of spiritual care should be deliberately open and ambiguous, whereas 'worship' and 'sacred space' within religious care should reflect the specifics of a given religion. Western spiritual care developed out of Christian pastoral care, hence the tendency for the two types of care – religious and spiritual – to overlap with each other. In contrast, spiritual care in Japan was imported in conjunction with the hospice movement, making it easier to distinguish from religious care. I belong to a group of practising researchers advocating the necessity of this categorical distinction, between religious and spiritual care, but there is as yet no consensus on the issue in Japan.[8]

Through my experience as a Vihāra monk, I am aware of the effectiveness of religious praxis in helping people to overcome their difficulties, for example through praying, reciting scriptures, and discussing their faith. However, if chaplaincy work in places such as hospitals must involve religious elements, one has to consider current Japanese sensitivities towards the open expression of individual religiosity in public space. And one must of course gain the consent of the recipient of care beforehand.[9] Whereas with religious care the recipient enters the world and accepts the worldview of the care provider (usually a member of the clergy), with spiritual care it is a prerequisite for the provider (who is not necessarily clergy) to enter the world of the recipient of care.

The recipient of spiritual care may not be religious, thus the provider should aim to help the person to express his or her own spirituality by abstaining from giving advice and focusing instead on listening. To put this another way, whereas in religious care the provider (chaplain) takes on the role of a 'key person', by performing religious rites and giving necessary advice, in spiritual care the recipient is the key person, and religious rites and advice are unnecessary. The examples of field care that follow in this chapter illustrate the practical difficulties in separating these two types of care. 'Grief care', in this context, should be understood as an umbrella term encompassing various approaches – involving medical, social welfare, psychological, legal and religious experts and organizations – of which religious and spiritual care are but two.

## Case studies

In the aftermath of the Great East Japan earthquake, Buddhist temples, Shintō shrines and Christian churches were used as evacuation centres, and clergy were quick to provide relief supplies alongside helping to clear rubble, providing counselling and listening, organizing tea parties, and bathing people's feet. All of these things could be considered 'spiritual care', but in the interests of avoiding too broad a definition of 'chaplaincy work' I will focus, in what follows, specifically on care of the sort that can only be provided by clergy.

It is not difficult to imagine counselling/listening as a form of spiritual care. Whether it is also a form of religious care requires an investigation of the precise details of a given conversation. Offered here are four cases that I consider to be religious care, unmotivated by any scope for proselytization. I will use the term 'chaplain' to describe those clerics concerned, regardless of whether they would use the term of themselves. In order to protect the privacy of individuals, I will limit my discussion to details that are relevant to my topic here. Four cases are discussed, in chronological order.

### Case 1 Sutra recitation

Countless sutra recitations have been conducted for the victims of the Great East Japan earthquake. Kimura Toshiaki has divided these into two categories: religious funerals conducted at places such as crematoria, immediately after the disaster, for those who were unable to contact their family temple;[10] and memorial services for unidentified/unclaimed corpses resting in morgues.[11] As an example of the former category, on 15 March 2011 the Sendai Buddhist Society [Sendai Bukkyōkai[12]] held a meeting with Sendai City municipal staff to organize sutra recitations at various crematoria. The resulting plans came into operation two days later. They created a manual, in order to avoid interdenominational confusion, encouraging co-ordination between monks to conduct an appropriate sutra recitation depending on the faith of the deceased. This activity, which lasted until 27 April, mainly involved members of Sendai Buddhist Society who were living in or near the disaster areas. As an example of the latter category, the Jōdo Shinshū Hongwanji-ha Northeast Tohoku Parish Disaster Volunteer Centre[13] started aid supplies on 17 March 2011. They began the recitation of sutras on 23 March at a morgue in Minami-Sōma, Fukushima, later expanding their activity to fourteen other morgues in Miyagi, Fukushima and Iwate prefectures, lasting until 14 August.

Aside from Kimura's categories, individual/group pilgrimages [*angya*] should also be recognized as a context for sutra recitation. On 4 April 2011, a monk set out on a pilgrimage from Miyako, Iwate, to Ishinomaki, Miyagi. This came to be widely known about after featuring on NHK News and in an *Asahi Shimbun* article entitled 'A Praying Monk'.[14] There was also

*Figure 12.1* A Tohoku memorial service.

a case of a Buddhist monk and a Christian pastor making joint pilgrimages, on 28th April 2011 and on 1 March 2012, in Minami-Sanrikuchō, Miyagi Prefecture.[15] In both cases, sutra recitation and prayer were intended for unspecified people, dead or alive, who had been affected by the disaster. The term 'sutra recitation' only really applies to the activities of Buddhist monks, but large-scale interfaith funerals have been organized through the combined efforts of Buddhist monks, Christian clerics and Shintō priests.[16]

My own involvement in sutra recitation came via the Jōdo Shinshū Hongwanji-ha Tohoku Parish Disaster Volunteer Centre, as well as on a private basis visiting morgues and temporary burial sites in Miyagi and Iwate prefectures. For this work I wore simplified religious dress and met the relevant officials in advance – police officers, fire fighters, municipal staff and volunteer workers – in order to gain permission to recite Buddhist sutras.[17] In most places, I was given a very warm welcome and people were grateful for what I was doing – a vivid reminder of what it means to be a monk. Although I couldn't call this activity a 'pilgrimage' as such, since I was travelling by car, in addition to the morgues I visited I was able to recite Buddhist sutras in twelve other locations in Miyagi and Iwate prefectures – from hilltops to the seawall overlooking the areas struck by the tsunami. Some people joined me in *gasshō* [a brief moment of prayer or thankfulness] along the way.

Similar activities have been carried out by Christian and Shintō clerics, along with other religious groups, making for a truly interreligious endeavour in which religious personnel both local and coming from far away have taken part. It is difficult to ascertain the extent to which disaster victims who were present at sutra recitations and ceremonies had expected to receive this sort of care, but those who reacted positively may be said to have been receiving a form of religious care.

### Case 2 Counselling room for the heart

'Counselling Room for the Heart' was opened towards the end of March 2011, through the co-operation of the Sendai Buddhist Society, Sendai Christian Alliance, and the Miyagi Prefecture Religious Institution Liaison Council. Co-operation from the Religious Institution Liaison Council meant that the project was supported by virtually all the (registered) religious organizations in Miyagi prefecture. Many more supporters came from outside the area. Activity began in earnest at Kuzuoka Saijō, a crematorium run by Sendai City, on 4 April,[18] and initially comprised Christian, Buddhist and Shintō clerics, later joined by Tenrikyō and Risshō Kōsei Kai. Activity at the crematorium was permitted until the end of April, after which Counselling Room for the Heart was re-launched[19] with the addition of new clergies and medical professionals, alongside experts in grief care and religious studies. An office was opened in Tohoku University's Department of Religious Studies. The new Counselling Room for the

Heart aimed to provide consolation and grief care by telephone, via a mobile counselling café ('Café de Monk'), via radio (Radio Café de Monk), and through the giving of talks.

Until the end of September 2011 the Counselling Room had the use only of mobile phones, but from October a toll-free landline was set up. Christian clerics, Buddhist monks and Shintō priests now take calls every Wednesday and Sunday. The service is not only for those affected by the disaster; calls are accepted on a wide range of topics, such as domestic and relationship problems. Some callers seek practical advice, whilst others ask for sutra recitation or prayer over the telephone. Needs are met according to the circumstances and religious background of the callers.

Café de Monk is intended as a means of listening to people's troubles and sharing their suffering.[20] Kaneta Taiō, head of the Sōtō Zen temple Tsūdaiji in Kurihara, is one of its main organizers. The service began in Minami-Sanrikuchō, Miyagi on 15 May, later expanding to Fukushima and Iwate, with a total of 140 events by May 2013. These have taken place in evacuation centres, in meeting halls in temporary housing complexes, and in temples. Café de Monk is predominantly run by Sōtō Zen monks wearing monks' working clothes, though it is common to find monks from other Buddhist sects taking part, alongside Christian clerics. The regional Councils of Social Welfare and municipal staff of the area are consulted prior to events, and they provide the venue and other support. Although the basic purpose of Café de Monk is to listen to people, depending on the circumstances they sometimes also provide religious advice or distribute mortuary tablets and prayer beads, as well as palm-size images of the bodhisattva Jizō – stone, cloth, or drawings (visitors to the Café can also make their own images in clay).[21] Occasionally, upon request, monks may make private visits to individual homes to recite sutras after these communal events. Kaneta reports meeting an elderly lady who had lost her husband in the tsunami. He recited a Buddhist sutra for her husband and told her: 'please keep moving forward, because he lives within you now'.[22] When giving out prayer beads, monks put them around the receiver's wrist, with a *nen* [wish] and a handshake. Sometimes people begin to talk about their experiences at this point, in which case monks may gather around to reinforce the *nen* and to reassure the person concerned that 'everything is okay ... you're protected: let's live on'.

No sutras are recited in public places, and chaplains of the Counselling Room for the Heart abide by the *Chaplain Activity Regulations*,[23] which are composed of two parts: a 'Code of Ethics' and 'Information for Providing Quality Care'.

The *Regulations* can be summarised in three key points:

1  Compliance with confidentiality obligations.[24]
2  Respect for victims.
3  Avoidance of missionary activity.

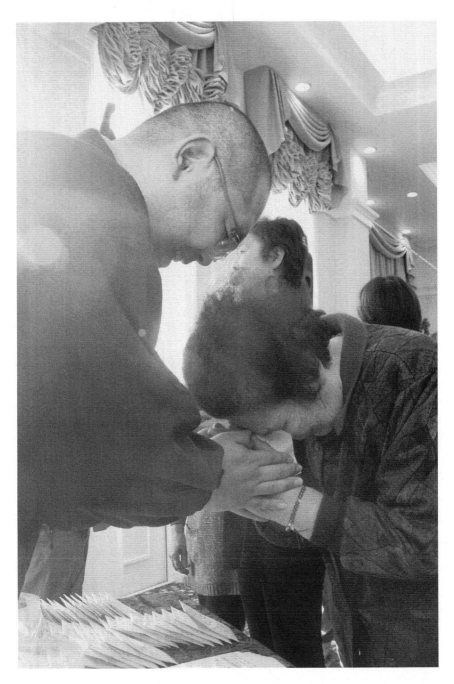

*Figure 12.2* Distributing Buddhist devotional materials.

On 20 December 2011, the Counselling Room for the Heart held a Café de Monk Christmas party at a wedding venue in the biggest temporary housing complex in what used to be the commercial area of Ishinomaki. With the help of Sendai Christian Alliance, more than ten Buddhist monks and Christian clerics took part in this event. I was handing out Buddhist prayer beads, trying to inject a little humour into the proceedings – describing them as something that 'might' bring good luck. Though there was a long queue of people I tried to provide a *nen* for each individual. During a break I spotted a lady sobbing quietly. I went and sat next to her to ask her why she was crying. She told me that she had lost her child in the disaster. Finding out that she was Christian, I called a pastor over and left my colleague to counsel her. It is upon this sort of basic co-operation between clergies from differing religions and backgrounds that a viable 'mobile counselling service' fundamentally depends.

### Case 3  A Catholic chaplain: Une Takashi[25]

Une Takashi was living in Kōbe before the Great East Japan earthquake. On 21 March 2011 he headed to the Tōhoku region and put himself on stand-by to move to spiritual care projects as and when required, initially joining a Buddhist monk of the Shingon sect in Kamaishi on 27 March. At Hudōji temple, which was being used as an evacuation centre, he met a Protestant pastor and went to join him at his church, Shinsei Kamaishi Kyōkai. A marquee was set up in the car park, for Japan Overseas Christian Medical Cooperative Service (JOCS) to provide medical and emotional care along with food and other necessary material aid.[26] As a member of the local 'care for the heart' staff, Une listened to many of the people who came to the church, and he took part in some of the JOCS visits. On 2 April the Catholic charity Caritas set up a base in Kamaishi Catholic church,[27] and Une joined their activities too, signing a contract to become a member of their care for the heart staff.[28] On his left arm, Une wore the 'care for the heart' armband of Hudōji and Shinsei Kamaishi Kyōkai, and on the other a 'Caritas' band. During the day, he volunteered at the café in the Catholic church and in the evening he joined JOCS visits. When the evacuation centre closed down, he went to a temporary housing complex and started a 'tea salon'.

The term 'care for the heart' was often perceived negatively by victims of the disaster. In part this was because of enduring preconceptions in the region about psychiatry and mental illness, including a particular fear of stigma attaching to a diagnosis of schizophrenia.[29] Another factor, however, was that sometimes people fraudulently claiming to be counsellors would enter one of the temporary shelters, put two chairs up on a stage, and ask people living in the shelters to come up onto the stage and talk – as though for the purposes of entertainment. As a result, some temporary shelters refused to allow any form of 'care for the heart' at all.

Une sought gradually to build trust with people via gentle physical contact, waiting for what he called their 'cry of the spirit'. He took on the identity of a 'spiritual care worker', downplaying his particular religious background. He wore casual clothes and kept his rosaries in his pocket, maintaining his listening stance regardless of whether the conversations turned out to be religious or not. He took care in deciding when and if religious intervention was necessary, and depending on the circumstances either gave advice based on his own faith or introduced one of his Buddhist, Protestant, or Shintō colleagues. When asked by non-Christians to teach them how to pray, he taught them the Lord's Prayer. On one occasion, Une accompanied a Shingon monk in prayer at a Buddhist altar.

## Case 4  Food radioactivity measurement station 'Inori'

On 18 March 2011, Catholic and Protestant churches around Sendai created an organization called Sendai Christian Alliance Disaster Relief Network (Touhoku HELP). Touhoku HELP emphasizes the need for 'spiritual care, and giving attention to the soul', as well as 'care for the dead'.[30] As part of Touhoku HELP's activities, the Sendai Food Radioactivity Measurement Station, 'Inori' [prayer] started operations on 25 March 2012.[31] Government officials and NGOs also run measuring stations, but a charge tends to be made – between ¥3,000 and ¥5,000 per measurement – and usually people are required to operate the machinery themselves. No charge is made at Inori, where radiation levels are measured in food, breast milk, and urine. I volunteered along with Christian clerics and Buddhist monks to provide support for those who might have strong anxieties about the invisible threat of radiation. Inori staff dress casually so as not to intimidate their clients, and in addition to measuring radioactivity they also listen to clients' daily problems. The technical support staff, nutritionists, and social workers are all Christian, and they go through spiritual care training programmes. A chaplain is always present when a radioactivity measurement is given, and with the consent of the client each session ends with a prayer. If asked, Buddhist monks also pray in a Christian style (which we learn from our Christian colleagues), out of respect for the faith of the client.

From my experience of working at the station, clients experience such diverse and contrasting anxieties that they are sometimes reluctant to broach these with one another. Some accept the fact that their food will inevitably be contaminated but visit the centre in the hope of consuming less contaminated products.

What is important here is that the station offers an opportunity for people to talk freely about their worries, which many show a great need to do. The act of listening to clients' anxieties sometimes constitutes a form of spiritual care, but prayer should be considered an example of religious care.

## Chaplaincy work

These four cases exemplify chaplaincy work involving consolation, grief care (through listening/counselling/spiritual care), and the alleviation of anxiety through spiritual and religious care. Chaplaincy work of this sort will be required for several years and possibly decades to come. In principle, the chaplains involved are expected to respect the faith and denomination of victims, but in times of emergency these needs have not always been met. Sutra recitation, prayer, religious advice, and distribution of ceremonial objects are examples of activities that could be considered religious care. In carrying out these activities, it was important first to gain the consent of the person receiving religious care, and second to make sure that it was not done in public spaces or in such a way that it could be considered an act of proselytization.

Even though chaplaincy work, as a whole, was organized by groups consisting of people from various religious backgrounds, when analysing the precise details of a given encounter the attitudes and work of individual chaplains should be considered separately from the general policies of their organizations. Chaplains were expected to accept other forms of faith while remaining rooted in their own, and though for funerals and formal ceremonies they wore religious clothes, for counselling Buddhist monks wore work or plain clothes, while Christian clergies wore clerical collars or plain clothes. Some people, like Une, wore plain clothes at all times, on the basis that 'religious clothes might limit conversation'. It is clear from these case studies that clothes are a powerful factor in advertising a person's objectives and role – whether this is intended or not – making group and individual choices here a crucial dimension of disaster relief care.

Okabe Takeshi, the manager of the Counselling Room for the Heart and an expert physician in home palliative care,[32] has commented on the clergy who were involved in Café de Monk and telephone counselling as follows:[33]

> In working with them, I have once again realised that 'there is work that can only be done by religious people'. People who came to the Counselling Room for the Heart were able to talk about their suffering because they were talking to clergy. People choose the topic of conversation depending on whom they are talking to. There are things that they can tell clergy but not necessarily medical professionals. The details of conversations of course vary, however they are almost always heavy and filled with grief. It is not easy to be the listener. I suspect psychiatrists or psychotherapists might not be able to continue long listening to the suffering of these victims, who are neither patients nor clients but simply people who are suffering. In other words, they are not the subjects of 'treatment' per se. However,

clergy are able to accept them. This was something of a discovery for me! Religious people are able to listen, receive, share the sadness, and 'pray' – which leads to liberation from suffering.

People are starting to recognize the potential of the 'work that can only be done by religious people'. Okabe hopes for chaplains to 'overcome religious/denominational differences, and work together to provide spiritual support for the victims of disaster'.[34]

## Future challenges

Where the potential and future challenges of chaplaincy work are concerned, the definition of 'interfaith' activity is the key factor. 'Interfaith' implies an agreement to abandon the aim of proselytization. Without such a covenant, religious care might turn into a method of proselytization disguised as charity work. How can this agreement be achieved? The simplest answer would be to encourage a comprehensive form of interfaith cooperation, not just between religiously similar groups such as the Sōtō Zen and Rinzai Zen sects, but also where the difference between groups is stark, such as between traditional and new religions. This way it is easy for people who have little or no interest in religion to understand where the general motive of religious care lies. A good example of this kind of cooperation is the Religious Institution Liaison Council, mentioned above, which includes most religious groups in Miyagi prefecture. It is essential for these kinds of administrative bodies to share common guidelines, e.g. *Chaplain Activity Regulations*, to respect each other, and more importantly to respect the faith of disaster victims. This sort of co-operation would, in turn, make it easier for chaplains to collaborate with secular and public organizations, and might help to ease public scepticism about religious activities.

What is required of the people who do this work? In the aftermath of a disaster, volunteers can be divided into those who live within the area affected, those who live close by (commutable each day by car), and those arriving from further away, for whom accommodation and other arrangements have to be made. Immediately following the 2011 disasters, the loss of transport infrastructure meant that only the first two groups were able to provide help. Communication, too, has often a problem: some of the people living in the areas affected by the Great East Japan earthquake have strong regional accents, and Une Takashi, for example, found the Tohoku accent particularly problematic. In my case, even though I spent my university years in Sendai, and was able to understand most of what was being said, I was not able to speak with the required accent. Given that chaplaincy activity often requires delicate acts of communication, it is imperative that chaplains from the area affected by a disaster help colleagues in this regard, and that all chaplains be prepared in advance for these sorts of basic problems. The Department of Practical Religious Studies at Tohoku University, which opened in April 2012, aims to help in this regard.

What can chaplains usefully do? What *is* religious care, under these circumstances? As illustrated in *Psychological First Aid: Field Operations Guide*, the distribution of prayer beads and mortuary tablets is a form of grief care that may help victims to come to terms with their losses. Palm-size *Jizō* may function as a physical symbol of the dead, and as such function as an aid to grief care. In addition, the life experience of chaplains is crucial to the effectiveness of their advice: ceremonies are important, but sensitivity of thought and act far more so – clergy must be capable of considering the context in which they are operating, and try to understand the victim as best they can.

There is a need for further investigation into how religious care can be improved, and to find out what is currently lacking. There are many things to be learned from Western examples and experiences, but the simple importation of Western methods would not be sufficient in Japan, not least considering the social status of religion within the country. There are also regional differences in religious, cultural and social conditions, and these too must feature in chaplain training programmes, in preparation for future disasters.

## The chaplaincy training programme at Tohoku University

Through the Department of Practical Religious Studies and the Chaplaincy Training Programme at Tohoku University – which is the first of its kind established in a national university – we are now training what we call 'interfaith chaplains'. In Japanese, we use the word *rinshō shūkyōshi*, whose close English translation would be 'clinical clergy'. However, 'interfaith chaplain' better reflects our goal of putting proselytizing to one side in favour of a focus upon providing spiritual and religious care. A new, Japanese version of the well-known chaplaincy training programme, Clinical Pastoral Education (CPE), which started in America during the 1920s and later became the standard for chaplain training around the world, was created in the 1960s by a number of Christian groups co-operating with one another. The Japanese CPE, with which I have been involved as a supervisor since 2006, is innovative in two ways: it involves co-operation with Buddhists, and it accepts non-religious students. Before the tragedy of 2011 this was the general trend: towards the secularization of religious care. Now, Japanese society is reconsidering the significance of religion and its potential to heal and care for people in distress. This is one of the premises of the new training programme.

The main qualification required for candidates to the programme, around a quarter of whom are women, is to be in a position to listen to believers. This implies the need for a tremendous amount of experience, so applicants must be ordained clergy in their own traditions or else 'leaders' in the case of some of the new religions. Even people with the necessary experience have often acquired it in 'protected', private environments such as temples and churches. Interfaith chaplains, on the other hand, are expected to work in public spaces, and need to know how to enter those spaces. To this end, the training programme at Tohoku University includes ethics, spiritual care, and the gaining of practical experience of the sorts of environments in which they might be expected to operate. Trainees are encouraged to look back on their life histories and, through exposure to co-trainees from various religious backgrounds, to contemplate and explore their own faith and learn to be genuinely accepting of different values.

Some of this training takes places in the context of Café de Monk, the telephone counselling service, the Food Radioactivity Measurement Station, and sutra recitation and pilgrimage work. Supervised field practice for palliative care is also provided by Okabe Clinic Home Care Service, the Vihāra ward in Nagaoka-nishi Hospital, and the Share-house Nakai in Osaka. The contributions these organizations have made to this training programme is of great significance for the future development of chaplaincy work in Japan.

Finally, supervised field experience must be part of a cycle of self-evaluation: new learning experiences, reflection on those experiences, and reflection on oneself. Once the initial 'challenge to oneself' is accepted, one's subsequent period of training as interfaith chaplains continues, in effect, for a lifetime: the chaplain training programme should be considered as merely the start of a long journey, rather than as the means to an end. Moreover, the programme is still under construction, and must itself develop and deepen, just as its students are expected to. In order to help this happen, the training programme strives to accept candidates from all walks of life, allowing them to learn from each other how to become 'interfaith chaplains'.

## Notes

1 Translated by Inoue Yoshinobu and Christopher Harding. This essay is a modified translation of Taniyama Yōzō, 'Saigai-toki no chapuren no ugoki: sono kanōsei to kadai'.
2 See Taniyama Yōzō, 'The Vihara Movement'.
3 National Child Traumatic Stress Network and National Center for PTSD, *Psychological First Aid*, p. 40.
4 Okabe, 'Higashi Nihon Daishinsai to Kanwa-Kea', p. 9.
5 Robert and Ashley (eds), *Disaster Spiritual Care*.
6 Ibid., xviii.
7 Ibid., xvii–xviii.
8 See Fukaya and Shibata, 'Supirichuaru-Kea to Enjosha no Shūkyōsei ni tsuiteno Jisshōteki Kenkyū' and Konishi, 'Rinshō Genba deno Shūkyōteki-Kea no Kanōsei to Supirichuaru-Kea'.

9 Taniyama, 'Supirichuaru-Kea to Shūkyōteki-Kea' and 'Bukkyō no Shiseikan to Supirichuaru-Kea'.
10 Kimura, 'Shinsai to Mukiau Shūkyō', p. 30.
11 Ibid., p. 31.
12 Sendai Buddhist Society (website) 'Higashi Nihon Daishinsai Shien Katsudō Hōkoku' [Great East Japan Earthquake Support Activity Report] (www.sendai-bukkyoukai.jp/?page_id=121).
13 Jōdo Shinshū Hongwanji-ha Northeast Parish Disaster Volunteer Centre (website) 'Katsudō Kiroku' [Activity Records] (http://otera-vc.jimdo.com/活動記録/).
14 *Asahi Shimbun*, 4 May 2011 and YouTube, 'Hisaichi no Sōryo' [Monk in a Disaster Area], (www.youtube.com/watch?v=DAsC1gaQBP4&feature=related).
15 Kaneta, 'Kokoro no Sōdanshitsu no Katsudō', pp. 12–13; *Kahoku Shimpō*, 29 April 2011; *Kahoku Shimpō*, 3 March 2012.
16 *Kahoku Shimpō*, 11 March 2012.
17 In some areas, particularly urban parts of Japan, such permission has not always been forthcoming for Buddhist monks. Soon after 11 March 2011, a group of monks were forbidden entry to a mortuary in Tokyo, where they had gone to chant sutras for victims of the disaster. The incident made the national news.
18 Touhoku HELP (website), 'Working With Other Religious Leaders' (http://tohokuhelp.com/panel/120605a.html).
19 Kimura, 'Shinsai to Mukiau Shūkyō'; Kaneta, 'Kokoro no Sōdanshitsu no Katsudō'; Taniyama Yōzō, 'Shūkyōsha ni yoru Kokoro no Kea'.
20 Kaneta, 'Kokoro no Sōdanshitsu no Katsudō'.
21 *Kahoku Shimpō*, 26 May 2012. Jizō Bodhisattva, Kustigarbha in Sanskrit, is believed to save the souls of the deceased. Jizō is generally portrayed as tender and baby-faced, and as such is a familiar and popular figure in Japan.
22 Kaneta, 'Kokoro no Sōdanshitsu no Katsudō', p. 15.
23 Counselling Room for the Heart (website) 'Chappuren Kōdō Kihan' [*Chaplain Activity Regulations*] (www.sal.tohoku.ac.jp/kokoro/data/upfile/25–1.pdf).
24 Besides these regulations, Article 134 of the Japanese Penal Code (Unlawful Disclosure of Confidential Information) is applicable to religious professionals. For more information, see 'penal code' via www.japaneselawtranslation.go.jp/.
25 Une Takashi, Interview on 29 May 2012.
26 Japan Overseas Christian Medical Cooperative Service (website), 'Higashi Nihon Daishinsai Kyūen Katsudō' [Great East Japan Earthquake Relief Activity] (www.jocs.or.jp/jocs/tinyd3+index.id+13.htm).
27 Caritas Japan, *The Great East Japan Earthquake & Tsunami Activity Report*, 2012.
28 Caritas Japan commended Une for his 'inter-parish -denominational -faith coordination', especially his leading role in 'Care for the Heart' activities in Kamaishi (www.caritas.jp/hotnews/current/tohoku.html).
29 See Harding (Introduction), this volume.
30 Touhoku HELP (website), '"Spiritual Care" and Our Souls' (http://tohokuhelp.com/ panel/SpCareandSouls.html).
31 Food Radiation Measurement Project 'Prayer' (website) (www.foodbq.com/).
32 Okabe Takeshi died on 27 September 2012.
33 Okabe, 'Higashi Nihon Daishinsai to Kanwa-Kea', p. 9
34 Okabe, 'Higashi Nihon Daishinsai to Kanwa-Kea'.

# References

Caritas Japan, 'The Great East Japan earthquake & tsunami activity report' (Tokyo, Caritas, 2012).

Fukaya Mie and Shibata Minoru 'Supirichuaru-Kea to Enjosha no Shūkyōsei ni tsuiteno Jisshōteki Kenkyū' [Empirical research on the religiosity of spiritual care and the provider], Kenkyūjo Nenpō, Meijigakuin Daigaku Shakai Gakubu Huzoku Kenkyūjo [Institute Annual Report, Meijigakuin University Institute of Sociology and Social Work], Vol. 42 (2012).

Kaneta Taiō, 'Kokoro no Sōdanshitsu no Katsudō' [Counselling Room for the Heart activity], Kanwa-Kea Vol. 22, No. 1 (2012).

Kimura Toshiaki, 'Shinsai to Mukiau Shūkyō – Higashi Nihon Daishinsai Ikō no Dōkō' [Religion facing the disaster – trend since the Great East Japan Earthquake], Watanabe Naoki (ed.), *Shūkyō to Gendai ga Wakaru Hon 2012 [Introductory Book on Religion in Modern Times 2012]* (Tokyo: Heibonsha, 2012).

Konishi Tatsuya, 'Rinshō Genba deno Shūkyōteki-Kea no Kanōsei to Supirichuaru-Kea' [Spiritual Care and the Potential of Religious Care in Clinical Settings], *Kanwa-Kea [Palliative Care]* Vol. 22, No. 3 (2012).

National Child Traumatic Stress Network and National Center for PTSD, *Psychological First Aid: Field Operations Guide, 2nd Edition* (Los Angeles: NCTSN, 2006).

Okabe Takeshi, 'Higashi Nihon Daishinsai to Kanwa-Kea – Zaitaku to Hisai no Genba kara Kangaeru' [The Great East Japan Earthquake and palliative care – thoughts from home and from disaster areas], *Kanwa-Kea [Palliative Care]* Vol. 22, No. 1 (2012).

Stephan B. Robert and Willard W.C. Ashley (eds), *Disaster Spiritual Care: Practical Clergy Responses to Community, Regional and National Tragedy* (Woodstock, VT: Skylight Paths Pub., 2008).

Taniyama Yōzō, 'Bukkyō no Shiseikan to Supirichuaru-Kea' [Spiritual care and the Buddhist view of life and death], *Rinshō Seishin Igaku [Clinical Psychiatry]*, Vol. 38, No. 7 (2009).

Taniyama Yōzō, 'Supirichuaru-Kea to Shūkyōteki-Kea' [Spiritual care and religious care], *Kanwa-Kea [Palliative Care]* Vol. 19, No. 1 (2009).

Taniyama Yōzō, 'Saigai-toki no chapuren no ugoki: sono kanōsei to kadai' [Disaster chaplaincy and its task in the wake of the Great East Japan Earthquake and Tsunami], *Shūkyō Kenkyū [Journal of Religious Studies]* 86/2 (2012).

Taniyama Yōzō, 'Shūkyōsha ni yoru Kokoro no Kea' [Care for the heart given by clergy], Watanabe Naoki (ed.), *Shūkyō to Gendai ga Wakaru Hon 2012 [Introductory Book on Religion in Modern Times 2012]* (Tokyo: Heibonsha, 2012).

Taniyama Yōzō, 'The Vihara movement: Buddhist chaplaincy and social welfare in Japan', Jonathan S. Watts and Tomatsu Yoshiharu [eds.], *Buddhist Care for the Dying and Bereaved* (Boston: Wisdom Publications, 2012).

Asahi Shimbun, 4 May 2011. YouTube, 'Hisaichi no Sōryo' [Monk in a Disaster Area], (www.youtube.com/watch?v=DAsC1gaQBP4&feature=related).

Caritas Japan: (www.caritas.jp/hotnews/current/tohoku.html).

Counselling Room for the Heart (website) 'Chappuren Kōdō Kihan' [Chaplain Activity Regulations] (www.sal.tohoku.ac.jp/kokoro/data/upfile/25-1.pdf).

Food Radiation Measurement Project 'Prayer' (website) (www.foodbq.com/).

Japan Overseas Christian Medical Cooperative Service (website), 'Higashi Nihon

Daishinsai Kyūen Katsudō' [Great East Japan Earthquake Relief Activity] (www.jocs.or.jp/earthquake/325.htm).

Jōdo Shinshū Hongwanji-ha Northeast Parish Disaster Volunteer Centre (website) 'Katsudō Kiroku' [Activity Records] (http://otera-vc.jimdo.com/).

Sendai Buddhist Society (website) 'Higashi Nihon Daishinsai Shien Katsudō Hōkoku' [Great East Japan Earthquake Support Activity Report] (www.sendai-bukkyoukai.jp/?page_id=121).

Touhoku HELP (website), 'Working With Other Religious Leaders' (http://tohokuhelp.com/panel/120605a.html).

# Conclusion

*Christopher Harding*

Taniyama Yōzō's chapter on chaplaincy work in disaster areas brings this volume full circle. Where Japan's late nineteenth-century encounter with western modernity placed temple and shrine therapies under implicit threat, their survival dependent upon congruence with the rationalizations of Japanese psychiatry backed by the law, Taniyama reveals a present-day 'revival' of involvement in psychological and medical care on the part of religious institutions and their personnel. The uncertain nature of this revival, made vivid in the delicacy of the disaster chaplaincy work Taniyama describes, tells us a great deal about what has happened in the intervening century or so.

We see a negotiation of prerogatives between three worlds: the state, civil society, and organized religion. Hospital staff might remove Buddhist monks from their premises if the latter were to turn up in religious dress, while clergy participating in disaster relief efforts after 3/11 went out of their way to affirm their respect for the sacrosanctity of civil space – engaging in careful and unassuming co-operative dialogue with municipal authorities, police, firefighters, and others. For the roots of this we could go back to public revulsion at Aum Shinrikyō in 1995, and to the social and constitutional marginalization of traditional religion in the 'New Japan' half a century earlier; we might recall violent early Meiji attempts at Buddhism's suppression – the *haibutsu kishaku* discussed by Yoshinaga in his chapter – and flare-ups of political hostility towards Buddhism and Christianity in earlier centuries.[1]

And yet across these same stretches of time religious organizations and individuals have found sufficient resonance for their values and concerns that they retain an audience amongst large proportions of the population and enjoy ready-made channels of engagement with both society and the state. Helen Hardacre gives the example of an enduring concern with peace as a means by which religious groups and individuals have (re)entered civil society since 1945.[2] If we expand our definition of 'peace' to include self-understanding, calm, and the social-psychological integration of new or changing values, then perhaps Hardacre's argument can be read back a few decades further: to Hara Tanzan's 1886 lecture on

'Experiences in Indian philosophy', positing a revived and embodied Buddhism as the Japanese people's best hope for escaping pain and achieving peace; and to temple and shrine cure pioneers who sought to render western psychotherapies more effective by domesticating them to the local 'natural and historical environment'.[3]

The work of Japan's celebrity Buddhist nun Setouchi Jakuchō offers vivid examples of how compelling religious messages of peace can still be for many Japanese today, her social activism – most recently in debates over the reactivation of nuclear power plants after 3/11 – running alongside a knack for presenting Buddhist insights as everyday emotional and interpersonal good sense. In this she is not so much a maverick as part of a lineage. Setouchi was inspired by and learned much about personal style and technique from her therapist in the early 1960s: one Kosawa Heisaku. Kosawa, in turn, owed much to Chikazumi Jōkan and to the concerns and methods of Inoue Enryō's generation.[4] Another aspect of Setouchi's appeal is the way that Buddhism's relative peripherality from everyday life in Japan lends it a certain transhistorical aura and appeal – an impression powerfully conveyed by images of Buddhist monks praying in the debris of Tohoku.

In her definition of civil society Hardacre has stressed the building of horizontal ties that extend beyond family without becoming political or

*Figure C.1* Zen Buddhist monks pray with a Christian pastor amidst the debris in Miyagi Prefecture, 28th April 2011.

commercial. Whereas this kind of civil society was largely smothered by Japan's prewar bureaucracy – as interest groups were 'envelop[ed] and coopted' by the state rather than allowed to exist outside and in potential opposition to it[5] – after the war and particularly in the wake of a new Non-Profit Organization Law in 1998 small-scale civil society groups have boomed in Japan. This in turn has created new space for Japan's religious organizations: the months and years that followed 3/11 have been rich in civil society voluntarism, with whose spirit of improvised generosity religious organizations' interest in peace and 'care' – interpreted increasingly broadly in recent years[6] – has dovetailed rather neatly. Moreover it is possible that where civil society leads, in welcoming, or at least tolerating, religious personnel and initiatives, the state may begin to follow – just as it did in the prewar era, passing mental health legislation that reflected existing social and cultural practices rather than imposing new norms.[7] Already in Japanese medical institutions, the labelling of care as 'spiritual' rather than 'religious' tends to make a great difference to its acceptability.

Alongside these shifting relationships between state, civil society, and religious organizations, Taniyama gives us hints as to where the modern history traced in this volume has left the cultural power of 'religion' more generally. On the one hand Buddhist monks are valued for their ability to humanize the medical; to mediate – philosophically and emotionally – scientific medicine's terminology, processes, and outcomes. And yet this seems precariously dependent upon the shifting connotations of Buddhist dress or Buddhist talk to particular sections of Japanese society. The image of a hospice patient participating in a sutra recitation via a television screen seems to capture a fleeting generational moment, and it is not unreasonable to ask whether the demand for places on Vihāra wards may drop dramatically as today's middle-aged Japanese – whom surveys show tend to be rather indifferent towards religion when compared with their parents[8] – become the elderly of tomorrow. Amongst the predominantly rural, ageing population of Tohoku there seem to have been many for whom the ministrations of a religious counsellor were more welcome and more soothing than those of a psychiatrist or psychotherapist, but again one wonders about the situation a generation hence – or for that matter even today, were disaster to strike an area of Japan with a more even age distribution and where secular mental health services had reached a higher level of community integration and cultural acceptance.

One could argue, of course, that such objections rest on a reduction of *shūkyō* (religion), with its complex modern history and resonances, to particular forms of religious engagement: the televised sutra recitation, or the senior Buddhist monk who enjoys an easy rapport with rural Japanese of his own generation. In that case, are there new, more favourable associations for 'religion' out there that might render it less vulnerable to demographic change and more able to bring forth and sustain fresh forms of engagement with Japanese society? How successful have religious organizations and personnel been in attempting to refine their long-standing concern with care of the human person in tandem with modern psychological findings and institutional change? Have they done enough to ensure themselves a place in Japanese society, at least as a counter-cultural resource for occasional consultation, once the present elderly generation passes away? Taniyama is upbeat: he quotes a claim by the Japanese doctor and palliative care expert Okabe Takeshi that 3/11 and its aftermath revealed aspects of care that *only* religious organizations or individuals can provide, such are the personal qualities that religious faith fosters in care workers and the power of religious narratives to contextualize suffering in a way that secular systems of care simply cannot match. Secular psychiatrists and psychotherapists might of course object to the claim that they are unable to cope in some circumstances, but it is striking that Taniyama sees 3/11 as something of a turning point – so much so that trends towards the secularization of pastoral care may, he says, need to be halted or reversed, such has been the apparent change in how Japanese society views the potential of specifically religious care in disaster situations.

It is too soon after 3/11 to know its full impact upon popular impressions of religion, spirituality, and mental health in Japan, but perhaps in combination with trends towards religious counselling and end of life care 3/11 will contribute to the achievement of a goal that unites many of the pioneering individuals featured in this volume: the repositioning of the religious in relation to Japanese modernity, such that it appears not as pre- or anti-modern but as 'supra-modern' – incorporating rather than rejecting modern rationality; assimilating secular and professional values and working these into a broad, transhistorical and trans-sectarian vision of the human person. The multi-faith internationalism of the 3/11 relief effort – neatly symbolized in the multiple armbands worn by the Catholic priest Une Takashi[9] – and of the Tohoku University Chaplaincy Training Programme seems to reflect a modest move in this direction. The latest innovations in disaster relief care are adopted, while the utilitarian and the material are laid aside as ultimate points of reference. Future studies will discover whether these emerging initiatives manage to surmount the confusions that have arisen over what counts as 'religious' versus 'spiritual' care, what the meanings are of prayer, worship, and sacred space in mixed and sensitive contexts, and above all whether these new forms of psycho-religious care actually work and are wanted.

What might the long-term importance be here of *supirichuariti*, as opposed to *shūkyō*? Horie Norichika's contribution to this volume, together with his writings elsewhere, serves as a warning that it is in the nature of fads and booms to come and go, with most people investing in them partially or instrumentally – albeit, as we shall see, the latter need not have solely negative connotations.[10] Ioannis Gaitinidis offers similar cautions in his analyses of the passing economic circumstances that underpinned the early twenty-first century 'spiritual boom' in Japan, while Ian Reader and Timothy Fitzgerald point in their differing ways to the role of religious studies scholars in talking up the significance of trends and concepts, well beyond anything that can be shown to be happening 'on the ground'.[11] That said, the enduring questions that the 'spiritual' takes as its starting point and goal are unlikely to fluctuate as dramatically as the televisual appeal of Ehara Hiroyuki or Japan's post-1990 economic fortunes. From evidence offered in this volume it seems that much will continue to hinge upon 'boundary work' between religious and psychotherapeutic systems and their representatives, vying to cater to that territory, in people's experience of life, where distress and meaning meet.

The question of whether or not the coming together of religion and psychotherapy secures the former a long-term place in Japanese society – successfully re-presenting itself as 'supra-modern', and banishing dusty, death-obsessed, or cultish counter-images – may matter greatly for established religious organizations, both old and new, but there is more to the 'religion–psy' encounter than this. A focus upon the boundary work that goes on between institutions, small professional classes, and their concepts (operating, as Josephson reminds us, within parameters set by the state[12]) ought not to eclipse shifts in ordinary people's attitudes, aspirations, and beliefs: these may be influenced by dominant concepts and institutional norms but are not, of course, neatly coterminous with them. This means that it is important to look not just at how modified religious and psychotherapeutic vocabularies are produced and disseminated in the course of boundary work, but also at why people select as they do from these vocabularies when they seek to name, explore, and exercise agency over the complexities of their lives – helping to sustain and even alter these vocabularies, from one generation to the next.[13] A key dynamic here has been the way that religion and psychotherapy are increasingly 'relational entities' since the latter half of the twentieth century. As mutual hostility has given way to an appreciation of religion and psychotherapy's need of one another[14] a degree of intermingling has occurred of their resources, ideas, practices, and dispositions. These come to be separated out again into 'religion' and 'psychotherapy' in people's minds on the basis not just of old and new institutional rationales but also shifts in popular perceptions about each of them.[15] A brief look at the comparable situation of 'religion' and 'spirituality' perhaps serves to underscore this point. As 'spirituality' comes to be associated, across many parts of the modern world, with individual freedom, exploratory interiority, true prayer, and relational openness to others and their worldviews, 'religion' starts to lose these associations and is lumbered instead with their unenviable antitheses: dogmatism, empty formalism, exclusivism, and intolerance. And yet relationality is complex and multi-directional: alongside its more flattering connotations, 'spirituality' has come to be construed also in terms of self-indulgence, short-term experiential highs, and that phobia of serious commitment that is held to be one of the hallmarks of late capitalism. This has allowed 'religion' to take on the feel of something solid and communitarian, its self-sacrificial wisdom more enduring and sophisticated than the soundbites and phony philosophies of the spiritual marketplace.

Just as a person might describe, then, more or less the same constellation of thoughts, emotions, and intentions as 'religious' one day and 'spiritual' the next, depending on these relational shifts as she experiences them, so similar switches may occur in the way she invokes 'religion' versus 'psychotherapy' in framing and pursuing possibly rather inchoate aspirations for development and change. While her awareness of the availability of competing systems and their vocabularies gives rise to a sense that she is making her own decisions here, no-one can fully objectify their deeper orientations and everyone is of course shaped by and making do with the resources given to them by their time and place. In that sense, 'boundary work' over long stretches of historical time plays off against, as opposed to being trumped by, 'relational shifts' in people's perceptions: a person may make choices within their situation, as psycho-religious practitioners and their clients in modern Japan have done, from Hara to Ehara, but it is equally true that their situation has chosen them. As Robert Bellah puts it, writing about religion in the modern world and the impossibility of fully stepping outside a given cultural-linguistic community:

> Reform and re-appropriation are always on the agenda, but to believe that there is some neutral ground from which we can rearrange the defining symbols and commitments of a living community is simply a mistake, a common mistake of modern liberalism.[16]

Rarely is a straight 'choice' being made between two poles and their associations. The human territory explored in this volume in terms of 'religion' and 'psychotherapy' is shared with aesthetics, philosophy (see below, on Tanabe Hajime), belonging, relationship, love, and identity, to name but a few. It lies well beyond the power of any single institution or idea to influence decisively the combinations in which people draw on the resources offered by these worlds. This means that the religion–psy encounter in modern Japan is at once more complex and more integrated with broader historical trends – beyond the institutional or cultural status of religion and the psy disciplines – than might at first appear to be the case. The aim of what remains of this chapter is to point readers in the direction of these broader connections, by teasing out three areas of tension that are evident in the psycho-religious ideas and practices explored in this volume and which extend into other areas of Japanese modernity: tensions between the personal and the (con)textual, between creation and discovery, and between instrumentalism and engrossment.

## The personal and the (con)textual

In their chapter, Kondo Kyoichi and Kitanishi Kenji argued that one of the things that distinguishes Japanese psychotherapies from western counterparts is the extent to which Japanese therapists, in formulating and administering their therapies, have been prepared to draw upon their own personal and interpersonal experiences while moving outside the received boundaries of particular traditions or modalities: 'A therapist is not so much a theorist as an ordinary person who lives life, relying on his or her own experiences and understandings of human beings'.[17] There is always the risk here of overstating distinctions between imagined blocs of 'Japanese' versus 'western' therapists – not least because the biographical research methodology that looms so large in the present volume naturally points us towards the pivotal importance of psycho-religious pioneers' backgrounds and personalities, at the expense, for example, of hard-to-come-by information about patients and their families. In addition, the work of Kosawa Heisaku, Doi Takeo, and Kawai Hayao suggests not so much that they prioritized pragmatism over theory as that they understood the latter always as a work in progress. This was Freud's view too, albeit the line between legitimate development of psychoanalytic theory and wrong-headed departure from it was one that he and his inner circle in Europe found themselves constantly having to negotiate.

Nevertheless, the essays in this volume make very clear the centrality of the personal: the way in which pioneering psychotherapists were injured and shaped by their circumstances, becoming in the process conduits for the ills of their ages to be expressed and addressed. This begins, in our volume, with creators of new forms of temple-based therapy at the dawn of the Meiji era: the *shugenja* Yamamoto Shūsen turned his own practices and experiences with healing into a new form of *settoku* (persuasion) therapy, which came to be so closely associated with his family's own lives and states of health that a local newspaper ended up writing about 'the mad curing the mad'.[18] And it runs all the way through at least to 2007, with the death of Kawai Hayao: as Japan's first Jungian, Kawai was perfectly at home with the idea of the 'wounded healer', sharing with Yamamoto's *shugen* tradition an understanding of good mental health and self-cultivation as two sides of the same coin, with the implication that the former is less a state than a never-ending process across the course of every human life.

One could read this as a vindication of the point made by the American psychiatrist Gerald May, referred to in our Introduction, that the encounter between religion and the psy disciplines occurs most profoundly and profitably at the level of the practitioner's own inner life. The flipside to this is that such a practitioner might all too easily find, as Kosawa did, that much of what made his brand of psychotherapy successful at one time becomes the source of its unacceptability later on. Kosawa's major theory – the Ajase Complex – was modified significantly by one of his students,

Okonogi Keigo, while another, Doi, shared Kosawa's interest in religion and his practical concern with managing relationships of dependence, and yet repudiated Kosawa's therapeutic style in the strongest terms. Neither Kosawa nor his rival psychoanalyst, Ohtsuki Kenji, were succeeded by true 'heirs' in the sense of people whose approaches closely and approvingly matched theirs.

Natural systematizers, those like Hara Tanzan who are prone to pay attention primarily to ideas, text and context, fared little better than those such as Kosawa and Doi who represent what we might call the 'embodiment–enactment' approach to religion–psy integration: embodying the tensions of their times as a means of integrating them, and enacting their view of the world via their activity as therapists. Hara's speculative mixing of religious with biological and psychological concepts, and his experimentation with new bodily 'technologies of the self' – to the point of putting his own health at risk – may have been an inspiration to later generations, as Yoshinaga points out. But Hara seems a less compelling figure than Kosawa or Doi (or indeed Morita and Kawai), perhaps because hybrid conceptual systems tend to appear more superficial and to date faster than individual personalities. For Kosawa's clients and students, his personality and approach made a far stronger impression – for better in Setouchi's case, for worse in Doi's[19] – than his theories. The words of one of his students, Maeda Shigeharu, are worth reproducing here from Iwata Fumiaki's piece in this volume:

> [Kosawa] neither molly-coddled nor attempted to enrapture his patients. Instead, his therapeutic motherly attitude – his fundamentally maternal approach – facilitated positive transformation and restoration of a basic level of internal unity. It was a profound interpersonal experience.

So too with Doi: although the work of his *Amae* theory in helping people cope with rapid social change in postwar Japan may now be at an end,[20] his personality and life story, as someone who allowed himself to embody the dilemmas of that period in order to find a way of overcoming them, continues to impress Japanese psy professionals today and to serve as a marker for engaged and compassionate psychotherapeutic care.

However, the importance of the personal in how religion and psychotherapy come together against a rapidly changing historical backdrop lies not just in therapists' ability to embody rather than (only, or inadequately) to conceptualize the contradictions and dilemmas of their age. It lies too in the power of one individual to inspire and draw out another, in a way that ideas alone might struggle to achieve. Kosawa's writings focus far more upon Chikazumi Jōkan, Shinran, and Freud as people with life stories than as theorists with theories: Chikazumi's transformative period of illness; Shinran's realization of his own hopelessness as a monk; Freud's dispiriting experiences with fractious followers. One of Kosawa's analysands in the 1940s, Mr Fukuda, expressed something similar when he recalled that his wartime schooling had left him searching vainly for the meaning of *jinkakusha*, a 'man of character', until he encountered Kosawa. Fukuda did not always find Kosawa a reasonable or even likeable person. On one occasion, when problems with the trains resulted in Fukuda being late for a session, Kosawa sent him straight home, saying that if Fukuda really wanted psychoanalysis he would turn up on time. But something about Kosawa, both inside and outside of the therapy room, struck Fukuda more directly than any of the ideas he had encountered in his wide reading up until that point.[21]

Alongside themes of embodiment and inspiration in this volume runs the question of subjectivity, and the difficulty, as Iwata puts it in his chapter, of 'achieving personal autonomy in modern Japanese society'. For critics of Morita, Kosawa, Doi, and Kawai, their embodiment of contradictions was all too passive, even masochistic. They failed to master these contradictions, and instead created psychological theories premised upon acceptance (Morita), weakness (Kosawa), dependence (Doi), or a necessarily flawed integration (Kawai). They were victims of context, of sociohistorical circumstance, rather than critical commentators or shapers in the way that Freud sought to be in the West. Some of this criticism comes from within the Japanese psy disciplines: for all their respect for Kosawa, senior psychoanalysts in present-day Tokyo and Kyoto explain the religious elements in his therapy as a feature of his times that he was unable to overcome – a means by which he 'coped' with professional isolation as one of very few Japanese followers of Freud.[22] And indeed Kosawa himself affirmed, in a letter to Karl Menninger, a sense of isolation along with his commitment to embodying his discipline: 'It is really a sad truth', he wrote in 1953, 'that I have been the only one who not only propagated psychoanalytical knowledge *but practiced and lived it*'.[23]

And yet Iwata's revised understanding of Kosawa's Ajase Complex, as not primarily a psychoanalytical theory but rather – initially, at least – a shot across the bows of modernist anti-religionists in the 1930s, suggests that Kosawa did indeed seek to understand and push against the tide of his times. The same was true of Doi in the 1950s: just like Kosawa twenty years before in Vienna, Doi rejected certain elements of western psychoanalysis as he came to know it, seeking to make creative use of his disappointment at western life. It is no surprise that Doi was drawn, in later years, to the work of Japan's great Meiji-era novelist, Natsume Sōseki, who turned his own miserable experience of living in the United Kingdom into the raw material for considering the plight of the individual in modern society. We see the result of all this in Ando Yasunori's account: Doi carefully staking out terrain in between what he regarded as Kosawa's overbearing motherliness and the emotional frigidity of American psychoanalysis *c*.1955.

Judgements such as these are largely a matter of perspective, and for many towards the end of the Second World War and immediately afterwards it seemed clear that Japanese individual autonomy in the prewar era – and with it the possibilities of resisting the gradual militarist takeover from the late 1920s onwards – had been undermined by what the Marxist philosopher Miki Kiyoshi regarded as a dangerous strain of 'Eastern naturalism'. As Laurence Kirmayer has pointed out, whereas self-awareness and self-representation are the shared stuff of human experience, psychotherapy involves the objectification of self-representations and a series of choices about which of them will be 'supported … as more "true"'. People are encouraged to search for their truest 'self' or deepest subjectivity in quite specific ways, depending on the therapeutic context, with equally specific assumptions at play about what that deepest subjectivity will feel like and how it will be validated as such once found. To define the self as 'the locus of attribution of conscious experience', for example, and to imagine that it can straightforwardly be sought by means of introspective self-awareness is but one amongst other options, and a deceptively simple one at that.[24] What worried Miki was that Eastern philosophy and naturalism appeared to insist upon the truth of – and so sought to foster – a form of subjectivity in which one regards feelings of autonomy as often illusory and eventually self-destructive. Such was Morita's worldview, in which therapy ought to involve 'recovering the power to harmonize with nature, by experiencing and expressing one's own nature – one's desires and emotions – just as it is, and making adjustments, through bodily experience, to the desires that have created an inflated sense of self'.[25] Whether formulated as psychological or psycho-religious subjectivities, these were in danger of looking complacent, in the post-1945 world, in their privileging of passive personal, interpersonal, or transcendental experiences of self at the expense of alternatives that focused on history, on politics, and on challenging injustice.

The choice after the war was, however, not simply between, on the one hand, fatalism, harmony, and the dissolution of the self into a broader reality, and on the other hand ego and a unitary individual autonomy. Just as Doi's *Amae* seemed to bear somewhat of a resemblance to Kosawa's understanding of *tariki* – the Jōdo Shinshū Buddhist ideal of our abject and ultimate dependence upon Other-power – so *tariki* itself, together with its great advocate Shinran, was undergoing reassessment at this time by three major figures: the historian Hattori Shisō and the philosophers Miki Kiyoshi and Tanabe Hajime. Hattori was significant for his effort to situate Shinran as a man of the people, someone whose religious development was bound up with the emergence of a powerful class-consciousness and a vision of a new egalitarian social order. Clearly such a figure held great appeal for leftists and liberals after 1945, seeking to put Japan back on the course from which they believed it had deviated in the 1930s.[26] But let us focus briefly here upon Tanabe and Miki, since their understanding of *tariki* takes us beyond clichés of accommodationist versus assertive forms of psychotherapy and shows us instead how closely related surrender and autonomy can be, and why the personal and the contextual genuinely exist in tension rather than being simple binaries in everyday experience.

Tanabe was an influential voice in Japan's 'Kyoto School' of philosophy,[27] his sympathies previously with the *jiriki* – self-power – element in Japanese Buddhism. But his late-wartime indecision over whether someone in his influential position should stand up and criticize government policy or steer clear of traitorous and destabilizing commentary at such a critical moment for Japan brought about a dramatic experience of *zange* – contrition, or 'metanoesis' in Tanabe's usage. This led him to understand the individual's situation in a radically new way: he argued that as 'reason, faced with the absolute crisis of its dilemma, surrenders itself of its own accord', one comes into contact with a processual 'absolute nothingness' that operates through and continuously transforms one's limited, relative self. 'It is no longer I who pursue philosophy', Tanabe wrote, 'but rather *zange* that thinks through me'.[28] There is little evidence that Kosawa was much interested in either philosophy generally or in the Kyoto School in particular.[29] But he was deeply concerned with the transformative potential of *zange*, and the new form of subjectivity described by Tanabe here (with a rare personal openness) bears a striking resemblance to experiences described by Mr Fukuda and Setouchi Jakuchō in the contexts of psychotherapy. Setouchi found at the deepest level of her subjectivity something she described in terms of '*umaresaserareru*' – being caused to be born/created by something, or being sustained by something – while Fukuda was struck by a vivid feeling of 'being lived through'. When Fukuda reported this to Kosawa, the latter replied that Fukuda had had a taste of the altered sense of selfhood at which psychoanalysis aims but which it seems to struggle to achieve.[30]

Kawai Hayao too found in his analysis of Japanese myths and folk tales that Japanese narratives tend to be marked not by 'heroic conquest but rather perseverance and endurance supported by a sense of absolute nothingness'.[31] As Tarutani has it in this volume:

> [These narratives] revolve not around a dominant male hero but a spacious or hollow centre that has a balancing and harmonizing function.... The hollow centre is not merely an empty nothingness; rather, it is more like an active nothingness, in the sense of receptive sensitivity. According to Kawai, it is not that 'nothing happens' but rather that '*the* nothing *happens*'. The entirety of the folk or fairy tale narrative gives expression to this nothing that is happening.[32]

For Tanabe, *zange* gives rise neither to an effacement of self nor to a self bent on capitulation to circumstances; rather, this is a 'radical self-awareness', in which one finds at the depths of one's self the dynamic activity of absolute nothingness. All this took place 'in the philosophical [as opposed to the religious] realm'[33] for Tanabe, and with *zange* both he himself and the entire project of philosophy with him was at once lost and re-found.

Miki Kiyoshi sensed in *tariki* a similar dynamic, but his concern lay with how psycho-religious subjectivity (concerned with the ego and with subjective self-awareness) and socio-historical subjectivity (concerned with a self that is enmeshed in historical time) could be bound up one with the other. Miki died in prison in 1945, just days before the Allies freed Japan's political prisoners, his essay on Shinran incomplete. But according to Melissa Anne-Marie Curley's analysis, Miki understood the process in Jōdo Shinshū Buddhism by which a practitioner realizes the futility of reliance upon self-power and instead calls the name of Amida Buddha – the quintessential act of reliance upon Other-power – to be *both* a psycho-religious *and* an historical turnaround, in other words both personal and contextual. This occurs as two simultaneous processes: the practitioner realizes himself as a powerless part of history, but in doing so he experiences his historical situation not merely as an objective fact but 'as internal, subjective reality'. This restores to him his subjectivity, in a new form. For Miki, Shinran was the model of this two-part turnaround: '[Shinran] realized himself in the age [part 1], and the age in himself [part 2]'.[34]

We see here in Tanabe, Kosawa, Kawai, and Miki the idea that at the far end of a process of self-realization guided from outside us but set off by our own contrite admission of utter helplessness one finds a renewed subjectivity and autonomy. For Tanabe and Kawai in particular this was not a once-for-all-time experience. Rather, it was truly a tension, through which one passes innumerable times. The personal and the contextual are here reconciled, in a way that we might label religious, philosophical, or psychological almost as a matter of taste or preference. Attempts to systematize or to establish conceptual solutions to religious or philosophical questions are abandoned in an 'absolute crisis' of reason. Reason is forced, in Tanabe's words, to 'surrender itself of its own accord', and the reasoner himself along with it: 'the personal subject [who] is undertaking the critique of pure reason cannot remain a mere bystander at a safe remove',[35] but instead experiences a kind of re-birth. One might summarize what happens here as the conceptual dissolving into the personal (as reason falters, a person's attempt to exercise it is turned back upon him), and the two together – reason and reasoner – then fragmenting into absolute nothingness. From this a new subjectivity emerges, given rather than owned. What makes this a tension rather than a once-for-all-time occurrence is a person's temptation to turn this new subjectivity towards old projects of categorizing or reasoning about himself and the world – a working against *zange* that could variously be described in Tanabe's philosophical terms as a failure of absolute criticism, in religious terms as self-centredness or ingratitude, and in psychotherapeutic terms as avoidance.

## Creation and discovery

One of the problems that follows from this recasting of the tension between person and text or context is that Tanabe cannot demonstrate in conceptual terms the 'truth' or naturalness of the experience of self he describes, so much as hold out a hand for readers to join him. This points us towards a second tension in the religion–psychotherapy encounter in Japan: between creation and discovery. Peter Dale, in an excoriating chapter of *The Myth of Japanese Uniqueness* entitled 'Omnia Vincit Amae', locates Doi's work and in particular his reaction to American psychoanalysis within a broader Japanese tradition of rejecting western intellectual trends and personality types as cold, aloof, and unreasonably objectifying of the world and its inhabitants.[36] In other words, Doi's work does not really amount to discoveries about how Japanese or western people think and feel; rather, he is creating psychological typologies that suit more general preconceptions, some inherited from a long Japanese tradition of cultural essentialism – what Harumi Befu has called 'auto-Orientalism' – and others picked up in the postwar environment in which Doi reached intellectual maturity. The illegitimacy of creation masquerading as (or genuinely confused for) discovery here is made all the more egregious, for Dale, by its amplification in Japanese studies and popular culture, courtesy of the *nihonjinron* publishing boom of the 1970s and 1980s: what started out with Doi and others as 'creation' – whether or not they would understand or admit it to be such – ended for millions of Japanese and western readers as 'discovery', albeit at second hand, of apparently real and long-standing psychological truths.

The picture changes somewhat, however, if we see Doi as Amy Borovoy does: not as cynically dreaming up absolute claims about the Japanese psyche to fit a particularist agenda, but rather as someone seeking a balanced approach to the powerful intellectual trends of his day – someone who, in Borovoy's words, was a relatively 'tempered critic of Japan's wartime experience and... cautious inheritor of American liberal individualism'.[37] It is clear that Doi himself was alive to the tension in psychoanalysis and in science between creation and discovery: 'I admit that such explanations [about the Japanese mind] would be hypothetical ... [but] any explanation about any subject is hypothetical in the last analysis, and the validity of hypothesis hinges upon how much it can explain'. In the same article, Doi went on to reject Dale's critique of his work, which Doi saw as resting 'solely on [Dale's] ideological interpretation of history'. Doi rejected too both cultural relativism and ethnocentrism, as 'two sides of the same coin'. He claimed that what is most fundamental is our shared humanity, and that Japanese and Americans are 'dependent' and experience 'ambivalence' in equal measure – two of the social-psychological concepts in which Doi was most interested – but that Japanese culture homes in on both of these while American culture tends to work around them.[38]

Perhaps Doi's theorization of 'ambivalence' – a concept he drew from Freud's analysis of children simultaneously experiencing conflicting emotions or desires – helped him cope with and justify his dual advocacy of humanism and Japanese particularism. Though Doi rejected the excesses of prewar and wartime nationalism, we might fairly regard his hope that *Amae* would be a means for Japanese psychoanalysis to teach the world something of value about being human as itself a form of low-level cultural nationalism. Doi ended the piece quoted above by expressing the hope that the 'soul' of Japan would never change – 'soul' suggesting essence rather than historically contingent tendency, and this in a nuanced piece of writing in which Doi was choosing his words carefully (the better to refute Dale).[39]

Doi can be understood here as one of the most recent in a line of thinkers stretching back to the Meiji era who were keen to draw attention to the richness of the psycho-religious insights to be found in various corners of Japanese culture. Hashimoto points out in his chapter that 'in general, Japanese psychiatrists [in the late Meiji and early Taishō periods] were inclined to look for elements of contemporary European therapies in Japanese traditional or religious ones'. So too Inoue Enryō's advocacy of contemporary Japanese Buddhism (over its Indian counterparts and western rivals), Kosawa's critique of Freud's ideas about religion, and Morita's invocation of East Asian philosophy: we see the enthusiasm of medical and psy practitioners for new western ideas and techniques tempered or inflected by self-conscious reference to the older ideological and practical wisdom of Japanese tradition.[40] Shiotsuki Ryoko's work on *yuta* in Okinawa offers a regional complement to this theme: for centuries occupying an uncertain space at the borders of mainland Japanese consciousness and identity, Okinawa's *yuta* and the phenomenon of *kamidāri* began in the 1990s to offer new sources for psycho-religious insight and new avenues for professional reflexivity on the part of Japan's psychiatrists – some of whom have gone against the legal trend initiated in the Meiji era by starting to discuss the 'usefulness of possession'.[41]

The creation/discovery tension is in part interpretative, the result of historians' perspectives bumping up, here, against religious and philosophical subject matter. Historians are concerned with relationships amongst people and ideas, bracketing out metaphysics or epistemology in a manner similar to Carl Jung who felt that, as a psychologist, it was not his place to delve into the ultimate possible referents of the psychological phenomena with which he dealt (as Tarutani points out, 'Jung treated the unconscious or "soul" phenomenologically, as a field of real experience, without venturing metaphysical speculations about it'). The danger with this, however, for historians and psychologists alike, is that methodological agnosticism may give rise to analyses skewed towards functionalism or instrumentalism: understanding psycho-religious concepts and practices fundamentally in terms of coping or self-improvement, as creating rather than pointing to (or 'discovering') objects or essences, and as working to sculpt a new person rather than chip away at the false to reveal the true.

Chikazumi Jōkan's use, in his teaching, of the classic Japanese folktale 'Obasuteyama' is a case in point. The story, as Iwata relays it in his chapter, is of a son who carries his ailing mother into the mountains on his back, with the secret intention of abandoning her there – 'Obasuteyama' means, in Japanese, the mountain (*yama*) where the old woman (*Oba*) is to be discarded (*suteru*). The mother has known her son's intention all along, and has been laying a trail of twigs as they go, so that he may find his way safely home once he has left her. For Chikazumi, this story tells us something about the morality and psychology of good parenting and about Amida Buddha's mercy – a mercy defined by its operation far beyond the understanding and calculations even of the smartest and the most self-regarding. Chikazumi would say that all three together – folktale, ideal parent–child relationships, Amida's mercy – help us to get at an essential truth about the way reality is. But if this triple complementarity was a matter of 'discovery' for Chikazumi, historians are more likely to see 'creation' at work. Chikazumi was led to create – or, rather, re-create – the meaning of 'Amida's mercy' by identifiable historical and personal circumstances: early twentieth-century social and technocratic concerns about how the next generation was to be raised; Chikazumi's own upbringing and adult experiences, as someone whose father read him *Obasuteyama* as a child and who in later life sat beside his sickbed and wished out loud that he could suffer in his son's stead. If we do wish to call this 'discovery' we are constrained to mean only that it was something novel and meaning-laden for Chikazumi and profound too for many others besides, not that it was the revelation of something truly universal – the latter judgement not being ours to make. One could broaden this point to argue that both in and of themselves and especially through the way in which methodological agnosticism constrains scholars to discuss them, many modern psycho-religious theories and practices end up not so much peeling back new layers of an objective world (operating, as it were, as a handmaiden to theology, broadly construed) as helping to kill off in people's minds the very possibility of an objective reality capable of revelation. They do this in two separate ways. First, by contributing to the 'psychologization of religion' in the negative sense put forward by the philosopher Herbert Fingarette: the reductive co-option of religion into materialist psychology, as part of a broader ideological relegation to the ranks of the inconsequential of anything in contemporary culture that is non-public and non-physical.[42] And second, by lending vigorous and intimate support to a postmodern emphasis on the constructed nature of all meaning and the inescapability of one's own subjectivity.

We could pursue the creation–discovery tension in one final direction by asking what effect psycho-religious commentaries on folktales, such as those of Chikazumi and later Kawai Hayao, had upon the previous balance within these tales between reflecting (discovering) and didactically shaping (creating) people's behaviour. We might look critically at Naikan or Morita therapies in a similar way. What is happening when a Morita therapy patient reads comments in his diary written by his therapist, or when he sits in front of that therapist having his progress evaluated? Is he discovering new facts about himself through guided introspection, or is a new self being created (see Kirmayer, above)? After all, progress from one stage to another in Morita therapy – from bed rest through to light and then heavier work, and finally resumed contact with the outside world – is decided on the basis of whether a patient has yet become a certain kind of person and has started to respond to his environment in the sought-for way. Similarly, with Naikan therapy, as Shimazono points out in this volume, the walls between individual rooms are thick enough for silent introspection to be feasible but thin enough that something of the emotional content of others' interviews with guides comes through. Add to this the playing of recordings of 'model reflections' during mealtimes at a Naikan centre, and the validation of new selves through tears shed and deep indebtedness realized, and we see the tension between discovering someone and creating them.[43]

## Instrumentalism and engrossment

Important though it is to recognize this creation/discovery dynamic at work in psycho-religious practices and subjectivities, to dwell upon it for any length of time is to be wearied by its apparent insolubility. With each attempt to state and restate it, no matter how exploratory and precise we might seek to be, we do not so much move towards resolution as frustrate ourselves with new layers of uncertainty or bore ourselves with the recurrence of old ones. To the extent that critical thinking seems here to raise questions that it cannot answer we begin to see the attraction – in theory, at least – of Tanabe's idea of a salvific 'absolute criticism'. We begin too, perhaps, to sympathize with the strong feeling of nostalgia that runs through this volume, in the voices of the therapists whose ideas are explored and in the voices of many of our contributors. It is as though people drawn to religious and psychotherapeutic themes share a certain sympathy with the argument made by prewar novelists like Tanizaki Junichiro, that Japan's Meiji-era contact with the modern West was a 'loss of innocence' in terms of how its people experienced both the world and themselves. If there is a difference here with religious, therapeutic, or poetic ambivalence about modernity in the West it is surely one of degree and of timing only: regular paroxysms of doubt and rejection on the part of post-1868 Japanese politicians, journalists, schoolteachers, artists, farmers, military men, or union leaders have their analogues in Britain or France or Germany, with the only difference being that Japanese people were free to disown modernity as something entirely foreign.[44]

At play somewhere in this nostalgia is a realization that such innocence is probably largely imagined and in any case cannot be restored, only attained in a new form. The search for this new form gives rise to a tension between instrumentalism and engrossment, in how people interact with the world and conceptual representations of it. In modern historical terms, this instrumentalism has at least two sources in the Meiji era. First, a sense, exemplified in Fukuzawa Yukichi's *jitsugaku*[45] and in the breakneck nation-building conducted by the period's politicians, that the best sorts of ideas were those that were 'for' something – those that had a purpose. Acceptable purposes, aside from building and strengthening a new Japan, included 'self-cultivation' – an interest that Janine Anderson Sawada has shown was inherited from older themes in Japanese life and culture[46] – and the achievement of peace and better interpersonal relations. As Shimazono shows in his chapter, many of Japan's new religions and 'psycho-religious composite movements' across this period helped to shift – or helped cater to an on-going shift in – people's focus, from 'salvation' within a grand transcendental scheme to 'healing' in this present life. The second source for instrumentalism in the Meiji era was the prevalence across medical, therapeutic, religious and popular spheres, of competing and seemingly incompatible epistemologies and worldviews. From Hara Tanzan through to the leading lights of hypnotism and *seishin ryōhō*, Yoshinaga has shown us how powerful was the desire in the late nineteenth and early twentieth centuries to demonstrate the ways in which one system of philosophical or medical explanation mapped onto another (in the interests of sectarian apologetics or new forms of commerce). This attempted mapping encompassed everything from Buddhist consciousness-only theories, Daoism, and electricity to mysterious gases and fluids operating within and between human bodies. And partly because ends mapped onto one another more readily than means – it was easier to suggest that different understandings explained or facilitated the same goals, such as enlightenment, than that they were mutually consistent in their detailed workings – synthetic theorizing such as that of Hara focused primarily on what ideas and systems achieved.

Offering a rare glimpse at the client perspective in psycho-religious practices, Horie's account of late twentieth and early twenty-first century narratives of reincarnation reveals the coincidence of this long-term trend towards instrumentalism with the dissolution of old family structures in Japan, especially since the Second World War. Horie reveals a shift from understandings of personhood that were fundamentally communal, or only 'individual' in some limited or temporary sense (a person being formed from a plurality of past lives and losing that singular identity at death, splitting apart again or merging with some greater entity[47]), to late twentieth century understandings that posit a single reincarnating Self. These new understandings share with their older counterparts a certain relativizing of the present self, but only in respect of this larger and no less 'individual' Self who moves through successive incarnations and can be known, to some extent, from within the psychological confines of the present life – through a form of 'expanded sensibility'. Similarly, bonds from a past life are still seen as carrying through to the present one, but whereas in the past this was a matter of reincarnation back into the same family or village – the all-too-vivid example of a dead infant buried beneath the family's floorboards bears this out[48] – now these bonds are 'chosen' by the reincarnating Self for its own purposes. As Horie puts it, in this shift 'the naturalness of the family unit collapses', with memorialism 'becoming subservient to the narrative of a reincarnating Self'. These shifts appear to reflect a re-formed individualism in which interpersonal bonds and responsibilities take on new meanings. Neither is any longer socially or metaphysically 'given' or imposed: instead, bonds are formed and used instrumentally by a reincarnating Self, while responsibilities exist primarily between successive incarnations of that autonomous Self. The cases outlined by Horie speak not so much of an instrumentalism of casual fantasy, superficiality, or self-indulgence here as of people trying to cope with existential and social situations not of their own making: an individualism given and coped with rather than chosen or necessarily welcomed, which 'romanticizes' rather than rejects interpersonal relationships and all the problems they create. Nor is this an entirely claustrophobic sort of subjectivity, since awareness of a reincarnating Self inspires awareness of and solidarity with reincarnating others.

This kind of instrumentalism turns ideas constantly towards the ends that they can achieve. Doi Takeo, quoted above, gave us the central idea in the philosophy of science that 'the validity of a hypothesis hinges upon how much it can explain'. The validity of ideas from the point of view of instrumentalism, on the other hand, differs: it turns not primarily upon the power of ideas to explain experience as to re-create, or re-deem it. Horie finds it useful to draw here on Paul Ricoeur's insistence that even a fiction can 're-describe' reality: 'a narrative of the self', writes Horie, 'constructs a narrative identity'. Moreover, the importance of creating and sustaining such a narrative may render it permissible to subscribe to two incompatible belief systems at the same time – '[using them] for different purposes and disregard[ing] the contradictions'.

There is an alternative, however, to responding to a loss of innocence by seeking to circumvent modern uncertainties through a kind of agnostic instrumentalism: engrossment. In Ricoeur's view (somewhat in common with Morita), part of the process that we describe as a loss of innocence has been a distorting of our ideas about how language functions, and with it our own agency more broadly. We find ourselves caught in a relatively new habit of relating to all utterances as though they were literal, allegorical, or analogical. We leave little space for the proper functioning of symbol, as something that is both literal *and* points beyond itself. Both Ricoeur and James Heisig, the latter writing about Japan's Kyoto School of philosophy, describe symbols as 'inexhaustible'.[49] For Heisig, they are 'inexhaustibly intelligible ideas that engage us, provisionally, with reality at its deepest ground'.[50] To (mis)treat a symbol, on the other hand, as something exhaustible is to indulge two false assumptions: that a symbol's meaning can be fully unpacked at a cognitive level, using some alternative form of words (this is to mistake symbol for allegory); and that literal or analogical language is able adequately to describe an objectively given reality (this would be a crudely representational theory of knowledge, in which a knower is believed able to transcend what is known).

Symbols, understood this way, are one means by which engrossment becomes possible. 'It is by living in the first [literal] meaning [of a symbol]', Ricoeur wrote, 'that I am led by it beyond itself'. As an aspect of experience prior to rational reflection, symbols can open the way to a 'second naiveté', a 're-immersion in our archaism'.[51] This aspiration of Ricoeur's did not amount to a rejection of modernity or modern criticism: it was aimed at the full enjoyment of modernity's 'gifts'. It is criticism, as long as we pass all the way through it, that allows us to 'recharge our language': 'beyond [this] desert of criticism', wrote Ricoeur, 'we wish to be called again'.[52]

This sort of engrossment is a process both more immediate than reasoning, because symbols are pre-reflective and tied up with human intuition, and far more drawn out, since it is a matter of unlearning and then relearning how to interpret and live in the world. A great many of the psycho-religious practices featured in this volume seem geared towards this kind of engrossment: one that is both immediate and far-reaching in terms of how one experiences oneself. A particularly vivid form is described by Terao Kazuyoshi, in his essay on Catholic Naikan and its developer, Fr Fujiwara Naosato. Engrossment begins to exercise its vacuum pull as folding screens loom over and seclude the practitioner: she enters tearfully into a 'purgatory for the living',[53] sensing the presence of the dead and her connection with them ('tens, hundreds, thousands of people are stretched out behind every single Naikan practitioner'[54]). She gains in the process 'a view from the borders of death'.[55] Terao describes this engrossment as 'a shamanistic exercise.... Watched over by a priest as their selves empty out, practitioners seek to achieve an altered state of consciousness of sorts that functions as a "communion of saints" with their dead fellows'. He goes on: 'While Yoshimoto secularized Naikan, Fujiwara has "re-religionized" it ... the priest plays a primordial role in bridging the worlds of the dead and the living'.

At the heart of the necessary and fruitful tension between instrumentalism and engrossment is the fact that neither one makes intellectual or practical sense without the other. What might appear from one perspective to be the instrumentalism of Past Life Therapy, with participants openly agnostic about the reality of past lives and seeking to use the idea to address present-life problems, is also the groundwork for engrossment or re-engrossment in life: from general day-to-day experiences to one's relationships with one's children. Practices such as Naikan and Morita therapies are both transparently instruments of re-engrossment, focusing on engrossment in relationship (construed both transcendentally and socially), while Kosawa and Doi's therapies can both be read in a similar way – the former with a focus on the transcendent, the latter on the postwar social. Words too can be instruments of re-engrossment, both in the case of symbols and also more complex devotional or metaphysical concepts. One might re-read Chikazumi in this light, asking (as Inoue Enryō, with his interest in the usefulness of faith, might have done): if a mother's wisdom and forgiveness (both in folktales and in present-day parenting) is pointing us towards Amida's mercy, what is Amida's mercy pointing us towards? Anyone sincere about *tariki* couldn't possibly imagine himself to mean by 'Amida' or 'Amida's mercy' some entity fully and accurately encapsulated by those words. Such words simply mark the endpoint of available descriptive reference: an invitation or plea to the Other to do the rest of the work of understanding in us and for us – even *as* us. One might put it another way: what could possibly lie at the end of any given sequence of references, if not engrossment?

\* \* \*

It is in coping with and making the most of these tensions – between the personal and (con)textual, creativity and discovery, instrumentalism and engrossment – that the encounter of religion and psychotherapy in Japan has sought to respond to modern problems of criticism and pluralism described by Fingarette:

> It is the special fate of modern man that he has a 'choice' of spiritual visions.... Although each requires complete commitment for complete validity, we can today generate a context in which we see that no one of them is the sole vision. Thus we must learn to be naïve but undogmatic. That is, we must take the vision as it comes and trust ourselves to it, naively, as reality. One must have a home [though] there is no Absolute Home.[56]

We might regard this as a tackling of modernity not by somehow trying to undo it but rather by trying to see it through. For Tanabe, this meant moving all the way into 'absolute criticism', while for Inoue, Kosawa, Morita, Yoshimoto and Doi – in a Jōdo Shinshū, Zen, or Christian humanist spirit – it meant realizing where the limits lie of our own autonomy, resisting passing generational pressures to under- or over-estimate it. For Kawai it meant striving for an ever more 'intimate' application of rationality, just as for psychiatrists taking an interest in temple and shrine cures and in possession phenomena it has meant making culture and patient perspectives a part of the critical assimilation in Japan of imported scientific epistemologies. For clients of PLT it means appreciating the texture of hair: pursuing therapeutic goals with sufficient sincerity that instrumentalism opens out into experiential engrossment. For Fujiwara, it means locating oneself 'among the coffins or in the graveyard', undergoing a kenosis through the unflinching practice of Catholic Naikan. And for Taniyama and his colleagues in Tohoku it is starting to mean probing the limitations of the secular, both in everyday life and *in extremis*.

## Notes

1  For a recent account of 'religion' in Japan and its shaping by political interests since the sixteenth century, see Josephson, *The Invention of Religion in Japan*.
2  Hardacre, 'Religion and civil society in contemporary Japan', pp. 389–415.
3  See Yoshinaga and Hashimoto, this volume.
4  See Harding, 'Japanese psychoanalysis and Buddhism'. On Chikazumi, see Iwata, this volume.
5  Hardacre, 'Religion and civil society in contemporary Japan', p. 394. A similar fate befell Buddhist philanthropy, as Hashimoto points out in this volume.
6  See, for example, the expanding involvement of religious organizations in medical and hospice care, and in the provision of counselling and psychotherapy.
7  See Harding (Chapter 1), this volume.
8  For a recent account of the statistics here, see Reader, 'Secularisation, R.I.P.?' pp. 7–36.
9  See Taniyama, this volume.
10  Horie, 'Spirituality and the Spiritual in Japan'.
11  See Gaitanidis, 'Socio-Economic Aspects'. Reader, 'Secularisation, R.I.P.?', and Fitzgerald, *The Ideology of Religious Studies*.
12  Josephson, *The Invention of Religion in Japan*, especially 'Religion Within the Limits' and 'Conclusion'.
13  A striking example is what has happened to Zen in Japan and in the West, under the influence of wealthy and demanding laypeople in the twentieth century. See Sawada, *Practical Pursuits: Religion, Politics, and Personal Cultivation in Nineteenth-Century Japan*, (2004) on koji Zen, and Robert H. Sharf, 'Buddhist Modernism and the Rhetoric of Meditative Experience,' *Numen* 42 (1995): 228–283.
14  See, for example, the account given in James Alistair Ross, ' "Sacred psychoanalysis": An interpretation of the emergence and engagement of religion and spirituality in contemporary psychoanalysis'. Doctoral Thesis, University of Birmingham (2010).
15  I take the term 'relational entities' from William Sax, who has used it in regard to 'superstition' and 'modernity'. Sax, 'Ritual and the problem of efficacy'.
16  Bellah, 'Religious Pluralism and Religious Truth', p. 484.
17  See Kondo and Kitanishi, this volume.
18  See Hashimoto, this volume.
19  'He was a truly lovely man', Setouchi recalls, 'wonderful ... so gentle. When he saw me to the door he would always compliment me on some little thing – my kimono, or my handbag. He never commented on my looks, though ...'. Setouchi Jakuchō, interview with the author, October 2012.
20  Borovoy suggests that 'Japan has outgrown Doi in many respects', though no comparable figure has yet emerged to take over the reins. Borovoy, 'Doi Takeo and the rehabilitation of particularism in postwar Japan', p. 294.

21 Mr Fukuda (pseudonym), interviews with the author, April and November 2012.
22 Kano Rikihachiro, interview with author, July 2011. Matsuki Kunihiro, interviews with author, June 2011 and October 2012.
23 Letter from Kosawa Heisaku to Karl Menninger, 29 June 1953. Menninger Archives (Topeka, Kansas, USA). Emphasis added.
24 Kirmayer, 'Psychotherapy and the cultural concept of the person', pp. 232–239.
25 See Kondo and Kitanishi's account of Morita, this volume.
26 Curley, 'The subject of history in Miki Kiyoshi's "Shinran"'.
27 For an introduction here, see James W. Heisig, *Philosophers of Nothingness: An Essay on the Kyoto School* (2001).
28 Tanabe Hajime, *Philosophy As Metanoetics* (1945), extract reproduced in James W. Heisig *et al.*, *Japanese Philosophy: A Sourcebook*, pp. 689–690.
29 There is little philosophy to be found either in Kosawa's writings or on the shelves of his personal library, which was preserved until recently in his Tokyo home.
30 See Harding, 'Japanese psychoanalysis and Buddhism'.
31 Tarutani, this volume.
32 Tarutani, this volume.
33 Tanabe, *Philosophy As Metanoetics*, extract reproduced in Heisig *et al.*, *Japanese Philosophy: A Sourcebook*, p. 690.
34 Quoted in Curley, 'The subject of history in Miki Kiyoshi's "Shinran"', p. 83.
35 Tanabe, *Philosophy As Metanoetics*, extract reproduced in Heisig *et al.*, *Japanese Philosophy: A Sourcebook*, p. 691.
36 Dale, *The Myth of Japanese Uniqueness*, p. 125. See also Harding (Introduction), this volume.
37 Borovoy, 'Doi Takeo and the rehabilitation of particularism in postwar Japan', p. 280.
38 Doi, 'The Japanese psyche', pp. 149–154.
39 Doi, 'The Japanese psyche', p. 154.
40 See Tarutani, this volume. A classic move of this sort by an Indian thinker of Inoue's era was a speech made by the advocate of Vedanta, Swami Vivekananda, to the World's Parliament of Religions. See Koppedrayer, 'Hybrid constructions'.
41 See Shiotsuki, this volume. On Meiji-era legislation marginalizing superstition and possession, see Yoshinaga, this volume.
42 Fingarette, *The Self in Transformation*, pp. 228–232.
43 On client autobiography in Naikan, see Chikako Ozawa-de Silva, *Psychotherapy and Religion in Japan: the Japanese Introspection Practice of Naikan* (2006), chapters 2, 3 and 4.
44 For a revealing overview of how moments of doubt and reversal of course played out in Japan's education system from the mid-nineteenth century onwards, one need look no further than arguments over what new generations of Japanese youngsters ought to be taught. See Marshall, *Learning to be Modern*.
45 See Harding (Chapter 1), this volume.
46 See Harding (Chapter 1), and Yoshinaga, this volume.
47 As posited, for example, by the folklorist Yanagita Kunio. See Horie, this volume.
48 Horie, this volume.
49 Ricoeur, *The Symbolism of Evil*, p. 15.
50 See Heisig, *Nothingness and Desire*, p. 3.
51 Ricoeur, *The Symbolism of Evil*, p. 13.
52 Ricoeur, *The Symbolism of Evil*, p. 349.

53 Terao, this volume.
54 Fujiwara Naosato, quoted in Terao, this volume.
55 Fujiwara Naosato, quoted in Terao, this volume.
56 Fingarette, *The Self in Transformation*, pp. 236–237.

## References

Bellah, Robert. 'Religious Pluralism and Religious Truth', in Bellah, Robert N. and Tipton, Steven M. (eds), *The Robert Baker Reader* (Duke University Press, 2006).

Borovoy, Amy. 'Doi Takeo and the rehabilitation of particularism in postwar Japan', *The Journal of Japanese Studies* 38, no. 2 (2012).

Curley, Melissa Anne-Marie. 'The subject of history in Miki Kiyoshi's "Shinran"' in *Neglected Themes and Hidden Variations: Frontiers of Japanese Philosophy Volume 2*, ed. Victor Sōgen Hori and Melissa Anne-Marie Curley (Nagoya: Nanzan, 2008).

Dale, Peter N. *The Myth of Japanese Uniqueness* (London & Sydney: Croom Helm, 1986).

Doi Takeo. 'The Japanese psyche: myth and reality', in Doi Takeo, *Understanding Amae: the Japanese Concept of Need-Love* (Folkestone: Global Oriental Ltd, 2005).

Fingarette, Herbert. *The Self in Transformation: Psychoanalysis, Philosophy, and the Life of the Spirit* (New York: Harper Torchbooks, 1963).

Fitzgerald, Timothy. *The Ideology of Religious Studies* (Oxford: Oxford University Press, 2000).

Gaitanidis, Ioannis. 'Socio-economic aspects of the "spiritual business" in Japan', *Shūkyō to Shakai* [*Religion and Society*] 16 (2010): 143–160.

Hardacre, Helen. 'Religion and civil society in contemporary Japan', *Japanese Journal of Religious Studies* 31, no. 2 (2004).

Harding, Christopher. 'Japanese psychoanalysis and Buddhism: the making of a relationship', *History of Psychiatry* 25, no. 2 (June, 2014).

Heisig, James W. *Nothingness and Desire: An East-West Philosophical Antiphony* (Honolulu: University of Hawai'i Press, 2013).

Heisig, James W. et al. (eds), *Japanese Philosophy: A Sourcebook* (Honolulu: University of Hawai'i Press, 2011).

Horie, Norichika. 'Spirituality and the spiritual in Japan', *Journal of Alternative Spiritualities and New Age Studies* 5 (2009): 1–15.

Josephson, Jason A. *The Invention of Religion in Japan* (Chicago: University of Chicago Press, 2012).

Kirmayer, L.J. 'Psychotherapy and the cultural concept of the person', *Transcultural Psychiatry* 44: 2 (2007): 232–257.

Koppedrayer, Kay. 'Hybrid constructions: Swami Vivekananda's presentation of Hinduism at the World's Parliament of Religions, 1893', *Religious Studies and Theology*, 32/1 (2004).

Marshall, Byron K. *Learning to be Modern: Japanese Political Discourse on Education* (Boulder: Westview Press, 1995).

Ozawa-de Silva, Chikako. *Psychotherapy and Religion in Japan: The Japanese Introspection Practice of Naikan* (Abingdon: Routledge, 2006).

Reader, Ian. 'Secularisation, R.I.P.? Nonsense! The 'rush hour away from the gods' and the decline of religion in contemporary Japan', *Journal of Religion in Japan*, 1 (2012).

Ricoeur, Paul. *The Symbolism of Evil* (New York: Harper & Row, 1969).

Sax, William S. 'Ritual and the problem of efficacy', in ed. William S. Sax, Johannes Quack and Jan Weinhold, *The Problem of Ritual Efficacy* (Oxford: Oxford University Press, 2010).

Tanabe Hajime. *Philosophy As Metanoetics* (1945; translated edition Berkeley: University of California, 1992).

# Index

Page numbers in *italics* denote tables, those in **bold** denote figures.

3/11 triple disaster 43, 175, 269, 270; *see also* chaplaincy work in disasters
abnormal psychology 84, 85
Adler, Alfred 150
aging, and Catholic Naikan 174
Ajase Complex 1, 11, 39, 40, 121, 123, 124–8, 129, 130–1, 132, 274, 275
Allison, Dale C. 169
*Amae* theory 39, 40–1, 137–40, 141–2, 143–5, 274, 280
ambivalence 280
Amida Buddha 30, 78, 128–9, 132, 156–7, 159–60, 196, 278, 281, 286
ancestor worship 205–6, 207–8, 209, 222–3, 225–6
Ando Yasunori 137–45, 275–6
anger, and Naikan 171–2
animal magnetism 85, 86, 90, 111, 151
anti-hypnotism legislation 32–3, 85, 95
anti-psychiatry movement 42
Aoki Tamotsu 138–9
Araki Giten 82
*arugamama* (accepting reality) 35, 115, 116, 195
Asaba, Michiaki 209
ascetic practices 54, 157, 159
Association of Japanese Clinical Psychology 42
asylums *see* mental hospitals
Aum Shinrikyō 3, 41, 42, 210
authority, of practitioners 33, 37, 38
autonomy, personal 130, 131, 133, 275–8
Awai Shrine, Naruto 64–5
Awaijima Mental Hospital 65

Baelz, Erwin 28
Bain, Alexander 87
Ballhatchet, Helen 27
Barthianism 165
bathing: in hot springs 57–8, 64; at seaside 65; under waterfalls 54–7, **56**, 60, 63, 64, 66–7, 68
Beard, George Miller 30, 111
Befu, Harumi 6, 7, 279
Bellah, Robert 153–4, 272
Ben-Dasan, Isaiah 138
Benedict, Ruth 6
Blocker, H. Gene 26
body, relationship with mind 76–8, 113, 116–17, 150–1
Borovoy, Amy 40, 279
Bose, Girindrasekhar 1
boundary work 10, 11, 271, 272
breathing exercises 30, 31, 78–9, 82, 96, 172
Buddhahood, attainment of 205, 207
Buddhism 1, 8, 25–7, 36–7, 41; and Catholic Naikan 169; and Christianity 26–7; esoteric sects 55–7, **56**, 60, 66, 79, 92; Funeral 205, 208, 209; in Hara's thinking 79–84; hidden 189, 195–7; influence of lay practitioners 13; in Inoue's thinking 87–8; intellectual outreach 26–7; in Kawai's thinking 185, 189, 194–7; materialist dilemma 77–8; medieval Japan 194–7; and mind 77, 78; Morita's use of 114; Nichirenshū sect 58–9, 60, 62, 64; original enlightenment 80, 195; philanthropy 62; as psychology and religion 40; Pure Land 78, 126–7, 132, 169, 195, 196–7;

Buddhism *continued*
  reincarnation 205–6, 207, 208; and science 26, 27, 77; in *torokashi* technique 142; traditional therapies 54, 55–7, **56**, 58–9; Zen 12, 13, 78, 79–84, 95, 185; *see also* Amida Buddha; Jōdo Shinshū
Buddhist monks: in disaster chaplaincy work 254–5, 256, **257**, 258, 259, **268**; in medical care 250, 251, 269; Vihāra monks 250, 251, 269
Bussensha 82, 84

Café de Monk 255, 260–1, 263
care for the heart 258; *see also* Counselling Room for the Heart
Caritas 258
Carpenter, William Benjamin 87
Catholicism 140–1, 165–7, 189; Catholic Naikan 167–75, 285; exorcism 151
*Chaplain Activity Regulations* 256, 261
chaplaincy work in disasters 250–63, 269, 270; case studies 253–61; future challenges 261–2; spiritual care and religious care 252–3; training programme 251, 262–3
Chikazumi Jōkan 27, 87, 120–1, 122, 123, 126, 127–9, 132, 275, 281, 282, 286
China 115–16
Chinese medicine 83, 84
Christian humanism 41
Christian priests, in disaster chaplaincy work 255, 256, 258–9, **268**
Christianity 26–7, 36, 37, 43–4, 140–1, 165–7; and Buddhism 26–7; Catholic Naikan 167–75, 285; Catholicism 140–1, 165–7, 189; collective consciousness 189; exorcism 151; in Kuwabara's thinking 93; Protestantism 7, 140, 165; and science 26, 27, 77, 88
Chuang-tzu 116, 181
Civil Law (1947) 38
civil society 267, 268–9
clairvoyance 91, 211–13
Clinical Pastoral Education (CPE) 262
clinical psychology 38, 42, 139
cognitive psychotherapy 114
collective consciousness 188–9, 194, 195–6
collective unconscious 188–9, 194, 195–6
commitment, of therapist 192–3

community care 38, 42, 68
Community Health Act (1947) 244
confession, and Catholic Naikan 174–5
confinement 27–8, 38, 62, 67, 243, 244, 245
consciousness 80, 83, 84; collective 188–9, 194, 195–6
constellations 191–3
contextual–personal tension 273–9
contrition (*zange*) 277–8
counselling 7, 38–9, 168, 270; telephone 255, 260–1, 263
Counselling Room for the Heart 251, 255–8, 260–1
CPE *see* Clinical Pastoral Education (CPE)
creation–discovery tension 279–82
creative illness concept 138
Cryns, Frederik 84
cultural psychology 40
culture-bound syndromes 5, 238
Curley, Melissa Anne-Marie 278

daily Naikan 155, 159
Dale, Peter 6, 11–12, 279
*dana* 80–4
Daoism *see* Taoism
death: and Catholic Naikan 169–74; rebirth in Pure Land 156–7, 159–60, 205, 207; *see also* reincarnation
DeMartino, Richard 39, 40
Department of Practical Religious Studies, Tohoku University 251, 255, 262–3
dependence *see* Amae theory
disasters, natural 42, 43, 175, 251, 269, 270; *see also* chaplaincy work in disasters
discovery–creation tension 279–82
disposition: as source of neuroses 35, 110–11, 113, 114; *see also shinkeishitsu* (nervous temperament)
Dobbins, James C. 13
Dods, John Bovee 86
dog-spirit possession 109
Doi Takeo 7, 137–45, 273, 275–6, 279–80, 284; *Amae* theory 39, 40–1, 137–40, 141–2, 143–5, 274, 280; and Kosawa 8, 11, 37, 120, 129, 140, 142–3, 274
dream analysis 181, 182, 184, 186, 194
dualism of mind and body 76–7, 94, 113, 116, 150–1
Dubois, Paul 112, 113–14

duration bathing 64
Dutch medicine 79, 83–4
dynamic psychiatry 111, 150, 151–2; *see also* Freud, Sigmund

earthquakes 42, 43, 251; *see also* chaplaincy work in disasters
efficacy debate 36
Ehara Hiroyuki 204, 210, 211–13, 223–4
elderly, and Catholic Naikan 174
Ellenberger, Henri 111, 138, 150–2
emperor 66
end-of-life care 250, 263, 270
engrossment–instrumentalism tension 282–7
enlightenment 39, 77, 78; Hara's theory of 80–4; original 80, 195
erythrophobia 32, 110
esoteric Buddhism 55–7, **56**, 60, 66, 79, 92
*esse in anima* 187, 193
Europe 58, 104
evenly suspended attention 192–3
evolutionary theory 27
exorcism 52, 151, 152
experiential reality of reincarnation 207, 208, 212, 213, 223, 224–5

familial relationships 34, 39, 130, 132, 281; *see also* mother–son relationships
fear of blushing 32, 110
fear of interpersonal relations (*taijinkyōfushō*) 5, 31–2, 103
Fingarette, Herbert 281, 286
Fitzgerald, Timothy 9–10, 271
Flournoy, Thèodore 186
fluid theory 86
folk beliefs: mental illness 51–2, 54, 109; reincarnation 206–7; *see also* possession phenomenon
folk health care 105
folk tales 129, 188–91, 194, 198, 199, 281, 282
Food Radioactivity Measurement Station 'Inori' 259, 263
forgiveness 129, 131, 132
fox possession (*kitsune tsuki*) 51–2, 67, 79, 109
free-association technique 123
Freud, Sigmund 1–2, 35, 36, 106, 122–3, 138, 150, 152, 273, 280; evenly suspended attention 192–3; helplessness 143; influence on Jung 186; and Kosawa 1, 120, 121, 123, 125–6, 131, 275, 280; Morita's critique of 111, 113, 114; Oedipus Complex 1, 11, 121, 124; totem theory 125–6
Fromm, Erich 40
Fujiwara Naosato 167–8, 169–71, 173, 174, 285
Fujiyama Naoki 137–8, 139–40
Fukurai Tomokichi 33, 34, 35, 91, 94
Fukuzawa Yukichi 29–30, 283
Funeral Buddhism 205, 208, 209

Gaitinidis, Ioannis 43, 270–1
Ganryūji Temple, Hyōgo 66
Gassner, Johann Joseph 151
gender, and reincarnation 225–7
*Genma Taisen* (Hirai) 209, 210
God Light Association (GLA) 208–9
Godart, Gerard 7
Gorer, Geoffrey 6
Great East Japan earthquake *see* chaplaincy work in disasters; triple disaster (March 2011)
Great Mother archetype 184–5
group souls 209, 223, 224
guardian spirits 204, 209, 223, 224
guilt, sense of 131, 132, 159, 161; *see also* Ajase Complex

Hakuin 79, 82
half-child folk tale 198, 199
*Han* theology 175
Hara Tanzan 30, 78, 79–84, **81**, 88, 95, 267–8, 274, 283
Harada Genryū 95
Hardacre, Helen 29, 267, 268–9
Harding, Christopher 1–18, 25–44, 267–87
Hasegawa Kanzen 62
Hasegawa Seiya 35
Hashimoto Akira 28–9, 51–68, 280
Hattori Shisō 276–7
Hayami Yasutaka 52
Health Inspection Committee 53
Hearn, Lafcadio 206
Heisig, James 285
helplessness 143–4
Heuvers, Hermann 140–1
Higashi Honganji 87, 121
*hikikomori* (acute social withdrawal) 5
Hirai Kazumasa 209, 210
Hirai Kinza 91
Hirata Atsutane 206–7
Hiruta Genshirō 51–2

Hito-no-michi 153, 154, 161
Hokekyōji Temple, Nakayama 58–9
home custody 27–8, 62, 243, 244, 245
Hōnen 195, 196–7
Horie Norichika 8, 42–3, 204–28, 270, 283–4
Horney, Karen 39
hospice movement 250, 252
hospital care *see* mental hospitals
hospitalization 28–9, 66, 67
hot spring bathing 57–8, 64
hot water prayers (*yukitō*) 59–60
Hozumi Shrine 59–60
Huayan Buddhism 185
hydrotherapy 63, 64
hypnotism 32–3, 78, 79, 84–92, 94, 111–12, 283; *see also* past life therapy (PLT)
hypochondria 103
hypochondriacal temperament 111, 114

ideal mother figure 129, 132–3, 190
*ie* system 206, 207, 225
Ignatius of Loyola 9, 172
Iida Fumihiko 210
Imura Kōji 79
incantations, in traditional therapy 58–60, 63
individual autonomy 130, 131, 133, 275–8
individual–universal principle 223–5, 227
individualism 208, 223, 284
individuation 42
'Inori', Food Radioactivity Measurement Station 259, 263
Inoue Enryō 13, 26, 30, 37, 40, 76, 77, 84, 85, 87–9, 90, 280
Inoue Tetsujirō 77
Inoue Yōji 166
institutional histories 5
institutionalization 28–9, 66, 67
instrumentalism–engrossment tension 282–7
interfaith activity *see* chaplaincy work in disasters
International Transpersonal Conference 185
internet, past life divination 211
introspection *see* Naikan
invocation psychosis 109
Ishibashi Haya 5
Ishikawa Hanzan 30–1

Ishikawa Sadakichi 76
isolated bed rest therapy 111, 112
Isomae Junichi 7
Iwashita Sōichi 140
Iwata Fumiaki 120–33, 274, 275, 281
*iyashi* (healing) 42, 43
Izutsu Toshihiko 185

James, William 91
Janet, Pierre 150, 186
Japan Overseas Christian Medical Cooperative Service (JOCS) 258
Japan Psychoanalytical Association 120, 124, 130, 142
Japanese Society of Neurology 94
*jiriki* (self-power) 78, 84, 122, 157, 277
*jitsugaku* (practical learning) 29–30
JOCS *see* Japan Overseas Christian Medical Cooperative Service (JOCS)
Jōdo Shinshū 12, 250; Chikazumi Jōkan 127–8; influence of lay practitioners 13; Inoue Enryō 87; Kosawa Heisaku 120, 122; Kuwabara Toshirō 93; *tariki* (other power) 78, 84, 122, 157, 276–7, 278, 286; Yoshimoto Ishin 39, 156–8, 159–60; *see also* Pure Land Buddhism
Jōdo Shinshū Honganji-ha Tohoku Parish Disaster Volunteer Centre 254, 255
Jōgi Onsen 57, 64
*Jōriki* 82, 95–6
Josephson, Jason 7
Jung, Carl Gustav 138, 150, 280; and Kawai 42, 181–2, 191–3; problems of exclusion 197; spirituality 185–8, 193, 194, 198–9
Jung Institute, Switzerland 184

Kadokawa Haruki 209
*kaku* 80, **81**
*kamidāi* (spirit possession) 235, 238–42, 243, 244, 245, 280
*kaminchu* (Okinawa priestesses) 234, 235, 236, 237
Kan Osamu 53, 62
Kaneta Taiō 256
Kant, Immanuel 187
Kashida Gorō 53, 54, 55, 56–7, 58–60, 63, 64–5
Katō Koyuki 211–12
Kawada Ryukichi 85
Kawahara Ryuzo 39
Kawai Hayao 7, 41, 42, 137, 181–5,

188–99, 273, 275, 277, 278;
  Buddhism 185, 189, 194–7; folk tales
  188–91, 198, 199, 282
Kawai Shinsui 165
Kawai Toshio 199
*Keishin Sūsokyōkai* (Society for the
  Worship of Deities and Ancestors) 34
kenotic theology 169, 170, 171
Kihara Kibutsu 95–6
Kimura Tenshin 34
Kimura Toshiaki 253–4
Kirmayer, Laurence 276
Kitanaka, Junko 3
Kitanishi Kenji 103–17, 273
*kitsune tsuki* (fox possession) 51–2, 67,
  79, 109
Kiyozawa Manshi 78, 87
Kleinman, Arthur 105
Klopfer, Bruno 181
Kobayashi Yasuhiko 53–4
Kobe earthquake 42, 43, 251
Kodama Sakae 63–4
Koga Renzo 94–5
*kokoro naoshi* 41, 42
*kokutai* ('national body') 31
Kondo Akihisa 39, 40
Kondo Kyoichi 103–17, 273
Kondō Yoshizō 33, 85, 89–90
Konsenzan Seiyōjo (Konsenzan
  Sanatorium) 65–6
Korea 175
Kosawa Heisaku 5, 8, 9, 36, 37, 38,
  120–30, 133, 268, 273–5, 277; Ajase
  Complex 1, 11, 39, 40, 121, 123,
  124–8, 129, 130–1, 132, 274, 275; and
  Chikazumi 27, 120–1, 122, 123, 126,
  127–9; and Doi 8, 11, 37, 120, 129,
  140, 142–3, 274; erythrophobia 32;
  and Freud 1, 120, 121, 123, 125–6,
  131, 275, 280; science and religion
  26; *torokashi* technique 128–30, 142;
  translation of counselling books 39
Kraepelin, Emil 105, 106
Kraepelinian neuropsychiatry 28, 38,
  111
Kudokukai 62
Kügelgen, Wilhelm von 140
Kure Shūzō 5, 28, 76, 109; research on
  traditional therapies 52–3, 54, 55,
  56–7, 58–60, 63, 64–5
Kuroiwa Shūroku 77–8
Kurosawa Yoshitami 110
Kurozumikyō 29
Kuwabara Toshirō 32, 78, 85, 91–4, 96

Kyoto School of philosophy 31, 277,
  285

Lao-tzu 115, 116, 181
legislation: anti-hypnotism 32–3, 85, 95;
  Civil Law (1947) 38; mental health
  27–8, 38, 62, 63, 66, 243–4, 245; Non-
  Profit Organization Law (1998) 269
legitimacy debate 36
Leider, Norman 143
Lewis, I.M. 235–6
life regulation therapy 112, 113
lobotomy 42
logocentrism 114–15, 116

Maeda Shigeharu 120, 129–30, 274
magic 79, 90
magnetism 85, 86, 90, 111, 151
Majima Tōhaku 85, 89
Mann, Thomas 121
Marui Kiyoyasu 35, 36, 122–3
Mass, Catholic 173, 174, 189
materialism 77–8, 89, 94
maternal themes 184–5, 197–8; in folk
  tales 129, 189–91, 198; *see also*
  mother–son relationships; mothers
Matsumura Masami 64
May, Gerald 9, 273
media, and past life boom 209–10
meditation *see* Naikan
melting technique *see torokashi*
  technique
Melton, J. Gordon 221
memorial services 254, **254**
memorialism 205–6, 207, 222–3, 225–6,
  284
memories 168
Menninger Clinic, USA 142
Menninger, Karl 38–9, 275
mental health legislation 27–8, 38, 62,
  63, 66, 243–4, 245
mental health nursing 244
Mental Health Preservation Movement
  110
mental hospitals 28, 30, 38, 42, 67,
  242–3; and emperor 66;
  hospitalization 28–9, 66, 67; lack of
  trust in 63–4; Okinawa 242–3, 244,
  245; replacing traditional therapies
  59, 62, 63, 65
Mental Hospitals Act (1919) 27, 28, 62,
  243, 245
Mental Hygiene Law (1950) 38, 62, 66,
  243, 244

## 296  Index

Mental Hygiene Law (1965) 38
Mental Patients' Custody Act (1900) 27–8, 62, 63, 243, 245
Mesmer, Franz Anton 86, 151, 152
mesmerism 84, 152, 186
Meyer, Adolf 35, 123
Miki Kiyoshi 121, 276, 277, 278
Miki Tokuharu 153
Miki Yoshihiko 167
Minami Hiroshi 107
mind: Japanese words for 76–7; relationship with body 76–8, 113, 116–17, 150–1
mind cure methods (*seishin ryōhō*) 76, 78, 79, 84, 85, 91–7, 283
*mishirabe* (looking into oneself) 39, 157–8
*mishōon* 132
missionaries, Christian 26, 140–1, 165
Miyake Kōichi 59
modernization, as cause of mental illness 30–1
Momose Fumiaki 166
monism 77–8, 88
Morita Masatake 8, 9, 31–2, 34–5, 36–7, 103, 104, 105–15, 116, 275, 280
Morita therapy 8, 34–5, 37, 39, 40, 103–5, 109–17, 154, 282
mother–son relationships 39, 124–5, 126–8, 129, 131, 132, 198, 281
mothers: ideal mother figure 129, 132–3, 190; reviewing relationship with 154–5, 168
Motora Yūjirō 91
mountain asceticism *see* Shugendō
mountains, holy 54, 55
mourning work 169–74
*Mū* (magazine) 209, 210
*muga* (no-self) 34, 115, 224
Muramatsu Kaiseki 165
Murata Tadayoshi 174
*mushi* (self-lessness) 115
Myōe 194–7
Myōgyōji Temple, Baraki-san 59

Nagaokanishi Hospital 250, 263
Naikan: Catholic 167–75, 285; daily 155, 159; Yoshimoto 8, 39, 43, 154–61, 168, 171–2, 282
Nakae Tokususuke 77
Nakamura Kokyō 35, 76, 96–7, 110
Nakamura Yūjirō 112
Nakayama Ryōyōin (Nakayama Mental Hospital) 59

Narumi Zuiō 65
national identity 40
Natsume Sōseki 117, 275
natural disasters 42, 43, 175, 251, 269, 270; *see also* chaplaincy work in disasters
nature 114–17, 276
Neijing medicine 83
nervous temperament (*shinkeishitsu*) 35, 36, 103, 106, 108–9, 110–12, 114
Neumann, Erich 184, 191
neurasthenia 30–1, 34, 108–10, 111
neuroses 30–1, 103, 106, 108–9, 110–12; disposition as source of 35, 110–11, 113, 114; *see also shinkeishitsu* (nervous temperament)
New Age 97, 152
new new religions 41, 210, 224
new religious organizations 41, 152, 153–4, 160–1, 283
New Spirituality Movements 152–4, 160–1
Nichirenshū Buddhism 58–9, 60, 62, 64
*nihonjinron* 6, 7, 40
Nishida Kitarō 31, 185
Nishimoto Taikan 157
Nishizono Masahisa 31, 120
Nissekiji Temple, Ōiwa-san 55–6, **56**, 68
Nitta Kunimitsu 61
no-self (*muga*) 34, 115, 224
non-directive counselling 7, 38
non-medical institutions *see* traditional temple and shrine therapies
Non-Profit Organization Law (1998) 269
Nonchurch Movement 140
Nostradamus 210
nuclear crisis *see* triple disaster (March 2011)
nursing, mental health 244

Obasuteyama (folk tale) 129, 281
obesity therapy 112
obsession (*toraware*) 114
occupational therapy 61, 109, 112, 113
Ōe Ryōken 62–3
Oedipus Complex 1, 11, 121, 124
Ohnuki-Tierney, Emiko 8
Ohtsuki Kaison 35
Ohtsuki Kenji 34, 35–6, 37, 38, 274
Ōi Gen 174
Oka Minzan 58
Okabe Clinic Home Care Service 263
Okabe Takeshi 260–1, 270

Okada Torajiro 79
Okinawa *see* spirit possession, Okinawa
Okonogi Keigo 11, 40, 120, 121, 124–5, 130–1, 132, 137, 274
Okumura Ichirō 167–8
Omata Waichirō 53–4
Ono Fukuhei 91, 94
*onsen* cure (hot spring bathing) 57–8, 64
openness, of therapist 192–3
original enlightenment 80, 195
Ōsawa Kenji 86–7, 94–5
Ozawa-de Silva, Chikako 8, 11, 43

palliative care 263
parent–child relationships 39, 129, 130, 281; *see also* mother–son relationships
parental self-sacrifice 126, 127
past life boom 208–10
past life divination 211
past life readings 211–13, 221
past life therapy (PLT) 204, 210, 213–23, *215–20*, 224–7, 286
paternalistic relationship, of practitioners 33, 37, 38
Pauline teachings 170
Pentecostalist movement 43–4
personal autonomy 130, 131, 133, 275–8
personal–contextual tension 273–9
personal cultivation 7, 29–30, 78, 96, 283
personal growth through reincarnation 207, 208, 212–13, 223
persuasion therapy 60, 112, 113–14, 273
philanthropy 62
philosophy 77, 88, 112
pilgrimages 54, 55, 58, 68, 254–5, 263
PLT *see* past life therapy (PLT)
popular health care 105
positive thinking 161
possession phenomenon 51–2, 67, 79, 109; *see also* spirit possession, Okinawa
practical learning (*jitsugaku*) 29–30
prayer 9, 172; in traditional therapy 58–60, 63, 79; *yukitō* (hot water prayers) 59–60
primitive therapy 150, 151–2
private life principle 223–5, 227
proselytization 253, 260, 261
Protestantism 7, 140, 165
psycho-religious composite movement 152–4, 160–1, 283

psychogenesis 34–5
psychological complex 186
psychosomatic medicine 80, 142
psychotherapeutic attitude 153–4
psychotherapy, history of 150–4
public hygiene nurses 244
Pure Land, rebirth in 156–7, 159–60, 205, 207
Pure Land Buddhism 78, 126–7, 132, 169, 195, 196–7; *see also* Shin Buddhism
purgatory, living 170

qualification debate 36
Quimby, Phineas Parkhurst 152

radioactivity measurement 259, 263
Reader, Ian 10, 43, 271
reality, accepting (*arugamama*) 35, 115, 116, 195
rebirth in Pure Land 156–7, 159–60, 205, 207
Reed, Edward S. 86
regression therapy *see* past life therapy (PLT)
Regulation for Control of Hospitals and Clinics (1933) 65
*reieki* 83–4
reincarnation 204–28, 283–4; and ancestor worship 205–6, 207–8, 209, 222–3, 225–6; Buddhist view of 205–6, 207, 208; experiential reality of 207, 208, 212, 213, 223, 224–5; folk views of 206–7; and gender 225–7; individual–universal principle and private life principle 223–5, 227; past life boom 208–10; personal growth through 207, 208, 212–13, 223; spiritual boom 210–13; testimonies of past life therapy 213–23, *215–20*; transcultural 207–8, 212, 221, 223
Reischauer, Edwin O. 38
*reishi* (spiritual clairvoyance) 211–13
Reiyū-kai 161
religious care 252–3, 262–3, 269; case studies 253–61
religious funerals 254
Religious Institution Liaison Council, Miyagi Prefecture 255, 261
Resurrection, Christian 169, 170
Ricoeur, Paul 284–5
Rieff, Philip 12, 153–4
Riklin, Franz 184
Risshō Kōsei Kai 255

## Index

Rogers, Carl 7, 38, 41
Rorschach testing 181, 183
Rose, Nikolas 3
Ryōzen'an retreat centre 62–3
Ryūfukuji Temple, Iwai 66–7
Ryukyu Kingdom 234, 237
Ryukyu Mental Hygiene Act (1960) 243, 245

sacraments, Catholic 174–5
Sagara Tōru 117
Saitō Mokichi 107, 110
salvation: new religious organizations 41; religious 127, 128, 129, 132; Shin Buddhism 156–8, 159–60; through family relationship 127; *see also* Ajase Complex
San Francisco Psychoanalytic Institute 143
Sandplay therapy 182, 193
sarin attacks, Tokyo 3, 42, 210
Satō Ichizō 67
Satō Migaku 169
saviour consciousness 142, 143
Sawada, Janine Anderson 7, 13, 29, 78, 283
science: and Buddhism 26, 27, 77; and Christianity 26, 27, 77, 88
seaside bathing (*suigyō*) 65
secularization: of religious care 262, 270; Yoshimoto Naikan 158–60
Seichō-no-ie 153, 154, 161
Seishin Kenkyu Kai (Society for the research of mind) 92
*Seishin-Reidō-Jutsu* 92–3
*seishin ryōhō* (mind cure) 76, 78, 79, 84, 85, 91–7, 283
*seishin sekai see* Spiritual World movement
self-actualization 208
self-cultivation 7, 29–30, 78, 96, 283
self-deception 186
self-emptying 169, 170, 171
self-lessness (*mushi*) 115
self-reflection *see* Naikan
self-sacrifice, parental 126, 127
Sendai Buddhist Society 254, 255
Sendai Christian Alliance 255, 258, 259
separation, pain of 138
Setouchi Jakuchō 268, 277
*settoku* (persuasion therapy) 60, 273
shamanism 54, 150, 171; Okinawa 234–42, 244, 280
Share-house Nakai, Osaka 250, 263

Sherrill, Michael J. 43
Shimazono Susumu 12, 41, 44, 150–61, 282, 283
Shin Buddhism 12; Chikazumi Jōkan 127–8; influence of lay practitioners 13; Inoue Enryō 87; Kosawa Heisaku 120, 122; Kuwabara Toshirō 93; *tariki* (other power) 78, 84, 122, 157, 276–7, 278, 286; Yoshimoto Ishin 39, 156–8, 159–60; *see also* Pure Land Buddhism
*Shingaku* (heart learning) 78
*shinkeishitsu* (nervous temperament) 35, 36, 103, 106, 108–9, 110–12, 114
Shinran 127, 195, 275, 276–7, 278
Shintō priests, in disaster chaplaincy work 255, 256
Shintō Shūseiha 61
Shintoism 25, 38, 41, 55, 79, 206; traditional therapies 54, 59–61, 64–5
Shiotsuki Ryoko 234–45, 280
Shōmyōji Temple, Kamakura 65–6
shrines *see* traditional temple and shrine therapies
Shugendō 54–5, 60, 67, 79, 93
*shugenja* 54–5, 60, 64, 273
*shugyō* (self-strengthening) 29, 30
*shuhō* 58–9, 64
*shūkyō* 7, 10, 79, 93, 269
six-realm reincarnation 205, 206
Society for Japanese Psychiatry 35, 110
Society for Psychiatry and Neurology 110
Society for the Worship of Deities and Ancestors (Keishin Sūsokyōkai) 34
Society of State Medicine 94
Sōka Gakkai 41
Sōtō Zen temple, Tsūdaiji 256
soul: relationship with body 76–8, 113, 116–17, 150–1; survival of individual 77
spa treatments 57–8, 64
Spencer, Herbert 87
Spiegelman, Marvin 181, 184
spirit, relationship with body 76–8, 113, 116–17, 150–1
spirit possession, Okinawa 234–45; *kamidāri* 235, 238–42, 243, 244, 245, 280; phases of 236–8; and psychiatric care 242–5; *yuta* (shamans) 234–42, 280
spirit tablets (*tōtōme*) 236–7
spiritual boom 210–13, 271
spiritual care 252–3, 262–3, 269

spiritual readings 211–13, 221
Spiritual World movement 41–2, 97, 152
spirituality 8, 227–8; Catholic 166–7; definitions of 204–5; in Jung's thinking 185–8, 193, 194, 198–9; in Kawai's thinking 193, 194; and religion 271–2
Starling, Christopher L. 26
steam showers 64
still-sitting 79
subjectivity 31, 275–8
*suigyō* (seaside bathing) 65
Suizu Shinji 59–60
superstitions: eradicating 7, 26, 88, 89, 96; and mental illness 109; *see also* folk beliefs; possession phenomenon
*supirichuaru* 42–3
sutra recitations 253–5, 256, 263
Suzuki, Akihito 29, 31
Suzuki, D.T. 39, 40, 77
Suzuki Manjiro 85–6
symbols 285
synchronicity 192

*taijinkyōfushō* (fear of interpersonal relations) 5, 31–2, 103
Taikan-an temple, Fuse, Osaka 156, 157–8
Takahashi Shinji 208–9
Takao Hoyōin 66
Takeda Makoto 36, 120, 122, 123
Takeuchi Nanzō 91
Takizawa 64
Takuma Iwao 85
Tamiya Masashi 250
Tanabe Hajime 276, 277–8, 279, 282
Tanaka Teruyoshi 168, 169
Taniguchi Masaharu 153
Taniyama Yōzō 250–63, 269, 270
Tanizaki Junichiro 282
Taoism 54, 82–3, 115–16, 181
*tariki* (other power) 78, 84, 122, 157, 276–7, 278, 286
Tarutani Shigehiro 181–99, 277, 280
Tateyama, Mount 55
tears 171
telephone counselling 255, 260–1, 263
temples *see* traditional temple and shrine therapies
Tenrikyō 29, 255
Terao Kazuyoshi 165–75, 285
Terayama Kōichi 63
Thelle, Notto R. 27

thinking, changing one's way of 153
Tillich, Paul 39, 41
Tōhoku Help 259
Tohoku University 251, 255, 262–3
Tokunaga Manshi *see* Kiyozawa Manshi
Tokyo Psychoanalytical Society 35–6
Tokyo subway sarin attacks 3, 42, 210
*torokashi* technique 128–30, 142
totem theory 125–6
*tōtōme* (spirit tablets) 236–7
Toyama Masakazu 87
traditional temple and shrine therapies 51–68; bathing in hot springs 57–8, 64; bathing under waterfalls 54–7, **56**, 60, 63, 64, 66–7, 68; changing views of public 65–7; doctors' views of 63–5; history of research on 52–4; incantations and prayers 58–60, 63
training, chaplaincy work 251, 262–3
training institutions 33–4
transcultural reincarnation 207–8, 212, 221, 223
triple disaster (March 2011) 43, 175, 269, 270; *see also* chaplaincy work in disasters
True Pure Land Buddhism *see* Shin Buddhism
tsunami *see* triple disaster (March 2011)
Tsurumi Shunsuke 189

Uchimura Kanzō 26–7, 140
Uchimura Yūshi 38
Uchiyama Takashi 67
Udagawa Genshin 83–4
Ueda Noriyuki 43
Ueda Shizuteru 185
unconscious 150, 186–7; collective 188–9, 194, 195–6
Une Takashi 258–9, 260
unified religious mentality 126
United States 104, 152; Doi's visits to 142, 143; Kawai's studies in 181, 183–4; reincarnation 210; US Civilian Administration, Okinawa 243–4, 245
Urashima Tarō (folk tale) 189
urbanization 30–1, 90

Vienna Psychoanalytical Research Institute 123
Vihāra monks 250, 251, 269
vitalism 77–8

Wakamatsu Eisuke 175
Wang Jianhua 116

waterfall bathing 54–7, **56**, 60, 63, 64, 66–7, 68
Watsuji Tetsurō 6
Watts, Alan 40
Weiss, Brian 210
Westernization 198–9
willpower 82
word association 191–2
Wu Yu-chuan 33

Xu Kangsheng 116

Yabe Yaekichi 1, 35
Yakuōin Temple, Takao 57, 66
Yamaguchi Sannosuke 94
Yamamoto Ichiji 61
Yamamoto Kyūgosho (Yamamoto Relief House) 60–2, **61**
Yamamoto Shūdō 60
Yamamoto Shūsen 60, 273
Yamamura Michio 123
Yamauchi Tokuma 94
Yanagita Kunio 206, 225
Yanaihara Tadao 140
*Yōkai Gaku* 88–9
Yoshikawa Takehiko 242
Yoshimoto Ishin 8, 39, 154, 155–60, 167
Yoshimoto Naikan 8, 39, 43, 154–61, 168, 171–2, 282
Yoshinaga Shin'ichi 76–97, 274, 283
Yoshino Kosaku 6
*yukitō* (hot water prayers) 59–60
Yunoyama Onsen 57–8
*yuta* (Okinawa shamans) 234–42, 280

*zange* (contrition) 277–8
Zen Buddhism 12, 13, 78, 79–84, 95, 185